THE LIVES OF LITERATURE

THE LIVES OF LITERATURE

Reading, Teaching, Knowing

ARNOLD WEINSTEIN

PRINCETON UNIVERSITY PRESS

PRINCETON AND OXFORD

Published by Princeton University Press
41 William Street, Princeton, New Jersey 08540
6 Oxford Street, Woodstock, Oxfordshire OX20 1TR

press.princeton.edu

All Rights Reserved

Library of Congress Cataloging-in-Publication Data

Names: Weinstein, Arnold, author.
Title: The lives of literature : reading, teaching, knowing / Arnold Weinstein.
Description: Princeton : Princeton University Press, [2021] | Includes
    bibliographical references and index.
Identifiers: LCCN 2021026491 (print) | LCCN 2021026492 (ebook) |
    ISBN 9780691177304 (hardback ; acid-free paper) | ISBN 9780691232324 (ebook)
Subjects: LCSH: Literature—Philosophy. | Weinstein, Arnold—Books and reading. |
    Characters and characteristics in literature. | Self in literature. | Best books. |
    BISAC: LITERARY CRITICISM / General | LITERARY CRITICISM /
    Semiotics & Theory | LCGFT: Literary criticism.
Classification: LCC PN45 .W357 2021 (print) | LCC PN45 (ebook) |
    DDC 801—dc23
LC record available at https://lccn.loc.gov/2021026491
LC ebook record available at https://lccn.loc.gov/2021026492

British Library Cataloging-in-Publication Data is available

Editorial: Anne Savarese, James Collier
Production Editorial: Terri O'Prey
Text Design: Karl Spurzem
Jacket/Cover Design: Karl Spurzem
Production: Erin Suydam
Publicity: Alyssa Sanford, Carmen Jimenez
Copyeditor: Plaegian Alexander

This book has been composed in Arno

Printed on acid-free paper. ∞

Printed in the United States of America

10 9 8 7 6 5 4 3 2 1

CONTENTS

ACKNOWLEDGMENTS

It is a pleasure to acknowledge the help I've received in writing this book. Some of it is obvious, some of it less so, since it is not easy to see the actual support structures that undergird anything one does.

I want, first of all, to recognize the assistance I have gotten over the past two years from my former student, Julian Fox. I enlisted him not only as assistant during the pandemic but also as junior colleague in this project: to aid me in tackling the work involved in permissions, production matters, and much else. His intelligence and generosity have been instrumental in the final stages of this work.

I want also to thank, formally, Anne Savarese at Princeton University Press for the sustained good will, critical acumen, and belief in me that I have felt during this entire project. Her diplomacy and clear-eyed sense of both my argument and my words have been invaluable to me. And I am in debt to the whole Princeton team, as I went through the copyediting and proofing of my manuscript. What might have been daunting turned out to be engaging.

My remaining acknowledgments are less obvious and direct, but arguably deeper still, longitudinal, and constituting much of the ground I stand on. Brown University has been the locus of my entire professional life, and I have benefitted immeasurably from its liberal culture and its student-centered curriculum, open to experiment and interdisciplinary forays. Some of this appears directly in my text. Much of it goes unsignaled, not easy to see. I can scarcely imagine what my life and work would have been elsewhere.

Finally, as in all my books, I salute the central influence of my wife, Ann Weinstein. Her wisdom, wit, and critical spirit have, sometimes like a whetstone, sharpened my mind; her native compass and sense of relative weights and measures have ever played a role in shaping my vision. She is my North Star.

Credits

Excerpt(s) from "A Dream Play" in *Miss Julie and Other Plays* by August Strindberg, trans. Michael Robinson (Oxford UP, 2009). Reproduced with permission of the Licensor through PLSclear.

Excerpt(s) from *The Three Theban Plays* by Sophocles, translated by Robert Fagles, translation copyright © 1982, 1984 by Robert Fagles. Used by permission of Viking Books, an imprint of Penguin Publishing Group, a division of Penguin Random House LLC. All rights reserved.

"Ithaca" from *Cavafy: Poems* by C.P. Cavafy, translated by Daniel Mendelsohn, translation copyright © 2009, 2012, 2014 by Daniel Mendelsohn. Used by permission of Everyman's Library, an imprint of the Knopf Doubleday Publishing Group, a division of Penguin Random House LLC. All rights reserved. Reprinted by permission of HarperCollins Publishers Ltd © 2014.

Excerpt(s) from *The Poems of Emily Dickinson: Reading Edition*, edited by Ralph W. Franklin, Cambridge, Mass.: The Belknap Press of Harvard University Press, Copyright © 1998, 1999 by the President and Fellows of Harvard College. Copyright © 1951, 1955 by the President and Fellows of Harvard College. Copyright © renewed 1979, 1983 by the President and Fellows of Harvard College. Copyright © 1914, 1918, 1919, 1924, 1929, 1930, 1932, 1935, 1937, 1942 by Martha Dickinson Bianchi. Copyright © 1952, 1957, 1958, 1963, 1965 by Mary L. Hampson.

"An Urban Convalescence" from *Collected Poems* by James Merrill, copyright © 2001 by the Literary Estate of James Merrill at Washington University. Used by permission of Alfred A. Knopf, an imprint of the Knopf Doubleday Publishing Group, a division of Penguin Random House LLC. All rights reserved.

INTRODUCTION

The Lives of Literature: Reading, Teaching, Knowing

We go to literature because it houses human lives. The books one most remembers deliver their quarry so wonderfully that those (fictional) lives actually exist in people's minds alongside the "real" people one knows. Oedipus, Hamlet, Don Quixote, Faust, Heathcliff, Jane Eyre, David Copperfield, Ahab, Emma Bovary, the brothers Karamazov, Huckleberry Finn, Gregor Samsa, Marcel, Leopold Bloom, Mrs. Dalloway, Gatsby, Quentin Compson, the Invisible Man, Yossarian, Celie, Sethe—among many others—occupy a good bit of human real estate, and some have claimed that we may know them better, more fully, than we know the "actual" people we know.

Further: one actually sees the arc of those fictional lives: Oedipus's transition from proud King back to cast-out infant and closing as blind exile; Lear's trajectory from estate magnate to madman on a heath; Jane Eyre's arc from unloved and abused child to monied, married woman; Gregor Samsa's trip from "bug-hood" to garbage. This, we say, is the work of plot. But consider the true magic here: how all these transformations (which can take weeks, months, years, even a lifetime to happen, which therefore escape our vision, our knowing) are compressed, contained, or delivered in the scope of a few hundred pages, requiring mere hours to access, to process. We enter the bookstore, see all the books arrayed there, and think: so many books, so little time; but the truth goes other way: books do not take time, they give time. They enable us to see the dimensions of life, a gift and a vision that are un-available to us as we live day to day. *Reading lives,* in every sense: litera-ture brings us, virtually, into the experiences and fates of its characters, but it is the act of reading that turns long-ago and faraway printed words into life, our life.

"Long ago and faraway" might seem like forbidding barriers, but the books we love crash right through, and into us. Why does this matter? When a friend of mine who'd devoted her life to Shakespeare was asked how much she knew about him, she replied: "Not as much as he knows about me." Isn't this why we turn to art and literature? It's more than curiosity or even education. We sense that they are intended for per-sonal use, not in the self-help sense but as mirrors, as entryways into who we ourselves are or might be.

Our own trip through time and space, even for the oldest and most far-flung of us, is limited. And then over. Unlike real people, literature's people live on, over the centuries, through the act of reading. This is amazing: you cannot go back to fifth-century BCE Athens and "meet" Oedipus, and yet Sophocles's play takes you there. And no less remark-able: they change. Not only does Coleridge's Hamlet have little in com-mon with Freud's, but you, too, can experience this. A second reading of a classic can astonish. It hasn't changed, but you have. And it will read more differently still when your spouse or child or grandchild reads it and sees in it things you never imagined. But books cannot speak: reading brings them to life.

They live through us. And we live—other—through them. That is literature's gift. That is what a lifetime of teaching has taught me, and it is what I have taught.

This will sound strange: I was born to do this.

In a letter of 1871, the poet Rimbaud uttered a phrase that announces the modern age, "'I' is someone else" ("Je" est un autre). Some sixty-nine years later, I entered the world as an identical twin, and Rimbaud's claim has an uncanny truth for me, since I grew up being one of a pair. Even though our family and close friends could readily tell us apart, most people could not, and I started the world with a blurrier, more porous, more fluid sense of my contours than most other people have. This iffiness shaped me, in ways I'm still coming to understand. I have never lost my conviction that one's outward form—the shape of people, but also of surfaces and things—may not be what it seems.

This applies especially to feelings. I remember little from the visual fare provided in the 1940s and 1950s, but the 1941 film *The Corsican Brothers*, with Douglas Fairbanks Jr., derived from a Dumas novel, conveyed something that seemed intimately true to me: each of the "separated" twins (who'd been conjoined at birth) was doomed to *feel* whatever happened to the other. Later films such as *Dead Ringers* and *Face Off*, each about glued-together doubles, spoke to me the same way. At some level, I believe my twin brother and I do have this extrasensory bond, this connective tissue.

That personal intuition goes a far piece toward explaining my career as literature professor, and also the views you'll encounter in this book, since I am convinced that great works of art tell us about skewed vision and shape-shifting and secret sharing, about both the world and ourselves as more mobile, more misperceived, more dimensional, more "spread out" than science or our senses would have us believe. Feeling—the actual motor force triggered by reading—is more promiscuous and outward bound than we think. On this head, all literature can be construed as a form of science fiction, since the very act of reading a novel or poem or play is a mix of time travel and space travel, constituting the finest cultural bargain ever to come your way. And most significant of all: it is how you become—even if momentarily, vicariously, "exitably"—someone else.

Math, science, philosophy, history: they are invaluable but offer none of this. The works of literature interrogate and stretch us. They are surprisingly morphological. They challenge our sense of who we are, even of who our brothers and sisters might be. When President Obama said of Trayvon Martin, "This could have been my son," he was uttering a truth that goes beyond compassion and reaches toward recognition. *It could have been me* is the threshold for the vistas that literature and art make available to us.

Belated Knowledge

One of the oldest stories in the West is about a man who misperceived his most basic relationships: the bullying old man he killed at the crossroads was actually his father; the woman whose bed he shares and who has mothered his children is actually his mother. Only an idiot would claim such news to be good, but alongside the horror of this plot, there is a strange yet persistent and gathering "bookkeeping" imperative: Oedipus ends up knowing who he is. He ends up, we might callously say, with the right résumé. He stubbornly works his way toward a final *optic* on his life, even if it is so unbearable that it will lead to his self-blinding.

The move toward self-knowledge, toward getting your story straight—even when it may be rife with doubles and others, even if it's fiasco-fed—strikes me as one of life's most exigent and profound requirements. Obviously, one wants, at every stage of life, to have some grasp of how the pieces fit together and what kind of story they tell. But aging adds further urgency and point to this project, in the nature of a final harvest, a narrative duty to accomplish before dying. This is not an aesthetic injunction but an existential one. Nor need such matters be depressing and mortuary—they can be filled with humorous surprises and discoveries, as well as laden with cadavers and regrets—but this book is my bid in this direction, my effort to get that final sighting, that final accounting.

"What is the creature that is on four legs in the morning, two legs at midday, and three legs in the evening?" the Greek Oracle asks, and Oedipus answers, "man." But Sophocles tragically scrambles time's "natural" forward march, so that the King is at once child and adult, lover to his mother, murderer to his father, sibling and father to his children. The King discovers his many selves. Nor are there any correctives or remedies in sight. Thebes must first be dying of plague before he can learn, via the Oracle, that he is the cause. His knowledge is belated: retrospective but hardly retroactive. Could that be Sophocles's direst message: that knowledge is always belated? If so, what are the consequences?

John Barth wrote of the *Oedipus*: "The wisdom to recognize and halt follows the know-how to pollute past rescue. The treaty's signed, but the cancer ticks in your bones. Until I'd murdered my father and fornicated my mother, I wasn't wise enough to see I was Oedipus. Too late now to keep the polar cap from melting. Venice subsides; South America explodes." Published in 1968, these words remain ghastly prescient. Not merely are Oedipus's "private" transgressions only knowable as such, long afterward, but other "broader," impersonal, even planetary horrors join the list: the polar cap is melting today; Venice is sporadically under water; we have polluted perhaps past rescue; countries and states across the globe are, often enough, exploding; and no signed treaty can undo the (not yet detectable) cancer ticking in our bones. Here is a terrifying system-wide purview: crime, disease, environment, and politics all obey a heinous logic of unknowable dormancy, so that we know them only when they explode, when they present the bill, when the damage is done. It is the damage that constitutes our knowing.

If you think this is unnecessarily bleak, consider further: the detective story cannot begin until there is a crime, a corpse; the heart attack and the tumor precede diagnosis and treatment; greenhouse-gas emissions occur long before the scientists see or measure their effects (and even then, the citizenry resists registering the awful cause-effect pattern because it is not "visible"); the erosion of polity and political order has roots, is the final part of a causative chain including elections and a whole welter of prior socioeconomic failings. "A man reaps what he sows," the Bible says, but this still upbeat, even if grim, model of responsibility is beset by the nasty perceptual truth that, all too often, we do not know what we have sown until we reap it: belatedness of knowledge everywhere you look, involving the fate of body, the body politic, and the planet.

The French poet Mallarmé made, in his most majestic poem, an astonishingly artisanal prophecy: "Le monde est fait pour aboutir à un livre" (The world is made to become a book). This grand claim for the book may sound like a librarian's dream—especially dubious in our high-tech world of smartphones, streaming, and other forms of evolved media—but it touches on something elemental: our ever-present and ever-foiled need to see the actual pattern, the actual meaning, the actual texture, of our own life. And he is right as well, to use the splendid verb "aboutir"—to become, to end up as—putting us on notice that the work of time is not only the currency of our long lives but also the key to our evolving grasp of what they signify. Only late do we know.

A phrase you'll often come across in this book is Paul's famous utterance in 1 Corinthians 13:12: "Now we see through a glass darkly, but then face to face." Paul has no interest in art or literature: he is referring to our ultimate encounter with God, presented as a moment of final knowledge, of truth (as indeed the remaining verse makes clear: "Now I know in part; but then shall I know even as also I am known"). One is familiar, as well, with the notion that the end of our lives produces its own final light. One might argue, more gently and generally, that all traditional societies saw *wisdom* along these lines, as the precious residue of experience garnered by the old—but that scheme has little play in the modern world. And science itself—with its cargo of ever-increasing facts and data—rules out such a model. The old are more likely to be seen as outdated rather than wise.

And please note as well: culture cannot structure its arrangements differently either, according to this time-release model. From the moment we draw breath, we are absorbing information, inscribed in a programmed forward trajectory that can last decades, even longer. The entire project of *school* hinges on the belief that we can and must acquire knowledge from the very earliest stages of life.

How does one get it?

"Aboutir à un livre," Mallarmé wrote. Livre. Life's experiences eventuate finally into a book. And books are what we serve up in school, to those who have little life experience. This is one of culture's most intriguing equations. Can pages with print deliver—seed—experience? Books are of course used in all fields, including the sciences and social sciences, but the ones I'm making my most extravagant claims for are what we know as *literature*. I am not speaking of "wisdom literature": the kind of things one finds in so many religious texts, where all the required dos and don'ts are posted. Great literature does not behave this way, does not sermonize, and if critics use the term "didactic," it is almost always pejorative. No, literature is precious for a different reason altogether: because of how we engage it, how we process it, what it brings to us, what it demands of us. Here would be its gift, its price.

Literature vs. Information

I have come to see literature as an alternate (invaluable) source of knowing. Alternate to what, you may ask? Alternate to *information*. Information surely seems to be our modern guide. Its delivery system has, of course, evolved. Everywhere I go, people stare into small phones, experiencing connectivity, linked to data and to others, networked. This has been a long time coming, extending back at least to the telegraph and its successors, as McLuhan argued, but perhaps ultimately to the arrival of print itself in the Renaissance. Big data would seem in the driver's seat today.

But my focus is on the actual status and reach of facts and information, located in archives and libraries as well as provided by today's high-tech devices, and I want to claim that literature's "testimony" is of a different sort. My quarrel may seem quixotic. Rationality and information seem, after all, to be more than ever in demand, insisting on their due, if we are to understand our world. And I agree entirely.

But life is more than reason or data, and literature schools us in a different set of affairs, the affairs of heart and soul that have little truck with information as such. Your heart is understood differently by your lover and your cardiologist. It is not sentimental to state that literature and art illuminate—engage, constitute—our experience in ways that other fields do not. The terrible deeds and punishments on show in Greek tragedy do not cheer us up, but Aristotle claimed that "watching" them unfurl onstage was a purgative, cathartic experience for the audience.

Aristotle's focus was on spectating—some ten to fifteen thousand people attended the performances of the Greek tragedies, constituting a media event closer to the Super Bowl than to our seeing an off-Broadway play—but I want to apply his insight to the experience of reading. After all, the Greek philosopher was drawn to the very mechanics of how we negotiate stories, and he was struck by their seminal, engendering effects, in his words, "pity" and "terror." Useful pity and terror. What I see here is a remarkable dialectic between the doom-ridden stories of tragedy and the potential social benefit they might provide: the "afterlife" of the text. Something beyond information or even exhortation was sensed and became real, was triggered and passed on, "live," big with its own futurity. Aristotle thought this to be purgative, but it is arguably more than that, and it can happen via reading as well as via performance. The *huis clos* of tragedy—no exit, caughtness, entrapment—spells eventual death for its people but also potential life for its readers and spectators. Those readers and spectators grasp more than a lesson: they grapple with the birth of knowing. The performance is over, the book is closed, but something has been seeded.

The Cost of Knowing and Life Writ Large

Remember Oedipus again. The middle-aged man realizes—*realizes*, makes *real* to himself—late in life, as omnipotent King, who he (plurally) is and has been, and what he has done. Hindsight, retrospect, belatedness, corrosive surprises: I have come to believe that many of the books I love most stage exactly these types of reversals. Wreckage of prior assumptions, emergence of new knowledge, would appear not just to be the very pulse of Sophocles's *Oedipus* but to be found at the core of *King Lear*, in poems of Emily Dickinson, in tales of Melville and Kafka, bringing to light both personal and political trauma in Twain and Faulkner, delivered as toxin in Strindberg and Proust, kept at bay in Joyce and Morrison, commanding the field in still others. Literature's very signature—like, at times, life's—is the cashiering of old (beloved) beliefs, as new (unsurvivable?) truths emerge. Literature is about the birth and cost of knowing.

It is also about expansion, about discovering one's emplacement in far-flung networks. Oedipus arrives at a form of fourth-dimensional portraiture, and that bristling portrait, coming into view over five acts, explodes forever the tidier coordinates he had thought were his. Art writes large. It bursts open the contours we knew, to show us others, including ourselves as others. Here, too, I believe our current informational model plays us false, because it hews to our "comfort zone," our known and chosen linkages and connections, but it ignores the larger scene that both contains and interpellates us, that refashions our boundaries.

Why should the young (or the old) read such fare?

Because reading itself is immersive, for it enables us to *taste* the lives of others, to acquire a *sentient* awareness of another, and then—unharmed but armed, even "increased"—to return to life. Reading is never retrospective, no matter how long ago the text was written, but always of the present, hence prospective, cued to possible futures. That is its unique gift. In some grisly yet beautiful way, "they die so that we might live." (This phrase would not have met with Aristotle's pleasure.)

"A book must be the ax for the frozen sea within us," Kafka wrote. Kafka knew a great deal about frozen seas, and he located them where no geographer would have: within ourselves. Yes, the ice in the Arctic melts today, but the ice inside retains its thickness. (Each of us can gauge the truth of such an inconvenient claim, challenging all notions of charity and empathy.) In fact, Kafka's own greatest texts are testimony to coldness of heart; his characters talk and think and talk and think nonstop, but there is little affect to be found and even less "shared" affect. One is astonished this is so, given the horrors he routinely depicts: being turned into a bug, being arrested for an unknown crime, being lost in bureaucratic labyrinths while trying to find one's way to truth or salvation, being unable to heal the sick child, or to manage the beak-like machine that dispenses justice, or just to go on fasting forever. What kind of "ax" did he have in mind?

As I see it, Kafka's narratives, unheated though they are, disclose nonetheless a remarkable structural pattern that goes a long way toward chopping through one's frozen sea: *metamorphosis*. As a twin with porous boundaries, I batten on to this drastic logic of people becoming other, becoming altered, even transmogrified. Kafka limns the fundamental action proper to art: transformation. Figurative, vicarious, exitable transformation. Not for the doomed denizens of his stories, of course, but for his readers.

Claims for reader-identification with art have been argued before but would be scoffed at by most scholars in my field both yesterday and today. And the academy's current interest in ideological matters—from race, class, and gender on to intersectionality and beyond—is at a huge remove from the emotional imperative I'm articulating.

And famous writers have targeted the notion of "identification" as well. When Rousseau—champion, one would have thought, of the bonds of feeling—wrote *against* the founding of a theater in Geneva in 1758, one of his most striking arguments had to do with the facileness and "short-windedness" of spectator-identification: one wept in response to the events on stage, and then, after exiting the theater, walked coldly right past the beggar on the street. Bertolt Brecht, in his programmatic efforts to found a Marxian theater praxis, railed against what he termed "kulinarisches Theater"; in such "bourgeois" theater, the audience "followed" the actors, laughing when they did, weeping when they did, whereas the kind of "episches Theater" he had in mind would bring about a radical critique by *reversing* this situation, so that the audience would cry when the actors laughed, and laugh when the actors cried, thanks to their new critical awareness of the "unnecessity" of the arrangements depicted on stage. It's a noble aim. Can it work?

At my university, modern theory—in its many different guises, including "anti-theory"—has enormous sway in literature course offerings and in scholarly publications. Critique is desired, not identification. I cannot help thinking that theory's great seductive promise is that it explains power, and that it does so in ways that appear to be historical, rational, unsentimental, scientific. In some sense, this is, for today's academy, the humanities' "last stand." The scholars' sights, like those of many of our best students today, are often on the ideological arrangements that subtend all moments and periods of history; and they rightly feel that literature is a rich quarry here. True enough.

But power is not only ideological. Of course, literature illuminates the operation of power in the stories it tells, and we do need to attend to that. But the driving question (for me) has to do with literature's own power: its experiential impact on readers, its payload. We process the books we read, and I believe they process us as well. There are no evident metrics for gauging such transactions, yet this is the central *commerce*, the unwritten pact, of both reading and teaching. I believe that these are primordial matters and that they underlie and underwrite our investigations and the work we do, both in our books and in our classrooms. And, inevitably, these are the issues that loom largest, as I come to the end of my career and wonder what it has all been about. As quasi-Corsican brother, as readerly, temporary identifier with Oedipus and Gregor Samsa (and a whole host of others, waiting in the wings), as old man who has incessantly cheerleaded and pimped for literature for so many different audiences, this is my moment of exploring what it all amounted to.

All Together Now

What I had not anticipated in this plenary volume was the surprise of seeing, at long last, the clear common ground in three distinct areas: my education, my teaching, and my books. This was my Ali Baba moment of discovering treasure. In recognizing these shared properties, in sensing that I have been cultivating the same garden in each of the major arenas of my career, I felt I had gained a precious "cohering" treasure. Or, put less flatteringly, I was reminded of Molière's Monsieur Jourdain, who learns that he has been speaking *prose* all his life, even though he'd never heard of the term.

What, you might ask, do education, teaching, and books share? Each is about transmission, about the language bridge that can carry us into other minds and hearts. And these arenas cohabit, cheek to jowl, in this book. So, you'll find here accounts of my schooling interwoven with commentary on my career, all of which is buttressed and outright writ large by discussions of the actual books that I have not so much taught as been taught by. That is who I am and what this book is. It may initially look varied and different, but it's not. Drumstick and thigh and wing and breast meat have different textures and forms, but they're all chicken. So it is here: my commentary on my writers probes and is fueled by the same existential questions that animate my career and life.

To begin with, each—as I have experienced them, as I present them—can be bristling, explosive, even lawless (despite all the rules we've ever learned), linked by a view of *language as armament*, language as the most powerful tool meted out to *Homo sapiens* for bringing our inner world to expression so that it is shareable, thereby bridging the immense divide that separates all living creatures in time, space, and flesh. Yet I termed language "armament" for still other reasons: it possesses a charge, a potential violence, a kinetic power (of persuasion, of rending, of bonding, of transport) that runs roughshod over docile dictionaries and differential systems such as sign/referent or word/meaning. This isn't always pretty or well behaved; this is not the familiar, steady, impersonal discourse of information. But it is my version of the Second Amendment: we are endowed with *words* as our most intimate and overlooked form of power; these are the arms we bear.

Second, I believe that *understanding* is keyed to this same array of unruly forces. I don't know how to overstate this. "Understanding"—the goal of both teaching and reading—can often be a wrenching yet potentially transformative proposition. I want to challenge our staid, rational "safe" view of cognition, of knowing. Knowing can be lethal. Characters are altered, erased, undone; what seemed fixed and stable is blown apart or disintegrates. Characters bleed and die.

But—and this is quintessential as well as self-evident—there is no blood in my classroom. Elementary, my dear Watson, you're probably thinking. Of course, reading is safe. But the question is, How have (unbleeding) readers nonetheless been changed? The answer I've spent my career arriving at is: they have encountered, vicariously, the cost of knowing. They have collided with a form of understanding that is unlike anything they meet in all other fields of study. Or on their phones and laptops.

Third, literature and teaching are kinetic forms of transportation, even though we may think them static. Both are fueled by words, and both may be said to yield energy fields, power systems, that are every bit as basic as the utility companies that provide you with electricity, gas, and water. Each quietly bids to wreck our conviction of being bounded figures, for they incessantly throw us into other times, places, and selves. This is not some form of cultural tourism on the cheap; rather, it extends our reach and thereby displays our truer actual dimensions. I said that words fuel this type of travel, but it is evident that imagination is the motor that drives our machine.

Mind you, this seemingly upbeat, perhaps overheated, liberal picture of the expanded self is also rife with threats. Without ever saying it, literature is drawn, like moths to the flame, to the question of how much any of us can afford to imagine. I see something at once precious and troubling here. All of us have been told that it is ethically good to "walk in others' shoes," that occupying others' subject positions may be the only way of understanding who they are, of understanding that they are real. But does such "outreach"—or "inreach"—have a price tag? Could some forms of identification be unsurvivable?

One thing is certain. None of our smart machines can even fathom such questions, much less exercise us in fathoming the answers.

Literature's Maps

Frequently in this study, I will speak of two religious philosophers—Pascal and Kierkegaard—who offer some of the pithiest accounts that I know of this type of understanding and boundary stretching. Let me acknowledge that Pascal and Kierkegaard are at pains to delineate the nature of *faith*, whereas my view of literature and my teaching are utterly secular. But, in ways they could not have intended, each of them is telling us that our ordinary cognitive operations—the machinery that enables us to understand mathematics or to read the newspaper—play us entirely false when it comes to the momentous affairs of heart and soul. Each of them challenges our conventional sense of epistemology, the nature of knowing. Each rebukes the lazy assumptions and outright hubris of the purely rational worldview, especially its defects as "search engine" (a term they would have understood if not used). Pascal has his sights on the immense stage of time and space that we, without purchase, inhabit, and Kierkegaard faults our traditional "reporting" habits (our reliance on "outcomes" and hence our ignorance of the "unknowing" experiential drama itself). Is this not literature's very turf? Literature's map?

As I said at the outset, the miracle that novels routinely pull off is to depict a person's trip through time and space in the scope of a few hundred pages. But literature can also represent our doings, our actual comings and goings, both the external ones and the others as well, the neural ones, the emotional ones. It records the mercurial, kaleidoscopic activity that roils nonstop inside brain and heart.

That spread-out, layered, *networked* picture dwarfs today's electronic testimony. Yes, literature enlists the hoary old technology of print, but its rendition of the human subject nonetheless turns out to be *wired* beyond compare. Yes, you can now summon, with the flick of a finger on your iPhone, a humongous range of faraway things, but literature's storehouse has a drastically different salience and economy, for it registers entries and arrivals that are not subject to our control; instead, it follows a regime of breaking and entering, of nodal points that connect us unbidden, of long-ago linkages that flay us still, that sit inside us like radioactive or cancerous deposits. Or perhaps fill us with delight, enable a recovery or vision of lost or imagined love and beauty? To use an embattled term, literature brings to visibility a sentient *ecosystem* that no machine can capture but whose captive we are.

Is it too much to claim that a lifetime in the classroom is also a fourth-dimensional, far-flung exercise, with its peculiar nodal points? The teacher participates in an evolving human chain, no less than a cultural contract between the old and the young, and although no one can either say or map how much "life" goes into or remains vital in this project of dissemination, I'd argue it is the transport system that school is designed for. A single classroom looks bounded, although it isn't, and the composite classrooms of a career have serious scope. In addition, I've personally had rare luck in still farther-flung ventures, such as with video, audio, and DVD courses and with online programs, such as Coursera, in the past and with Zoom more recently, in our time of plague. What kind of face-to-face or shape-shifting could happen in these precincts so different from the brick-and-mortar containers we're used to? Teaching cargoes us into others' lives and is thus endowed with a futurity that outlives the classroom, sometimes outlives the teacher.

Literature's Knowing, Teaching's Mission

Likewise, the "cost of knowing" is, I firmly believe, a signature feature of teaching, inasmuch as one seeks not only to impart information but to convey something even greater: its *value*, its wider reaches, its stakes in human life. Young people approach instruction the way animals regard food: as sustenance. Or not. Perhaps the most fateful decisions in a classroom are rarely conscious as such, for they involve the young (and the not young) determining whether they do—or do not—find nutrients in what is presented. I actually think this true for every field, for every classroom, but it is the very rationale for teaching literature (a field all too easily dismissed as frills, or half-processed as merely dead letters). "Does this bear on me?" is the unstated but severe test question that students put to what they read, and the teacher, as well as the text, either passes or fails it. The best books interrogate their readers—jostle their assumptions, challenge their own sense of "me"—and the teacher's calling must be to convey this "live." There are myriad ways of doing so.

What, you may ask, does literature teach? Literature's news has nothing in common with what you might find in so many other sources: CNN or the *New York Times* or your smartphone or a politician's tweets or Wikipedia or indeed the *Encyclopaedia Britannica*. We are now awash in an era of suspicion regarding the veracity of what we read or hear, thanks in part to social media in all its forms. "Fake news" is, all too often, the term applied to news we disagree with. But my sights are elsewhere: could *all* of it—liberal or conservative, blogosphere or dictionary, rumor or historical record—be, at some key level, *fake*? I'm pointing not to conspiracy theory but, rather, to the actual reach and tidings of what we *know*, what has galvanized our heart as well as our mind. $2 + 2 = 4$ is something I "know"; my feelings for my wife, children, and brother are something I know differently. What do we know? How do we know it?

Philosophy might also be said to begin exactly here. I wonder how many people take seriously Socrates's nugget of wisdom: "All I know is that I know nothing." In my view it brings terrible news to us, and I have to think it especially noxious for young people, given that their entire education has told them the opposite, has claimed to increase their knowledge. And today, when we can access facts and data with a touch of a finger, this now labor-free belief is even more entrenched. By the time folks get to my classroom, they have good reason to feel they are already possessed of a serious amount of information, firmly documented by reams of grades and standardized tests. And they're hungry to expand their base even further.

Hard to imagine Socrates a welcome guest at their feast, or to imagine him a tenured professor at a university today. Literature crawls with people discovering they know nothing. Do universities?

I invoke these critiques of personal knowledge, to continue pointing the way toward literature's peculiar endemic truths. And, again, I'll enlist as guide Søren Kierkegaard, whose astonishing *Fear and Trembling* (1843) not only straddles philosophy and religion but also posits the germinal thought that underwrites, as I've said, so much of my book, my life, and my career: what we think we know turns out to be fake news: not so much bogus or wrong as radically inadequate. All educated people believe they understand the story of Abraham and Isaac, but do they really? Remember Genesis 22. I've read it; I suspect you've read it. But even if you haven't, *you know what happened*. God told Abraham to sacrifice his son Isaac at Mount Moriah, but at the last minute the angel and ram appeared, Isaac was saved, and he went on to play his role in founding the Jewish people. Basic stuff: a story we know. Because we know how it ended.

But as Kierkegaard sublimely points out, Abraham went to Mount Moriah not knowing the ending. In this light, consider what you know of all recorded history, legend and fact, and ask yourself: how much of it is dependent on knowing the outcome? (Some outcome dates to ponder: 1066; 1492; 1776; 1789; 1861–65; December 7, 1941; November 23, 1963; September 11, 2001; and, for that matter, your birthday.) Kierkegaard has many purposes in this short, maddening text, but the one that matters most is signaled by the very title: *fear and trembling*. How much do you know about the fear and trembling that inhabited Abraham, that not only was the warrant for his faith but informs so much major human doing and undoing?

Literature's testimony teaches us about what never makes it into the world of numbers and facts and archives: human sentience. Any record that ignores—or cannot plumb—human feeling is alien to the actual texture of living. In that respect (and only in that respect) I will claim that the realm of data or information is, humanly speaking, fake news. The world of information is more Gothic than its believers believe, because it is so often ghostly, silhouettelike, deprived of human sentience.

The humanistic model is sloppy. It has no bottom line. It is not geared to productivity. It will not increase your arsenal of facts or data. But it rivals rockets when it comes to flight and the visions it enables (or the shibboleths it exposes). And it will help create denser and more generous lives, lives aware that others not only are other but are real, felt as such, encountered as such. In this regard it adds depth and resonance to the shadowy and impalpable world of numbers and data: empirical notations that have no interest or purchase in interiority, in values, notations that offer the heart no foothold.

Mitempfinden, or Feeling With

In this sense, my job of the past half century—to impart a knowledge of literature—has been a great ride but also tricky, tricky. Students have every right to anticipate knowing something substantive by course's end, whereas I am the Mephistophelian figure, the one bent on sabotage as much as discovery. After all, what do you know when you know a literary work? A reading of *Hamlet* produces nothing comparable to studying linear algebra or molecular biology or computer coding. As teacher, I have no ax to grind, no personal view of the world that I am trying to foist on either my writers or my students. Literature, I want my students to see, above all, is not window dressing, not an anthology of quotable phrases or beautiful language or stirring plots. Instead, it honors human sentience. It recognizes that our lives are bathed not only in fear and trembling, but in joy, pain, happiness, horror, excitement, anxiety, and much else that resists notation, that "passes show" as Shakespeare's prince said, and thus eludes our monitoring devices and the public record, even as it underwrites our existence.

There is a line spoken by Goethe's young protagonist, Werther (1774), that I've always admired, even though it is rarely quoted: "Only insofar as we empathize, is there honor in speaking of things" (Denn nur insofern wir mitempfinden, haben wir Ehre, von einer Sache zu reden). Goethe rightly enlists the word *Ehre,* honor, as the prerequisite for judgment or commentary, and I see something programmatic here: our discourse *must* embrace feeling if it is to be worthy as well as credible. *Mitempfinden* means "to feel with." There is nothing touchy-feely about this assertion; it acknowledges human feeling as life's very ground, and it goes on to mandate a rule: your account must include this. What it does not quite say is, How do you get there? How do you "feel with"?

Try It On

When approaching a piece of literature, I frequently urge my students to do something rather intimate: "Try it on." I then remind them that they'd never purchase clothes or shoes without first trying them on, and they then remind me that online shopping has turned my exhortation into something quaint and nostalgic. OK. But visualize those angled mirrors that still exist in clothing stores, whereby you see yourself not only in the front but also from the side and even in the back. You see your butt. (The mirror is indispensable: you can't do this without it.) Books of literature are mirrors of this sort. They see "inside" their characters (we can't), but they also see their characters in the round (also off-limits to our vision of ourselves and others).

And they often see into the "beyond," a place where the individual can be lost or eclipsed. This can range from delivering an entire city rife with change, even alienation (as Baudelaire does for Paris and as Joyce does, in countless different modes, for Dublin in *Ulysses*), to imagined, fantasized voyages (such as the masochistic speculations of sexual betrayal generated by Proust's jealous narrator or the Faulknerian one made, in *Absalom, Absalom!*, by two Harvard students in 1910 into a Confederate camp in 1864). Or the fictional voyages can be literal, such as the one on a raft on the Mississippi undertaken by a runaway white boy and an escaped black slave. Sometimes literature reprises actual historical documents, such as Melville's narrative of the real sea captain Amasa Delano who encountered things on a Spanish slave ship that exploded his worldview entirely, while challenging ours.

Readers who have never been to Dublin or Harvard, or on a raft or slave ship, find themselves fellow travelers, and this strange readerly perch opens onto the truer mysteries, the ones involving ethical and spiritual transformation, confronting us with the shocking truths of art, reconfiguring—sometimes obliterating—the players themselves as well as the things we thought we knew. As said, the literary characters thrust into these larger realms can be transformed, undone, annihilated. But what happens to the reader who negotiates such landscapes? This would be literature's knowledge.

Take It Out for a Spin

The discussion sections in my courses used to take place in Brown's science and engineering buildings, and for years there was a beguiling poster on one of the bulletin boards that spoke directly to my heart: it was a picture of a human brain (not a heart). This particular brain was figured like an automobile chassis, and it was outfitted with four spiffy wheels. The caption under the image read: "Take it out for a spin." This is sage advice, and eminently more palatable than Socrates's severe insistence that we know nothing, because it aligns with the outward voyage that all new learning generates inside us. In the past I chided my undergraduates, telling them that they seem willing to engage in the most strenuous physical exercises imaginable (such as I see in the huge, crowded gym rooms I walk past, with their shiny equipment and their sweating youths), whereas the exercise I am urging on them is different, at once cardiac and neural, but distinctly undisplayable by today's electronic monitors, whether EKG or EEG.

That brain-on-wheels, making its way through time and space, is unsurpassable as image, for it figures the very engine itself that is needed for the explorations and trips that lie ahead. Try it on! Strap yourself in! Far too long we've subscribed, in our schools, to a *work ethos*, drumming into our students the need to labor mightily, to strain with all their might—as if they were constipated—so as to absorb and ingest the materials we put their way. Have we missed the larks of it all?

Very often, today's literature courses are courses of correction: how the author was either blind or ideologically at fault. And I know how much good can come from this. Of course, we need to know about the sins of the past and the present, and we need to see how tenacious old, encrusted beliefs can be. But we are nonetheless talking about literature. Writers and artists are not primarily trying to reform the world; their mission is to imagine it, to deliver it. Yes, there can be a profound ethical payload in such work, but it is rarely prescriptive or amenable to legislation. Works of literature do demand work, but, as I see it, of a different sort. What sort? The academy's reply is often: rigor, objectivity, theory; those have their place and their value, but you won't find very much of them in my classroom or in my book. In my crazier moments I think that rigor may be akin to rigor mortis. I am after other game: synthesis as well as analysis; connections that both bind and expand; even might-have-beens that never came to fruition but still live in the human heart.

Dead Letters, Live Letters

But the tenor of the text, whether comic or tragic, whether declarative or subjunctive, does not alter the basic exchange in play. The umbilical cord linking teacher and text and student—with its implied imperative of nurturance, from the one to the other, of hallowing *life*'s basic needs—that compact, indeed that covenant, writes large the very rationale of school as institution. Teaching, as I've said, is a vital generational compact, involving teachers and learners, hinging on the fact that *books do not speak for themselves*. Teachers speak them, make them live, help convert them from dead letters to living script.

Dead letters. You recognize the words but you don't get the meaning. Think about that. How much of your verbal world—books you've read, conversations you've had—consists in dead letters? Any honest tally would be immense. As my own mind starts to rot, I find this generic threat even more depressing than usual. We're not far from Kafka's frozen sea either, since the failure of communication is more often existential than merely lingual. Is there anything more miraculous than the unsimple event of words becoming alive, real? This entails more than some linguistic view of sign and referent; it is closer to magic, to the kinds of faith central to Pascal and Kierkegaard, when the language bridge works.

Education = to lead out. It's a trip. These matters are *vehicular*. The teacher does more than guide or contextualize; he or she lights the fuse, explodes the dynamite, sees to it that it goes off, where it is meant to, in the minds of the students who are brought into this age-old contract between the word and the life. For too long, we've thought these matters to be docile and discreet, a quiet affair of language and pedagogy; but they can be eye-opening, heart-opening, as the ceaseless semiotic miracle takes place, and we discover how volatile these forces are, how inflammable they and we are. I've intentionally enlisted melodramatic, fiery language here, because good teaching, even when it proceeds via whisper or wink or ironic aside, opens doors, so as to blow you through them.

Going Out, Coming Home

How does one put teaching and writing—the two activities I've poured my life into—together, in such a way that highlights their remarkable common ground? My solution is: I want this book to do justice to the exploratory, expanding vistas of literature and teaching, while also attending to the pitfalls and reversals that can stud the entire enterprise. These two perspectives do not cancel each other out. One way to describe this two-way street is to see it as the "voyage out" and the "return home," a round-trip model that is at once kinetic and reflective, or centrifugal and centripetal, committed to both the life voyage each of us makes and the sense we might make of it, before, during, and after. These terms risk seeming esoteric, but I have my sights on elemental things.

I have learned that my books inhabit me every bit as much as I inhabit them. The cohabitation makes clear boundaries and origins impossible. If I opine on any topic whatsoever, it is likely that the usual suspects (Sophocles, Shakespeare, the Brontës, Melville, Dickinson, Baudelaire, Mallarmé, Twain, Strindberg, Kafka, Proust, Joyce, Woolf, Faulkner, Morrison, Coetzee, the whole crowd) are financing the party, whether or not I quote them, whether or not I even know they are there. The opposite is no less true: when I teach or write about the books that matter most to me, I not only find/bring myself into the equation, but I seek overtly to translate them into the sentient and existential terms and issues that impact on my students, our society, our lives. Transport, *transport*.

However, I am acutely aware that the above paragraph could not possibly make sense for my students. For them, the words of the whole gang, from Sophocles to Morrison and Coetzee, are likely exotic, new, unknown. Untried. Perhaps even soporific. Certainly at risk of being or becoming dead words. And I wonder what they must think of the old man who seems larded with them, who claims his own inwardness is stocked with these words and thoughts, making up this payload he seems so intent on delivering. It is as if my mission were to dig into my own depths—for that is where my writers now live—and find ways to get these materials into theirs. I have no shovel or pickax available. Just a classroom with a couple of hours a week.

Isn't it odd that we know more about the etiology of disease than we do about the origins of thought? Or the deposits and transfers that take place in the dark?

For all these reasons, this book is *interwoven*. I write about my life path, about teaching as career, and about literature itself.

The account of my voyage from Memphis six-year-old to senior Brown University professor displays a version of those centrifugal energies I earlier mentioned, whereas my looking back with questions obeys the homecoming injunction no one escapes: what does it all mean? The very enterprise of teaching is cued to this same duet of exploratory and critical moves. Finally, the book harvest that will be central to many of these pages is no less keyed to these same matters: the cost of knowing, the dimensionality of narrative, the gathering retrospect. The books I discuss, and the "I" who is discussing them, have kept each other company, had their affair, for many long years. I don't want to separate them.

Yet that particular couple—the books and me—live by different rules, despite my conviction of what they share. Life itself has a way of talking back, and a half century in the trenches can teach the teacher a great deal that is not in the lesson plan. I am not speaking about the predictable failures: that the students don't read or understand either the books or the teacher; that particular booby trap is baked into the system. There's worse. Anyone who has put in fifty years doing anything becomes a specialist about other types of wreckage as well, going well beyond classroom fiascoes to further more intimate threats involving the teacher's own machinery. There'll be a place for this too.

Working for Your Bread

"Old men ought to be explorers," T. S. Eliot wrote, but exploration carries its own risks, especially for the old. And my openly incendiary account of what teaching entails has, as anyone can see, little in common with the subtle Socratic manner of gentle prodding and strategic indirection. (I wouldn't have gone far in a philosophy department.)

Working for your bread: my guess is that everyone reading this sentence has, at some time or another, come across or invoked this venerable phrase, to denote what they do to earn a living. It states a core algorithm in human life: the relation between effort and reward. It may surprise you that my mentor, Kierkegaard, explicitly brings it up—"Only one who works gets bread"—in order to blast it as blatantly untrue: many people work and receive no bread; many others receive bread without working. Here would be the elemental material injustice that resides deep within so many social and economic systems. Yet the philosopher goes on to claim that things are different in the soul. There, he says, it does not rain on the just and the unjust alike. There, in the soul, labor and reward align. What does he mean?

Kierkegaard is, I believe, talking about the severe law of *understanding*. You have to work through to knowledge. You cannot merely receive it or log on to it. His primary example, as I've said, is Abraham: you won't understand him until you factor in the fear and trembling he experienced, in obeying God's command. But we are free to apply this austere, beautiful notion to our own labors and to our grasp of mankind's efforts at large. We are awash with outcomes, but do we grasp the human drama that preceded and produced them?

"Working for your bread" has, of course, an unmistakable further fit with this book as well. After all, I am writing about fifty-plus years of working for my bread: what I did, what it meant, what its value was. My students received grades, I received a salary, yet I am still pondering that critical relation between work and reward. There was a time when these matters seemed more self-evident and required no special pleading. It seemed to make obvious sense to study literature. CEOs even told us that the critical skills we were teaching would be highly valued in all walks of life. And few argued that it was foolhardy to spend time (and money) reading Shakespeare. These issues were uncontroversial.

But the world has changed. Today's students come to our universities well aware of the great prestige of STEM fields, and of its inevitable corollary: that a major in the humanities is impractical at best and a dicey choice or even death sentence at worst. Therefore, in a gnawing, unwanted way, the phrase also applies to the basic dilemma of my field itself: students (and their tuition-paying parents) today must suspect that the study of literature fails exactly this stubborn real-life test: it will not lead to a job or career; it will not yield bread. So, at least, the naysayers say.

This book is about what it does yield.

Satyr Play

And here's the rub. We know the books are ageless. We also know the books are unflinching in their bookkeeping, about comeuppance, lost illusions, and cashiering of prior beliefs. What about teachers? The Greeks mixed comedies with their tragedies, and they included satyr plays as well. I cannot quite fill the bill on that front, but my retrospect would be hollow and fraudulent if it did not shine its critical, indeed satirical, light on the teacher (*moi*), to expose the foibles, hubris, failures, and other asserted messes that are threaded into my career but that I've never acknowledged or earlier noticed. I've come to see them all too clearly now, shiny and embarrassing, in the murky mirror. I now see that my end-of-career tale is also one of occasional pratfalls and error, of occasional purblind ignorance regarding my audience, of frequent arrogance and benightedness. Of only sensing now how inflated and pretentious many of my moves and claims might actually be.

And so there's a late chunk of this otherwise drum-beating book that delves into what the French call gaffes—errors, mistakes, or screwups. I don't find it easy to laugh at myself—my tone is frequently exalted, puffed up, declamatory; I suspect you've noted that—but these lower-to-the-ground gaffes have their own overdue, corrective, salty truths to deliver. They are owed in late reckonings. They demand their place in the trip home. Maybe, maybe, they will allow the teacher to learn some belated final lessons. Or, if not, at least they round out the story. We're never through discovering who we are.

CHAPTER I

My Voyage Out

I think teachers stand in relation to their students somewhat the way Walt Whitman's spider stands:

> A noiseless patient spider,
> I mark'd where on a little promontory it stood isolated,
> Mark'd how to explore the vacant vast surrounding,
> It launch'd forth filament, filament, filament, out of itself,
> Ever unreeling them, ever tirelessly speeding them.
>
> And you O my soul where you stand,
> Surrounded, detached, in measureless oceans of space,
> Ceaselessly musing, venturing, throwing, seeking the spheres to
>   connect them,
> Till the bridge you will need be form'd, till the ductile anchor
>   hold,
> Till the gossamer thread you fling catch somewhere, O my soul.

Is the bridge ever formed? Does the ductile anchor hold? Does the gossamer thread of our days and years truly catch somewhere? Such are the scary questions that the teacher as well as the writer must eventually ask.

I write this book—anyone who ever writes a book does so—with the hope that the bridge can hold, that the thread can catch. Has held, has caught. But such hopes can never be more than hopes. Certainties in this arena are not to be found, and that is astounding in its own right. Had I been a teacher of mathematics or computer science or even

26

history or political science, there would be a more comforting, reliable sense that I have imparted the basic facts of a field, and that all parties *know what they know*. A career of teaching literature is closer to Whitman's existential uncertainty. Yes, they've (probably) read the books, but then: what has been learned? One is reminded once again of the reply given to the question, "Do you believe in baptism": "Yes, I've seen it performed many times." Heaven knows I have performed teaching many times. What does it mean?

Starting Out

In writing about how I got here, it is clear that I am embarking on a quest that is personal as well as professional. I have already spoken of how being an identical twin shaped my perception of literature and of others; this account of my further "formation" shines a broader light on what teaching means and why I do it. It will be seen that "Ithaca" is a motif in several of my chapters, and for good reason: the project of returning home—fueling great texts well beyond Homer's *Odyssey*—amounts very often to a critical, even shocking discovery of what home actually was or is. This is inevitably the final turn in one's voyage out, whether it be the path from child-reader to old professor or the tally of what any lifelong career has wrought.

I who write obsessively about memory—it cannot be haphazard that Proust and Faulkner mean so much to me—have very little of it myself. My wife often teases me that, as identical twin, I outsourced my memories (my bookkeeping) to my brother. She may be right.

When I go back to the beginning, I encounter the memory of standing in front of a small easel in first grade at White Station School in Memphis, in 1946, an easel with colored pictures of Bob and Nancy and their exploits, accompanied by *letters* and *words* underneath the bright images. I have no recollection of how this material was taught—and I had not gone to kindergarten—but I knew even then that I was encountering the basic semiotic miracle of life and culture: written words that signify things. "Semiotic miracle"? Imagine explaining that to a six-year-old. Yet this long-ago memory still bristles with a hedonist, indeed, fateful sense of excitement and rendezvous, an excitement that was even more miraculously repeatable, time and again, each time I looked at print. I loved being at that easel. Even thinking about that long-ago easel with Bob, Nancy, and the markings underneath, I salivate. (I salivate but I also reflect: yes, every child undergoes the Bob-and-Nancy initiation in some fashion, but professors of literature spend their very lives drawing on that encounter, pondering what actually happens when letters become people, when people become letters.)

Yet I did not become a reader back then, nor do I remember being read to, as a child. *Literature* was a term that meant nothing to me. We had a *Compton's Encyclopedia* in my house—my parents were told it was indispensable for the intellectual and cultural development of their children (those must have been the very words)—but I never consulted it in the least. I sailed through my primary, secondary, and high school years, finding it embarrassingly easy to get A's on tests—why didn't everyone, I wondered?—yet with no curiosity whatsoever as to what those tests were meant to evaluate or promote.

Bob and Nancy had of course done their work: I could read and answer all the questions put to me. But the hallucinatory pleasure that attended the birth of reading died out almost immediately thereafter. And I realize now, with some seventy-plus years of retrospect and a good dollop of sadness, that my school accomplishments, however much lauded by my teachers and parents, were entirely devoid of the adrenaline I'd experienced at the age of six, in front of that long-ago easel. Good grades, but no "understanding." That's why I so often critique "information." It's as if my apology for teaching were a (doomed) effort to reach back in time and rescue that dull, complacent little boy, to jostle him and wake him up.

Hot Stuff

Then, years later, came the first tremors of the second awakening. The eye-opening, heart-opening moment was occasioned by my eleventh grade English teacher, Mr. Hazelwood, doing a one-year stint at our sleepy Memphis public high school—a somewhat awkward young man, a newcomer bent on doing things differently—whose teaching style *got through*. He managed to jolt me on a regular basis: regularly electrifying many of us, the until-then-torpid students now sitting bolt upright in his classroom, as he held in his hands a book of poems, pointing to Keats or Shelley, telling us that this is *hot stuff!* Not "was" but *is* hot stuff. I can still see him in my mind's eye: a rather ill-at-ease man who *came to life*, who *crossed borders* when he had a book in his hands and read from it. I was shocked: why did his entire manner change? How can a poem be hot stuff? What was happening? As I look back, I realize I've spent more or less the whole of my later professional life measuring the in-dwelling heat and seismic life that he—like a scientist or excavator digging into hidden recesses, digging right into my heart—first helped me see.

But I did not then think back, as I now do, to Bob and Nancy and the elemental logic of linking word to picture to reality—it would have been mortifying; after all, this was poetry, and I was in the eleventh grade—but something of the same thrill, the same frisson was at hand, was tasted and enjoyed. I sensed there were dimensions out there ... or in here. Where, I wondered?

My Swedish wife's story is rigorously parallel. She remembers how Fröken Kronwald used to read poetry to her and her sixteen-year-old peers in the girls' school she attended. The girls were bent on important things—examining their nails, thinking about the café they would go to when class let out, about the parties scheduled for that weekend—but they were discomfited by what Kronwald was doing: this sixty-year-old woman was reading aloud from nineteenth-century Swedish poetry, and she would reach—furtively but at regular intervals—toward the lace handkerchief tucked in the edge of her sleeve, so that she could quickly and discreetly wipe away the tear (the tears) that could not be kept down, that seemed inseparable from the poems being read, as if they welled up from the same source.

And my wife tells me she thought, I do not know what this poem means, but I am shocked by how much it means to this old woman. Such thoughts whispered to her then, as to me in Mr. Hazelwood's class: is it possible that poetry has a kind of power that does not age or die, that is as irrepressible and invincible after decades of acquaintance as it was when first encountered? Is it possible that teachers are *conduits*, power stations, sending energy and news from afar into the young? Utilities such as light, gas, and water; coal, electricity, solar and nuclear power—we've known forever that each town or city or country requires them for its energy needs, but it hasn't occurred to us that we also find them closer to home, in classrooms.

This book is about that power.

Paris Pleasures

From high school in Memphis, I went on—excellent grades and boards, yet unawakened, "unawoke"—to Princeton, where I immediately felt my woeful lack of sophistication, on so many different fronts, social as well as intellectual. How, I wondered, could my new peers from Andover and Exeter have possibly acquired the rhetorical poise they displayed? Would I ever catch up? Those memories come to mind each fall, in my first-year seminars at Brown, where I recognize the frequent panic in my students' eyes, as so many of them secretly feel that the Admissions Office made a mistake, that they shouldn't be there, that they'll be found out. I certainly wondered the same when I was in their place. Nor did I have any clue about the future.

I began to get a fix on these existential matters only when I crossed the ocean—for the first time—to spend my junior year in Paris. Paris was, as it has so often been for Americans in the past, my stirring and unmistakable wake-up call: I found that my intensive but newly acquired college French was enough, when combined with a kind of curiosity and momentum and staying power never felt earlier, to propel me into uncharted territory.

Therefore, when I try to understand why Paris was what it was— beyond the existential discoveries that came to a young, untraveled person of twenty encountering that magical city for the first time well over half a century ago—I realize that *language* was a key element. I had learned both Latin and Spanish in high school and could decipher simple texts, but there had been zero emphasis on the oral side. In

Memphis of the late 1950s, in my circle, there seemed, as far as I could tell, to be no one to talk with in Spanish (even if I could have understood a word of it). And it hadn't fully dawned on me back then that that's what languages were for. Hence, the heady, even disorienting experience of *speaking* and *hearing* French day and night roused me, primed me, seemed to target and expand my own voice by making it more "independent," by making me lingually other, perhaps bringing out whole selves that English had not served. This is not an uncommon experience—"You're different when you speak a foreign language," people have said forever—but I felt it as liberating, as freeing up a wilder and unknown side of me (another twin?), and I now see it as the first steps in my growing sense of language as means of self-enactment.

The written side of this equation matched the oral side, inasmuch as I read exclusively French literature for an entire year, and wrote accordingly in French as well, luxuriating in its resources, as if I only now *saw language*. Above all, I owe a debt to a yearlong course at the Sorbonne on the poet Mallarmé, a wizard of suggestive and haunting verses as well as a mythmaker of poetry as its own universe. (You've already run into him in this book; you will hear still more about him.) Through Mallarmé I discovered what his younger peer Rimbaud rightly called "l'alchimie du verbe," the metamorphic and colonizing power of language. It did not then occur to me, as it does now, that Bob and Nancy had pointed the way.

Voice

Most life-changing of all, this immersion into French and Paris—into Mallarmé's daunting poetic world (studded with words I had to guess at, words whose multiple meanings sent me far and wide, requiring neural energies I did not know that I had or that anyone had)—coincided with (more likely catalyzed) the discovery of my own *voice*. Some kind of fateful consonance between language and feeling took place inside me, taking *hot stuff* to a new plateau that I could actually inhabit, could use as stepping stone or platform. I began to write papers with (French) fire in them. (*Words* look staid enough, but they can surprise you by being thermal, and I was now sensing the heat, turning it up: in my writers, in myself. To paraphrase Whitman, I was simmering, simmering, simmering, and Paris brought me to a boil.)

Something incendiary had happened. A door had opened. I knew, then, at the ripe age of twenty, that I wanted to teach. And that literature would be my field. Much later, as professor, I would find a "purple" moment in James Joyce's *Portrait of the Artist as a Young Man*, where young Stephen Dedalus swoons at the entry of a prostitute's tongue in his mouth; and I would sense that maybe this is what "foreign tongue," or "langue étrangère," might actually betoken: a quasi-sexual entry of something live, quick, and arousing inside oneself, adding to oneself. No linguist would agree, but my "thermal" theory accords with this view.

The stint in Paris was followed by a summer of immersion in German in Heidelberg, filled with the same adrenaline, adding to my growing conviction that I would be headed for some kind of future with languages. One unexpected discovery my new command of German led to happened in Memphis at summer's end, back at home with my parents and my ailing Jewish grandmother, a woman I'd never much liked or known well, given that her duty in life seemed to shield my mother from demands posed by my twin brother and me, but also because her only workable language was Yiddish. But that late summer in 1961, for a few weeks, we did something momentous: we *spoke*—she in Yiddish, me in German—she showed me her Yiddish newspapers (which I could actually read), and . . . I grudgingly began to realize that she might actually be a person, not just a grandmother. But I went briskly off to my senior year up north, and never saw her again. She died later that fall. Belatedness.

I returned to Princeton a different person, and I had the great good fortune of encountering Laurence Holland, whose legendary course of "Four American Authors" not only provided literary fare (Melville, Twain, James, and Faulkner) I plumb to this day (and in this book, as you will see), but it also modeled a form of teaching that seemed to me an outright version of Mallarmé's poetics of suggestion. Holland could not know this "French connection," nor could any of my Sorbonne professors have seen or validated it. But I did. In each book I've written, I've saluted Holland's impact (as have many others who came Holland's way), but this is the book where I will be investigating the longitudinal *teaching chain* itself, the formative bonds that reached all the way back to Bob and Nancy, to Mr. Hazelwood, in my earlier life. Retrospect's bounty.

Senior year at Princeton changed me in yet another way, even more life-altering, for I then met—right at Labor Day—a young Swedish au pair, Ann, whom I fell in love with, whom I married fifteen months later, whom I'm still married to, whose spirit is all over this book. When we first met, at a party given by a German professor, I smoothly passed myself off as a French graduate student—surely languages count for something, don't they?—and spoke halting English to her with what I felt was a convincing French accent. She immediately saw through my pose and called me out, as indeed she has continued to do for going on six decades.

As said, we did indeed marry (in Sweden), during the following year (she and) I spent in Berlin, studying German literature, going to German plays and restaurants, walking all over war-torn, unrebuilt Berlin, including on Kurfürstendamm, where the Gedächtniskirche looked like so many other bombed-out buildings. It was a momentous year, the equal of my Paris stint: as one of the handful of American students on German Fellowship in Berlin in 1962, I was invited to stand a few feet from the charismatic JFK when he spoke at the Freie Universität, thrilling me with his eloquence and learned references to Goethe, Bismarck, and others, giving me a strange pride in being American. It was a time of immense geopolitical strife: the Berlin Wall was still new, just beginning to acquire its bloody history; and each time we left Berlin for Sweden, the train went through the Communist "East," meaning that each return trip stopped regularly at the Friedrichstraße Bahnhof in the Russian zone of Berlin, where Vopo agents swung actual bayonets under the train wagons, searching for escapees; only afterwards did one make one's way to West Berlin and seeming security.

Married, I said. Is it ever that simple? Ann was working for an American colonel who told her, when the Cuban missile crisis happened in October—causing many to expect Khrushchev to order a Russian countermove on Berlin—that she'd "better get that American boy to marry her right away" because war was coming, and I would immediately be sent back home and drafted, whereas she (not yet American citizen) would have to return to Sweden. We did. She still likes telling the story that she had to create an international crisis to bring about our wedding.

After Berlin came graduate school: comparative literature at Harvard, a field that beckoned because I (naively) viewed it as *artisanal*, open to unsuspected pairings and amalgams, resistant to legislating formalisms and binding categories. Our acts of reading and thinking, I felt in my bones, have a lawless life of their own, and there is—or should be— a freedom in the very act of comparison. As an older French colleague once told me later, "Influence is the most untrackable thing in the world, like the smoke in a bar." Smoke in a bar: how do you pin that down? Should you even try? But my graduate program had different views: the professional instruction I was indoctrinated in seemed filled with defini- tions and fences and regulations and conventions and arcane rules regarding how one is to link literature 1 with literature 2 or 3. It also whispered to us: you can *never* learn enough to pronounce on anything. Is this professionalism's dirty secret?

But I was probably, at the level where it mattered, unteachable, for it was still the *freedom* of my field that most attracted me. Let me go fur- ther still, in a way I could scarcely have articulated back then: the human mind is arguably more jubilant, more empowered, more hedonistic, and more at home with *synthesis* than it is with stern requirements of *analy- sis*. (Why is this never emphasized in our curricula? Just imagine how much more pleasurable coursework might be.) And even *synthesis* is too poor a term for what I am arguing: *comparison* is the outward thrust of the mind and heart, for it is the pattern searcher, even the marriage bro- ker. As a newlywed, that term seemed right.

The Sense of a Mission

Teaching was, yes, the inevitable career choice. I had come upon some- thing quasi-demiurgic, outright spawning, in its energies, liminal, bring- ing news of new dimensions, further roads to travel. Each of these encounters was larded with power: the texts whose potency I was just discovering, the teacher whose role was at once seminal and midwifing, and myself being launched. That such a scheme might be at war with the regimes of information and data was not yet thinkable for me, given not only that our culture's love affair with information technology was still decades away, given also that I had scarcely heard of Kierkegaard or his radical critique back then.

It sounds awfully swollen-headed and pompous, but I sensed something almost contractual in all this. One reason that I knew all this viscerally, with an unmistakable sense of *calling*, was because I perceived—for the first time in my life—what I was actually good for. (Here was the luckiest turn of all; I know, from decades of talking to my students, how elusive such eureka moments can be, how they may never come. Mine banged me on the head.) I felt exalted, as all people do, when things crystallize. (Irony has never been my strong suit.) I would become, yes, a medium, a conduit for others to make similar discoveries, similar explorations. Literature was to be a storehouse of such possibilities, and I was to be the happy, empowered guide.

Thermal. I am aware that the overheated prose of the paragraphs above has an embarrassingly purple, sophomoric character, and although my (inherited) Jewish background would have vetoed thinking myself (as Joyce's Stephen Dedalus does) "a priest of the eternal imagination," I did obliquely sense a quasi-religious vocation. In fact, exactly that had been pointed out, and promptly forgotten, far earlier, when I was sixteen and took, as many of my peers did, an "aptitude test" whose results stated that the career I was *most* suited for was rabbi, adding that *least* suitable would be forest ranger. I still remember this episode from all those years ago: I laughed out loud when my mother transmitted this finding, and I laughed each time I thought about it. Rabbi seemed more outlandish than forest ranger.

But, it recently dawned on me, one doesn't have to go back far at all, since the evidence stares me in the face every day of my working life: rabbis are folks who spend a lot of time interpreting the culture's texts to their community. Hmm.

Brown and Human Studies

"Human Studies" may sound like a cliché today, but back in the late 1960s, when I started teaching at Brown, the term designated a brand-new program of study, the brainchild of a courageous professor who actually exited his STEM department (Applied Math) in order to devote himself fulltime to this large-souled venture, where the focus was kept on the "human." You may think this is unexceptional, the sort of thing any professor might elect to do, but I assure you that such behavior is *unimaginable* today. In fact, it was unimaginable then too. He was the only man "without a department" in the Brown faculty, and he paid for it, in terms of sacrificed faculty prestige. I have not forgotten the contemptuous remarks made by several deans (and doubtless shared by many colleagues) about Human Studies, indicating plainly that exiting one's department is a form of hara-kiri and cannot possibly be taken seriously.

Yet who turned out to be right? Human Studies was an elite program. Several of Brown's most illustrious graduates majored in it (one of whom went on to serve later in the Clinton cabinet). In fact, one of the senior honors projects done at that time in Human Studies was nothing less than the blueprint for what then became Brown's *New Curriculum*, written collaboratively by two brilliant undergraduates. The seeds for liberal change at Brown—removing requirements, introducing the Satisfactory grading option, encouraging interdisciplinary work—were *student-driven*. Neither the administration nor the faculty were the drivers here. Yet this marked the beginning of a new chapter—what one today would term a new "branding"—in Brown's mission, image, and appeal. It was launched. And even today, what is best and most seductive and indeed marketable about Brown bears this stamp.

I, too, bear this stamp. At the very beginning of my career, I had the great good luck to join this small cadre of professors to work with Human Studies students across disciplinary lines, and this experience changed how I understood literature itself. One of the core principles in Human Studies was: unlike the order of the university, life itself does not come packaged in disciplines; another was: you cannot see the conventions that shape your discipline (and your vision), until you exit it. (It is hard to overstate how against the institutional grain these two contentions still are. Disciplines and departments are the core structures of academic knowledge, even if real-world problems and challenges invariably cross these lines.) There was yet another principle that I personally stole from Human Studies, and it underwrites both my full career and this final book: the humanities offer an urgent critical optic on much that seems business as usual in other fields.

Two of my most ambitious courses were born this way. "The City and the Arts" explores the culture of city life from the vantage point of literature, painting, film, architecture, and urban theory. "Literature and Medicine" looks at the testimony of literature (along with the work of medical historians and theorists) over the centuries, depicting not only how doctors are seen, but also focusing on key matters such as pain, trauma, addiction, diagnosis, death and dying, and much else. These two offerings brought Urban Studies and premed students my way, young people already steeped in the sciences and social sciences, and it was bracing for me to make—and have to defend—claims for literature and the arts in areas where they are thought to have little purchase. All this I owe to Human Studies.

Tearing Down Walls

"The voyage out," as concept, stamps my teaching in still other ways, ways I could never have intuited at the beginning of my career; namely, I found myself involved in a number of experiments in "tearing down walls," even beyond the Human Studies paradigm. For roughly a decade I served as curricular advisor to the Dean of the College, and during that time we came up with a program called "Texts and Teachers"; the title is innocuous, but the aspirations were grand: to establish new partnerships in education. Anyone who has taught in a school or university knows how much red tape shows up when one ventures outside one's "turf." Over a period of years, with generous support from the National Endowment for the Humanities (NEH), I begged, enticed, and persuaded colleagues in four departments to come up with a battery of team-taught university courses—theme-centered ventures with a small number of texts, thrusting the issue of *difference* directly at us—by bridging literature and philosophy and religious studies, as well as the cultures of America and Europe and Asia. The disciplines had it out with each other. This was scintillating, perhaps most of all for the faculty, since our exchanges took place publicly on stage, as we argued with one another about the meaning of our diverse materials—something inconceivable in single-instructor classrooms with their unquestioned top-down authority structure—but I noticed that many undergraduates were discomfited by our quarrels, by our cacophony. And my cynical brain thought: When students pay our insane tuitions, they expect their courses to move inexorably toward harmonious conclusions, nicely wrapped up at semester's end; our debates were unseemly, making some of them wonder if they were getting their money's worth. Surely you shouldn't exit a course more confused than you were at the outset?

But we tried to go further still. We left the precincts of the university and went into the high schools, seeking to form a new teaching coalition that would wed secondary and higher education. This model was so exciting that, armed (again) with generous NEH-funding, we took it "on the road" and created a national model, inviting *teams* from Seattle, Chicago, Memphis, and Columbus to come to Brown for Summer Seminars geared to yield collaborative high school–university joint offerings in their home sites during the following years. I have italicized "teams" because it seemed—it still seems—outright revolutionary to ask these two populations to work together.

The most ambitious piece of all this was our desire to meld the two walled-off student bodies themselves, by having college professors and college students go into the high schools to participate in a *common course*. And it was a two-way street: high school seniors, as well as their teachers, participated in college offerings. As I look back in hindsight at these heady programs, I marvel at the scale of what we attempted. Knocking down walls in the service of a common vision, so that separate (and separated) constituencies could work together: this flies in the face of all bureaucratic models and conventional thinking. (I recall meeting with the superintendent of Providence Schools, in the beginning stages of our venture, seeking her ideas about which public schools to approach, and being told flat-out that our project was crazy, would never work. Why, she asked, were we doing it? What did we think we could achieve? I had no great reply then, and I'm not sure even now that I do.)

As I reflect back on Human Studies—now long gone from the Brown scene, a distant memory, a curiosity—and on those years of NEH-funded team-taught courses that wedded entire communities—equally disappeared, unremembered, dead—I see my own monumental naivete as well as the stirring fervor of the 1970s and even 1980s. The old disciplinary forms still exist, as strong as ever, even if there is a bit more crossover in the sciences. Yet surprises happen. A recent number of the *Brown Alumni Magazine* elected to focus on—you guessed it—Brown's "open curriculum," and by dint of serious excavation, it finally paid tribute (half a century late, in my view) to the pioneering work done by Human Studies and its visionary founder. I suspect I am the only Brown professor still teaching today formed by those faraway days.

If anything, Brown itself seems to have evolved in directions I could hardly imagine back then. We actually bragged, in those days, about the fact that Brown offered no "business courses"—"other" schools did that, we crowed—whereas today such offerings appear throughout the curriculum, garnering huge enrollments (and huge donors). Likewise, computer science was a fledgling field back then, but today it rules the roost and has gobbled up a huge chunk of the university's intellectual and research real estate, with massive support from students, faculty, alumni, and big business. Places change.

Still, I wonder, Did we achieve anything back then? I think back to the numbers of students from underfunded city and rural high schools, who participated in our experimental Brown program. After all, these young people were not naive, and they knew quite well that their chances of ever going to Brown were minimal (for economic as well as GPA reasons), yet here they were. And when my spirits are low, I want to think they may—may—have realized something potentially momentous: *I can do this.* There is much talk today, at the university and elsewhere, about *empowerment.* As self-indulgent humanities professor, I've always faulted myself for being only an armchair activist, for living so completely in the world of books, but then I reflect: this faraway decade of work in public and private education just might have nudged some lives. Again: isn't it strange how little we know about moments when new self-perceptions are born? *Hot stuff* moments in the classroom, taking place in the dark, surely unknown to Mr. Hazelwood in 1956, when he altered me and my path. We never know what, if anything, we seed. But regarding these team-taught experimental courses, at least one person was changed for sure: me.

The Great Courses

The next installment of my "voyage out" took place right after the NEH-funded initiatives came to a close: in the 1990s I was invited by The Teaching Company (now The Great Courses) to create literature courses for their broad public audience, to be marketed and disseminated in video format. I had given invited lectures before at many venues, but this was new: a nonuniversity adult audience, with no papers to write or exams to take, freed of the constraints of the academy, seeing these lectures in the privacy of home. What did these folks want from literature?

One of the most challenging features of The Great Courses was its attitude toward erudition and professional discourse. I was obviously expected to know what I was talking about, but it was imminently clear that I could not clog my lectures with little footnotes or grand chunks of academy-speak or theoretical jargon. Everything I said had to pay its way. I had actually run into this same challenge when I wrote some books for Random House (rather than university presses) during this same decade; it was tricky.

You might think that writing for (or teaching) a *general audience* is easy—I certainly thought it would be, initially—but you'd be wrong. Years in the academy have their enduring hold, and I discovered, over and over in the giving of these courses and the writing of these books, that all number of scholarly references or ornamental quotations crept unnoticed into my work, as a kind of crutch or filler that was virtually invisible to me. It is harder to take the academy out of the professor than it is to take the professor out of the academy. I was now required to think differently: does this reference or that line of reasoning have any significance to all these people? This, I came to realize, was a high bar, not a low one.

This clientele needed no persuading that literature mattered; many of them were returning to "school" in order to reread classics they'd either read or heard of, almost a lifetime earlier, to little avail, but that they were now eager to reencounter and possess. There is food for thought here: is it possible that my field (literature) actually makes far more sense to older folks than it does to college students? I do not think that maturity or life experience matters when you're being taught chemistry or mathematics; but *King Lear*? Over and over, I would get messages from these people I'd never met, saying that *now* these books make sense, whereas earlier, they seemed irrelevant.

No less essential, my Great Courses audience didn't need credit or a diploma or—crucially—a job. The fierce competition at the university— can you "afford" a literature course if you want to be a doctor or lawyer or if you know you'll graduate with significant debts?—disappeared from the equation. These adult students were actually free to study what they liked.

Today's neoliberal mantra—let the market decide—seems therefore especially dicey to me when it comes to education. Our expensive institutions of learning, despite their high-sounding rhetoric about liberal education, are finding themselves increasingly bound to the harshest of economic metrics, whereby entire areas of study thrive or founder, depending on what their job-getting utility might be. The sleuthing adage "Follow the money" applies more to the academy than one might think. It's not simply that the tuitions are absurdly high but that many of the university's most generous donors choose the STEM fields for their gifts, doubtless convinced that such areas of knowledge must be ever stronger if the (expensively) diploma'd-young are to make their way. I've spoken a lot about the "cost of knowing," as it pertains to human knowledge, but in a different sense altogether, the humanities are being priced out.

My own mantra has always been: The liberal-arts education prepares you for life, not for a job. I still believe that. But it is a belief that perhaps makes most sense to folks who are retired, who already have jobs, who don't need jobs. And I have a queasy feeling of being quite the hypocrite since I, in fact, do have a job: I actually get paid to try to convince young people that literature matters. No one has yet pressed me on this, but still . . .

A final word about my work with The Great Courses. In the mid-1990s my literature courses for this outfit were going great guns. Ads would appear in the *New York Times* or the *New York Review of Books* featuring this or that course, sometimes equipped with a sketch of me at the podium and often closing with the provocative hook "Can't get to Brown? You can take Professor Weinstein's course with us, by purchasing . . ." I recall getting irate letters from Brown's provost, telling me that such advertising was distinctly verboten, that sacred issues of intellectual property were at risk of infringement, and that I had to issue a cease-and-desist order to the folks running The Great Courses. (I did nothing of the sort.)

But what goes around comes around. My courses are still in circulation, but the people running The Great Courses have in recent years explained to me that my courses are awfully labor-intensive: after all, I am assuming that my audience will actually *read* long works of literature. But a cursory glance at today's huge panoply of Great Courses makes it clear that most of their offerings have very little in the way of "homework"; they are understood to be "enriching" all on their own. There is an interesting Catch-22 here: I had supposed that these video offerings would be utterly manageable, since the (university-imposed) bugbear of exams, papers, grades, and competing courses was removed from the equation. Nor would this audience need my course to get a job or a raise. Turns out that my book-crammed courses may nonetheless be too arduous, too "expensive" along exactly the lines Kierkegaard limned: labor versus reward. Hoisted by my own petard.

My MOOC

I have been charting the outward course of my career and my teaching, and its final capstone experience is of much more recent date: my stint with MOOCs (massive open online courses), when I created (for

Brown's trial run with Coursera) an online version of one of my signature university courses, "The Fiction of Relationship," in 2013–14. Here would be the most radical and the most contemporary form of disseminating teaching, and it drew, in its two iterations, an audience of close to one hundred thousand "students." After all, if teaching is a living chain of transmission, MOOCs provide outreach and economies of scale unimaginable in traditional precincts. Given, however, the suspicion in many quarters about online education versus brick-and-mortar schooling, and given the general view that such a data-based instructional model is particularly unsuited for the humanities, I discuss distance learning more broadly in chapter 2. But a few words here are in order.

Few people on the planet are as tech illiterate as I am—I want to wind up my computer each morning—but I came out of this experience persuaded that the phenomenon of online education was here to stay, and for good reason: instead of paying a six-figure tuition bill, the student needs only a modem; and with that modem, anyone can access the teaching of reputable professors throughout the world, but at one's own pace, in one's own time and space. (The advantages of this controllable form of access are huge; you can see and hear it, turn it off, take a walk or a nap or a pee, have a meal, turn it on again, see it again, see it yet again next week, next year; you do it, as Sinatra might say, "your way." No lecture hall provides that.) We are still in the early stages of this online-teaching revolution, and even though it has lost some of its luster and hype of a few years ago, I am certain it will alter the educational landscape. Finally, the benefits may surprise us, given the unrecognized promise such technology has for the basic mission of the humanities (and the central theme of this book): personal knowledge.

Let me close with a postscriptum about "me and MOOCs." My stint with Coursera happened in 2013–14, but our world changed in 2020, with the advent of the coronavirus and its enormous impact on schooling at all levels. As you will see, Coursera was not to be my last encounter with online education. As I write these words, universities throughout the world are obliged to use that model, and so, too, did I, over the 2020–21 academic year, via the miraculous benefits of Zoom. That experience— as complement to my account of MOOCs—will be dealt with in the next chapter.

The Book as Trip

I can still remember the closing words of an eminent Renaissance scholar who spoke long ago at Brown, saying that what most endured, most mattered, in his mind toward the end of his career, was essentially a core iconic image: the *figure* of a professor holding a book and speaking to the young about the book. He meant: what matters most, ultimately, is that books themselves matter, that holding them as meaningful, fruitful, even inexhaustible sources of knowledge can also be literally an affair of *holding* them up, cradling them in one's arms, as it were. (Today's digital culture makes my reference fairly nostalgic but not—yet—obsolete.)

And I think back to Hazelwood and Kronwald. Perhaps that is what our long teaching careers produce at best: that books matter. That is what is contagious: if it can matter this much to us, then just maybe it might for them as well. Books themselves look bounded, but, as I've argued throughout, they fuel a transportation system, a series of bridges that bear much traffic, that need no maintenance.

For years and years I have received messages—letters initially, emails now—from students who'd graduated long before, telling me that they *still* remember vital words of mine about Shakespeare or Faulkner or some other writer; and they sometimes go on to quote what they remember. Often enough, the quotation embarrasses me: can I possibly have said something like that? And then, I say to myself, does it really matter? Neither Mr. Hazelwood nor Fröken Kronwald ever published one word about poetry, and yet I am comfortable saying that they have done as much for the afterlife—the mix of appreciation and continuous belief and discovery—of poetry as the most exalted scholars have ever done. They never got much recognition for their work. Maybe they did not need it.

In this light I recall the career of a senior colleague, regarded as the country's top authority on Neoplatonism, but memorable to me because of his astounding rhetorical gifts. This man put no stock whatsoever in undergraduate teaching—he retired early, disenchanted, because of a scholarly slight regarding one of his books—despite the fact that he was legendary at Brown for the high drama of his introductory courses. And I feel that he created his most enduring legacy in just that arena: via the hush that attended his talking about Milton in a dark room, or wearing a pot on his head when he discussed Cervantes, or doing poetry readings before Christmas break, eagerly and gratefully attended by masses of students who would never go on to graduate school or think of going into the academy. I see a conundrum here. Where and by whom, I wonder, should one most want to be remembered? By other scholars? Or by students who today are bankers and lawyers and computer scientists, who today have little to do with the humanities, who've never given much thought (then or now) to Neoplatonism?

Teaching and the Afterlife

Teaching stages an elemental contract between the young and the old. Teaching reverses the dreadful Oedipal story that Freud theorized, by means of which life demands of us that we slay our elders in order to make our way, because teaching enacts a decorous form of generational continuity. Perhaps not always decorous. I sometimes joke with my students that my job is to suck their blood, yet this vampirish notation gets at a certain truth in our arrangements. They, the ever young, bring their hungry minds and curiosity to us, the seasoned ones, and we not only dispense our wisdom and our wares but also batten on to our students, find our own nourishment in these exchanges, this ongoing cultural compact about what endures. Here is an evolutionary-biology account of teaching, positioning us as carriers in a moving chain, necessary for the conversation to go forward. In some respects, it may never end. (I know, I know that this bond can be abused, exploited, sexualized; all the more odious, given its promise and purpose.)

Here's a question I rarely hear at my university: What is to be said of/ for the *bulk* of students who come our way and fill our classrooms and lecture halls, the ones not at or even near the top of the class, the ones that don't "go on"? They, the "great unwashed," as a snide colleague of mine once intoned, are an unheralded, never interrogated, quite unseen form of continuity (since they, too, "go on," don't they?): they, the (often "silent") majority, can be almost invisible, quite unappreciated, given the peculiar optics and valuations of our profession. "Who will (have to) teach the intro course in our department?" is a question that reliably comes up each year and is more often than not seen as a burdensome one, leading to the assignment of such "grunt work" to the junior folks who can't say no.

Graduate seminars, however: now, those are the plums of the profession. This was the cherished (painful) belief of my former Neoplatonist colleague, and this is the belief system that governs today's academy. What do these priorities tell us about *teaching*? About the value accorded to it? About the actual *uses* our materials might have? I sometimes think there is an element of narcissism in the profession's love affair with graduate seminars, with "the happy few" who just might follow in our footsteps. Have we properly seen to it that all the "others" got their fill? Have we figured out what their fill might be?

The Credit Rating of Teachers

I have opted for the ironic rubric above in order to address a stubborn fact of life that I have encountered at every level of education: the *devaluing* of teachers. I have no clue what my first-grade, Bob-and-Nancy-introducing teacher earned, nor do I know what either Mr. Hazelwood or Fröken Kronwald received as salary. But I have to think it modest. Yet the inequity that galls me still more is the low esteem often accorded to teaching at our universities, an esteem that seems paradoxically lower and lower, the more elite and respected the university is. Here we are dealing with a complicated problem quite distinct from the dilemma in our secondary school system.

The meat market for my part of the academic world takes place every year shortly after Christmas: it is called the Modern Language Association Convention, and it features two major kinds of events: learned presentations given by scholars at every rung of the ladder, but also interviews with candidates looking for jobs. These two events are joined at the hip, for each is cued to what is thought to be "cutting-edge" research, and that research (promise) goes a very far piece in determining who gets invited to campuses to give talks and—if they win the lottery—get an offer. Sometimes I think that the judgment call made at the convention resembles the ratings meted out to the world's wines just after the grapes have been picked and they are still in casks: it is something of a guessing game. To be sure, one also has the recommendations of the senior faculty vetting and championing their candidates, but one is essentially trying to look into the future and to gauge whether this young person is likely to continue doing significant research and writing important books in the decades to come, well beyond the doctoral dissertation that is usually the major piece of evidence at this stage of the game. This all makes sense in its own way, and there are no villains in the story I'm telling.

The crunch comes seven or eight years later, when these no longer quite young people must encounter the Great Reckoning: the tenure decision. Note that I am speaking of our top universities where tenure-track positions still exist and where armies of underpaid graduate assistants and adjuncts haven't yet been marshaled to do all the teaching. The march of time is felt at tenure: how much have the young hires actually accomplished? Equally important: how is their work evaluated? This last question gets me to the crux of the matter: they are evaluated by the top scholars in the specialized field of their research. Do these young professors' articles or books pass muster, when examined by the experts? Here is the rationale that matters, since no respectable department will even put forth for tenure a candidate whose reviews are dubious; the university-wide tenure committee would never approve such a recommendation, since the institution's own stature and ranking are ultimately on the line. The all-important outside scholarly evaluations ("outside," hence, putatively free from "politics")—which by definition can take no account of the candidate's teaching or service to undergraduates—are tantamount to fate itself for young professors coming up the ladder.

I've taught long enough to see what can sometimes happen in this scheme. Obviously, the system often enough works, and those who are promoted go on to do a creditable or even excellent job of teaching, during the years ahead. And all tenure committees have information about the teaching record of the candidates. But the classic challenge to this model occurs when a truly talented teacher fails the scholarship test: the outside letters sink him or her. Quite recently at my institution, in the case of a young, charismatic teacher, we recommended against tenure, because the outside experts largely concurred that the research was not up to the highest standards. Here's the rub: I had sat in on this teacher's lectures and had seen, firsthand, how numerous, devoted, and enthused his students were. He was a Shakespeare specialist, and I still remember one of the written student evaluations that essentially said, "I've had Shakespeare shoved down my throat for years in high school; only *now* do I understand why he's a great writer." As far as I could tell— and I do teach the Bard, even though I'm no expert—there was nothing "dumbed down" in this man's presentation of Shakespeare: he was smart, learned, provocative, even dazzling in the lecture hall; yet none of this made it over to the supreme "accounting," that of the outside specialists.

The ironies here are palpable. The outside experts claim that our candidate doesn't truly get Shakespeare, whereas the students claim the opposite: only now do they get Shakespeare. The experts say that our candidate seems unaware of the existing research on Shakespeare; our students have no interest in Shakespeare scholarship, but they are capable of falling in love with Shakespeare. Two rather different missions are on show here: whether your published work gets high marks with the experts or how well you convey your materials to your students. In this instance, these two missions collided, and his career with us came to an end.

I am sufficiently old to be skeptical regarding both these mission statements. Teaching is said to be ephemeral—so the old chestnut goes—because it cannot outlive its classroom utterance, whereas scholarship is eternal, stored in libraries. Both claims are dubious. Scholarship can often be marginal, towing the line of what is fashionable among the scholars, not to mention that it can lie rotting in the stacks (or online) and that it often holds little light for the uninitiated. Teaching is no less vulnerable, and even advocates such as me recognize how impressionable the young are, how much irresponsible "Pied Piperism" is possible in the classroom, and how transient its outcomes may be.

But if I were a dean, I'd be torn indeed. To go with the scholarly ratings, but to lose talented teachers as the cost of doing so, seems to me a peculiar view of what the institution's priorities should be. It's not merely a question of *which* audiences—the outside experts or the undergraduates—most matter, but it has to do with how we define our mission and what purposes our field serves. (Don't deans want the "great unwashed" to be thrilled by their courses?) The knee-jerk reply one hears is: "There is no contradiction here, no incompatibility between scholarship and teaching." And there's an edge to it that you can't miss: surely, surely, one doesn't want to award tenure (at Brown!) to folks whose evaluations from the experts are weak. Not only deans but students themselves confidently tell me that, insisting that scholarship and teaching do not compete with each other. It's win-win. And often that's true. The trouble comes when it's not.

So, it stuns me how little the students—rightly thought of as shrewd consumers, aware of the power of the purse—understand this tenure system and its impact on their education. When a star younger teacher "disappears" from our ranks, it does not occur to undergraduates that promotion was denied and on what grounds it was denied. (This last point is thorny and a trifle absurdist: I don't think my students have a clue as to how my books and articles, or those of other scholars, have been received; worse, I could conceivably trot out whopper after whopper in my lectures, but how would they know? The undergraduates and the experts constitute two radically distinct juries.) But I often wish the students were savvier and more informed about these matters and that they could better defend their interests; after all, their tuition dollars keep these universities afloat. It is possible that we will acquire stronger scholars in this fashion, but the price tag sometimes seems very high to me, given the inspirational value of what can be lost. I've titled this whole section "The Voyage Out," but all too many gifted teachers voyage out of the academy because the gift they have is not the one required.

I think back to Hazelwood's "hot stuff" and to Kronwald's tears: the adrenaline they unleashed and the doors they opened do honor to the very project of school. This happens at university also, but I wonder if it gets its due. "Pedagogy" is the term often used, as in the phrase, "he is fine at pedagogy, but his scholarship is weak." I take umbrage with that implied snub. Don't for a minute think that good teachers are cheerleaders. At their best, they are transformational. Despite the appearances, there is something aristocratic, not plebeian, in reaching the young who come our way for a passing moment, as they follow their forking paths toward careers in law, medicine, business, and much else that seems to have nothing to do with my field. One of the beauties of the American liberal-arts model—a model fighting for its life today, and not to be found in other parts of the world—is that it inculcates a belief that Shakespeare enriches everyone: stockbrokers as well as poets.

Voice Redux

I know that the ear-nose-and-throat specialists explain *voice* in physiological fashion, concerning vocal cords and the like, but, as I've said, mine was "born," in a deeper, vocational sense, via my commerce with literature. I sensed this in Paris in 1960, and I understand it ever more fully today. Reading literature—unlike, I think, reading history or the newspapers or anything else—does something remarkable to our lingual and rhetorical equipment. As you probably know, it is today axiomatic to assert that our subjectivity is a welter of discourses not of our own making. And I well know that students, especially younger students, rightly bridle when they are confronted with this theory, since it must look like outright theft to them, implying that "their" words are in fact "others" words, even counterfeit at some severe level. I remember once presenting this deconstructive view to a senior dean, asserting that the sacrosanct charge of *plagiarism*—high on the list of college sins—is a tad foolish, given that all of us incessantly plagiarize, that the words we speak and write are scarcely "our own," but likely echoes or redo's of what we've read or heard or internalized long ago. It's hard, likely impossible, to be original. Fired up, I even added that plagiarized papers at least mean the student has seen (and stolen) something probably good, whereas many many "honest" essays are low wattage indeed. Are we interested in virtues or ideas? The dean thought I was insane. And perhaps dangerous also.

But these matters extend still further, and I would again like to take the offensive, but to make a more artisanal point: we are building and shaping our voice all our lives. The encounter with literature fuels and layers this; and teaching disseminates it.

Even if we do not subscribe to Matthew Arnold's canonical definition of the classics as "the best that has been thought and said," we are nonetheless chockablock full, stuffed, larded with the words of poets, dramatists, and novelists. (We're also chockablock full of garbage, of ditties and rhymes from advertising and old songs that have crept into us, taken up lodging there, to stay. They must like hobnobbing with Shakespeare.) One goes badly astray if one construes this commerce as an affair of quotation and memorized lines. Nor do I fully agree with the familiar charge that each of us is *scripted* by culture's discourses, even though it has its share of truth. No, a life of reading literature creates a subsoil of its own, and subtends/nourishes what we think, as well as how we say it. All this is what passes over (or sneaks under) teachers' tongues as they speak to their classes, and it needn't be a conscious exercise in the least. Here would be the accretive work of education and of life: internalizing, disseminating, and unpacking the words of others over time, "*les mots de la tribu,*" "the words of the tribe."

Teacher as Cannibal

I feel passionate about this communicative bridge—this "blood transfusion" from afar—because it is how I now understand my answer to the question I've often been asked: "Are you a writer, yourself?" (This means: Do you write novels or poems?) No, I always replied. I'm a critic. (The disappointment registered in the student's face comes at once.) But the fuller, more accurate, and further-reaching reply is: I am a parasite, I am a poacher, I ingest, I cannibalize (verbally, conceptually, spiritually) the writers I teach, and they become part of me, they grow

me, they yield my voice. It is all too easy to gauge these transactions as
the brainwashing baked into culture and professional formation—
which is real—but to do so is to miss what is enriching and liberating.
Yes, we may well be plagiarists all, but these matters are oddly organic
as well, and personal voice may be what is most emancipated, most
surprising, most creative about lingual creatures reworking what they've
absorbed, extending the life of what they've read.

For a long time I lazily regarded this rich legacy as merely the inevitable accumulation of materials resulting from years and decades of
reading and teaching. I draw on them, I told myself. And then I realized
that it is a far more profound, intimate, visceral, and transformative relationship than such terms suggest. I have been molded by my writers.
The scenario is not far from Frankenstein and his monster: I seem to be
made up of foreign parts. But this Gothic takeover schema gets it entirely wrong. What is so fulfilling about this model is that it emancipates
and enriches and instrumentalizes me, in just the sense that Emerson
meant: they (the poets) have become the *commonwealth*.

I now see with ever more clarity that my love for lecturing is cued to
exactly these same arrangements: my authors feed my thoughts and
words, and just like all nurturance, it produces energy. For I am then
free to continue to grow, to *use* the munitions they provide in order to
go out on sallies of my own, to move into precincts of my own, to generate horizons of my own. Horizons of my own, yes, but generated by my
sources. Is it not possible that the elemental appeal of (good) lecturing—
often dismissed today as woefully undemocratic, as "the sage on the
stage"—is not merely a homage to the dimensionality of books but
proof positive that books are actually imbued with futurity? The teacher
models the still living power of the book. And where it goes, nobody
knows.

I do not prance around my lecture hall, nor do I turn off the lights or
put a cooking pot on my head, but I do *play*, attempting to show how
alive my materials actually are. Such lecturing and the smaller classroom
discussions that complement it constitute the up-to-now repeatable
pinnacle experience of my life: to convey what is living in the materials
I assign. And nothing here is as predetermined or rehearsed as you may

think: neither lectures nor discussions. Things actually happen on the fly: that is what taking it out for a spin can produce. Often enough an entire session devoted to a single poem or short story can be filled with surprises, galvanizing perceptions that none of the parties involved, including me, quite knew about on the front side, but that are catalyzed by the pulsing force of art, which packs tight its materials, expecting us to unpack them. Seeing these connections and vistas can be startling: for me, for my students. Teachers do not resemble each other—there are countless styles and methods—but the best are always arsonists in some fashion.

CHAPTER 2

Distance Learning:
Yesterday and Today

The first part of this chapter focuses on a teaching experiment I was asked to participate in, back in 2013 and 2014: to offer my "Fiction of Relationship" course under the aegis of Coursera, one of the country's major purveyors of MOOCs, as Brown tested the waters of online education. MOOCs uniquely illustrate what I have been arguing as the *reach* of teaching itself, as they utterly reconceptualize the teacher–student bond, by exploding the boundaries of the "classroom," as well as translating the key educational exchanges into digital form, along with all the trumps and liabilities involved. Traditional brick-and-mortar arrangements were being tested as never before. The "outcome"—a notion so central to this book—remains to be seen.

Yet I have termed this two-year stint "yesterday" for good reason. Fully aware of the trail-blazing potential of MOOCs, and thus excited to be in the front line (as it were) of such a movement, I obviously had no clue about what was to come some five years later: the coronavirus pandemic. What looked edgy, maybe even quixotic, in 2013, became, grudgingly and by necessity, educational "business as usual" across many parts of the United States and all over the world, as schools and universities sporadically closed their doors and shut down in-person learning, in response to the massive coronavirus threats to the health and safety of both students and teachers. Distance learning was all that was left, and we are still measuring what it has cost us.

As I write these words, we are still "in medias res" as far as this in-structional paradigm shift is concerned, but it is fair to say that the no-tion of distance learning no longer seems exotic or futuristic. The future is now, by force majeure, and it is decidedly a mixed picture, with un-even outcomes. Much of the modern world has had a crash course in distance learning, and it has shone a light, as the pandemic itself has, on the long-term inequities and problems and sores of modern society, now seen up close.

I, like so many teachers and professors, have had to learn how to use Zoom in order to teach my university courses, and even though my earlier Coursera venture taught me a great deal about such a model, today's experience differs entirely from the more utopian scheme I worked with, back in 2013 and 2014. Both stories warrant telling, and both stories belong in this book, for each episode—Coursera back then and Zoom-cum-pandemic now—bids to reconceive the very no-tion of *transmission*. I have elected to offer my testimony regarding MOOCs as I experienced it (and indeed wrote about it) *back then*, in the trenches, yet filled with curiosity, where, as you will see, I display considerable optimism about the new technology and the new vistas. I want that enthusiasm to show, since it reflects how I felt during this experiment, back then. The issues were essentially pedagogic. Lives were not at stake.

But the second part of this chapter, focusing on my experience of teaching via Zoom in the time of the pandemic, must needs have a darker coloration. What became horribly visible was the precariousness and fragility of teaching itself, for it had always taken for granted a mea-sure of social and psychic stability, a floor to stand on; what came in-stead, and continues as I write these lines, is a setting of existential dread, and no account of Zoom *today*—its promise, its costs—can ig-nore the larger stage where our structures and means of teaching and learning are located. That is why I used the phrase "Zoom-cum-pandemic." Pandemics destabilize all the networks we are accustomed to, and teaching is no exception.

Let's start with the happier story.

MOOCs: My Experience with Coursera

Online education: these two words taken together may seem more like a problem or even an oxymoron than what I want to argue here: they constitute a promise, an unanticipated "open sesame" that taps into what is most vital in the field that seems least suited to the digital model: the humanities. MOOCs, generated, yes, at specific university sites, but reaching far and wide across the globe, needing only a modem (here, there, anywhere) for realization—are to be seen as a portentous juggernaut in the United States, even if tongues are no longer quite wagging about them today, as they did a few years ago. I would wager that soon enough other societies not only will take note but will find themselves impacted to the very core of their mission: teaching, the dissemination of knowledge (and, by extension, the challenges to a faculty professoriate long thought to be the primary drivers here). The general repercussions of this movement are going to be momentous. It is well known that the sciences and social sciences, as well as mathematics and technology and business and law, will receive an unheard-of boosting power, thanks to these engines of information-spread, commanded by some of the major scholars at the most eminent universities. How will the humanities fare?

Let me begin by briefly rehearsing the obvious. The humanities are said to be in dire shape, in terms of dwindling college and university enrollments and no less dwindling departmental rosters. They are said to be the academic victims of a culture that seems to want ever more in the way of science and technology. Pious defenses continue to be mounted, along the lines of crucial critical skills (the humanities' arguable payload) being as highly prized as ever today, yet students do vote with their feet (when it comes to majors), and university administrations vote with their purses (when it comes to programs), and even legislatures do weigh in on curricula (when it comes to public funding): none of this is good news for my area of the university.

Less touted, but no less crucial in my own view, is the nagging suspicion that the crisis in the humanities is, at least in part, of its own doing: it has created a way of doing intellectual business (arcane vocabulary, theory-speak, massive concern with ideology, arguable proneness to political correctness) that can seem off-putting to a public that has not followed professional developments of the past half century. What used to be thought, by the larger public, as "reading the books" is now understood to be a far more rigorous and complex set of critical and intellectual moves, on the order of a foreign language with its own grammar and idioms and procedures. A glance at the titles of professional publications and conference topics will prove my point. Not everyone can "buy in." When one couples these two lines of force—a general culture increasingly focused on technology and information-gathering and an academic culture increasingly hermetic in the eyes of the "great unwashed"—then the headwinds look daunting and the odds bad.

Further, online education itself seems often enough cued to the same empiricist paradigm that is most at home in fields such as computer science, mathematics, principles of business and law, and the like. One need not be, as they used to say, a rocket scientist, to understand this alliance, since one of the defining characteristics of online education is its enshrining of *information* as essential given, "information" now digitally accessible and pried apart from—liberated from?—its traditional institutional, educational home. It now seems feasible—inevitable?—that significant numbers of "students" from around the world can partake of this new educational paradigm. The elitist givens of an earlier age—only the "lucky few" could be expected to attend the premier institutions of higher learning—are yielding to a new order: democratic, inexpensive, everywhere available. The old classroom is being reconceived.

So, too, is the role of the professor. The old Socratic model of mentoring—a model of both complexity and immediacy—depended on the wise guidance and thoughtful questions put by the master to the student(s). I still believe this scheme is the gold standard for education, for it seeds thinking, and it capitalizes on the energies of exchange that are in play when the seasoned teacher artfully poses questions, teases out responses, plants ideas, and—no less crucial—*listens* to the responses of the students. One thinks of the tutorial system made famous at Oxford and Cambridge, at Harvard and Yale, and emulated at the finest educational institutions, perhaps most perfectly at the smaller elite colleges (and independent secondary schools prior to college) where such a model is enshrined as the most humane, achievable, and invaluable path toward both knowing and thinking that has been devised. It is precious; it is expensive. MOOCs cannot deliver this.

MOOCs do something else. *Access* has been drastically redefined. It is as if the story of "The Emperor's New Clothes" were being retold, and it appears that *learning* may no longer have any need of its former institutional clothing or frame. Here is a *positive* argument that needs examining. So much of the rationale for online learning has been pragmatic, and often enough it is taken for granted that MOOCs will never be more than "second best" . . . at best. I believe this attitude misses the point. This is a serious shake-up, because a rival model, with its own striking digital advantages, is coming into view and into operation. Much of this we know. Wired instruction is a cogent, perhaps overdue move, in harmony with some key principles of knowledge acquisition. Not surprisingly, most online courses operate along well-known Cartesian analytic principles, principles perfectly embodied in both the matter and the manner of the digital model: the use of bullet points and diverse critical/pedagogical procedures to illuminate and convey the key matters in the material at hand, but also the possibility of a no less empiricist, denotative assessment model, whereby a student audience sometimes exceeding one hundred thousand can be efficiently examined via computerized exams, to document whether or not the major principles of the course have been mastered. From a certain angle, one could say the promised land (of learning via universal access) is coming into view. Will the humanities benefit?

Folks are still seeking to understand the likely impact of this new juggernaut in higher education. The well-known examples of San Jose State and Amherst several years ago—each refusing to go along with the MOOC scheme—signal some of the opposition roiling out there in the academy. It is evident that a course with more than one hundred thousand students, taught by a luminary in the field, represents an undreamed-of economy of scale, yet many are worried about its possible dystopian consequences along institutional lines: drastic and widespread curtailment of faculty positions (leading to a tiny super-elite professoriate, with countless minions doing the grunt work of "administering" the courses); potential disappearance over time of brick-and-mortar education (with its real-time instructional scheme and its dense social texture); severe reduction of "local" teaching, where individual departments and instructors set the agenda, tone, and pace (in clear contrast to the one-size-fits-all approach now threatening to take over); and utter loss of personal interaction between students and professors, as face-to-face yields to talking heads–on-monitors. Accounts of this movement seem decidedly mixed in their assessment: delivery of information on a radically expanded scale is undeniable, perhaps inevitable, but—many would argue—coming at a steep human and educational price.

It was against this powerful, indeed threatening, backdrop—and for just these reasons—that I elected to give my literature course, "The Fiction of Relationship," for Coursera, when Brown University asked me to do so in 2013. I especially felt that there was an unarticulated challenge to the humanities that was quasi-hardwired in the digital project. First of all, grading a MOOC in my field seemed an inherently doomed proposition. A novel or poem may well be information-rich, but, as teachers of literature have known forever, the "right answer" testing-model will scarcely be commensurate with the things one wants students to ponder and learn. From the outset, therefore, the assessment component of my online course was dogged by problems that could be insoluble.

My courses are also writing-intensive—short analytic pieces every other week, a longer reflective and comparative paper at semester's end—and this model works fine in a university setting (where I am assisted by professionally trained TAs), but in a course with thousands of students, how could this be carried out? Let me therefore acknowledge, at the outset, that this problem remains arguably the Achilles' heel of the MOOC concept. Peer grading is a valiant effort to step into the breech, and it may be the only solution that is feasible, but it has its own indigenous drawbacks, and—perhaps fatally—is bereft of precisely the professional authority that underwrites classical "grading." The evaluation challenge will therefore need to be (somehow) met, if ever the next epochal step in this revolution is to take place: the bestowing of actual academic *credit* for MOOCs, a goal that the founders of this scheme must indeed have had in mind since the outset.

Beyond even this pragmatic challenge, however, there existed, in my mind as humanist, the *operational* one: Would it be possible to use the digital classroom and online technology to promote *interpretation* itself?—a posture that depends as much on emancipated imagination as analytic acumen, that examines the quiddity of the literary work (in my field) but goes on to trace, even to project, its links to realms beyond the text itself, such as history, ethics, feeling, and life. Given that the course I gave was "The Fiction of Relationship," my entire venture (substantive and conceptual as well as methodological) was committed to the view of art as special map of human connection on every possible level: emotional, moral, political, environmental, verbal. Here would be the acid test. Could this enterprise possibly work, I wondered, online? Might it actually be possible to enlist the digital scheme for my own humanistic purposes?

The answer to that query—and the rationale for this account—is a massive YES. Let me begin with the easy part. My own role was not all that much different from what it is at Brown. My lengthy lectures—now subdivided into digestible bytes of eight to twelve minutes—built on the same skill set I've developed over a lifetime in the academy. I was even able to insert some vital student discussion pieces into these taped presentations, so as to yield in this new format something of the roundedness and variousness of the teaching and learning experience that I aim for at the university. I'm pleased with the outcome. But, in some crucial sense, this turns out to be the least interesting discovery for me. What I could not anticipate was the utterly remarkable *afterlife* of these taped lectures and discussions as seen in the stunning number of threads and posts appearing each week in the discussion forums. There is the payload of the MOOC experiment, as I see it. Its ramifications are huge.

The discussion forums for my MOOC excited and gratified me, because they are inseparable from my remarks about "no right answer." Indeed, "*answer*" is the wrong term; "response" comes closer to the mark. This is the line in the sand that separates humanistic from scientific inquiry. I am not advocating relativism of any and every stripe ("My view is as good as yours") but rather *interpretation* as the desired goal of the humanistic enterprise. I often recall snide remarks sometimes made at faculty meetings by colleagues in the sciences: "We actually teach materials where there are *wrong* answers, unlike what you do." OK: not nice, but fair enough. What I had not foreseen was the made-to-order fit between the energies and vistas of interpretation, on the one hand, and the digital modus operandi of MOOCs, on the other. There is dynamite here.

I had stated in my introduction lecture, half in jest, that this literature course had very little pragmatic benefit to offer. It would not teach mastery of literature (if there is such a thing); it would not get them a job (no surprise there); it wouldn't yield anything very measurable of any sort whatsoever. But, I added, that's the bottom line for the humanities in general: that they don't have a bottom line, that they don't add to a bottom line, that they are meant as exploratory, open-ended, bristling reading experiences, where the essential task is to align the text with the world: the world of its own provenance, but also the world of readers, yesterday, today, and tomorrow. Information certainly figures in these two trajectories, but the *experiential* payload of literature is less data-dependent than it is a product of reflection, speculation, projection, and vision. Literary meanings are generated by the encounter between a text and a reader, separated by time and place, linked by the alchemy of reading. *Teaching*, as a discipline, adds a crucial social component to this equation: the production of meaning is shareable. Are bricks and mortar required for that generative act? Might MOOCs catalyze it in unheard-of new ways?

Moreover, I had suggested, the two revolutionary features of the MOOC scheme—courses are accessible to anyone in the world with a modem; courses are free—might well be liberating in ways we'd never predicted. Taking a MOOC course is thought to be bereft of the thick social atmosphere that bathes the teaching experience at brick-and-mortar institutions. Couldn't this condition also be a liberating one? Is it possible that virtual access is enlivening and catalyzing in ways we had not suspected, in ways unavailable to traditional "real-time," "face-to-face" instruction. "You" (I said to my invisible audience) "are free from the multiple stresses that beset my university students: you don't need credit for this; you are not paying (a fortune) for it; you're not trying to balance it with three other high-intensity courses; in short, you're in it for the sheer intellectual stimulus. You get to read ten great novels, you get to see my lectures and my students' discussions, . . . and you're off to the races." Off to the races: how often does the "real class-room" send its participants into the beyond?

My MOOC students were, week in and week out, to put it gently, on the move. So much so that most of my preconceptions about this entire venture were simply overturned. I have conceded that the assessment piece remains problematic, but what astounded me—and fuels these remarks—was the vitality, range, texture, and "legs" of the discussion forums. There was something fissionable happening. It is here that I see the revolutionary element, and it is entirely cued to the core humanistic principle that I started with: *interpretation* as the royal road for our field. Shakespeare lives each time his plays are read or seen: *experienced*. In like fashion, my sequence of narratives, from Prévost's *Manon Lescaut* of 1731 up to Coetzee's *Disgrace* of 1999 (passing through Charlotte Brontë, Melville, Kafka, Woolf, Faulkner, Borges, and Morrison) triggered a kind of call and response, give and take, and ongoing chain of reflection and reply that went on and on, at the speed of electricity, creating a virtual community of readers who both challenged and built on one another's views, yielding a tapestry of interpretative moves that dwarfed anything I've ever encountered, whether it be in the classroom or conference hall or scholarly publications.

This river of readings, with its vigorous current and multiple partici-pants in the swim, was no less surprising for its civility, curiosity, fre-quent erudition, and persistent focus on both personal and public matters. Not being a great fan of social media, I had expected a consider-able dose of narcissism, of folks trotting out their private views for any and all to salute (and this does happen), but what I mostly found was something deeper, more caring and more insightful, quite wonderfully fresh and independent, and always *building*, reaching for common ground, respectful of local differences, ceaselessly unpacking our materials and threading them into the very texture of human experience: their joint experience. These threads and posts were also—it bears repeating—*intelligent*; the allegation that online teaching sacrifices subtlety, ambiguity, and the like makes no sense to me, since the discussion forums are utterly hospitable to nuance and innuendo, even if scholarly discourse as such is either absent or given short shrift.

One of the other novelties here was my own diminished role in all this. Of course, I was credited with good points I made in lecture, as well as critiqued for assertions that were more dubious, but for the most part I was only there as the origin of this unfolding discourse. I was cited now and then, as reminder or measuring stick or gauge, but not much more than that. Well, maybe, something more than that after all, since I was the one who chose the books, articulated the original lines of coherence of the course, and was responsible at least for its "originary" form. This matters, and it distinguishes MOOCs from, say, online reading groups or book clubs where such a structure is missing.

Nonetheless, my views did not rule the roost. Far from it. What I actually encountered was the rich, variegated, sometimes impassioned "street life" of *interpretation* itself. Interpretation as the truly democratic thing it can and should be. Interpretation rescued from the authority of the priesthood (professors like me). Online education bids to be the freest engine imaginable of interpretation. Online education bids therefore to be profoundly attuned to the very lifeblood of the humanities. After all, I cannot imagine this kind of endlessly inventive, interpellating, interpretive chain in a course on computer science or mathematics or any of the information-centered fields I had thought were the favored purview of this new enterprise. Au contraire, discussion forums flaunt, by their very suppleness and vitality, the muscular pluralist life of art. And of experience. Above all, these discussion forums embody the true seriousness of my field: literature is about the complexity and drama of mind and heart; the threads and posts are testament to just that, as students align these texts with what they've read and felt and then go on to relate it to what others have read and felt. This sequence of signifying could go on forever (and this shocks me, given how delimited and thin classroom discussion—and book reviews—usually seem).

And there is nothing populist at hand here. Of course, one could claim that these respondents were perhaps unprofessional in their take on these novels, that they may have known little of the intricate scholarly conversation that exists about these books. This quibble is dicey—they did sometimes cite chapter and verse from other scholars, other courses, other books—and ultimately unimportant, since what was being manifested was the vigor and binding strength of interpretation as the key activity of a virtual community, linked only by common readings and a common course. One might infer from this spontaneous activity that literary scholarship as such has little purchase in these matters, and I suppose my position is not far from that inference, inasmuch as the scholarly discourse is all too often a rather closed circuit, aimed at a specialist community with particular lights. Indeed, the very nature of professional specialization in my field undergirds such a scheme. Careers and the entire pecking order of the academy (cued to "experts" and to others seeking to be that) follow such a hierarchical logic. But the lifeblood of literature exists, it seems to me, on another plane altogether—a level playing field, as one might say today—and it is that plane that comes into view in the digital project. After all, writers do not write, in the last analysis, for critics, but for readers. I realize I may be sawing off the limb I'm sitting on, but so be it.

I suppose I subscribe to a higher utilitarianism when it comes to the field of literature. Voltaire's Dr. Pangloss posited that God created noses in order to support glasses, and I'd be comfortable claiming that we have literature in order to deepen our sense of life's issues and textures. There is a great cultural gift at hand here, a storehouse of *usable* notations and discoveries (and warnings). The texts pay their way. Edvard Munch once claimed that the reason he left many of his paintings outside in the harsh Norwegian climate, subject to wind, rain, snow, and bird shit—the "Hestekur," horse cure, he called it—was that the work would thrive in such a setting. Is it too much to claim that literature lives out its life in comparable fashion, in the gritty but vital, unprofessional, and egalitarian world of readers opening covers (or Kindles or iPhones), negotiating pages, absorbing stories, pondering what they've encountered or ingested, and invariably doing so in light—not of scholarly opinion—but of their own human experience? Getting Melville or Faulkner "right" or "wrong" is completely irrelevant here. What counts is they are "getting" Melville and Faulkner, and they're doing it in the most remarkably interactive and constructive fashion. They are putting my writers to work. The multiple payoffs amaze me.

Work; payoffs. (Is there bread here?) These terms would appear, figuratively at least, to be part of that empiricist metric that I've repeatedly claimed to be alien to the humanities. What's measurable here? The results that I'm so struck by had everything to do with the ubiquitous, never quiescent, oddly contagious interests of my large swath of students, and by that I mean: literature tends to apply to life (in all its guises) everywhere you look. (This could not be claimed for computers, mathematics, or law, at least not in the sense I have in mind.) The discussion forums in my course were structured according to the enormous variety of topics brought up by my students in this venture. One rubric was that of students "over fifty" sharing their specific, age-related views (try this one at college); another was keyed to issues of psychology as a university discipline; another explored connections between our course and the tenets of modernism and postmodernism; another debated the crucial gender conflicts that animate so many of my texts; many of them reflected on the ideological arrangements on show (or hidden) in our materials; most of them cited chapter and verse of our texts, as well as invoking other relevant texts well beyond my reading list.

The breadth of perspectives should not surprise, since these students came from all over the globe, ranged in age from twelve to eighty, and represented professions, points of view, and life choices of incalculable variety. It's hard to exaggerate this last point: I remember one email from a student in Egypt, explaining she'd fallen behind in a particular week because she was busy protesting in Tahrir Square in Cairo; yet another (older) student brought his hospital experience with crushed limbs and a long stint in a strapped-in container to bear on Kafka's "Metamorphosis," with its protagonist become giant insect. (I was unused to such perspectives in my Brown classes.) Further, the sheer flow of responses was huge. Some of the threads had hundreds of posts, and they continued to evolve long after the book in question had been finished. Other threads had only a few posts, but there's no reason to think they might not have started to grow and mutate in the weeks ahead, in the twelve-week course, or still later. *All* of them were, as it were, to the point, inasmuch as they displayed the shimmering, unbounded, unpredictable, weirdly intimate, deeply philosophical life of both art and interpretation.

There would appear to have been *nothing* that these books failed to touch on, but the only way to see this was to have a live, even if virtual, audience doing the touching, illuminating the reach, exhibiting the network, making the connections, feeding on the books, and therefore feeding the course. And feeding one another, for that is what shocks: the spectacle of people invisible to one another, separated by continents in some instances, conducting exchanges about literature with such heft and vigor. I do not for a minute believe this could have happened in any other format. A flesh-and-blood classroom—especially if equipped with a professor—could not possibly trigger the avalanche of personal reflections, anecdotes, and suggestions that I found in these posts. The digital scheme brings to visibility the otherwise invisible censorship of our real-time model. (Yes: censorship; I wonder how many teachers will agree that their own presence might stymie as well as promote?) These threads grew in front of my eyes, on the order of a digital photosynthesis. "Play of meanings" would doubtless be the semiotic take; I'd prefer to invoke Jack and the Beanstalk, with the proviso that Jack seeds the Beanstalk, makes it happen and evolve.

The cumulative field-picture of these discussion forums is what intrigued me. It was not so much a patchwork quilt as a living, breathing critical organism, possessed of its own indigenous life, independent not only of me but even of those who contribute to it, since the moving thread appears to have its own indwelling energy and directional pattern. As someone who has taught literature for more than five decades, I feel even today—several years after the experiment—that I am only now discovering the actual reaches of criticism as student-driven connective tissue, because the sheer scope of these unfurling responses was so impressive. By contrast, I feel ever more acutely the constraints of the classroom framework that otherwise governs my teaching: how can I expect my (brilliant) undergraduates to match—in staying power, in diversity, in responsiveness, in the richness and perspectival mellowness that time alone brings—the performance of my online students? Their joint "play"—"work" seems an inappropriate term—had a leisureliness (even at instantaneous digital pace) that constrained university settings rarely allow, a rhythm of building blocks and exploratory routes, each post usually outfitted with personal trappings that seemed more freely offered because of the medium, coursing not only forward but also sideways and backward, reminding me at times of Laurence Sterne's digressive manner in the quirky eighteenth-century narrative *Tristram Shandy*.

Were these posts at times intimate and self-referential in a way that scholarly discussion and classroom etiquette prohibit? Yes. But this is a mark of power, I believe: the power of literature. If Melville's "Bartleby" raises questions of resistance-in-the-workplace, if Kafka's "Metamorphosis" triggers accounts of personal alienation and estrangement, if Charlotte Brontë's *Jane Eyre* taps into still roiling gender issues about women's roles, if Woolf's *To the Lighthouse* refigures those matters even further by endowing them with rare poetic intensity, well then my own students' vivid appropriations and back-and-forth responses seemed to me to be right at home in our course. The in-your-face thematic examples I've cited are arguably predictable, but the threads themselves were not, since they could (also) be witty, provocative, and erudite, with insights ranging from contemporary modern feminist theory to learned commentary on the kinds of Protestantism that subtend Faulkner's *Light in August*. Once again, the discussion forums constituted the signature and living heart of this enterprise: they are the finest flower of this new technology, and they are beautifully attuned to the depths, pulsions, and vistas of my field.

At the risk of a sensational analogy, I'd want to compare the instructional and learning paradigm on show in these threads and posts with the epochal significance of the Bible being translated into the Vulgate so that common readers could read the Word without the mediation of priests. It is as if removing the instructor from the podium (again, could "we" be in the way, in our own classrooms?) were akin to opening the gates or the spigot, so that the current might truly flow. I can remember a comparable claim made for the new discipline of semiotics by my former colleague Robert Scholes, especially in his fine book, *Textual Power*, but I believe the dialogic revolution happening online via Coursera and other new ventures is robust and communal in ways that are new, far from what scholars such as Benedict Anderson meant by his own term, "imagined communities." Neither semiotic play nor shared ideological beliefs came—as far as I could tell—to the fore in what I was seeing. In my online course, literature itself was being rescued from the academy in order to take its rightful place in the very questions, responses, concerns, and insights of active readers. Borges would have had no trouble designating the interpretive chain that so enthralls me as a *forking path*, and I invoke that metaphor as an illuminating figure for the unpredictability and generative character of these posted reactions to texts.

It would be gratifying to close this account by claiming that ventures in online education bid to rescue the humanities from the threatened position they now occupy in today's academy. But even my boundless optimism does not go that far. I've already acknowledged the "faculty personnel" threats in plain sight here, since I can easily imagine the "savings opportunities" envisageable here, if you were a dean or congressman looking for cuts; just write pink slips for the untenured professors and plug in a MOOC to replace them: not a pretty narrative. We know that automation is going to savage large parts of our workforce; I'm not thrilled at contributing to further raids on the academy. So, I confess that I do not know how one might channel the energy and the forms of what I encountered in my course into some kind of institutional relief package. And I remain stymied by the assessment—and eventual "accreditation"—challenges embedded in this model.

But I find it heartening—especially at this stage of my life and career—that this much discussed and often maligned new form of instruction is so big with life and promise. I am grateful to have been part of it. What is happening via the offices of Coursera, Udacity, edX—and perhaps other more recent ventures now in place—may not bode well for departmental rosters and may produce other problems beyond my ken. But it does write large, via vibrant discussion forums and ebullient energies of interpretation, the good health and abiding strength of our field, as it links students together into an evolving community of readers who perform the time-honored work of bringing literature to life; this matters.

Zooming Away: Distance Learning in a Time of Plague

My current experience with Zoom differs, in signal ways, beyond even the presence of the pandemic, from the two MOOC stints I did in 2013 and 2014 (discussed above), and it is good to highlight them. One of the great rewards in teaching for Coursera had to do with the immense, remarkably diverse audience I had at that time, with close to one hundred thousand registered "students"—that is, students who were of all ages and likely not enrolled in university courses. I translate: students free to take what they felt like taking from my Coursera offering; students often "returning," after a long hiatus, now "ready" to read books they had read or heard of in their past; students who had no requirements (from me) at all: no papers to write or exams to take, nothing to hinder the simple experience of reading some ten great novels and then discussing them with their online peers.

That large audience still exists. And the pandemic no doubt whetted far more people's appetites for such distance-offerings, given the cooped-up lives so many Americans were leading in 2020 and 2021. Podcasts and Zoom-cast lectures: such "available" fare, already quite robust before the pandemic and its attendant shutdowns, became even more irresistible and in demand, headed for still more "markets" and audiences. Dissemination of knowledge is a-changing.

But my personal Zoom-work, the subject of this second stint with distance learning, is part of my Brown University job, limited to undergraduates enrolled in my course, and hence larded with assignments, grades, pressure of all stripes. Nothing leisurely in sight here, none of the "personal enrichment" scheme that drives and supports MOOCs, that had so much to do with my views on the Coursera adventure. Things were now different, at the workplace itself. What had been university business as usual—meeting one's classes in person for eighty minutes a pop, several times a week—had radically changed. The time was out of joint. And we all know why.

Much has now been written about the overt and hidden costs of the country's Zoom teaching season. Zoom, though just a teaching aid of sorts, brought the socioeconomic injustices of our society to obscene visibility (just as the pandemic itself did), as we recognized who the privileged and who the underprivileged are. My students and I are among the privileged: we have access to this technology, my job does not oblige me to "be at work," and my salary is secure. Many, many others, perhaps most others, are not so lucky. So many young people from underserved communities have either poor or no access to computers, not to mention access to still more basic goods such as the food and human contact that schools "naturally" deliver(ed), as communities try to figure out whether they can be open or not, often lurching from one scheme to the other and back. Zoom may have been tricky for my students and me; it proved impossible for so many less fortunate others.

The numbers of students across the country failing their distance-learning courses are through the roof as I write these pages, and that is only the academic price tag. The emotional and existential ones are yet to be gauged, assuming we find a metric for that. Failures resist metrics because the "downstream" consequences of such matters never stop being real, never stop unfurling, whether or not anyone is counting or knows how to connect cause and effect. If public education was always a site with known problems—in worst-case scenarios: underpaid teachers, overfilled classes, and substantial numbers of students from indigent or broken families—it has now become still more dysfunctional, leading to anomie, boredom, and "dropping out" among the disaffected young, as well as predictable confusion and lack of know-how even for those who try their level best to make things work, to follow their teachers and acquire knowledge through peering into a small screen. Who can be surprised that many give up, that many lose not only a year, but perhaps everything, as they exit the entire learning-compact?

But I do know what my fall semester of 2020 Zoom-instruction at Brown University taught me about my materials, my students, and myself, and it belongs in this book. I had assumed, given my past with The Great Courses and MOOCs—where I had easily, fatuously, spoken my words of wisdom, via microphone, into the wild blue yonder—that Zoom would be a piece of cake. I was not ready for the massive displacements that eroded the very teaching compact: students back in homes they'd thought behind them, struggling for space to work, for a viable computer, for staying—the hardest of all—focused. The very air we breathed was toxic: not only with putative viral load but with anxiety and fear, fed by the ever-rising amount of infection and death and tribalized public squabbling (protests, masks, the US presidential election, etc.) that invaded our TV screens. When hordes of people were dying, or afraid of dying, much that had seemed "normal" (workloads, concentration, caring) started to look and feel iffy. School had never existed in a vacuum, but somehow this sense of exposure seemed to target our entire enterprise: reading books, writing papers, taking exams—all began to seem abstract, unreal, crazy, undoable.

Let me start on the light side, with one of Zoom's minor but unanticipated disturbing features: *I see myself*, sharing a screen with my students. And I realize that I have been mercifully spared exactly that visual truth during my entire career: whether meeting students in person or delivering a lecture to a live audience or into a microphone for taping and further dissemination, I have only seen *them*, never me. It was and is an unwelcome shock, jolting me each time, as in "What's wrong with this picture?" Who is the ancient old man in this sea of young faces? Why is he there? I've earlier spoken positively and sentimentally of the age–youth bond that underwrites teaching, but *seeing* it up front made me sense how unnatural such arrangements arguably are, involving even different species. It also seemed like a death sentence of sorts, a visual warning that I wouldn't long be at such a party.

And then, closer to the nitty-gritty of the Zoom screen itself, there is the slight but inevitable time lag between face and voice, so that the communicative chain seems fractured, broken into stubborn units, far from the fluidity of in-person teaching, where the spontaneous exchange of words and views is actually possible. (Each year in the first session of a seminar, I tell students not to raise their hands during our classes, but to interrupt—something, it turns out, as hard to do as to forget one's toilet training—and I add that my ideal scenario is the one they have all experienced: a spirited conversation with friends where words erupt, where one ends up saying things one had not rehearsed or even known one knew. At its best, in-person teaching can capture some of that give-and-take: moments where one is surprised, maybe where insight or growth take place.) Zoom is tough on spontaneity.

Everyone today is aware of this tiny but nasty little gap between speakers and listeners: when we see it on our TV screens in so-called interviews, we feel, with discomfort, the amount of time needed for the question to reach its interlocutor, for the reply to reach us. It's a bit like measuring the speed of sound, now coming to us as checked by a series of relays, as interruptible. Likewise, those still more common moments when faces simply freeze, even as sometimes the voice continues, as the system briefly hiccups, giving me the uneasy sense of seeing something close to facial paralysis, the sort of thing that accompanies stroke. The old man in me senses trouble, even though I do know it's just a technical glitch, nothing nefarious, and sure enough, eyes and lips start to move again and life is restored. And there's occasionally far worse, when someone's audio all of a sudden goes berserk in mid-speech, so that a voice gets stretched out of all recognition, turned into a monstrously slow evolving sound, a sound that has severed its connection with meaning, with living people.

Perhaps there, too, upon reflection, there's an unsuspected upside: one understands perhaps better the issues long experienced by those who stutter, those with injured vocal cords, those who freeze with fear when called on. Processing Zoom as it processes us, we begin to realize how precious real-time, in-person dialogue is, the kind one has with people in the same room, where transmission itself seems unfettered, immediate, and automatic. No more.

One further technical remark: Zoom demands that one pay attention to those pesky little commands such as "chat" or "security" or "breakout-rooms" or "reactions" and the like. Recently a student in my lecture course hadn't realized she was "unmuted" as she murmured, "there he goes again, rambling"—denoting no one other than me, *moi*—but now available for group consumption. Consternation followed: I continued lecturing (come rain or shine) but was soon deluged by other students apologizing, telling me that they listened to my every word and that it was an utter breech of decorum (and decency!) that this student had committed. Soon enough the student herself wrote, begging forgiveness, telling me how much she liked the course, what a bad day she was having, even informing me that her mother had studied with me a generation earlier. I told her not to worry, that it was a tempest in a teapot, and that I do ramble, and to say hello to Mom.

MOOCs deliver a smooth, finished product for folks to consume when they are ready. Zoom aims at something relational, which is fraught with challenges. Still other glitches can occur when folks talking to each other can't be next to each other. The whole country has now become accustomed to "losing" people onscreen, being (calmly) told "We'll get back to you when the problem is cleared up," as their audio or video goes out; this is true when you watch mainstream channels, and it was even truer with Zoom, given the rickety connections and installations many of my students were dealing with. It will sound paranoid, but I personally seemed outright targeted by such mess ups, and my classes (conducted in my living room) seemed regularly threatened by disruption, by the whole system crashing, so that the students, forewarned, learned to be patient, to wait until Professor Weinstein could reset things.

Equipment failure, yes, but whose equipment? And located where? Does the breakdown in my computer or Wi-Fi augur something darker still? I couldn't help wondering what it would feel like if, in an in-person setting—what we used to call a regular classroom—someone simply disappeared or became incommunicado. If that someone were me? It seemed like a message, and it did not bode well. And if it were a student? Maybe they turned off their video, not because of a stroke or breakdown but so as to go to the bathroom or, equally plausible, to exit our class and check out things on Amazon. These are things you cannot do—or get away with—in an in-person classroom.

More sanely, Zoom helped me see that all learning is distance learning. As I argue so often in this book, getting through to the other is a threatened, freighted proposition in the best of times. Exchanging the in-person classroom for a face-filled small screen turned out to be precious in its own way, at this fraught moment. Our Zoom-reality actually seeded something I couldn't have predicted: a strange kind of generosity, with young people courteously referencing what a peer had just said, or what I had said, making the small moves of recognition and respect and "building" that exchange thrives on, that makes exchange the civilized thing it can be. And I gather that they strangely credited me for trying to make Zoom work as our delivery system—doubtless visually cued that I did not know what I was doing, that I was out of my element—as if everyone began to realize how fragile and needy and needed communication might actually be, how much plural effort and good will (and luck?) are needed to bring it off. A curtain seemed to have gone up. The now all-too-visible artifice of our arrangements lent them an unsuspected authenticity, a price. A sweet surprise.

As old print-formed professor who still views computers as typewriters-cum-email, I am scarcely knowledgeable about the astounding array of apps, digital forays, and formats in use today and familiar to my students, children, and grandchildren. But even I enlisted and recommended programs such as Slack, where I saw a vigorous pulsing form of traffic and exchange going on between the students themselves, yielding something on the order of the posts and threads I had encountered in my two Coursera stints, constituting at times a complementary, even rival discourse to my own. Here I eavesdropped on a student-driven call-and-response, a welcome form of connectivity, yielding what one might even call "community spread." I choose this loaded, edgy metaphor for transmission because I see a genuine link here, one I intend to explore further. Zoom, with its "Hollywood Squares" array of diverse faces on screen, shining when speaking, is democratic and egalitarian. As is the pandemic.

One might assume—even I halfway assumed—that pandemics tend to weed out the trivial from the essential, that folks set their sights on what most counts. By this reckoning, it might be thought that *literature*—with its lousy track record of securing a job for you—would fare poorly, would appear even more esoteric and marginal, a frill, having little to do with young people's needs and futures. Yet I found the opposite to be true. My "Rites of Passage" course, with first-year students spread all over the globe using Zoom as access, had an urgency to it that I had never seen before. The readings for this course begin with medieval France and move forward to our day, and my aim is to show these eighteen-year-old students that their own passage from childhood to adulthood can be, surprisingly and profitably, aligned with the difficult maturations on show in my texts from many different centuries and cultures. The unstated rationale for this offering—a rationale the students quickly grasp and take to heart—is that they are undergoing precisely a rite of passage themselves, in real time, as they negotiate the move from home and community to university.

Except that pandemics and distance learning wrecked my claim. These young people, virtually imprisoned in their family homes, had been cheated out of exactly the social immersion that customarily defines entry into university (and accounts for one of its most meaningful and long-lasting benefits). This is what I particularly learned in reading their final essays: almost uniformly, they wrote about alienation, being adrift, being stopped in their tracks, anxious and uncertain of the future. But this experience seemed to turn them into astute readers of our materials, to give them special lights about how growing up is supposed to happen, how it often (in our own texts) runs into obstacles that require overcoming: our twelfth-century knight must go temporarily mad before learning to be selfless rather than vain; Jane Eyre must find a way to move beyond the abuse experienced in her childhood (at home, at school, even romantically) so as to find a kind of love that would grant her equality (class and gender arrangements in Brontë's 1847 Britain were coercive on both these fronts); Huck Finn comes to sense (with astonishment) that an uneducated black man, escaped slave or not, is the father he's never had; Faulkner's Isaac McCaslin will elect to relinquish his inheritance as he measures the fault lines of his culture: ownership of land and ownership of people.

These stories of difficult, life-changing growth, of being caught in the web of culture itself, and of the grit or even luck needed to make one's way resonated with my home-confined young people. And I am willing to propose that Zoom-the-miraculous was the little engine that could, the means of establishing a virtual community where books and ideas could be discussed, debated, shared, and turned into personal knowledge—all at a time when just going outside had its portion of threat. I did not fully realize this during our sessions—I'm not sure the students themselves did—but all of us came gradually to appreciate it, when we had time to reflect on what we'd been doing for three months and what it had meant, in a regime of lockdown, infection, and death. I am fully aware, as I stated earlier in this chapter, of how privileged I myself am, and I know my students felt this as well, but this teaching experience helped me understand why literature matters in times of crisis, why a writer such as Boccaccio focused on storytelling as the logical response to the Black Plague, not merely to combat boredom but also to imagine and enact human connection.

These matters were still more front and center in my large lecture course, "The Fiction of Relationship," the very one I'd earlier given for Coursera. The title of my course advertises its great theme: human relationship. But in a pandemic, the elemental forms of exchange—talking, touching, sharing a meal or a bed—acquired a toxic, possibly lethal character. Exchange can kill you. For just these reasons, I began my course this time with Defoe's remarkable *Journal of the Plague Year*, published in 1722, dealing with the London Plague of 1665, and yielding a sometimes journalistic, sometimes hallucinatory, rendition of what mass death does to a great city. My students experienced a shock of recognition in reading how Londoners from more than three centuries ago negotiated a pandemic that killed seventy-five thousand people; Defoe wrote of the horrors brought on not only by the plague but also by quarantine: London authorities forcibly locked people up in their dwellings, if the dread "tokens" appeared on anyone in the family, sent special Watchmen out to enforce such regulations, so that loved ones ended up killing their own children and parents. Defoe makes clear that mania was seen in the streets, feverish confessions erupted from the dying, and perhaps worst of all, London experienced the "epistemological" terrorism of *not knowing* whether or when they were infected, hence condemned to living as carriers prior to dying as victims. Here was our go-to, start-up text for our cultural moment, and it was followed by more palatable, less threatening fare about relationship, including love stories, familial narratives, even monstrous pieces such as Kafka's fables, as well as many accounts of how large race and gender loom when it comes to human linkage and connection. It's a broad theme.

But I now closed the course with Ingmar Bergman's film of 1956, *The Seventh Seal*, depicting a knight's return from the Crusades, as well as the fate of a family of performers (husband, wife, and child) during the Black Plague of the mid-fourteenth century. Bergman reprises the very motifs he has seen since childhood painted on the walls of medieval churches: Death playing chess, Death sawing off the limb of a tree, the Dance of Death. Bergman himself acknowledged that the riskiest move he made was to personify Death as a character in the film, replete with black cape and hood, tracking the "players" at every turn, laying waste to the land and the people. Bergman's own religious crises may perhaps no longer engage cinema audiences, but 2020 was an excellent year to see this film, for it staged the central dynamic of our moment: Death stalking the land. Bergman has written about *seeing*—opening the Seals—as both the modus operandi of film itself and also its priceless gift. This, too, is why it served us so well. You cannot see the actual bacteria or viral load when you are infected with the plague—this is the central horrid riddle of infection—but you can definitely see the figure of Death, in the film . . . and, I believe, as the lurking, ever-harder-to-ignore threat in our very lives today. At one early moment, Death opens his cape wide, and the entire screen goes black: Apocalypse is nigh.

I have loved and taught this film for many decades and have always closed my lecture by reminding students that Bergman did indeed have Apocalypse on his mind: as seen in the two evocations of the Book of Revelations, where one-third of humanity and of the land and the sea and the rivers and the sun and the moon and the stars dies; as seen in the on-screen plague that actually destroyed one-third of Europe; and as feared in 1956 (by Bergman and many other intellectuals) as all too possible an outcome of nuclear warfare, of the genie let out of the bottle in 1945 at Hiroshima and Nagasaki. But in 2020 nuclear war seemed almost abstract in comparison with the here-and-now, 24/7 flowing images of coronavirus's inroads throughout the world: hospitals, venti-lators, morgues, first responders, the dying, their families, masks, hys-teria, politics, and numbers, numbers, numbers: the mounting death tolls, the positivity rates, the ICU capacity, the comparative data of which countries and regions were doing better or worse. Defoe was back. Not one of my students needed my input on Bergman's film. And they all knew why we finished the course this way.

Bergman's film itself closes with Jof, Mia, and the baby Mikael—the family of minstrels—surviving the plague, escaping Death's rule, mak-ing us understand, in our minds and hearts, that the human family (and the love that makes them a family) is what will outlast destruction. So achingly simple. My sense is that my students, confined to their homes, had rediscovered the beauty and worth (as well as the aggravations) of family. And it made them more grateful for the peculiar yet real com-munity we still had: professors and their students. Zoom's portrait gal-lery of faces on my computer screen was testament to the living and to our common ground.

Human connection is what is targeted today: by the coronavirus and by the entire project of social distancing, mitigation, and the like. Zoom made it possible to see each other close-up but safely. No touching, no breathing. It is unquestionably the education vehicle for our moment. But literature's broader tidings, from Sophocles to our time, invariably open up the Seals, to deepen still further our knowledge of connection. And, amid our vexed efforts to get a reading on this key matter of expo-sure, could it even be that literature is culture's best diagnostic test? That literature shows us, as little else quite does, the company we keep?

Dickens's masterpiece *Bleak House* (1857) enlists smallpox as its bac-terial signifier for all intercourse and exchange: Jo, the novel's child of the slums dies of it, Esther (who tended the boy) is disfigured by it, but we cannot avoid seeing that the entire project of *distancing* is a fantasy: the great slum at the core of both London and the novel, Tom-All-Alone's, is a virulent, nonstop source of disease and death. Dickens him-self, tireless promoter of urban hygiene, knew that filth and rot *spread*, cannot be contained, and his "tentacular" plots inevitably expose link-age and connection. This is ultimately political: the haughty aristocrats who think themselves safe behind the walls of their mansions find that "immunity" is a fiction. Neither stone nor flesh are impermeable. Poe had dramatized the same invasion of disease in his "The Masque of the Red Death," where the revelers in the fortified castle are unable to keep out the lethal invader who closes the party.

Immunity is, at some level, a fiction, no matter what our medical people tell us to the contrary about the body's resources and the society's strategies. It's the mind and the heart that can't be protected. That is the bad news. Our most tragic American writer, Faulkner, knew a great deal about this, and it's no accident that one of his early novels is titled *Sanctuary*, for, in novel after novel, he shows us that all our hiding places are frivolous, that we will be found out. Faulkner's books take a wrecking ball to our pieties about human and social separation. His baroque plots are keyed to two stubborn taboos: incest and miscegenation. I regularly teach these books to Ivy League undergraduates, and, whereas they understand incest as transgressive, they are often mystified that somehow "miscegenation" mattered so much to the Mississippi writer in the 1930s and 1940s. But the marchers—some of them "fine people," we were told—in Charlottesville who chanted "Jews will not take our jobs!" were likewise as unsettled by black–white sexual relations as, yes, Abraham Lincoln himself was, in the mid-nineteenth century, as he pondered the potential postwar fate of emancipated slaves. Lincoln spoke, in the meantime, of a "house divided," and the reason that phrase is so pungent is that America has always been a house divided because division and demarcation and taboo have fed our politics and our nightmares since the founding. It's a history we're coming to know more about.

Faulkner's richest novel, *Absalom, Absalom!* is worth referencing one more time, for it magisterially probes these matters. In the convoluted, slowly emerging, speculation-fed story of an antebellum house divided, two Harvard undergraduates in 1910—one Mississippian, one Canadian—come to understand that Henry Sutpen's murder of his friend (and the fiancé of his sister Judith), Charles Bon, at the gates of the family plantation in 1864 not only was a fratricidal murder but was committed to protect the South's holy boundary of white-versus-black.

Henry, we learn by book's end, has killed his (half-black) half brother, and the two narrators imagine their last words, as Henry begs Charles to renounce Judith. Henry: *You are my brother.* Charles: *No, I'm not. I'm the nigger that's going to sleep with your sister. Unless you stop me.* It is hard not to see that Faulkner is telling us about the Civil War itself, also fratricidal, as stemming from a racial taboo that cannot be brooked, a racial taboo designed to keep black and white in their respective categories.

All of Faulkner's genius is enlisted in showing that this murder did *not* have to happen, that even this war did not have to happen. "The overpass to love" is how Faulkner words the alternative to bloodletting, an overpass that discovers and imagines—then hallows—the humanity of the other. That discovery is not cerebral, not the effect of education: it is physical, sensorial, sexual, cued to the most basic drive in human life: touch. *"Because there is something in the touch of flesh with flesh which abrogates, cuts sharp and straight across the devious intricate channels of decorous ordering, which enemies as well as lovers know because it makes them both—touch and touch of that which is the citadel of the central I-Am's private own: not spirit, soul; the liquorish and ungirdled mind is anyone's to take in any darkened hallway of this earthly tenement. But let flesh touch with flesh, and watch the fall of all the eggshell shibboleth of caste and color too."*

It's worth pausing over this astounding utterance. On the docket is not just race as the South's fault line but the ideology of the American project itself, arrestingly written in crude capitalist code as "the central I-Am's private own"; and we are to see that human touch—itself figured as a kind of mugging, as a kind of physical, carnal knowledge having no truck with spirit or soul—is both the most explosive force in the world and also the most *binding.* Touch is the very modality of love, familial as well as sexual. Is it too much to say, in our age of the coronavirus, of social distancing and quarantine and paranoia of the infectious other, that *touch* is what is outlawed, deemed threatening, even lethal? And that this is inhuman. Can we not also see that Sophocles, Defoe, Dickens, and so many of our great writers have been telling us this forever?

Plague exposes these taboos. Managing plague only separates and incarcerates us, but plague itself brings to visibility the very opposite:

the systematically occulted relations of our people. We now *see* that our country's most underpaid are its most overexposed, that the most ignored are the most likely to die, that the most privileged are at once the least threatened and the most parasitic, and that our very institutions are, in some sense, a collective form of "decorous ordering," of segregation and exploitation. Touch challenges all this.

"Winged words" is a familiar, delightful phrase for denoting the very power of phrases themselves. Today, when we know something about the toxic viral load that spoken words at close proximity might possess, it is good to retreat to literature as civilization's written form of touching. Literature teaches us that we have no immunity against others, nor do we want it. On the contrary, it initiates us, as fellow travelers, into the subjective lives of others, at least for a while. It shines a special light onto and into "the darkened hallway" of "our earthly tenement." In this way, it gives us a reading on our affairs that no scientific testing is likely to rival.

Zoom, I feel, enabled us to maintain this covenant. This past year my students and I occupied, I think, the same side of this equation: we saw in our books—in entering together the collective imaginative testimony of writers over the centuries—a strange bloodline, a writerly current that one could *travel* into the lives and fates of others, both fictive others and real others. And we could share what we saw. We were online.

CHAPTER 3

The Three R's

If my diverse experiences with distance learning have given me a taste of how today's cutting-edge technology bids to revolutionize teaching, I want, now, to go way way back, to return to the "basics," to the most venerable, elemental curriculum that we know: the three *R*'s: Reading, wRiting and aRithmetic. Those three fields were traditionally thought to cover all the bases: here, we were told long ago, is what all young people need to learn. You might well want to add to this trio of subjects—a cursory glance at education today, even at kindergarten level, will tell you how much has indeed been added on—but tackling these three core, founding areas of study remains hardwired in any model of school. No matter what else you study, this is where you start.

Oddly enough, at career's end, I think I have gained a special sighting on those essential matters, those three pillars that support the entire edifice of learning. I've already written about my personal trajectory from naive Memphian on through college, university, Brown, and beyond. I want to do something radically different here, and I will need to do it the way I have for the past half a century: to *use the books*. For it is in the books that I have learned who I am, what I believe, and why it matters. The "books," I want to argue, or at least some of the most provocative and unhinging ones among them, can shine a remarkable beam on just those three *R*'s. Let's rethink the basics. Might the three *R*'s shock us, when seen anew? Is it possible they are both wilder and more coercive than we've thought?

I do not expect anyone or any institution to use this chapter either as a blueprint or as a new foundation for education. Instead, I am following one of my masters, the Norwegian playwright Henrik Ibsen, whose fiery mission statement was "to torpedo the ark." I am quite intentionally reprising my "armaments" argument, but now with a view toward delivering the goods, the actual BOOM. Yet I have not gone mad entirely, since these "performances" are the best way I know for depicting the actual power at work and play here. I want, here as elsewhere in this book, to take off the gloves, so as to gauge what is elemental and fierce and destabilizing in my materials. I'm returning to school but with no concealed weapons of any sort, because the firepower I have in mind is lodged right there in plain sight, in school's own core activities.

Reading

The text I will draw on is Faulkner's *Go Down, Moses* (1942), a late, sometimes shrill, sometimes uneven work that registers, among other things, the author's discomfort with the cacophony of modern life—the book was published as Hitler was changing Europe—and his nostalgia for an earlier, vernal world, a (disappearing) primeval world that mandates human stewardship. Less acknowledged, but central for me, is the book's astounding focus on *reading*: reading the wilderness, reading one's history.

Faulkner did not make it past the eleventh grade. (His mentor Phil Stone, Yale graduate, deserves credit for exposing the young dropout to major nineteenth- and twentieth-century literature, with emphasis on England and France.) *Go Down, Moses* takes a number of shots at traditional schooling. At a key moment, when Sam Fathers, the Native American guide, lies dying at the camp after Old Ben (the totemic bear) has finally been brought down, the boy Ike—the "white" center of the story—begs to be permitted to remain longer at the camp to be with Sam (thereby missing school) and receives this reply from General Compson: "'All right,' General Compson said, 'You can stay. If missing an extra week of school is going to throw you so far behind you'll have to sweat to find out what some hired pedagogue put between the covers of a book, you better quit altogether.'"

Every time I read this passage, it stings. I, too, am a hired pedagogue, and I routinely urge my students to sweat to find out what is lurking between the covers of books. Not worth it, our author asserts; at least not when contrasted with the experiential learning afforded by the wilderness itself. Nowhere is this put more pungently than in this account of the boy's education as hunter: "If Sam Fathers had been his mentor and the backyard rabbits and squirrels his kindergarten, then the wilderness the old bear ran was his college and the old male bear itself, so long unwifed and childless as to have become its own ungendered progenitor, was his alma mater."

Reading one's environment is doubtless an old trope, but Faulkner quite explicitly literalizes it as the key hunterly skill. Ike, we learn, "knew the old bear's footprint better than he did his own, and not only the crooked one." This business of examining the legendary animal's footprints achieves high drama when Ike quite intentionally loses himself in the wilderness; this he does by relinquishing all his human assets— watch, compass, gun: tools of measurement in time and space, and armament—so as to *enter* the wilderness on a footing of equality with the wild ones. Faulkner cunningly chooses the verb *"relinquish"* to denote Ike's giving up power, because it foreshadows a larger relinquishment to come. For now, however, the covenant is with the mythic bear, and in a spellbinding passage we see Ike-the-reader intently pursuing the bear's ever-fleeing prints as the water fills them to unreadability; the passage is worth citing:

> seeing as he sat down on the log the crooked print, the warped indentation in the wet ground which while he looked at it continued to fill with water until it was level full and the water began to overflow and the sides of the sides of the print began to dissolve away. Even as he looked up he saw the next one, and, moving, the one beyond it; moving, not hurrying, running, but merely keeping pace with them as they appeared before him as though they were being shaped out of thin air just one constant pace short of where he would lose them

forever and be lost forever himself, tireless, eager, without doubt or
dread, panting a little above the strong rapid little hammer of his
heart, emerging suddenly into a little glade and the wilderness co-
alesced. It rushed, soundless, and solidified—the tree, the bush, the
compass and watch glinting where a ray of sunlight touched them.
Then he saw the bear.

One remembers—Faulkner himself remembers—the words on Keats's
tombstone, "Here lies One Whose Name was writ in Water," and there
is something unforgettable about Old Ben's fleeting/fleeing footprints,
ever poised to disappear and reenter the elements, challenging all efforts
to possess or decipher them. It is the epic struggle known to all writers
as well as all hunters. But what perhaps most moves us here is the visionary triumph: the bear is *read*, then *seen*. In teaching this passage, I ask
my students the unsimple question: Does the bear produce the prints,
or do the prints produce the bear? They are usually stymied. In "nature,"
an animal produces its prints, and even if the hunter enlists those prints
to track the animal, we understand the logical and temporal sequence.
But in a text—and surely the word *print* tells us that we have to do with
a text here—the directionality is reversed: the print produces the bear.
And it does so in the magic way proper to semiotics, as I first learned
long ago from Bob and Nancy, when I was even younger than Ike Mc-
Caslin, not yet knowing I would become a hunter of a different sort.

Teaching Faulkner is hard going. A high school English teacher I
knew well confided her secret for succeeding with *The Sound and the
Fury* in her twelfth-grade class: she *gifted* each of the eleventh graders a
copy of the book, signed by her, in June at the end of classes, with a
request that they read it over the summer. Smart. I often visited her
classes in those days and saw that her strategy produced results. But *Go
Down, Moses* is even harder going. Precious few of my Brown University
students have ever hunted before, and the great majority of them are
quite critical about the project itself. Faulkner did not know the term
"animal rights," but if he had, I believe he would have approved of it. My
students rarely grant this much. Killing animals is a no-no. Why, they
(silently) wonder, have I assigned this unappealing material? And, of

course, this book's hunting transgression is joined by a host of conceptual roadblocks as well, such as the opaqueness of Faulknerian prose and the taint associated with the South itself, all having to do with that "postage stamp of soil" that Faulkner claimed as his territory. Much to overcome here, on my end.

When someone earnestly told Mark Twain that all Standard Oil money was "tainted," he replied that it was "twice-tainted": Tain't yours and tain't mine. The taint my students ascribe to the South is no joking matter: it was the home of slavery in America and thus was the source of the bloodiest war in our history. Yet Twain's witticism about dubious, slippery "ownership" is rigorously appropriate here. The long and tortured fourth section of "The Bear," constituting the novel's vexed heart when it comes to matters of race and history, leaves the mythic hunt (depicted in the earlier sections) and its totemic animal in order to frame Ike McCaslin's *education* in a radically different way: once again as *reader*, yet not a reader of the wilderness's tracks but rather a reader of his own family history. This takes place in the commissary as a form of dialogue between the twenty-one-year-old Ike and his much older cousin Cass, as they read and interpret the old yellowed ledgers of the McCaslin history, going back to the great Patriarch, Carothers McCaslin, who founded the line.

Once again, relinquishment will be the order of the day, but it takes some time and considerable work on our part to understand *why*. What is at stake is no less than Ike's legacy, his inheritance of the family farm, and we are once again confronted with the taint of the South. The ledgers record, in the scribbled, cryptic writings of his two sons Theophilus (Ike's father) and Amodeus, a history of ownership: of land and of people. But it is not written in the clear, correct, sanitized language of traditional historiography or legal documents or political science courses; instead, we are given confused, garbled, misspelled notations of two uneducated old men seeking to transcribe the transactions of their own father over half a century.

And we see their text. There are some seventeen pages of mixed writing: the thoughts and words of Ike and Cass in the commissary, on the one hand, and the actual inserted (italicized) hard-to-read script of the ledgers, on the other. I will now offer you a sampling (over two pages of text) of these notations at their most potent, and I dare you to make them out:

> *3 Nov 1841 By Cash to Thucydus McCaslin $200. dolars Set Up Blaksmith in J.*
> *Dec 1841 Dide and burid in J. 17 feb 1854*
> *Eunice Bought by Father in New Orleans 1807 $650. Dolars. Marrid to Thucydus 1809 Drownd in Crick Christmas Day 1832*
>
> *June 21ˢᵗ 1833 Drownd herself*
>
> *23 Jun 1833 Who in hell ever heard of a niger drownding him self*
>
> *Aug 13 1833 Drownd herself*
>
> *Tomasina called Tomy Daughter of Thucydus @ Eunice Born 1810 dide in Child bed June 1833 and Burd. Year stars fell*
>
> *Turl Son of Thucydus @ Eunice Tomy born Jun 1833 yr stars fell Fathers will*

Some of the challenges here are small-bore: we correct the spelling of these two old men—dolars = dollars, blaksmith = blacksmith, dide = died, burid = buried, marrid = married, drownd = drowned, crick = creek, Cristmas = Christmas, niger = nigger; abbreviations are even easier: we also write the months in shorthand, much as Buck and Buddy did; and we can figure out that J. means Jefferson. Once you've made these mechanical corrections—not at all clear my students are entirely prepared to do even that—you're in a position to reconstruct the *sequence* that is being written/told here. This is where one begins to sort out the sheep from the goats.

The first part of Faulkner's written sequence goes, then, like this: *Thucydus was freed and paid cash in 1841, and set up as blacksmith* [doubtless by Buck {Amodeus} and Buddy {Theophilus}; Carothers had died in 1837]; *Thucydus died in 1854. Much earlier, in 1807, Carothers had gone to New Orleans and bought a female slave, Eunice. In 1809 Eunice was married to Thucydus. In 1832, on Christmas Day, Eunice drowned in the creek.*

Both brothers are bewildered by this last piece of information: three times they convey to each other, as if they were in a nineteenth-century chat room, their confusion at her drowning. *Who in hell ever heard of a niger drownding him self*, they memorably ask. I return now to Faulkner's italicized sequence: *A child, Tomasina, daughter of Thucydus and Eunice, is born in 1810, and she dies in child bed in June 1833, while giving birth to a son, Turl* [father unnamed]. Any student with the merest grasp of numbers (and some goodwill) can make out this much.

Now comes the harder part, the part that requires you to work for your bread: you must translate this sequence into a *story*. I have taught this novel for many decades, so allow me to offer you my version of the story that is being told/made/uncovered here: *Carothers went to New Orleans and bought a female slave, Eunice, in 1807. She is impregnated (by Carothers) and therefore married (off) to his manservant, Thucydus, in 1809. She gives birth to a girl, Tomasina, in 1810. On Christmas Day 1832, Eunice commits suicide by drowning herself, because she knows her daughter, Tomasina, has (also) been impregnated by Carothers. Tomasina dies in childbed in June 1833.*

Ike McCaslin has also deciphered these cryptic markings, and he has even added his own commentary: Carothers bequeathed to (his son) Turl $1,000 because "*that was cheaper than saying My son to a nigger*," and we even get an imagined rendition of Eunice's suicide: "He seemed to see her actually walking into the icy creek on that Christmas Day six months before her daughter's and her lover's (*Her first lover's* he thought. *Her first*) child was born, solitary, inflexible, griefless, ceremonial . . ." Yes, Ike parses these scribblings and derives from them the terrible truths of racial, sexual, and patriarchal abuse that they reveal.

Business as usual in the antebellum South, you might think. Yet, Buck and Buddy are stymied: "*Who in hell ever heard of a niger drownding him self.*" And I venture to say that most of this book's readers go right past this material, since no one is paid overtime for unpacking inserted, dense, cryptic, misspelled prose (except professors, I suppose).

Relinquish. It is largely this "packed" story—with its tragic, toxic view of ownership writ large—that catalyzes Ike McCaslin's life-altering decision to repudiate his inheritance, to give up the farm. Owning land, owning people: both of these hard-core principles that were bedrock truths in the antebellum South are rejected by Ike McCaslin. Ike and Cass deliberate on these matters for pages and pages, trading views about race, about John Brown, about God's "design" and God's "curse" on the South, but the luminous story that constitutes the ethical spinal cord of *Go Down, Moses* is that of Carothers McCaslin. Twice, Buck and Buddy referenced falling stars; twice they referenced Father's will. That *will* is a good bit more than the $1,000 inheritance he bequeaths to Turl; it is the entire belief system that made a white man feel entitled to own black slaves, entitled to impregnate his female servant (and then marry her off), and then entitled to impregnate his own daughter by that servant. Father's will. Eunice will not endure this double exploitation/injury. She takes her life as the only form of will-assertion available to her. Buck and Buddy cannot fathom it. Ike does. We can.

Ike takes stock of his inheritance: the land and the transgressions that regularly occurred on it. And he says no. Today in America, taking stock of one's history is big business. Ancestry.com is a major source of knowledge and, indeed, entertainment in today's media and digital landscape. Our understanding of DNA has made it possible for anyone to look back, to uncover roots and ancestors. Unlike decoding the yellowed ledgers in a commissary, unlike relinquishing a patrimony, today's sleuthing is easy, painless, and almost immediate. Log on—pay your fee and send in a spit sample—and you will receive a printout of your genetic past, writ large and clear. Is this enough?

Where you come from is more than a genetic issue. It is as much about the culture that produced you as about the individual people from whom you sprang. Those yellowed ledgers that Ike and Cass read tell Ike (and us)—once "we" have moved from sequence to story to ethics—"a tale of the tribe," a societal script, saturated with assumptions about gender and race, about ownership and responsibility. How do we make those moves? What looms large here is the ethics of reading, the necessity to open up your script (and yourself) in order to gauge its widest and deepest and most unhinging meanings. Gauging the violence done to Eunice and Tomasina by Carothers McCaslin, understanding the systemic nature of this abuse that turns the query "*Who in hell ever heard of a niger drownding him self*" into an indictment of the men who ask it: such labor on our part reshuffles our informational deck, transforms our facts into tragic and resonant knowledge. Facts do not speak for themselves. Buck and Buddy are confounded by their script. The very purpose of reading is to convert these markers into human sentience.

The first-year seminar in which I teach *Go Down, Moses* is titled "Rites of Passage." Given that the theme stems from anthropology rather than literature—tribal cultures devised liminal rituals for their young, with the three main stages being separation, transition, and reincorporation—my students are initially surprised (and then delighted) to find that they themselves, having just come to university to spend four years and then to graduate "into" society, are in the very midst of this process. Many different cultures possess some form of this scheme, and traditionally the young person's "coming of age" is signaled in two crucial ways: sexual puberty and the capacity to read. I think it fair to say that students at my university discover very quickly that being at college offers them a behavioral freedom of major proportions; I do not and cannot judge the sexual component of this freedom, but it exists. Needless to say, my job is cued to the second criterion of maturation: the capacity to read. I know, of course, that they know how to read—they, too, have had their version of Bob and Nancy many years ago—but I am at pains to challenge and deepen their reading habits, to help them see what a central, lifelong, intellectual, moral, and civic role reading will play in their university work and, still more importantly, in their future. My aims are very broad, and it matters little to me whether they intend to major in literature or not; they will be readers as long as they live, and there is great gravity and purpose here.

I point out to them that many of the religious coming-of-age rituals they are familiar with, such as Confirmation and Bar Mitzvah, center on a young person reading from the Bible or the Torah to the adult community or congregation. One is recognized as adult by the capacity to read the great books. All too often—as was the case with my own Bar Mitzvah—the task can be narrowly linguistic and mechanical: I simply had to read aloud a Hebrew text to the adults who were there. (I understood no Hebrew; I memorized the text; nothing more was required.

I don't think many people in the congregation knew any Hebrew either.) I had my rite of passage as reader. It did not feel like a passage, even though there were many presents.

Now it's my students' turn. So I want to begin shifting gears and to return to *Go Down, Moses*. It is no stretch to claim that Ike and Cass, who are reading about Carothers McCaslin's acts in the yellowed ledgers in the commissary, are performing a ritual that has much in common with Confirmation or Bar Mitzvah. Those ledgers are indeed the script, the book, of the South; Faulkner repeatedly goes out of his way to claim as much. But, unlike my performance at Temple Israel in 1956, Ike McCaslin will alter his life permanently because of what he understands in the text he is reading. He will repudiate his heritage. I can only imagine what a scandal it would be if a young person being confirmed or "bar mitzvahed" were to announce to the congregation: No. I now see (in the very text I'm reading) the values of this community, and I reject them. In some essential way, that is what Ike does. Faulkner later tells us that Ike's model is a carpenter from Galilee. Neither that carpenter nor Ike McCaslin is much appreciated by the community at large.

Mallarmé once wrote that the job of the poet is to "rendre plus purs les mots de la tribu" ("to make more pure the words of the tribe"); I would like to tweak the French poet's claim, by saying that the job of education is to *understand and assess* the words of the tribe. Frequently such activity is termed "critical thinking," and that is not a bad term for it; yet there, too, I would want to go further and to assert that critical thinking can never be only "analysis," for it must also be cued to human sentience and human values. That is what Ike and the reader do when they gauge the behavior of Carothers McCaslin. That labor is special, and it is the fundamental argument for the value of literature: it schools us in this broader, more far-reaching, more arduous, yet more humane form of understanding. This means we are to read with our hearts as well as our brains, that we are to "see, feelingly," as Shakespeare's (blinded) Gloucester, meeting the mad king on the heath, put it in *King Lear*. We are to open up the script we confront so as to recover the human story that subtends it, and that is our ultimate prey.

Is this reading challenge not the very mission of school itself? I began this discussion by referencing Ike McCaslin's education as hunter, an education that is demonstrably cued to *reading* the *prints* left by the great bear. Ike had learned to distinguish Ben's unique footprint from those of any other bear roaming the wilderness. And I have repeatedly said that my own calling as professor—as someone who is a professional reader—had its first intimations as far back as Bob and Nancy but was decisively vitalized by my encounter with French, with the poet Mallarmé. I can still recall poring over those hermetic poems—doubly so to me, who had a scant two years of French under my belt—and thrilling at the experience of opening them up, of tracking the many different vectors of allusion and motif that were coded into these brief lyrics. Those French words bristled for me—as Mallarmé had pointedly intended with his poetics of suggestion—as I negotiated them, transformed them from alien signs or markers on a page into pregnant and resonant meanings.

I have also referenced my sterile rehearsal of Hebrew script during my Bar Mitzvah, where I recited from memory, instead of actually reading the text. I can almost see that Hebrew text still, some sixty years later. So let me now summon all the teacherly, professorial clout that I have, and ask you to go through an exercise with me. We are going to return to Babel and confront the strangeness, the "otherness," of languages.

1. My name is Arnold Weinstein.   French: Je m'appelle Arnold Weinstein.
2. My name is Arnold Weinstein.   Spanish: Me llamo Arnold Weinstein.
3. My name is Arnold Weinstein.   Italian: Mi chiamo Arnold Weinstein.
4. My name is Arnold Weinstein.   German: Ich heisse Arnold Weinstein.
5. My name is Arnold Weinstein.   Swedish: Jag heter Arnold Weinstein.
6. My name is Arnold Weinstein.   Russian: Меня зовут Арнольд Вайнштейн.
7. My name is Arnold Weinstein.   Chinese: 我的名字叫阿諾德 · 溫斯坦.
8. My name is Arnold Weinstein.   Japanese: 私の名前は Arnold Weinstein.
9. My name is Arnold Weinstein.   Arabic: فاينشتاين أرنولد اسمي. .
10. My name is Arnold Weinstein.   Hebrew: ויינשטיין ארנולד שמי.

I confess that I myself can only read the first five entries. Once I get to Russian, I'm in trouble. Let's for a moment pass over the Russian in order

to focus on the Chinese, Japanese, Arabic, and Hebrew: 我的名字叫
阿諾德・溫斯坦 私の名前は اسمي أرنولد .فاينشتاين שמי ויינשטיין ארנולד.
Look hard at those four entries. If you are a reader of Chinese or Japanese or Arabic or Hebrew, you will "translate" the one or ones you can,
but if, like me, you do not know those languages, then I submit that
what you are looking at *looks like bear tracks.* Faulkner's text is about
reading. It is about looking at signs or markers—whether left by a bear
or left in a ledger—and converting them to their fuller meaning. Ike's
education as hunter of bears is inseparable from his education as reader
of the South.

I want now to say that there was a time, for all of you who are native
English speakers, when English also looked like bear tracks. I cannot
remember that time, and you cannot remember that time, but it has to
have been true, and it has to have puzzled or shocked you that these
markers were filled with significance: one's own name, later (in my case)
that of Bob and Nancy, still later the hot stuff of Romantic poetry when
Hazelwood held forth, the Swedish verses that made Kronwald weep
when my wife was a student, the sibylline verses of Mallarmé that I
pored over in Paris. It all started as bear tracks, as uninterpretable signs.
The entire project of school is about learning to convert those signs into
significance. This mission extends well beyond "foreign" languages
because it loops back to our very own first language, a script that looks
obvious to us, only because we may not have interpreted it as it deserves. Every subject studied in school—not just English but history,
social sciences, geography, science, even mathematics, I would claim—
is about learning to decipher scripts and bear tracks, to translate signs
and markers into meaning. This can mean going well beyond dictionary
entries and putting what you read (its numbers, its facts, its data) into
other crucial, critical contexts: ethical, sentient, ideological. That is
what Ike does. That is the labor of the humanities, in general, and literature, in particular.

It may well be replied that my argument *at most* applies only to literature. Other scripts require no decoding. Or do they? And you might
ask, How many of us are put in front of yellowed ledgers that depict the
evil abuses of our grandfather during the time of slavery? So let me close

with a final literary reference: to Ibsen's most sensational play, *Ghosts*, published in 1881. Its scandalous themes of hereditary venereal disease and incest and euthanasia were scarcely welcome reading in proper bourgeois sitting rooms. Why does Ibsen title his story of a woman coming to terms with all the lies she's both told and been told *Ghosts*? At a key early moment in the play, Mrs. Alving (the heroine and mother of the diseased Oswald) overhears her son flirting with their maid, Regina; she knows the maid is the illegitimate child spawned on their earlier housekeeper by her husband and that therefore Regina and Oswald are in fact half siblings. But listen to the way she explains what she has heard to her (Luddite) pastor friend:

> When I heard Regina and Oswald in there, it was as if I saw ghosts. I almost think we are all ghosts—all of us, Pastor Manders. It isn't just what we have inherited from our father and mother that walks in us. It is all kinds of dead ideas and all sorts of old and obsolete beliefs. They are not alive in us; but they remain in us none the less, and we can never rid ourselves of them. I have only to take a newspaper and read it, and I see ghosts between the lines. There must be ghosts all over the country. They lie as thick as grains of sand. And we're all so horribly afraid of the light.

Ibsen's play is overtly about the lies we tell, but it is covertly about learning how to see better, to read better, to understand better. His evidence of a "magic script" is not an English or Swedish or French poem or a Faulkner text but rather the *newspaper*. We read newspapers every day, whether in print or online. We expect to encounter there the "news of the day." What could be more prosaic than the prose of newspapers? M. Jourdain could handle it. No rhyme schemes, no misspelled words, no onslaught of Chinese or Japanese or Arabic or Hebrew or bear tracks. Just good old English (or Norwegian, as the case may be) staring us in the face, delivering the goods. Yet, Mrs. Alving looks at this docile, inert script and finds it teeming with life: ghosts between the lines, lying as thick as grains of sand. What on earth is she talking about? The only answer I can give is: the so-called record of today's events is a roiling display of yesterday's and last year's and last decade's and last century's events. Those "dead ideas" and "old and obsolete beliefs" that Mrs. Alving saw in the paper are just as alive and well—as thick as grains of sand—in our own world of print and document.

What are colonialism's legacies, along with tribalisms and sexism and racism of all stripes, if not "old and obsolete beliefs" that continue to live and thrive and to lie behind what goes into our newspapers and our laws? (How many old and obsolete beliefs go into writing *"Who in hell ever heard of a niger drownding himself"*?) Today's newspaper is a living script: the deeds it records are often of long, even tragic pedigree, have been gestating for great periods of time, are saturated (if we could see it) with blood and tears, are big with human life (and death). What kind of readers are we? Can we decipher the bear tracks? Can we see the picture?

School, in the broadest acceptation of the term, should be about learning how to read, learning how to see the fuller reaches of the facts and figures that may seem complete in themselves but that actually cry out for human interpretation. Otherwise, we are shipwrecked in an unechoing realm of numbers and data and dead words, bereft of meanings and implications, bereft of the human drama that subtends them and is in turn shaped by them. Let me repeat: "is in turn shaped by them." The cardinal lesson derivable here is: the fuller reach of words and facts and data is not the purview of poets and critics and experts; it is the inevitable human record itself, the inevitable "playing out" of facts and numbers into actual lives and fates. Our reading mistakes derive from both the "frozen sea" that Kafka located inside us and the legacies of culture that hinder our seeing their imprint, their price tag. Unqueried, unfelt data are no less than bear tracks, markers we see but cannot properly decipher.

Think back, once again, to Ibsen's view of the newspaper as living script. One wants students to have the eyes of Ibsen's Mrs. Alving when they read the newspapers and fact sheets of today so that they can see the ghosts between the lines, ghosts that lie as thick as grains of sand. Both the Norwegian dramatist and the Mississippian novelist are intent on awakening us (as Joyce's Stephen Dedalus said) from/to the nightmare of history. This means restoring to the signs themselves the fuller, sentient narrative that is concealed in them. And one also wants these young people to understand that our cultural record is teeming with such *news*: we find it in places that do not speak, such as cemeteries with their silent stone markers, and we must learn to recognize it in the great texts that come down to us, for they, too, do not speak on their own (as generations of dazed students have experienced every day) but must be made to speak, by dint of a reading practice that would be *dimensional*. I am not talking about close reading—what the French used to term "explication de texte," what the Swedes sweetly call "lusläsa" ["lice-reading"]—but rather about something far more expansive and trans-formational, whereby a culture's bear tracks are decoded so as to yield the often horrible news they contain, news that we ignore at our own expense as a society, as a people. And it is not a question of digging up corpses—even though they are there aplenty—but of endowing dead letters and inert numbers with the human, sentient plenitude they actually possess and deserve.

The larger picture always eventually emerges, often cadaver-ridden. Chou En-lai's famous quip regarding the impact of the French Revolu-tion, "It's too early to tell," testifies to many things at once: the belated-ness of understanding, the continuing unfurling effects of war (as of slavery and colonialism), the sheer difficulty in getting a fix on things. It also speaks to the time-release toxins that both nature and politics rou-tinely produce but that we cannot see . . . in time. Must truth always be retrospective? Must Kierkegaard's bleak dictum that we live our lives forward but understand them backward always be valid? (My genera-tion blissfully soaked up as much sun as we could every summer, never having a clue that skin cancer could, years later, be the result. My Mem-phis peers and I saw Confederate statues every day when I was a child, but, no matter how liberal we were, we white youngsters rarely thought twice about them.) When do we learn? Might reading yield something *prospective*? I believe we can indeed see better today, so much later, what the impact of the French Revolution, or indeed the Civil War, the World Wars, the Vietnam War, the Iraq War was to be (while still coming into focus): the changing of the world order, the ripping apart of the Union, the possibilities of mass extermination, the disillusionment of the public, the spread of terrorism, the unhealing/unfurling signs of PTSD and other forms of wreckage that accompany all wars and have a ghastly afterlife.

I can scarcely claim that *reading* might have helped us avoid these catastrophes. Yet, much of this has a verbal cast. Staying with the topic of war, one thinks of Hemingway's indictment of grand but empty words—*honor, glory*, the whole kaboodle, reliably trotted out during the Great War, during all wars—as utterly absent from the field of battle itself, where all he saw was carnage. Or we could move from war to other ills, such as the subprime mortgages, hurriedly concocted on bogus income data and then spewed out into the world via instruments laced with (camouflaged) toxic "tranches" leading to disruptions and destruction far and wide, as well as near and here. Vitriolic discussion of so-called fake news is more than partisan rancor; Daniel Patrick Moynihan's famous statement "Everyone is entitled to their own opinions, but not their own facts" is true, but doesn't go nearly far enough, since even the facts can require decoding: not to find some hidden key but to get a sense of the sentient reaches and ramifications that lie coiled there. We need a citizenry capable of *interpreting* the ubiquitous data-glut spilling out onto today's digital scene, capable of seeing both "the ghosts between the lines" and the ghosts yet to come. We need *readers* capable of working for their bread.

I remember a brilliant lecture given years ago, eliciting this response from one of my colleagues: "Well, of course, he is a good reader, but where is the theory behind it?" Now, at the end of my career, I can think of no more exalted title than being remembered as a good reader. This is what I, with my wrinkles and white hair and sometimes wobbly legs, still hope to bring to my university classes, and it is nowhere more essential than in my first-year seminar on "rites of passage," for I am the fellow who is to play the role of reading-guide to these young people on their own rites of passage. They come to me at the age of eighteen—they are always eighteen—whereas I who meet them have moved from my thirties to my forties to my fifties to my sixties to my seventies and accruing still, always playing out my part of this same schooling covenant. I, too, am making a passage.

The trip that began with Bob and Nancy, then moved on to Hazelwood and Princeton and Paris and Berlin and Harvard, to settle in at Brown for its long professional duration, has put me ultimately in the Sam Fathers slot, and I must eventually exit it, as Sam himself does. I wrote that Ike McCaslin begs to stay in the woods when Sam dies, and that General Compson permits him to do so, since the wilderness's lessons outstrip those of any "hired pedagogue." Sam himself is buried in ritual fashion, with offerings to mark the spot, but Faulkner has Ike return the next season, to realize that Sam's death-place is unfindable, that he is both in the earth and of the earth. Maybe, I like to think, that is also how hired pedagogues like myself who teach reading finish out: in the earth and of the earth, not merely in a cemetery but elsewhere, out there, in the soil and of the soil of the young whom they have taught, as time marches on. Have I seeded readers? What do they make of today's bear tracks?

(W)riting

If you speak to any older teacher (grade school, high school, university) thinking about retirement, and you ask what they will miss least in their work, it is possible that *writing* will be the subject they're happiest to let go of. A lifetime of reading and correcting the papers written by the young can take its toll. And these matters are rigorously democratic: a sampling of student opinion would almost certainly yield the same result: "writing" is arguably the single most painful and laborious discipline encountered at school, the one of longest duration. It may be the reason that so many people acquire a visceral dislike of school itself from the get-go, from their very earliest experience of having to sit still at a desk (!) and then produce writing; welcome to Foucault's "discipline and punish." Young people all too often find it (writing) rule-laden yet arbitrary, wooden yet elusive, cumbersome to the point of imprisoning, deeply resistant to their internal world of feelings and thoughts, hence "artificial" in the worst sense: an alien code that shackles them to systems not their own, an alien code they must try to master, to show what they have learned. They very often come off as "less" than, or "other" than themselves.

Schools at all levels (including university) offer a battery of writing courses to their students, and we the faculty are routinely urged to make sure that students needing help on this front receive it (at the hands of specialized centers and the like). The stakes are high. We in the humanities are often told that we should, above all, make special mention of our students' strengths as critical writers when we ourselves write recommendations for them down the road. Here would be our contribution to their education. One might even say that the humanities, in particular, are partly defined, in the eyes of many, as writing-centric and that this focus constitutes one of their (few) advantages in the competitive world outside the university. At least, folks think, these literature or philosophy majors know how to write. At least that.

Yet my experience has not been so good on this front. Not that there aren't loads of folks committed to this issue. My own teaching assistants have often worked out programmatic views on what good writing is. I have also seen what the Writing Center or the Writing Fellows Program put forth as essential in helping young people advance an argument. And, of course, I have worked closely with colleagues who are directing undergraduate honors theses and PhD dissertations, hence much concerned with students' writing. My abiding sense is that *all* these authority figures, at every level, have a confident conviction of how the job is to be done. Surely the vast array of resources thrown at this basic concern should yield results. They often do: many of the papers I receive, and find readable and persuasive, have benefited from such counseling.

But often enough, it doesn't work out this way in the least. Two memorable occasions come to mind. The first was more than four decades ago when I was directing a doctoral dissertation, with a distinguished senior scholar serving as second reader; he quickly led me to understand that we would constitute a "good cop–bad cop" team, that I would go easy with the writing, and he would do the hard labor. Well, he labored hard indeed: the graduate student in question came to see me, in tears, and showed me the pages my colleague had "corrected"; they were virtually unreadable because they were *scored*, outright torn and written through, by the violent pencil markings inflicted on them. It was an embarrassing moment of unwanted intimacy (with my colleague, not the student), since what was more than clear—it was *graphic*—was the queasy mix of passion and vehemence that fueled my colleague's penetrative markings. Nerves were touched. (The student eventually completed her dissertation; my colleague elected to go more lightly.)

The other instance that stays in my mind has to do with an earnest teaching assistant who week in and week out gave C's to virtually all the students' papers assigned to her section for discussion and grading. None of them, it seemed (over and over), could write. None of them knew how to make an argument. There, too, I looked at the evidence (frequently brought in to me by angry or hapless students) and saw that every sentence was being corrected, rewritten, made right. Nothing passed muster. (What kind of learning is this? I wondered.) I was reminded of how assiduously orthodontists inflicted young people of my generation with braces: no person's teeth seemed to measure up, seemed to be as straight and upright and in line as they should or could be (forced into).

My reference to braces is not as loopy as it may seem. We have learned that several years of teenage braces—a form of sadism a good bit of my generation experienced—may well serve the young during their "partnering" years when they need to look sharp, from a Darwinian angle, but that eventually nature will have its way, and your teeth will return (regress?) back to the original plan or lack thereof. And I suspect that writing has parallels. After all, many of my university students have been writing (badly) for at least thirteen years before they ever get to my classroom. I'm tempted to add: they've been "thinking" badly (uncritically) for just as long. But, not to worry. We will perform our miracle work. Once they have received our tender ministrations, all will be well. Their paragraphs will be concise, their logic clear (and their teeth straight). After all, there simply must be some tangible reward/outcome for them and their parents, after paying the tuitions routinely charged at the elite places where folks like me work.

But, alas, it doesn't always come out this way. All too many of my students exit my classes as hamstrung and limping (as far as writing goes) as they were upon arrival: fuzzy sentences, fuzzy thinking, fuzzy conclusions. And it may even be that they exit my institution, in an overall sense, far less changed and improved than our PR folks like to believe. I am not thrilled with the institutional/instructional Pandora's box I seem to be opening here, since if four years of (expensive) university work doesn't produce demonstrably good writing, one has to wonder what else it doesn't produce. What, I sometimes wonder, can actually be *taught* in twelve weeks of a literature class? Or in four years of college?

I assign a goodly number of one-page papers, to be written at a regular clip, and I tell them in my most avuncular voice: "craft an argument." But I am a bit slack when it comes to telling them *how*—and they do ask—since I think there are countless ways to put life into prose. Each good essay or novel we read proves this. I also entertain the unsuave belief that my courses should be fun. And not having a degree in "critical writing"—if such a thing exists—I sometimes do worry that I may perhaps not have all the expertise and clout I need to uphold my authority and generate results on this front. But then I perk up, as I reflect on their backgrounds and what they've already been put through. My Ivy League students have, after all, crawled or sailed through countless courses and standardized tests devised to document their skills in writing.

So, why is it that I am dismayed equally by their writing and by the legion of folks who lay claim to correcting their faults? Much is at issue here: whether there is such a thing as good writing (which I believe), and whether it is teachable (which I doubt). My expensively educated students still make mistakes in grammar, even in spelling; OK, spellcheck could handle that. But, worse still, and approaching the point I want to make—maybe my own writing stumbles a bit?—so many of them have so little *flair*. So many of them turn in work that is clumsy, laborious, rambling, and—worst of all, and not just for me—boring if not painful to read. That is the gripe I am airing and exploring in this book. (I am speaking in generalities: in every class I teach there are always some who write like the angels. Yet I wonder if teachers or angels ever taught them.)

Here is what I have gradually come to believe. Year in and year out, my students seem all to have been indoctrinated with the all-powerful schema of *thesis-argument-conclusion* as the very law (if not the soul) of how to proceed when writing a paper. This model is virtually sacrosanct;

to tell them to jettison this approach would be like telling them to wet their pants. They are (toilet)trained; they "know" what is to be done when it comes to writing an essay. Yet very very few of them seem to relish the labor. Hard labor: it's the term we used to use for prisoners and chain gangs. The standard way at my institution for determining how much hard labor any course entails is to ask the seemingly innocuous question "What is the workload"? This means: how many books and articles must we read? How many papers must we write? I often reply, caustically, that their term, "workload," seems quite out of place to me, and I propose another, more to my liking: "pleasure-load." They look at me in outright disbelief. (Some smile, the way one might in dealing with the senile.) Here is what it comes down to: *sentences*—to read, to write—appear to many of them as something both arduous and measurable, indeed as prison sentences. I sense it will be an uphill battle to convince them otherwise.

But it's a worthwhile battle. I try to explain that the very model they have all been taught—thesis-argument-conclusion—is itself a prison sentence, a form of incarceration. What is incarcerated? Ideas, thoughts, the living pulse of thinking and feeling as they are cargoed/coerced/straitjacketed into words and forms. What god ever told us that the way to convey one's thoughts is through the vehicle of thesis-argument-conclusion? (The ones in the Old and New Testaments, as well as other sacred texts—not to mention the literary works we'll be studying—do not use this schema at all.) I then expatiate on my writing-assignment model: regular forays limited to one page, but "free" in design, including the freedom to write in verse or to write less than a page; and I urge them to consider scrapping the thesis-argument-conclusion model in favor of something more sinuous, forking, surprising, fun. You might start with a false lead, I suggest—after all, life often proceeds in this tricky fashion, and learning almost always does—and in mid-page reverse course; or you might make unprovable but scintillating allegations, and you're allowed to, as long as you show me you know they're speculative, but that you think they produce light. I also require long final essays—this frequently frightens the first-year students, unaccustomed to building a more longitudinal argument—where I want to get a sense of what they've learned or imagined or construed about our fuller semester spent together reading and discussing books.

But, first, we focus on those one-pagers. I tell them I expect their single page to take me somewhere so that the end is not merely a confirmation of the beginning, but a venture outward, perhaps even a series of radii on the move. At bottom, I am seeking, via these suggestions and guidelines, something important for myself (in addition to not being bored): to encounter a personal voice, a personal point-of-view. This often stuns them, since many come to college having been told that the only legitimate way to write is the impersonal, objective, neutral (neutered?) way, as cleansed as possible of personal bias or agenda. Finding one's own voice is, I fully recognize, no easy proposition, yet it may well be what ultimately turns writing into pleasure and insight (into their material, into themselves). I myself had the great fortune of discovering a voice long ago in Paris; I now credit that discovery with as much hedonism and value and prophecy as anything else that happened to me in that life-shaping year.

One of my targets, as you can probably guess, given the rule-less scheme I am championing, is the holy Maginot line that separates *critical writing* from *creative writing*. They come to university convinced that *critical* and *creative* are antonyms, at war with each other. How, they wonder, could they have common ground? What, they ask—it is the professor's bane in life to never get clear of this question—am I looking for? I reply, This hybrid critical/creative model doesn't mean that you are encouraged to free-associate or to do some form of Surrealist "automatic writing" or just go off on a tear. But I want them to have more awe of the remarkable medium that is theirs, to begin see that writing has a pulse, an energy, and—often—a gathering coherence of its own, that it has a flow and reach that may well outrun the thin outline or premises they had in mind when they began. That it can have heat, that it can move. Your mind, I glibly tell my students, runs deeper than you think, and part of your job is to free it, rather than to coerce or overschematize it.

This course, I mischievously remind them, is a *literature* course; it is not a law school course, it is not about making an airtight argument or concocting an impeccable brief, it is not even about crystalline prose, much less mathematical precision. Tone, image, metaphor, ambiguity, *voice*, may all have a role to play. In essence, I expect their paper to be as commensurate as possible with the complexity, richness, thrust, and dimensions of our materials. See writing as a process of discovery. Think of it as how the framers saw our defining document: *a declaration of independence*. Think of it in the same terms we find in the First Amendment: *freedom of speech*. (I am aware that the framers were not a playful bunch of scribblers. The actual writing in the Constitution can put you to sleep, even though it is a brilliant document.)

Great writers have never aimed simply for "workmanlike" prose. Hemingway used to claim that even in a dry spell, he had only to be patient and wait to find "one true sentence," and it would open the door to more writing. (Theorists have observed that there are no "true sentences," but Hemingway had his own writerly truth here.) It is high time that we taught students to be poachers, to *use* the strange literary materials we put (in) their way, to enlist some of the firepower that fuels art. Writing is writing is writing (as Hemingway's mentor Gertrude Stein might have put it). It can do a lot of things.

Today's culture is abuzz about the unfurling, still ununderstood, powers of the internet, the smartphone, social media, artificial intelligence, the whole host of dizzily evolving gadgets and (for me) technospecters that dot our horizon, but perhaps our most potent armaments are older and of longer pedigree, and just as close to hand, located in great literature, in those "classics" that we've been lulled into thinking staid or even mute. Remember Ibsen's Mrs. Alving: she looked at the newspaper and saw ghosts crawling between the lines. What else might we find living there?

Now, as I warned, I shall proceed to go crazy. Let me invoke two texts—for the dark as well as the light they shine on what writing might truly be, for the sense of grandeur and surprise and vehemence each locates in the very *act* of writing—that stand at great length from one another, that flaunt to the full the power and the *stakes* of writing, showing it to be boundary-smashing, at once extending our reach and within our reach. As teacher, I want my students to begin sensing the sheer vibrancy and firepower of the medium they've been docilely using for years. I do this because I believe they can tap into this energy stream, even as they compose their measly little one-pagers for me. It's not unlike the astonishing range of uses this computer (that I'm using as a typewriter) actually possesses, a range I neither comprehend nor explore; they (my students) are quite conversant with machines such as mine. But it is time for them now to consider that writing a paper can be equally muscular, equally empowered, might even rival with the arsenal of apps they've grown accustomed to, which require only a touch of the finger.

I begin with the Norwegian Knut Hamsun, an author much revered in the past if not much read today, and I choose his most unhinged narrative, *Hunger*, published in 1891, and (mis)understood as the story of a down-and-out starving writer in Christiania (Oslo). Hamsun probably did not know Rimbaud's "cri de coeur" of 1871, claiming that the poet must become a "voyant" ("seer") by a "long, immense et raisonné dérèglement de tous les sens" ("a long, immense and deliberate derangement of all the senses"). Hamsun's protagonist lives out a good bit of the French poet's injunction, and the text insistently flirts with incoherence. *Starving* (and the mania it provokes) is presented as the subject's effort to break the biological—and behavioral—laws that govern us from birth to death. Might writing be his bid for freedom? Here is what it looks like when our man actually goes about it.

All at once, one or two remarkable sentences occurred to me, good for a short story or a sketch, windfalls in language, as good as I had ever come on. I lay saying the words over to myself and decided they were excellent. Soon other sentences joined the two; instantly I was wide awake, stood up, and took my paper and pencil from the table at the foot of my bed. It was like a vein opening, one word followed the other, arranged themselves in the right order, created situations; scene piled on scene, actions and conversations welled up in my brain, and a strange sense of pleasure took hold of me. I wrote as if possessed, and filled one page after the other without a moment's pause. Thoughts poured in so abruptly, and kept on coming in such a stream, that I lost a number of them from not being able to write them down fast enough, even though I worked with all my energy. They continued to press themselves on me; I was deep into the subject, and every word I set down came from somewhere else.

Despite the fact that Hamsun's own language here is controlled and easily read, this bravura piece seems nonetheless unhinged, untrammeled, in its pouring out of urgent verbal matter. Words spew from the writer in ways that mimic the vomiting that also parses this text about starvation. But it is essential to recognize that the words come *to* the writer, rather than *from* him—the Norwegian says "blir lagt mig i munden" (are placed in my mouth)—and in that sense echoes an ancient tradition of lyric inspiration seen in forms such as "invocation to the Muse," where the writer formally asks to be invaded, intoxicated, mesmerized, turned into a vehicle. I have written about Hamsun's passage in other contexts, emphasizing how many sober laws it breaks, even enlisting it as evidence why a Plato would have banned the poets from his ideal Republic. Perhaps Hamsun is closer to Plato than it seems, for he has the wisdom to sense that the deepest forms and truths he is capable of will come to him rather than from him, will ambush him, will enlist him as their conduit, not their source.

Hamsun's hero's finest creative moment comes when he *invents* a new word: *Kuboaa*. (Most of us cease to invent words about the time we learn to speak.) With pride and glee, our man trots out a worthy selection of possible definitions for his naked, new "unbaptized" noun—*God, Tivoli Gardens, cattle show, padlock, sunrise, emigration, tobacco factory, yarn*—and says, Nope, *Kuboaa* doesn't mean any of those. Admittedly, plugging *Kuboaa* into a cogent sentence would be dicey, since it would fatally burden Hamsun's term with a dictionary meaning. But one understands the inebriation as well as the hubris and fantasy that stem from this moment of seeming creation ex nihilo. We are at the opposite pole of Flaubert's famous mot juste, designating the perfect—indeed the only—"right" word for saying what the writer wants to say; Hemingway followed the Flaubertian suit. So do most of us who take writing seriously.

But Hamsun-Lucifer is pushing a verbal version of "Non serviam" (I will not serve); he is flexing his muscles by denying this referential yoke, by cashiering the semiotic choke hold that our differential view of language seems to present, for he is a true anarchist, bent on exploding the System. Please note: I do not tell my students to invent words. Yet, even short of such absolute verbal autonomy, we *should* sense, each time we speak or write, a kind of giddiness regarding the instrument at our disposal, so much more charged and potent than we often realize. We should salivate, with munitions of this sort. But there is still more to be said about Hamsun's writer: his best words *come*. Either from somewhere else or on their own. No dictionary or style book is required, no effort or discipline or deliberativeness, no groaning or straining, no outline. Very curious.

Of course, Hamsun is writing *fiction*, and Plato banished the *poets*: what use can my students—required to analyze texts—make of such verbal inebriation, when the words might come unbidden, on a wilding? Won't students counter that it makes sense (at most) to claim this kind of torrential verbal-flooding as the province of *creative* work? But what about *criticism*, which is what they're asked to do? What about thesis-argument-conclusion? After all, this is a literature course, and they need a grade. Is Hamsun's eruptive, lavalike outpouring a usable guide? And I imagine them turning on *me*, and asking, "Have *you* (who have tenure, who have written books, who's pontificating to us) done the 'Hamsun-thing'"?

Yes. I'm realizing that, yes, I have, at least in my own limited way. In a fifty-plus year career consisting of writing books and articles of literary criticism, as well as that same amount of time spent teaching, I now recognize and salute Hamsun as my mentor. Very often when I've made my best points, I've been "off script," followed a tangent, discovered that the words I am speaking or writing are awfully close to being placed in my mouth, rather than chosen. I am an amanuensis. Don't get me wrong. I do not rant and rave, I do not froth at the mouth, I do not appear in a trance. I even speak whole sentences. But, at my best, I follow as well as lead my words. But here's the catch: they are still *my words*, fueled by a kind of prior intelligence, a broader, even more lateral, inclusive intelligence, that amplifies me, surprises me, *coheres me*.

And now comes the final admission: this is a hoot, a trip, an experience of enormous hedonism. I always feel that such work is what I am meant for, what I do best, what gives me the keenest satisfactions. It is quasi-visceral. To be sure, these words are exiting my own mouth, and they absolutely bear on the topic at hand in my book or lecture or class, and, further, they definitely reflect decades of conversance with my materials. But they go further, have more authority, more *life*, than any outline or schema I might have or could produce. Writing connects me to a current that is me (all that I've thought and intended to say, all that goes beyond my wispy planning and intentions), yet more than me, as if the words were the prime movers, intent on doing it their way, virtually elbowing me out of the way.

Of course, I concede that the rants in my work are far more "prepared" and "strategic" than I'm letting on. But I feel that the essential takeaway from my courses and my books is deeply language-driven, with the key corollary that my students also might feel empowered, might have, at least now and then, a similar relation to language and writing, might also discover that words have an indwelling power of their own. The medium's reaches expand our own, turn the analytic project into something more vibrant and self-propelling. This is neither self-reflexive nor belletristic nor even anarchic, but rather a more robust critical and exploratory discourse. Writing reveals us to ourselves, makes our reaches ours. As Emerson said (and as I never tire of quoting), the poet apprises us not of his wealth but of the commonwealth. Ultimately, this centrifugal model is nonetheless centripetal as well, like a boomerang that returns, faithful to its signifying mission; and it helps us see that we might experience writing as not only on-target but also hedonistic, instead of laborious.

And funny. One of Hamsun's most endearing passages consists of a zoom shot of the very paper he is writing on, paper that has attracted a community of flies and gnats to its surface, hence requiring that the writer take action:

> I breathed on them to make them go, then blew harder and harder, but it did no good. The tiny beasts lowered their behinds, made themselves heavy, and struggled against the wind until their thin legs were bent. They were absolutely not going to leave the place. They

would always find something to get hold of, bracing their heels against a comma or an unevenness in the paper, and they intended to stay exactly where they were until they themselves decided it was the right time to go.

When I read this passage I think of what we have lost as well as gained, with the advent of electronic writing. Whether it be papyrus or vellum, whether it be the monks' beautiful script or the calligraphic traditions of Eastern cultures or the notebooks of yore handed out to us in school—a tradition that was still alive during my encounter with Bob and Nancy, which meant that my earliest grades for *writing* had to do with cursive itself—we do well to grant writing its materiality. Our modern knowledge of linguistics, which works via *difference*, via the traffic between word and meaning (sign and referent), is all too immaterial and disembodied, too abstract, too much a head game; and, of course, our digital arsenal has little use for handcrafted markings, even if it offers you a choice of emoticons.

But whether you're writing a one-page paper or a three-hundred-page book, you're working with/on ordnance. Hamsun presents us with no invoked muses, but the scene-of-writing is nonetheless one of great traffic, of entries and exits. Bugs resting their behinds on a comma may seem like small beer, but it is weirdly monumental in its own tidings: commas are as edgy as cliffs are; prose has reefs and shoals; writing has tangible markers. The very word *character* used to mean "stamping tool," even "pointed stick"; you could be stamped out or gouged. Writing is visceral; it can rip into your viscera.

Visceral. To make good on this (extravagant) claim for writing's power to rend, I now move to my second extremist example, Kafka's story, "In the Penal Colony." It is Kafka's grisliest story—and that is saying something—and I regularly encounter my students' distaste for it when I assign it. I understand why. Its plot features a grotesque form of archaic state punishment—the prisoners are laid, strapped and naked, in a "bed," and then a giant mechanical beak goes into action inscribing on their flesh the nature of their transgression—that makes guillotines and even cyanide showers look gentle. (Some critics have indeed suggested that the story, published in 1919, prefigures the Nazi doctors.) Worse yet, there is no trial, no assumption of "innocent until proven guilty." And, to cap it off, this entire brutal scheme, the customary form of meting out justice on this island, has (or had) major religious significance: in the old days, we are told, people would come from far and wide to witness these executions, with children having front-row seats. Any student who dislikes torture and believes in justice or a fair legal system must choke on this story.

There are three key players in the tale: the Explorer who has come to witness this model, the Officer who carries out the punishments with spiritual fervor, and the Machine itself. Others do exist, however: the Prisoner and the Guard, both of whom are described in animalistic terms as ignorant pawns in the story, each following orders they don't really understand. *Really understanding* turns out, in fact, to be the core issue of Kafka's story (as well as of this book you are reading). The Officer desperately seeks to convey to the Explorer the *rightness* of the penal system he serves: it cemented the Community, it meted out not only justice but also truth, and it even achieved this utopian result for the Prisoners themselves who, at the end of the first six hours of their twelve-hour stint "in the Machine" invariably began to show that they at last "understood." What they understood, we realize, is the actual Script that is being written on/in their flesh by the offices of the Machine. They *read* it. "Am eigenen Leib erfahren" is a time-honored German expression, signifying: to experience something in the flesh. Kafka's Machine achieves that. And we cannot fail to see that it is a Writing Machine. A horribly twisted but stubborn version of Eden appears here, a writerly paradise where word and thing are magically reunited, fused, embodied.

We begin to realize why the story has the religious overtones it does— the Officer served the former Old Commandant, but the new Commandant seems to have a different belief system; critics have spoken of Old and New Testaments—for the very word for *writing* in German is *Schrift*, which also is the term for holy texts. We are accustomed to thinking that holy texts command assent from their believers by dint of a shared belief system, but Kafka seems to be zeroing in on language itself, language that is imaged in this story as a giant beak that rends the body. At this point it becomes clear that Kafka's Machine overcomes the central impasse that has dogged language ever since the Tower of Babel: it creates an *immediate* (that is, *nonmediated*) *language*, a language that transcends the schism of sign/referent or word/meaning (as well as the busy work of dictionaries) that stamps all known languages as "differential" (with the possible partial exception of sign languages). Kafka's Machine would be a mechanized, materialized (and lethal) version of Flaubert's mot juste; poor Flaubert (whom Kafka revered) had to shriek out the words in his *gueuloir* (screaming room) to see if they were right. Kafka has modernized the process (although it's not clear the shrieking has disappeared). We are familiar with the phrase, "the Word becomes Flesh," but in this story it happens *in the flesh*. Try visualizing this. Kafka has.

It is impossible to overstate the ramifications of this scheme. A corporeal linguistics is at hand, a language that "gets through," that is, at one with "meaning." No interpreters needed, no mediation required. In real life we never—*never*—have this immediacy, this fail-safe communication. How can I prove this? Well, have you ever misunderstood . . . a poem? A page? A person? Have you ever been misunderstood? How often has language remained *dead letters* or "bear tracks" in your lifelong experience of communication? I personally experience this failure on a routine basis: in my teaching, in my human relationships, in my reading. (Kafka's "incisive" dead letters seem to be fighting back. His bear tracks become bears.) For most of us, the semiosis, or reading-of-signs, in daily life is incredibly vexed and uncertain: yes, we know what a green or red light or a price tag means, but do we know really what the words of the spouse or the friend or the lover or the child or the doctor or the lawyer or the report or the novel or even the newspaper article actually meant? (No spell-check can fix this.)

Kafka's Writing Machine obliterates this endemic problem in communication. The Prisoner's "understanding" is not cerebral or conceptual or linguistic in the least. His understanding takes place *in the flesh*. There is something horrible yet delirious happening here. Words now rend you, get inside you. And allow me to pose an impertinent question: does one not sometimes secretly desire exactly that power—that the words might actually get inside the person one is speaking or writing to? Medieval writers use the conceit of language moving through the ear directly to the heart without any blockage or mediation. (What would a heart surgeon make of this?) I wonder whether, at times, parents and teachers, as well as friends and lovers, haven't yearned to possess this kind of power. Isn't it possible that all writers and all speakers might—at some unavowable level—desire this (penetrative) kind of language? Might that be where one wants to be (understood)? Needless to say, I am talking about *words* reaching the other, not about some monstrous beak that opens up prisoners. And, yes, I am painfully aware of how abhorrent my terms are, given the ugly sexual and gender implications of my figure. Decide for yourself, nonetheless, whether Kafka's model is worth pondering.

There is a moment in Faulkner's *As I Lay Dying* where Addie Bundren offers us a chilling but recognizable avowal about *teaching*: "I would look forward to the times when they faulted, so I could whip them. When the switch fell I could feel it upon my flesh; when it welted and ridged it was my blood that ran, and I would think with each blow of the switch: now you are aware of me. Now I am something in your secret and selfish life, who have marked your blood with my own for ever and ever." Addie's special pedagogy has always seemed to me to be a direct version of Faulkner's view of language, of words: meant to enter us, to invade our secret life, to mark our blood and make it flow. It is not a pretty picture— she'd rightly lose her job in today's schools—but it does make sense to align this with Kafka's "language beak" as expressing a desire for invasive entry that warrants reflection as well as rejection.

One intriguing feature of Kafka's penal saga is how it inverts one of the oldest figurative binaries on record: surface/depth. We all know that the adjective "superficial," when applied to human utterance or writing or thinking or feeling, is no compliment; conversely, "deep" has long enjoyed a venerable reputation, since it points to reaches below the surface, hence reaches endowed with greater meaning and value. Think of how many notions are held hostage to this dyad: "deep-seated," "deeply felt," "profound," even "deeply entrenched," and then think of how "surface" plays out: "external," "ostensible," "apparent," "cosmetic." We revere the depths as containing truth; we critique the surface as being imperceptive or shallow or false. Now, bearing in mind what Kafka has wrought with his writing beak, let us ponder what happens when we *somaticize*—make physical—these terms. A "superficial wound" is what you want, not a "deep" one. When it comes to flesh, folks are a bit more prudent with their metaphors. An "open" person is not the same as an "opened" person. After all, *skin* is what gloves and protects our organs and bodies, and skin calls for respect and caution. Such caution is annihilated by the cutting work of the Machine; it murders those put in it.

"Cutting edge" is a darling (albeit surgical) metaphor in my line of work, for it signals research at the boundaries of a field, bidding to redesign its contours; "edgy" is itself a compliment when applied to a work of art or performance. But we are highly aware that these are metaphors. As my examples have repeatedly shown, language is precisely a form of communication and exchange that is figurative rather than literal, that gets through but does not maim. That might well be its greatest justification: *figurative* entry. (No reader of this is bleeding; if you are, it is not because of my words.)

And bear in mind: the species cannot survive if the feeding and seeding of a body—food and sex: two staples—does not take place. It's an old creatural logic, even if modern life offers alternatives to it. Yet, Kafka—in both his life and his work—seems remarkably unable to negotiate either of these "entries": starvation is preferred, repeatedly, to eating; the priesthood of writing is preferred to intercourse ("coitus as the punishment for the happiness of being together," he wrote). Dostoevsky's Ivan Karamazov famously "refused the ticket"; Kafka's work is keyed to elemental refusals as well, for it says No to the somatic exchanges required for life and procreation and continuity. Sometimes this is strikingly anti-Oedipal: Georg Bendemann and Gregor Samsa—each inscribed in a family he's been supporting—are both stopped in their (maturational) tracks, doomed. You can't get married; you can't grow up; you will be stymied or undone.

But the writing that delivers them is endlessly empowered, imbued with futurity. (This is proven each time the story is read.) This is why "In the Penal Colony" is so astounding: its very first line says it all, "Es ist ein eigentümlicher Apparat," and that special Machine is *language itself: a writing beak that rends flesh.* This is not nice; I do understand that it opens the door to cruelty, violence, torture, and much else that is heinous. But it begins to do justice to the verbal munitions all of us are equipped with. Language is our nonsomatic, unweaponized way to get "through": not through our assignments, but through to the other. Even through to ourselves.

What kind of lesson is this? Would student-writing be somehow less "penal" (to invoke Kafka), if its practitioners went about their work like sculptors or surgeons, attuned to the heft and materiality and cutting edge of the instrument they are using? Would students regard their written assignments as more charged, indeed more fissile—instead of laborious and rule-driven—if their view of language and communication were more *charged*? The revered power of our smartphones and computers is feeble in comparison to the engendering, life-altering force of language. This is not simply the province of art but rather the everyday realm each of us inhabits as verbal creatures; it is the terrain we enter with every argument, every declaration, every promise we make, including the ones we make only to ourselves. Shakespeare had told us that the senior Hamlet's death came from *poison-in-the ear,* which, unpacked, must mean: spoken language, lies. Iago's "poisoning" of Othello shows us how generative these toxins can be, as they work their will. Each of us knows something about the possible virulence of words: those we utter, those we hear.

But the oral side of it is matched by the written side. The words we read also enter and alter us. And "toxicity" is too dark a label for this quotidian form of exchange, interchange, relationship. What about "influence," the etymological *flowing in* of another's language into us? Culture itself—not just executioners—operates along these lines. Growth, discovery, and alteration are also cued to these encounters that a page of print can engender. No one with the slightest life experience would question whether language can be cutting, penetrative, bruising, undoing, awakening, crippling. I certainly do not expect to be cut or bludgeoned by my students' or authors' writing, but I want to be reached. Just as I want my words and our books to reach them. As critic, as

teacher, and as verbal creature, I find Kafka's work frightening and sometimes horrifying, but I also think it salutary and overdue to see these
dimensions of writing as "material" lingual event.

Hamsun's *Hunger* and Kafka's "In the Penal Colony" do not look like
writing primers. They offer no rules to be put into place. One of them
seems intoxicated and unhinged, and the other is both sadistic and lethal. Yet they possess, in my mind, the great distinction of restoring to
writing something of the generative and invasive energy, existential seriousness, and potent reach that few students ascribe to an activity that
will parse their very lives, not merely at university but for days and years
ahead. And it goes without saying (even though I'm now saying it) that
my own life and career have been no less cued to these two exemplary
texts. The élan, muscularity, coiled power, expressive magic, and social
impact of *language* have been my faithful guide, my firepower, whether
it be lecturing, discussing, or composing my books. I have not launched
into wildings as Hamsun's man does, nor have I strapped my students
into harrows, to receive my tidings, but I have drunk at the same well.

(A)rithmetic

I entered college thinking I might well major in math. (My high school
curriculum in this area stopped with twelfth grade solid geometry and
trigonometry.) Therefore, I hungrily signed up for a two-semester calculus course in my first year. A chance to continue my upward climb and
to see how far I might go!

Calculus almost destroyed me. I came to realize that my math profi-
ciency was of the most banal sort: I was great at adding and subtracting,
multiplying and dividing. Algebra and geometry gave me numbers and
forms I could still handle. But that was it. (This meant—it still means—I
am impressively able to figure out my grocery bill just about as fast as
the cashier does, with her machine and barcodes. And I can do it for
others, too, those standing in line in front of me, who don't seem to have
a clue what the total is going to be. I sometimes want to whisper figures
to them. I am also a whiz at balancing checkbooks, gauging interest rates
and monthly notes, and doing all kinds of finite number-chores.)

What I learned in freshman-year calculus was that I was utterly unable to *think* mathematically. What especially sticks in my mind and my craw is my collision with the "delta concept"—a little triangle that signified a new kind of incremental process, beyond the finite arrangements I could manage—and my abject failure to understand it. (I still don't.) It was my first encounter with outright classroom disaster. Math was terrain I had thought solid, but it was crumbling, and I was shaken. It seemed to tell me some unwanted truths, whispering a tune of failure I didn't particularly need or want to hear at that juncture. Memphis to Princeton had made me fragile enough as it was.

And I also recall, rather painfully, my freshman roommate taking the same course and lapping up the delta exercises, moving through them at a prodigious (no doubt accelerating) speed; this stunned me because I felt—with zero proof—this guy to be no smarter than I was, less good at imagination or thinking, but he was sailing through and I was stuck. It was at this point that I grasped there'd be no further math courses for me. I didn't know what I'd major in, but I knew what it wouldn't be.

But I think mathematicians might be surprised to see how often math figures in literature. (I do not believe literature figures in math.) The prime example I want to propose is the remarkable literary commentary surrounding one of math's elementary principles: $2 + 2 = 4$. You'd think there'd be nothing to say about such a self-evident truth, but if you go to Wikipedia and check it out, you'll find several pages of learned references, beginning with Johann Wigand in 1562 and recurring with Descartes, Molière, and Samuel Johnson and gathering steam with nineteen nineteenth- and twentieth-century writers, such as Byron, Victor Hugo, Dostoevsky, Turgenev, Bakunin, right on through to Orwell and Ayn Rand, and contemporary video games. But what I haven't told you is: I misrepresented my key numbers, for the Wikipedia references have to do with "$2 + 2 = 5$." Why does this jarring mathematical error get such a run?

One answer is: $2 + 2 = 4$ so epitomizes obvious, unarguable truth that any tweaking of it must be an effort to bend or alter or deny the truth. Much of the commentary on this equation moves into the area of either the absurd (to believe in God or miracles might be tantamount to

THE THREE R'S 117

believing that $2 + 2 = 5$) or evidence of the power of propaganda (thus critics of Napoleon III, Stalin, Hitler, and others have enlisted the notion of $2 + 2 = 5$ as a "truth-assertion" of the state, something we find today as well, under the rubric of "alternative facts.")

But the most interesting quarrel with this arithmetic axiom comes from Dostoevsky's *Notes from Underground*, where the protagonist vehemently declares war on this logical straitjacket, asserting that human freedom cannot/should not be bound by such laws. *Notes* is among the most overheated, manic novellas ever written, and its feverish antihero will stop at nothing to assert his independence: he will choose to be sick, mad, and even self-injuring—all in the name of liberty. It is as if Emerson's proud transcendentalist creed of "self-reliance" had become twisted into a petulant absolutist campaign against all constraints. One is not far from what Gide was later to call "l'acte gratuit": acts that are unmotivated, beyond logic or any form of utility. Dostoevsky's man sacrifices everything in sight (including possible happiness) to preserve his fierce (and fearful) autonomy.

What is modern about this text of the 1860s is its battle to the death against *Reason*, and therefore against the tyranny of $2 + 2 = 4$. Listen to our man: "I admit that twice two makes four is an excellent thing, but if we are to give everything its due, twice two makes five is sometimes a very charming thing too." There is something undeniably anti-Enlightenment in such a program, and in that direction lie the neurosis and paranoia of the text. But there is also a broad and deep recognition that human truths may be incommensurate with the clarity of numbers and arithmetic. Metrics are real but exist on a plane that may be at odds with heart and soul.

And maybe bodies as well, or at least our grasp of them. When the Grandmother in Proust's long novel begins her descent into terminal illness, the author remarks on the weird anomaly of taking her rising temperature with a thermometer, saying that the magical "silver salamander" of mercury attains a precision of measurement that nothing in this cultured woman's sensitive mind can approximate. I even think back to Shylock's dreadful bond with Antonio, entailing "a pound of flesh," and to Portia's brilliant intervention that hinges entirely on the messiness of bodies: "This bond doth give thee here no jot of blood. The words expressly are a 'pound of flesh.'" Sixteen ounces, neither more nor less, and no amalgams—flesh only—please. *Unruliness* is our lot; "rulers," whether they be yardsticks or sovereigns, don't get our dimensions right. I even feel that (the mathematician) Pascal's tribute to our perception of the divine works the same binary: "Dieu sensible au coeur, non à la raison" (God felt by the heart, not the head). You'd expect God to be beyond the reach of mathematics, but there's more.

The spiritual, the affective, the ethical—all resist numbers. We realize there is little that is existential about $2 + 2 = 4$, and its status as reductive baseline truth is nicely shown in Molière's *Dom Juan* when the rake title-character, bent on a "libertine" career of seduction and destroying, enlists exactly this math equation as the only thing he believes in. Faulkner has little of Molière in his tragic, dark novels, yet his Thomas Sutpen (of *Absalom, Absalom!*) is also a creature of logic and metrics, especially concerning his dealings with others (such as wives or children), and the word used to designate his grievous shortcomings is "innocence," defined in the following way: "that innocence that believed that the ingredients of morality were like the ingredients of pie or cake and once you had measured them and balanced them and mixed them and put them into the oven it was all finished and nothing but pie or cake could come out." Recipes won't cut it when it comes to people, as Sutpen himself learns the hard way when his head is cut off by an aggrieved man with a scythe, who speaks the last words Sutpen will hear: "*I'm going to tech you, Kernel.*'" "Tech" can mean both "teach" and "touch," and they come down to the same thing: knowledge in the flesh, "am eigenen Leib erfahren," has nothing in common with numbers or pies or cakes.

Going by the numbers: it seems nonetheless to be what we do, and we do it in so many domains where it may not work. Yes, a foot is twelve inches long. But when the hospital nurse asks you to rate your pain on a scale of 1 to 10, you sense that, yes, this is possible, maybe even useful (for the nurse), but not especially accurate when it comes to your pain. (Not to mention that men and women, athletes and nonathletes, give different scores to "comparable" pain.) It also seems that whole populations are often asked to rate their happiness on a similar scale, which has produced interesting results, so that countries thought to be melancholy turn out to be joyful, by this account. This is good to know. When, many years ago, one of my children brought home an English essay that had a grade of 79.5, my wife and I felt that something was deeply askew here: with the work, of course, but also with a teacher who could assign such a numerical coefficient to prose and thought. (No semiotic mystery here actually: 79.5 was to indicate "not quite B- level; get it?") Oliver Sacks and others have written about idiots savants who were capable of the most abstruse mathematical equations but could not otherwise reason at all. And one has read a great deal about "quants" being gobbled up by investment firms, hired on the strength of their mathematical prowess, hence likely to add to bottom lines. What actually does a bottom line mean? Is anyone asking about judgment? Does any university or graduate school transcript even whisper anything about judgment? Values? Priorities? Ethics? What do we measure when we measure?

Not too long ago (January 16, 2018) the American public was treated to the White House doctor's report on Donald Trump's health: a goodly number of numbers were shared with the TV watchers, ranging from cholesterol readings to body-mass equivalents, blood-pressure levels, and much else; the pièce de résistance came with the "mental competence" exam (that the president explicitly requested as well, given that doubts had been raised on this score), and we learned that he scored a grand 30 out of 30 on the test. This test required, among other things, the president to subtract 7 from 100 as far down as far as he could. He could, we gather.

Recently, at the dinner table, my wife, knowing that I had garnered a score of 800 on my SAT math test long ago, asked me to calculate the ratio of "cost" to "profit" entailed in the eight books I've written. "You can figure this out," she told me; "no problem." So, I began (in my mind) to tabulate the royalties and advances connected with my books, even the salary raises that arguably ensued—that was the profit—and then I approached (mentally) the cost-side of the equation. That's when trouble arrived. What metric do I use to assess the "price" of writing these books? How long it took? Let's assume that I could establish that numeric datum—x number of years—how would I go about actually gauging the cost itself? How would I measure the zero-sum game (math rules again) that measures the time put into each thing we do, against its inevitable opposite number: what we therefore are not doing? What was I not doing, while I was writing my books? Sadly enough, as I look back and do some existential computing, I think I can answer that: I have to have been, sporadically, even often, an absentee figure for my wife, my children, my friends, my larger world. Hmm. That's an algorithm that gives me pause. And I'm demonstrably at it yet again, as I type these very lines on my laptop, working for my bread. Numbers can be unforgiving if we gauge their unstated sentient ramifications. Perhaps, staying with economics, we call this "the cost of living"? We pay it every day.

And, yet, we are numbers creatures, all of us, whether it be depending on the clock or the calendar for appointments, buying and selling of every stripe, "counting the days," doing investments, planning retirement, purchasing insurance, measuring our calories, setting the alarm, and much else. This is our quotidian pensum. There is little poetry in these accounting exercises that parse our existence, although T. S. Eliot's "I have measured out my life with coffee spoons" gets the point across, with J. Alfred Prufrock's wistful sense of futility and misfit. Yet such figures do constitute a baseline for much of our lives as a metric of how we lived, as well as what we had or lost. Often enough, literature can be eloquent on this front. One remembers King Lear's anguish as his retinue is diminished from one hundred to fifty to twenty-five to even less, as his daughters Regan and Goneril suavely explain to him that he doesn't need servants; his reply is: "Reason not the need." I've always read that line as evidence that our vanity or self-respect, or both, is anchored in material possessions that indicate worth, but I now feel that Shakespeare is also questioning numbers themselves: numbers of daughters, lands, servants, days, and years. The tally matters. "Nothing will come of nothing," Lear admonishes Cordelia, never suspecting that he himself has just signed on for a long multiact trip to Nothing.

In the hands of a writer such as Samuel Beckett, we can see the often grotesque highs and lows of such a scheme, with regard to our dignity, as in the mathematical labors undertaken by his character Molloy when he seeks to establish his all-important fart pattern:

And in Winter, under my greatcoat, I wrapped myself in swathes of newspaper, and did not shed them until the earth awoke, for good, in April. The Times Literary Supplement was admirably adapted to this purpose, of a neverfailing toughness and impermeability. Even farts made no impression on it. I can't help it, gas escapes from my fundament on the least pretext, it's hard not to mention it now and then, however great my distaste. One day I counted them. Three hundred and fifteen farts in nineteen hours, or an average of over sixteen farts an hour. After all it's not excessive. Four farts every fifteen minutes. It's nothing. Not even one fart every four minutes.

This display of arithmetic pizzazz is the performance of a character who is leaking more than gas; in the course of the narrative, he is increasingly reduced in function, beginning lame and going steadily downhill from there, with major motor, perceptual, and verbal deficits. It is as if he were the object of an experiment in *subtraction* (as in: let's remove this function today, that one tomorrow, and then we'll see for the day after). Yet one might consider the fart exercise as a small Cartesian victory of the cogito as defining human characteristic, and I can even imagine Beckett's grade-school math teacher reading this savory prose and taking some grim delight in having at least passed on something to his former student, something that actually proved useful.

Molloy's arithmetic confidence might not win him a professional prize, or get him through a calculus course, but at least it falls under the can-do rubric. I would wager that the world is teeming with (uncounted) numbers-challenged people, folks who start to feel uneasy and inadequate the moment mathematical equations come into view. Literature rarely illuminates these low-to-the-ground, routine debacles; literature customarily treats anxiety and failure with the utmost seriousness, reserving it for discussions about love, God, fate, and other assorted ultimacies. We know that "math anxiety" has been a much used term, sometimes with gender accents, and we know as well that one should not be sloppy about such matters, as Larry Summers learned when he made the mistake of hinting at a biological factor, even while strongly urging for increased numbers of women in science.

Today's high-tech apps, able to register reams of crucial physiological information, promise to gauge with reliable precision your health and future, like it or not, whether or not you can do the numbers. Proust's silver salamander has morphed bigtime. In Don DeLillo's *White Noise*, the protagonist Jack Gladney, having been exposed to a "toxic cloud," gets himself tested, and is told he's "generating big numbers" He asks what they mean and is told that his entire history has been tapped into, yielding "bracketed numbers with pulsing stars." Gladney then reflects: "I wondered what he meant when he said he'd tapped into my history. Where was it located exactly? Some state or federal agency, some insurance company or credit firm or medical clearinghouse? What history was he referring to? I'd told him some basic things. Height, weight, childhood diseases. What else did he know? Did he know about my wives, my involvement with Hitler, my dreams and fears?" We have the machines. No need for Tiresias.

But the quotidian little mess-ups that occur when you can't do numbers constitute a familiar, unglitzy, doubtless widespread distress that warrants discussion. This is why it is interesting when we do come upon a literary version of "l'homme moyen sensuel" who happens to be lousy at numbers. (How many folks such a specimen represents we can only imagine; no statistics here; we never have numbers everywhere we need them.)

Strindberg's brilliant late drama *A Dream Play* offers us a world-class depiction of numbers torture, in a hallucinatory scene you'll not easily forget. The victim of this math deficiency is called simply the Officer, and we watch him, in the course of the play, fail in most of his pursuits, most notably in his love campaign for the beautiful actress Victoria: Strindberg stages this failure in remarkable fashion by presenting the Officer's courtship in successive snippets over time, so that we see him in the same position, same flowers in hand, awaiting Victoria's exit from the theater at three vastly different moments (youth, middle age, and old age). Same setup, same ecstatic hopes, same fizzled outcome. One wonders if Beckett read this play before writing his great "wait drama," *Waiting for Godot*.

But the Officer's love loss is weirdly matched by his numbers fiasco, and it goes like this:

Now the wall of the yellow house is removed and we see three school benches with BOYS *on them, among them the* OFFICER. *In front of them stands the* SCHOOLMASTER *with spectacles, chalk, and cane.*

SCHOOLMASTER [to the OFFICER]. Now, my boy, can you tell me what two times two is? [*The* OFFICER *remains seated, painfully searching his memory without finding the answer*] Stand up when you're asked a question!

OFFICER [*stands up, tormented*]. Two————times two . . . Let me see.————That makes two two!

SCHOOLMASTER. I see! You haven't done your homework!

OFFICER [*ashamed*]. Yes, I have, but . . . I know what it is, but I just can't say it . . .

SCHOOLMASTER. You're trying to get out of it! You know, but you *can't* say it. Perhaps I can help you! [*He pulls the* OFFICER'S *hair.*]

OFFICER. Oh, this is dreadful, really dreadful!

SCHOOLMASTER. Yes, dreadful, that's precisely what it is when a big boy like you has no ambition . . .

OFFICER [*pained*]. A *big* boy, yes, I am big, much bigger than them; I've grown up, I've finished school . . . [*as if waking up*] but I've a doctorate . . . What am I doing sitting here? Haven't I got my doctorate?

SCHOOLMASTER. Yes, of course, but you'll sit here and mature, you see, mature . . . Isn't that it?

OFFICER [*clasping his forehead*]. Yes, that's right, one must mature . . . Two times two . . . is two, and I can prove it by analogy, the highest form of proof. Listen, now! . . . One times one is one, so two times two must be two! For what applies to one must apply to the other!

SCHOOLMASTER. The proof is perfectly in accord with the laws of logic but the answer is wrong.

OFFICER. What is in accord with the laws of logic can't be wrong. Let us put it to the test. One into one goes only once, therefore two into two goes twice.

SCHOOLMASTER. Absolutely correct by analogy. But in that case, how much is one times three?

OFFICER. Three!

SCHOOLMASTER. Consequently, two times three is also three!

OFFICER [*thoughtfully*]. No, that can't be right . . . it can't be . . . otherwise [*sitting down in despair*] . . . no, I'm still not mature!

SCHOOLMASTER. No, you are still far from mature . . .

OFFICER. But, how long will I have to sit here, then?

SCHOOLMASTER. How long? Do you think that time and space exist? . . .

The initial stage directions—*the wall of the yellow house is removed*—put us on notice that we're in the realm of dream or hallucination, and that such places offer zero protection: the walls that protect us in daytime and in sanity are "removed." Trouble. What happens when walls go? Who, one wonders, is removing them?

Then the torture begins. Like someone being stretched on the rack, the Officer is "put to the test" by the Schoolmaster and comes up short over and over again. Repeatedly asked the very bedrock question with which we began this segment—$2+2=4$, now recast as multiplication, $2 \times 2 = 4$—the Officer repeatedly fails the quiz, is unable to reply. This grilling is old-school sadistic: stand up when you're called! Hair gets pulled when you mess up! Here is a form of humiliation that the very old among us may have experienced at some point early in our lives, very likely at school. Nothing genteel in sight. Accused of not doing his homework, of trying to weasel out of the question, the Officer receives the classic punishment for his crime: he's told he has no ambition, that he has failed life's test, that he is still not mature. *You'll sit here and mature.*

And we begin to realize that that is what the scene is about: *one does not mature.* "Do you think time and space exist?" We (and Newton) might have said, yes, they do, but our psyche would appear not to have gotten the message. Time's accomplishments—growing up, being an adult—are exposed as illusory and are being erased in front of our eyes. And space is just as alterable and evanescent: you can be hauled back into grade school at any moment, find yourself on a bench with the other "boys" (even though you have your doctorate), and *found out*: unable to answer the most basic equation there is. True enough, you try your best, trot out your analogies, bravely sputter your answers, but they fizzle. You are *undone*. Beaten by the numbers.

My students are jarred by the cruelty and viciousness of this punishment scenario, but they are incredulous and dumbfounded when I tell them *it will happen to them*. Their faces tell me: on what basis can you possibly predict that this kind of nightmarish humiliation will be meted out to us? How would *you* know? Here's how I know: *it happens routinely to me*. (There is no obvious way for me to prove that my personal experience has any wider validity or prophetic power; still, I believe it does. It's simple math: $1 = 1$, which can be translated as: professor = students grown old.) I am the Officer: I have my doctorate—in fact, I have even more: published books, tenure, at least some reputation—but it doesn't make a lick of difference. My recurrent nightmares teach me exactly the lesson that is being taught to the Officer: you will be brought back to zero; your attainments will go up in smoke; you will fail the test; you will be exposed in your nullity. And it is indeed a lesson, structured pretty much the way a boomerang is structured: the harder you throw it outward, the harder it returns home—that is, the more notches you have on your gun barrel, the more degrees and honors you've racked up, the more you're thought to have learned, the more that gun barrel is turned on you, *the more you will be erased and undone*. Note, please, the economy of this punishment: it is precisely the stuff you've achieved that will be taken away; it is precisely the armor you've thought yourself ensconced in that will volatize; it is precisely the heights you imagine yourself having scaled that will turn into descent and abyss.

I called this a lesson, and now I want to call it a math lesson. It is as rigorous as any sum you've ever learned. It is about *subtraction* as the heinous secret law of addition, humiliation as the ultimate residue of success. What you have achieved is what you lose. Here is the nasty lesson my own dreams bring home to me on a frequent basis. I earlier asked, Who is doing this to you? The obvious answer is myself. Here would be the disappearance act that one can experience over and over, before disappearing altogether. Life has its own ghastly arithmetic: not merely the numbers game that requires that we move from birth to death, and that our aging has its own gathering entropic power, but also the grisly fact that our minds do their own vigorous prep work in this arena, briskly undoing (on a trial basis? a form of calisthenics?) in our dreams what we have laboriously wrought (in our lives and careers). When I teach this play, I usually go light on these ghoulish matters, partly out of *pudeur* (that it would be unseemly for the old professor seriously to unload his nightmares onto the young) and partly out of a respect for their very youth, their own optimism and robust sense of life's challenges being *in front* of them, with little need of being hectored about the damage already done and the booby traps that might eventually await them. It's not a math lesson I feel good about teaching.

If Strindberg strikes the torture note—numbers move, psychically, from positive to negative, as a kind of punitive algebraic equation we are obliged to negotiate over and over, late in our run—I'd like to "add" to this account of "arithmetic" by coming up with at least one *positive* example, one instance where the very logic of arithmetic is transmuted into art. My example is drawn from the "Ithaca" chapter in Joyce's *Ulysses*, and it is offered as an "answer" to the text's seemingly innocuous demand to compare the respective ages of Bloom (the book's older Jewish adman, its Ulysses) and Stephen (the book's young Irish artist, its Telemachus). This should be easy, but hold on to your seat:

> 16 years before in 1888 when Bloom was of Stephen's present age Stephen was 6. 16 years after in 1920 when Stephen would be of Bloom's present age Bloom would be 54. In 1936 when Bloom would be 70 and Stephen 54 their ages initially in the ratio of 16 to 0 would be as 17 1/2 to 13 1/2, the proportion increasing and the disparity diminishing according as arbitrary future years were added, for if the proportion existing in 1883 had continued immutable, conceiving that to be possible, till then 1904 when Stephen was 38, as Bloom then was,

Bloom would be 646 while in 1952 when Stephen would have attained the maximum postdiluvian age of 70 Bloom, being 1190 years alive having been born in the year 714, would have surpassed by 221 years the maximum antediluvian age, that of Methusalah, 969 years, while, if Stephen would continue to live until he would attain that age in the year 3072 A.D., Bloom would have been obliged to have been alive 83,300 years, having been obliged to have been born in the year 81,396 B.C.

One hears of choice cultural documents being stored in outer space for the appreciation of some future galaxy or world once ours has long disappeared, and my vote would be for this sequence from a modern classic that few read (for pleasure). Joyce was, of course, Beckett's great mentor, but whereas Molloy seems caught up in entropy and headed for the void, Stephen and Bloom enter the promised land, the Numbers-Creation where the old rules can be sovereignly suspended and rewritten.

What is so splendid about this hallucinatory send-up is the sheer amount of fun Joyce appears to be having, as he "takes the gloves off" his numbers and sets them deliriously free, to cavort and prance on their own, obeying the giddy laws of multiplication while spiting those of flesh and mortality, all the while assigning the names of Stephen and Bloom to this sortie. When you consider the venerable gravitas surrounding dates of birth and death—on display in every cemetery and record book from time immemorial, established as the bedrock way of keeping our books about our species, as bottom-line truth that speaks the numbers and dictates of fate itself and that nothing can alter—then you can better savor the delicious freedoms and breakthroughs on show here. In some sense, this passage points its beam of light toward the ultimate zone that interests Joyce—Sterne had called it a "Northwest passage to the intellectual world" in his zany *Tristram Shandy*—a place of writerly independence, a place where the word—*no! the number!*—becomes the deed.

As a way of closing my treatise on arithmetic, I'd like to yoke Joyce's preening passage with its grand disregard of flesh and mortality to my own flesh and mortality. I cannot compete with Methuselah on the far side of Joyce's numbers game, but I can espy, in the very logic of this gonzo passage with its dizzily increasing numbers doing their dance, a version of something I encountered long ago, to my great and lasting humiliation: *delta*. Yes, this passage flaunts its own kind of "Delta Force," and it makes an unstated bold bid for arithmetic as worthy celebrant at literature's feast and rites. *Delta* meant nothing except pain to me at eighteen in my Princeton calculus class; I now know better.

Stephen and Bloom *age* according to the circus-like magic power that James Joyce has impishly, maniacally, derived from the sober storage room of numbers, thereby fueling and enabling his characters to carry out their magnificent romp through time, distributing new and altering dates of birth and death as the two figures make their merry way. None of the rest of us is likely to have multiple tombstones, nor will anyone find on those stones any delta icon appended to the staid numerals indicating birth and death, beginning and end. But I write these words at a time when there is feverish activity, especially in Silicon Valley, where serious money interests fuel it, to offset or even vanquish aging. Joyce's fantasia beckons to a kind of freedom and independence that are denied to flesh, whatever promises the Constitution may imply to the contrary, but those very freedoms testify to the ontology of art as well as numbers: a shimmering world beyond entropy.

I am not foolish enough to believe that my quarrel with numbers—with or without delta—will persuade most people interested in education. (I don't think my views on reading and writing will launch a revolution either.) A recent issue of *Harvard Magazine* outlined three major experimental templates for rethinking liberal arts in higher education: the Yale-Singapore NUS College curriculum, Nicolas Lemann's schema published in the *Chronicle of Higher Education*, and the Silicon Valley Minerva Project. Each of these models makes considerable space for "numbers": Quantitative Reasoning (Yale), "numeracy" (Lemann), and Formal Analyses + Empirical Analyses (Minerva); each is the child of a world dominated by big data; yet each is still seeking a way to keep humanistic thinking alive. Each is reasonable. None of those education architects is likely to be much taken by this book of mine. The diatribe against (a)Rithmetic that courses through my pages is to be under-stood as both a "last stand" and also tongue-in-cheek. Yet I hope this quixotic battle with metrics, this tilting at windmills, will make at least some intuitive sense, because the logic of the heart is not the same as that of the mind, and even the logic of the mind often sidles with Dostoevsky's sense that $2 + 2 = 5$ would indeed be "charming." And true. And then some.

As for delta, be patient: it's still on the move.

CHAPTER 4

Literature and the Cost of Knowing

Some of you may have come away from the three *R*'s with a sigh of relief that no university has yet entrusted its curriculum to me. And I confess that I have sometimes done worse still, even claiming that the patron saint of teaching should be Dracula, the fellow known to us as major bloodsucker; I have invoked this sanguinary figure to conjure up something of the vital, unruly exchanges that can take place when that venerable triad of teacher, text, and student goes into action, producing its multidirectional flows.

Of course, I also know that sweet reason has its place at the feast of learning, and I even know that logic and clarity have their own precious, essential, cooler light, crucial to the challenges of all problem-solving, whether those challenges accost us in a classroom, courtroom, or bedroom.

Precisely for all these reasons, we must do our best to *honor* knowledge by refusing the facile, the glib, the counterfeit, by ensuring that it is worthy rather than tinsel, that it is earned rather than memorized or downloaded, that it takes account of the dark in its pursuit of the light, and that it makes room for human sentience as it moves toward its truths. The richest and most beautiful books that I teach are astonishingly cued to wreckage, reversal, and comeuppance, not because they are sadistic and enjoy inflicting damage but because their final sights are on spiritual growth, which is never easy, automatic, or guaranteed. In the following pages, I will interrogate these unyielding, fertile texts. My authors are Sophocles, Shakespeare, Emily Brontë, Melville, Twain, Dickinson, Kafka, Faulkner, and Morrison. Each explodes pieties; each is at war with complacencies and readymades. Each is aware that our final truths may have blood on them.

Why are they like this? Because they are enemies of fraud, of fake news, of comfort zones, of cheap optimism, of rosy pieties. Because they hallow the Socratic dictum that wisdom can only follow the realization of ignorance, and the Pauline view that self-knowing must go through the murky mirror. And, in ways that none of them ever argued—but that I am using as the cornerstone for much of this book—they intuit that literature is precious to us for just these hard reasons, that the very purposes of art are wedded to the pursuit of difficult truths and the cashiering of frivolous ones. Finally, in ways I think my authors might actually contest or disavow, art's ultimate validity stems from its status as mere representation, its constitutive, enabling make-believe, its never even whispered acknowledgment that the reader's encounter with the abyss is vicarious, survivable, exitable, and usable.

We must therefore relocate "literature's home," by revamping our sights entirely—yanking books off pedestals, pulling them out of libraries and courses, even extricating them from their venerable academic frameworks and traditions and periods and genres—so as to encounter it, text by text, as you would a meal, treating it as basic nourishment for heart and mind. It will be seen that each of these books writes large—even if diversely—the painful route to knowing. Painful because there exist no shortcuts. These beautiful, sometimes awful, texts are big with tidings about *us*. My first guide is Søren Kierkegaard.

Kierkegaard and the Trip to Mount Moriah

The trip to Mount Moriah, as we know, is the trip made by Abraham and Isaac to the place where Isaac was to be sacrificed, pursuant to God's command to Abraham. As I indicated, Kierkegaard cites the old proverb "Only one who works gets bread" but then points out how false and untrue this proverb is in real life, where frequently those who work receive no bread, whereas many receive bread but work not, because in the "outward world" our labor may or may not lead to reward. Yet his grand conclusion, "it is otherwise in the world of spirit," is followed in remarkable fashion: "Only one who works gets bread, and only one who knows anguish finds rest, only one who descends to the underground saves the loved one, only one who draws the knife gets Isaac" (57).

It is an astonishing passage, for the references to Eurydice and Isaac indicate how far you must go to get your reward, transgressing limits of both life and ethics. Above all, Kierkegaard is sketching a way of knowing, and he annihilates any notion of shortcuts or freebies in the world of spirit. The effort–reward ratio is never contractual, never guaranteed. How do we, then, get bread? Orpheus and Abraham certainly worked for theirs. *How far you must go.* Kierkegaard's text is regarded largely as a theological meditation, geared toward an effort to grasp the nature of Abraham's faith, the incomprehensible faith of a man prepared to sacrifice not only his beloved, long-awaited son but also the future of the Jewish people. Most pertinent of all, the narrator, John of Silence, focuses on the voyage itself, repeatedly telling us that the only way to do justice to Abraham's "trial" is to take the proper measure of the trip to Mount Moriah. There was no "winged horse," no instantaneous arrival at the mountain or discovery of the ram. "One forgets that Abraham rode on an ass, which can keep up no more than a leisurely pace, that he had a three-day journey, that he needed time to chop the firewood, bind Isaac, and sharpen the knife" (80).

Chopping wood, binding the child, sharpening the knife: nothing theological in sight here. Just narrative. And *time.* "He needed time . . ." Have you ever pondered how long it actually took to get to Mount Moriah? What thoughts must have been in the mind of a man who had a little over three full days to think about the impending murder he'd pledged to carry out? John of Silence is intent on making us *understand* Abraham's *trial,* and here is his strategy:

> If I myself were to talk about him I would first depict the pain of the
> trial. For that I would suck all the fear, distress and torment out of the
> father's suffering, like a leech, in order to be able to describe all that

Abraham suffered while still believing. I would remind people that the journey lasted three days and well into the fourth; yes, those three-and-a-half days should be infinitely longer than the two thousand years separating me from Abraham.

Mathematically this is nonsense. Three-and-a-half days is roughly 1/210,000 of two thousand years; yet John tells us it should be *infinitely* longer. And the answer can only be: we are meant to *feel* the full measure of those awful three-and-a-half days, whereas the two thousand years that separate us from the story have no sentient weight at all; on the contrary, their ever-growing distance just adds to the gravity-free datum we've all grown up with: "Abraham's sacrifice of Isaac." After all, as Kierkegaard never stops telling us, *we know how it ended*. A ram replaced Isaac.

We know that. But for the three-and-a-half days (roughly eighty-four hours, or one thousand eight minutes, or sixty thousand four hundred eighty seconds) it took Abraham to get to Mount Moriah, he did not know that. Kierkegaard is trying not only to make us grasp the existential turmoil experienced by Abraham "en route" to Mount Moriah but also to force us to realize that the meaning of Abraham's *trial* inheres in the three-and-a-half days on the "front side" of the event. And *not* on the back side, the "outcome side," of the event. An interesting binary, this: Abraham knows only the anguish, indeed only the *fear and trembling*, caused by God's command, whereas we know only its "happy ending." And the brutal logic at hand here is: the "ending" teaches us nothing about Abraham; it is his fear and trembling that offers the only valid measure of his trial. Why call this "brutal"? Because either you understand the affective density of this event or you don't understand it at all; you merely "know" the story as "information."

At a later juncture in *Fear and Trembling*, Kierkegaard leaves Abraham in order to speak of Jesus. He knows this to be one of the world's most beloved stories. Yet might it not also be the most *unknown* story? Again, he asks if we have understood, if we have taken its awful measure:

One is stirred, one harks back to those beautiful times, sweet tender longings lead one to the goal of one's desire, to see Christ walking about in the promised land. One forgets the fear, the distress, the paradox. Was it so easy a matter not to be mistaken? Was it not a fearful thought that this man who walked among the others was God? Was it not terrifying to sit down to eat with him? Was it so easy a matter to become an apostle? But the outcome, eighteen centuries, that helps; it helps that shabby deception wherein one deceives oneself and others.

At this point we begin to realize that Kierkegaard is indicting an entire episteme of "received ideas"—including what we have taken to be history itself—as lazy, post facto, benighted, and deprived of understanding. Education itself is on the docket, and that is why Kierkegaard lashes out so vehemently against teachers themselves: "They live in their thoughts, secure in life, they have a *permanent* position and *sure* prospects in a well-organized state; they are separated by centuries, even millennia, from the convulsions of existence; they have no fear that such things could happen again; what would the police and the newspapers say?" There is a sauciness and punch in this diatribe that lays bare the fraudulence of so-called *instruction*: I see, in Kierkegaard's very terms from 1843, today's entire university professoriate (especially the tenured among us) exposed here in an "Emperor's New Clothes" critique that excoriates us for a philistinism we scarcely realize: our obscene reductionism, our accounting of life's turmoil as docile information, our after-the-fact transformation of fear and trembling into data or outcome.

But we might reply, Of course, we are inevitably after-the-fact; what can be done about that? The question is, Might that hardwired, inescapable temporal handicap be acknowledged, even overcome? Could grasping the experiential dimensions of recorded event (history or even fiction) be the only strategy for recovering the living pulsions that brought these events to pass? Might this be the labor required of literature?

I call this a theory of narrative, even though it flies in the face of modern theory (of almost every kind), because it relies on an embarrassingly simple (yet arduous) injunction: bring the heart to your reading. Make your text, as Pascal was to put it, "sensible au coeur" (felt by the heart). Or, as I often urge my students, *try on the text*. I call this procedure countertheoretical inasmuch as it insists on our vicarious and imaginative investment in the information we process—that is, it does battle with the *distance* that seems to me to be the (enshrined) cardinal requirement of academic thinking. Required so as to see as clearly as possible what there might be to critique in whatever it is that we read. That is, as I see it, the claim we most often hear, indeed the prowess that humanistic studies seek to inculcate. We are taught to be critical thinkers. *This*, the academy intones, is (in hard times) the justification for the humanities. And it may have some essential things absolutely backward.

I am no enemy of criticism. But I am saddened by the losses entailed by today's reading practices and interpretive procedures. What is lost? The imaginative sense not only of what produced the "information" in the first place but also of its ramifications and reverberations in the field(s) of human experience. I would argue that a key purpose of the humanities at large is to help us recover precisely those dimensions of "data," to turn dead numbers and dead letters into a living script. Kierkegaard's text is—I am the first to admit—diabolically complex, subtle, learned, and difficult to access. I know this from reading it many times; I know this from teaching it many times. In both instances it always outruns me. Yet its core meaning is shockingly elemental: if you are to understand the nature and scope of Abraham's trial, you must "imaginatively" make the trip to Mount Moriah.

What Our Great Books Tell Us about Knowing

"Great books" is a term that has fallen into disrepute. It has been rightly accused of Western hegemony, and its list of literary stars tends to include an awful lot of dead white male figures. Today's literature courses, in both high school and university, have become more inclusive, more attentive to diversity and cultural scope, race and gender. My own field, comparative literature, was entirely Eurocentric at the beginning of my career, whereas our contemporary curriculum has a healthy, much needed reach and breadth to it, extending into cultures all over the globe. Progress does happen.

Most of the books I discuss in this chapter, however, are familiar canonical texts—widely read and widely taught books many of us grew up with, were obligated to read, likely wondered (now and then) why, and very possibly forgot soon thereafter. I bring them front and center here because I feel that they are larded with unsuspected surprises and that a fresh new encounter with them might be a way of rediscovering old acquaintances and, hopefully, being shocked by how much pith, how many toxins, and how much trauma they contain. Each of the works I write about is big with horror, is indeed about the fault lines of the societies they emanate from, and each issues forth a very harsh light about crises both private and public. They jolt us. They jolt us into awareness of art's depths and thereby our own. But nothing here is easy. They are also wise about the price paid for knowing. We need them.

They are also the reason a career in teaching literature is a lucky career. I knew my own hunger when I went to university and became a professor, but I could not then know how inexhaustible my materials would be, how a lifetime of mining them would not be too much, how steadfast their company is, how they would bear on issues great and small, how capable they still are of knocking me off my feet. They do not belong on some ideal library shelf—which is how many visualize them, I fear—collecting dust, unread, prized at a distance, claimed (but not felt) as important, waiting to be known.

And they take the place they take in this final book because I see them not as my subject matter but as the motor forces of my career and my life. I see them as the source of my ideas about teaching and my belief in the humanities. They are vital to who I am, not as literature professor but as person, and I hope to convey that vitality. You need no erudition or prior knowledge or even much curiosity to read these forays. Further, these books were never meant to be the exclusive province of schools and universities, but of the broader world of readers everywhere. The airing I'm giving them is meant to be as democratic as air itself, for they are our living unpollutable human environment, out there until read, in here thereafter, alive. Breathing and reading. Your bookshelf is as intimate as your medicine shelf, for each contains powerful agents, waiting to be absorbed and come to life. But no doctors are required for these goods.

Oedipus the King

Sophocles's play stands as the West's most famous example of *not knowing* the things most of us take for granted: the identity of (a) the spouse in your bed and (b) the bullying old man you had to do in, at the crossroads, years ago. Further, Sophocles's own audience knew the story inside-out already, so there could be no surprises (for them). Why take another shot at it? Why did Sophocles? Why do I? After all, I've already focused on the *belatedness* theme, arguing that it posits a view of "knowing" that is inevitably stymied, after-the-fact. I've also posited a "bookkeeping" outcome for the play, inasmuch as the King finally sees the full picture, his fourth-dimensional portrait.

I want now to go to the heart of the matter: that the most powerful effects of the work, well beyond its "preknown" taboos of parricide and incest, are geared to making us grasp what the story's transgressions actually *feel like, as they are committed.* Nothing prurient here in the least, but rather a writer's ultimate sense of weights and measures. It's one thing to highlight major error; it's quite another to convey the sentient reach of these infamous misdeeds, a reach endowed with shocking staying power, shocking returning power, as will be seen. Further—and rarely acknowledged—Sophocles is out to show us that the familiar Greek world of prophecies and oracles causes far more day-by-day, unceasing human injury than we customarily recognize. We need to do justice to these affective dimensions of a story we've long thought we understood. Why, you might ask? Because the very life and law of literature say so. They mandate that our understanding go beyond "information" to become something more intimate, brutal, and coercive, something commensurate with Aristotle's own contention that "pity" and "terror" are the aimed-for responses to tragedy.

First, let's rehearse the givens. The city is dying of plague. No one knows why. The oracle explains that this mass dying stems from a concealed crime. The present horrors are to be understood as the *outcome* of past transgressions. How to fix this? By getting your facts right, by recovering the missing data, by reconstructing the causal chain that led to this morass. Smoking gun, origin of the crime, source of the disease, criminology, etiology: all are present. It has a medical feel to it, as well as a legal or courtroom or *policier* feel to it. *Information* is desperately needed. The King is the man to carry this out. He will conduct the investigation in order to get to the bottom of things. He will find out the missing truth. Light will come and then the dying can stop. It initially seems that Sophocles's play plays by the rules of an informational paradigm: get the facts straight, work out the sequencing, establish cause and effect, and all will be illuminated at last.

Fixed too? One wonders whether the plague exited Thebes after the blinded Oedipus does. The author doesn't say.

Oedipus is king but is in the dark about the basics. He will be exposed as unknowing, even though he solved the riddle of the Sphinx. As the scholars have pointed out, the text comes at a moment when the great achievements of Greek humanism in areas such as medicine, agriculture, mathematics, and navigation come to seem as perhaps illusory, given the reversals staged within the story: he is seen as Thebes's doctor, but he is the cause of the plague; he steers the ship of state, but he has taken it into the shoals. His courage will be seen not only as homicidal but as parricidal, even regicidal. On the marriage front, the man's seeding will be seen as a transgressive double-sowing, so that every *single* figure turns out to be *double*. He will challenge the Oracle's claim—we know that the institution of the Oracle was subject to increasing doubt at the time of the play—by asserting his own human authority, right through to the very end, indicting both Tiresias and Creon as conspirators out to get him. Yet, Oedipus's very rashness, his chutzpah (as shown in his aggressive treatment of all who question him: Tiresias, Creon, the Messenger), testify to an intellectual bravura that is more than arrogance or hubris: it signals a kind of daring and confidence that (also) speak for Periclean Athens's highest aspirations.

What does he know? And when does he know it? These (vulgar, oft-heard) questions, as I've already indicated, loom large for spectators and readers. They are asked in criminal investigations, and they matter still more, here, in terms of individual identity; by play's end, the facts have all been aired. But there is also enormous *pathos* here. We learn that when young Oedipus, living in Corinth and thinking Polybus and Merope his biological parents, got wind of the prophecy that he would murder his father, he was filled with dread, and he forthwith exited the family home, never (he thought) to see them again. He could not know that running *from* the curse would turn out to be its very opposite, since his flight led him, as it were, from the frying pan into the fire: "I abandoned Corinth, / from that day on I gauged its landfall only / by the stars, running, always running / toward some place where I would never see / the shame of all those oracles come true. / And as I fled I reached that very spot / where the great king, you say, met his death."

We hear the whirring of the "machine infernale" as it closes in on the protagonist. Motivation matters for naught. Fate rules. Mousetrap. Stacked deck. To be sure, young Oedipus is well-meaning and outright innocent. But this innocence will be blown sky high by the cascade of revelations that are to come, making it ever clearer to all parties— Oedipus, Jocasta, the other players and the Chorus, spectators, and readers over the centuries—that he is indeed the guilty one, the killer, the fornicator, the double-sower, the plague, the miasma that besets the kingdom. He simply didn't know.

The greatest minds in history have tried to make sense of these matters. Schiller focused on "analytical tragedy," noting that the greatest horror of all is not what we "know" happened but what "might" have happened. Such a view recognizes the engendering nature of imagination. Nietzsche saw in the play the seeds of scientific inquiry itself: "ein Verbrechen an der Natur," a "breaking-into" nature and its cycles. Freud read into this murder a universal desire on the part of the male child to sleep with its mother and to murder its father. To the question of whether Oedipus could have wanted to do this, Freud replied that he didn't need to "know," that it made no difference: his very acts tell us that he was programmed for such behavior. Lévi-Strauss was taken with the difficulty of walking and behaving "straight." René Girard has brilliantly analyzed the play's archetypal conflicts as keyed to the necessity of scapegoating, centered in a battle (between the three old guys) to see who will be "produced" as "cause" of Theban plague and mass death (given the need of sacrificial logic to come up with some figure on whom disaster can be blamed.) Jacques Lacan commented on the centrality of riddles and double meaning, leading to a view of alterity, of Oedipus as other unto himself.

One wonders not only what Sophocles might have thought of these theories but what Oedipus himself might have made of them.

One of the most telling features of Sophocles's rendition of the story is that he starts at the end. All the players are living with the outcome. Hence, we see none of the originary horrors unfurl, nor do we know what "went into them": the encounter with the Sphinx is over, parricide and incest have already been committed, all that remains is to discover and make knowledge of them. Hence, the only maneuvering room granted Oedipus is ratiocinative: he cannot reverse or undo the past, but he can do all within his power to come to an awareness of it and then make what amends are possible. At play's end, the pattern is revealed: Oedipus has solved the puzzles, the damning pieces are in place, and he responds by blinding himself, to exit the kingdom as exile. Solving the mystery, then acting on it: this would be the only action possible. The gods, he rightly claims, were responsible for his horrid misdoings, but he alone—Oedipus—has brought it to light and then turned out the light. His horrors are such, including his two daughters, who embody his crimes, that they cannot be looked at.

But the deepest penetrating thrust of the play—deeper than the gouging out of his eyes—must inhere in the transgressions themselves. Beyond medical or legal or political logic, beyond even justice as such, incest and parricide are Sophocles's quarry. They must be looked at. They must be made into knowledge, rather than simply error. Oedipus's knowledge and our knowledge. Information may suffice for the detective story, but more is needed for art. And starting at the end did not help matters in the least, given that the great transgressive acts cannot be seen as they "happened," much less "on the front side" (as Kierkegaard would have required).

But Sophocles was well aware of the need to bring each of these key cruxes *into* his story, and he did so by presenting them as vivid flashback, as two moments when the dialogue stops, so that this toxic but crucial material can be retrieved, vented, and made into knowledge: *ours*. The first such "eruption" comes when Oedipus for the first and only time talks to his wife about when a proud old man with a staff came bearing down on him at a crossroads. Watch how the narrative becomes cinematic:

> Making my way toward this triple crossroad
> I began to see a herald, then a brace of colts
> drawing a wagon, and mounted on the bench . . . a man,
> just as you've described him, coming face-to-face,
> and the one in the lead and the old man himself
> were about to thrust me off the road—brute force—
> and the one shouldering me aside, the driver,
> I strike him in anger!—and the old man, watching me
> coming up along his wheels—he brings down
> his prod, two prongs straight at my head!
> I paid him back with interest!
> Short work, by god—with one blow of the staff
> in this right hand I knock him out of his high seat,
> roll him out of the wagon, sprawling headlong—
> I killed them all—every mother's son!

Here, at last, is an accounting, done almost as filmic zoom shot, of one of the most famous murders in history. It is Laius's sole entry in the text, but it does him proud: arrogant, impatient, violent, undone. We sense here the creatural energies inherent to parricide: *Keep your place on the road! Do in the old man before he does it to you!* And we get our urgently needed "face-to-face" picture of the lethal encounter: the old man imperious, bullying, and striking; and the young man rising to the challenge, furious, unstopped, and unstoppable. Oedipus bridles with rage, recalls every physical particular in their mano-a-mano, since just the telling of this event is roiling with affect, almost breathless in its delivery and outpouring. Freud never comments on this passage as such—he seems content to rely on the *outcome*—but Sophocles has felt it necessary for us to *feel* what went into this murder, no matter how long ago it was. It cannot simply be "information" such as a court record might present. Oedipus's consistent anger and rage at *all* of the "old men" of the play—his threats to not only Tiresias and Creon but also the Messenger and the Shepherd—bristle with parricidal energies, help us to see an entire pattern of pulsions against "fathers" leading to murder. Yes, the time frame for the play would seem belated and foreclosed, but the playwright knows that the fateful actions must become present-tense, still-to-happen yet inevitable, indeed still happening, dripping with violence and power.

Critical focus on right-or-wrong "information" skews the fuller ramifications of Oedipus's life choices. One-liners of all varieties, including "Oedipus complex" and the like, may well be part of educated people's mental furniture, but the project of art is to give these facts and notions their proper density. I've already noted that Oedipus fled Corinth to escape the curse, but Sophocles forces us to realize that this decision never stops hurting. At play's end, the Messenger patronizingly explains to the King that he has some good news for him, that the death of old Polybus makes him safe from the curse, at last. But Oedipus speaks again of the pain his fateful moves caused: "Apollo told me once—it is my fate— / I must make love with my own mother, / shed my father's blood with my own hands. / So for years I've given Corinth a wide birth, / and it's been my good fortune too. But still, / to see one's parents and look into their eyes / is the greatest joy I know." The Messenger, delighted to be of service, moves in: "You're afraid of that? That kept you out of Corinth?" Oedipus's reply speaks volumes: "My *father*, old man — / so I wouldn't kill my father." It is a striking moment, revealing an injured King, a man haunted and wounded by prophecy, and living more or less in exile to avoid it. And it still hurts. Robert Fagles italicized "father" to convey the emotional weight of Oedipus's decisions: the heart knows nothing of irony or facts, and the King has lived every day with the threat of murdering his father, only by paying the full price: to never see his father again. This is real, and its sentience is on the far side of getting prophecies right or wrong. It's time we realized that this, too, is a mousetrap: fleeing the prophecy required its own butchery.

Likewise, the myth demands that the child be expelled from its true mother and father, because of the curse. But the myth is not interested in the human cost of such a loss—all it cares about is false information (wrong parents, wrong old man, wrong queen) and the ripening horror of the murder and incest—yet Sophocles has not forgotten that Jocasta is a mother who gave away her child; and it is close to unbearable, leading to the mix of pain and cynicism we see in her words to her husband, regarding this chapter of her life: "Apollo was explicit: / my son was doomed to kill my husband . . . my son, / poor defenseless thing, he never had a chance / to kill his father. They destroyed him first." Once again, we are confronting a type of miasma that has no truck with fate or prophecy, only with human pain and loss. The myth cares nothing for Jocasta's bitterness; it needs only to get its ducks in the right rows. But Sophocles presents her as more than a cog in a machine; he wants to hint at what is so monstrous in this plot: the dismembering of the family, a dismembering that happens twice, since its first iteration seeks to avoid the curse and its second iteration is when the curse gets enacted. Yes, the lost little boy was lost, but then horribly found, found in the worst possible way, as Jocasta's husband. And there's nary a word from her after she figures that one out: her only response is suicide.

At the risk of being trite and simplistic, I want to say that Schiller, Nietzsche, Freud, Lévi-Strauss, Girard, and Lacan have no interest in the *pain* of the story. Each of them is so bent on opening up the possible significances of the myth that they turn a blind eye and a deaf ear to the hurting creatures caught inside the mesh and the gears. What stuns me most is the economy of Sophocles's rendition; as said, by starting at the end, he would appear to have missed any chance at gauging the play's affective price tag, since all the deeds have already occurred. It's not the case.

If the murder and the loss-of-child have more resonance than we often realize, what is to be said for its most spectacular transgression: incest? Not merely the conventions of Greek tragedy but decorum in a larger sense altogether rules out taking the reader/spectator into the royal couple's bedroom where the incest (regularly) occurred. Here, too, we have to wonder at the cost of starting at the end: a middle-aged husband and (older) wife can scarcely be counted on for much in the way of erotic energy, since their union is of long date. But the wily playwright knows there is a living past—a sexual as well as a murderous past—*and it must speak*. And so it will; again, he makes us wait until the very end of the play, and sure enough a flashback comes to us via the tale of the Messenger who has followed Oedipus and Jocasta into the royal palace. There he has received an eyeful, which he then proceeds, breathlessly, to pass on to us; the sequence must be quoted in full:

> Once she'd broken in through the gates, / dashing past us, frantic, whipped to fury, / ripping her hair out with both hands— / straight to her rooms she rushed, flinging herself across the bridal-bed, doors slamming behind her— / once inside, she wailed for Laius, dead so long, / remembering how she bore his child long ago, / the life that rose up to destroy him, leaving / its mother to mother living creatures / with the very son she'd borne. / Oh how she wept, mourning the marriage-bed / where she let loose that double brood—monsters— / husband by her husband, children by her child.
>
> And then — /
>
> But how she died is more than I can say. Suddenly / Oedipus burst in, screaming, he stunned us so / we couldn't watch her agony to the end, / our eyes were fixed on him. Circling / like a maddened beast, stalking, here, there, / crying out to us— / Give him a sword! His wife, / no wife, his mother, where can he find the mother earth / that cropped two crops at once, himself and all his children? / He was raging—one of the dark powers pointing the way, / none of us mortals crowding around him, no, / with a great shattering cry—someone, something leading him on— / he hurled at the twin doors and bending the bolts back / out of their sockets, crashed through the chamber. / And there we saw the woman hanging by the neck, / cradled high in a woven noose, spinning, / swinging back and forth. And when he saw her, / giving a low, wrenching sob that broke our hearts, / slipping the halter from her throat, he eased her down, / in a slow

embrace he laid her down, poor thing . . . / then, what came next,
what horror we beheld!

He rips off her brooches, the long gold pins / holding her robes—
and lifting them high, / looking straight up into the points, / he digs
them down the sockets of his eyes, crying, "You, / you'll see no more
the pain I've suffered, all the pain I caused! / Too long you looked on
the ones you never should have seen, / blind to the ones you longed
to see, to know! Blind / from this hour on! Blind in the darkness—
blind!" / His voice like a dirge, rising, over and over / raising the pins,
raking them down his eyes. / And at each stroke blood spurts from
the roots, / splashing his beard, a swirl of it, nerves and clots— /
black hail of blood pulsing, gushing down.

This sublime speech displays a Sophoclean genius that is every bit as
much narrative as it is dramatic. Whereas the spectator/reader expects
a mere summarizing of the suicide and blinding, the Messenger in fact
opens up the precincts of the play, not just temporally but affectively,
and with a startling economy. Time no longer binds, and we cannot fail
to see that this account of what just transpired is no less the story of
what happened long ago. Repeatedly we are told of breaking and entering, of gates and doors being smashed open, and we sense that this is
the very iconography of incest: of a taboo opening, a taboo thrusting.
Yes, it describes Jocasta's death, but it also conjures up Laius, the haunter
of the play, the desecrated husband/father, the first lover, making us
understand that the same marriage bed has been the scene of transgressive sexual couplings, of a birthing that was to prove infamous; that
birthing is nowhere more perfectly instanced than in Fagles's exquisite
adjective "cradling" to describe, in close-up, mesmerizing description,
the hanged body of Jocasta.

But the Jocasta of this account seems scandalously alive, as well as
dead. We see Oedipus lift her down from the noose, lay her on the marriage bed, disrobe her, and the scene comes to poignant yet gruesome
life, refiguring/recasting their conjugal sexual intimacy as well as denoting her death. Finally, the phallic imagery of thrusting reaches its climax

as Oedipus gouges out his eyes with Jocasta's jewels, creating, via Sophocles's images, a cosmic, seminal hailstorm of gore, as if to show us that "penetration" always goes further than you know, that it lethally opens up harbors and gates and doors and vaginas and, finally, eyes. The Messenger's tale is a tour de force, and it cashiers any hackneyed notion that "showing" always trumps "telling." Art's telling is special.

For years I have read these two passages about the parricide and the incest as evidence of Sophocles's desire to convey the actual emotions of this story to his spectators, as if he realized that enactment on the stage (even if the standards of decorum permitted it) would nonetheless be *feebler* than a narrative account might be, where the language itself could resonate, take us back in time. He must also have felt that his starting-from-the-end rationale absolutely required this figurative trip back to the past, so that his viewer could experience the horrible fullness of time. And, of course, that is what the entire play records: a trip back to the past. But this time, thanks to the Messenger, we go too. *We* are meant to take measures.

For I now believe that Sophocles was most concerned to find a way to bring all of the story's toxic and transgressive passion to light and to life. *Parricide* and *incest* are horrible words, on the misdeeds docket, but they are only words, concepts. The project of the playwright was to inject these words with the indwelling heat, virulence, potency, and horror they "contained," to make us see their weight and energy and *life*, their doom-constituting truth. Hence, the play mandates that *we* make the terrible trip back to the crossroads and to the bedroom, to register the immediacy, the density, the shimmering power of those crucial taboo moments when the working of fate actually happens, moments *before* they became secrets, *before* the outcome.

The detective formula plays us false. Sophocles understood that parricide and incest can never be reduced to information as such and that the best way to get this across was the drastic act of self-blinding. Had Oedipus "merely" killed himself, it would have none of the horror that his blinding possesses. He is not simply a man who can no longer bear to look at his children/siblings or his world; he is a man undone by a knowledge so luminous, so utterly radiant, that he, like one who gazed directly at the sun, collides with the solar principle and puts out his own light. We are to understand the mesmerizing repeated thrusts of the jewels into his eyes as the final *act* he commits, the act that brings to completion the parricide and the incest. And we see these horrible gestures as inseparable, as a suite of moves whereby the transgressions of the past find their final penetrative conclusion. Time past and time present fuse together: the Messenger's story brings to us, in nuce, as one fluid moment, frozen in time, ballet-like, the living incest, brought to light and life and finally *completed* via the blinding. He has understood the price, and he pays it. Information has become knowledge: his, ours.

Sophocles's two astonishing speeches perform the cinematic role of flashback, and they do rare honor to the power of storytelling: Oedipus's words to Jocasta and the Messenger's words to us are "winged": they move *all* of us back in time—obliterating any sense that the "past" is past—by retrieving the originary violence of parricide and incest, so that we feel their force. We have long been told that oracles announce the future, and even in Sophocles's time, this contention was open to doubt; yet, at these two key moments, the play does hallow the despotic, unhinging, doom-ridden power of *words*: no longer those coming from any temple but those pronounced by people on a stage, written by a playwright, hurling all of us backward into a living past. I began by saying the Oedipus is the most famous example of not-knowing in history, but I want to end by claiming that the hallucinatory passages I've discussed transcend time and space, initiating us into the darkest knowledge. That would be art's light.

King Lear

To claim that *Lear* is centrally about the "cost of knowing" risks being fatuous, given how self-evident it is. The arrogant old man who begins by divvying up his kingdom and disinheriting the one child who loves him ends horribly chastened and even more horribly "knowing" about issues such as power and filial devotion. His "education" ranks among the most severe trials in Western literature. Unlike Sophocles's use of retrospect and retrieval, Shakespeare's procedure is dreadfully linear and progressive, tracking both Lear and Gloucester step by step as they stagger from pride and gross error toward horizons of truth they had never earlier dreamed of. There is a rigorous epistemological discourse here: two rash old men drastically misread the signs—each takes the false child or children for the true one—and each is slated to drain the cup of miseries as the price for eventually seeing clear.

The Fool never ceases to chastise Lear for giving away his estate to his two false daughters, while Kent actually risks his life in speaking up for Cordelia. No such figure exists to warn or berate Gloucester, but Edmund himself shares his villainy with the audience—producing the queasy complicity that Shakespeare's soliloquies often yield, making us want to intervene, to prevent the disaster waiting in the wings, all the while savoring the sheer cunning on show—as he gloats at how easy it is to deceive both his father and his brother. One is astounded at the rapidity of it all: Goneril and Regan make a show of devotion, Cordelia keeps mum, and that is quite sufficient for disinheriting; Edmund fakes a letter, does some smooth talking, and both Edgar and Gloucester immediately go along. Why are they so easily duped? One answer might be: they are slated for an *education*, for rethinking the testimony of tongue and eye.

We've always known that Shakespeare's play is about the illusory nature of appearances. Liars are believed, truth-speakers are suspected. Worse still, Lear will come to understand that his entire kingdom is a stage-set for cruel false appearances, where the *signs* of authority invariably cheat; if you dress the part, you'll be believed: "Through tattered clothes great vices do appear: / Robes and furred gowns hide all. Plate sin with gold, / And the strong lance of justice hurtles breaks; / Arm it in rags, a pygmy's straw does pierce it. / None does offend, none, I say none." Shakespeare wants us to see how "agony-fueled" that dread insight is. There is no shortcut to this searing vision that exposes the world's sham, its obscene charade of order and virtue, always at the expense of the weak and poor. My verb "exposes" has a facile curtain-lifting ring to it, for the reality of the play is a good bit more labor-intensive: it is Lear's suffering that makes him become a decoder, a *reader*, of power. The old king has, he says, been "bound on a wheel of fire," suggesting that one must burn through to the truth, as if light and fire were inseparable, and that you do not achieve the one without undergoing the other.

Burning through to the truth will require five acts of pain. Recall *Lear* at the outset, and gauge its simplistic, reductive, quasi-numerical vision: a kingdom is to be divided into three parts—no, wait: only two parts—and the offending child who says nothing is to receive nothing: "Nothing will come of nothing." It turns out that Lear's own portion will be nothing, as Goneril and Regan put paid to their old father's desire to keep his retinue at full strength, or to keep at least the accouterments of power even if not the substance. He is to learn that accouterments are at once everything and nothing. His authority is to be reduced ever downward, and once "nothing" is reached—as it is on the heath where he goes mad—well, then, he comes to understand (nay, to feel) that "nothing" is the bedrock condition of the poor and hungry who made up his kingdom (the one he pompously divvied up):

> Poor naked wretches, whereso'er you are
> That bide the pelting of this pitiless storm,
> How shall your houseless heads and unfed sides,
> Your looped and windowed raggedness defend you
> From seasons such as these? O I have ta'en
> Too little care of this. Take physic, pomp,
> Expose thyself to feel what wretches feel,
> That thou mayst shake the superflux to them
> And show the heavens more just.

Fire is required; *physic* is also needed. The imagery of shelter—"houseless heads," "looped and windowed raggedness"—is inverted to display utter exposure as the natural condition of "unaccommodated man," of the "bare forked animal" who has nothing to prop himself up, who discovers that all his prior power was but a prop, has become nothing. What is sublime in this play is the ever-widening vision of its hurting protagonists. Gloucester, like Oedipus, has been blind and must be blinded if he is to see; when, on the heath, Lear asks him if he can see "how this world goes," his answer is simple yet profound: "I see it feelingly." As for Lear, the newer optics are system-wide, for he now, "softened" (as they say in the military) by the kingdom-wide assaults coming his way, becomes horribly wise about the grisly theater of everyday life, about the spectacle of a topsy-turvy universe of predators and cheats, of humans doing and done to; and this joint discovery of his own nothingness and the world's counterfeit is too much: it breeches his defenses, turns his own head houseless, renders him mad.

Lear thinks himself more "sinned against than sinning," and many readers have felt the same: must this play be so implacable in its rebuke to power and arrogance and blindness? Must Cordelia die? But Shakespeare is less concerned with moral justice than he is with the cost of knowing. Lear's calvary installs a new mathematics. Kingdoms cannot be divided like pie or cake (as Faulkner's Sutpen will assume, centuries later), but rather they must be "seen, feelingly." Kierkegaard insisted that we make that three-and-a-half day trip to Mount Moriah; Shakespeare also teaches us something about the sentience of numbers. And the man who says "Nothing will come of nothing" must experience what it is like to be reduced to nothing. It is the fount of knowing.

Two kings, Oedipus and Lear, are undone—one gouging his eyes out and the other driven mad and soon to die—by what they finally come to know. Lots of horror here. And, yet, there are lessons, even if neither text is remotely didactic. The Theban king arrives at a face-to-face, 360-degree form of self-portraiture, and his "achieved" life story repackages every biographical item he thought he knew. His people have been dying of plague, but he comes to understand that he is, in more ways than one, the miasma. As for Lear, his calvary is unbearably instructive, for it illuminates the incessant, baroque, vile horror-show going on nonstop in his kingdom, as power goes through its paces: the strong devouring the weak, the charade of virtue veiling the work of evil, the merciless route to seeing clear. Shall we call this "the cost of knowing"? Or, perhaps, "the truths of art"? Where are *we* in this equation? My question is not rhetorical: "the cost of knowing" is not just the severe final tally of these works; it points to what we, the nonplayers, stand to gain by frequenting them, by trying them on. It would be the payload of literature.

Emily Dickinson: "And finished Knowing—then—"

It seems fair to say that poetry is widely regarded as the most esoteric of the literary arts. Its formal devices—rhyme, meter, stanza, and the like—immediately put us on notice that we are in rarefied territory, a regime of verbal conventions that differ entirely from the everyday prose we use to communicate with our fellows. Novelists, on the other hand, often—not always—seem denizens of the quotidian world of potlucks and paychecks and politics that we associate with "reality." (I have a hunch that most of you noticed the consonance and alliteration I just aimed for, with my 3 *p*'s, and of course our brains are overflowing with rhymes and the like, taken from the songs we love and even the ads we don't always notice. Poetry, or least doggerel, sneaks in, more than you think.)

Emily Dickinson would likely rank very high on anyone's list of *difficult* poets. She fractures syntax, disregards those pesky rules of singular/plural that most of us follow, makes use of (forgotten) nineteenth-century hymnal forms, capitalizes whatever words she is of a mind to, and splatters her verse with so many dashes that it almost looks like calligraphy. In many of her poems, each line seems to cry out for translation, for help. In short, she is diabolically hard to understand, and therefore I am taking a significant risk in using her as a major exhibit for why literature matters, for all of us (not just professors or specialists, but all of us). Is there a Dickinson for the uninitiated general reader, or, using the slur I've already invoked, for "the great unwashed"?

Let's begin with one of her most revealing pronouncements, found in a letter to Thomas Wentworth Higginson (minister, abolitionist, literary critic) constituting the most pungent definition of *poetry* that I've ever seen: "If I read a book, and it makes my whole body so cold no fire ever can warm me, I know *that* is poetry. If I feel physically as if the top of my head were taken off, I know *that* is poetry. These are the only ways I know it. Is there any other way?" I have forever read this utterance as being about poetry, but I now believe it is primarily about *knowing*, because the most spectacular fireworks in Dickinson's inimitable poems inevitably have to do with the unhinging, traumatic, indeed spectacular character of knowledge itself.

But her view of knowing is more than *son et lumière*; it is also word-resistant, belated, harrowing, and undoing. Like so many of the authors examined here, she tells us that we risk being destroyed by the process of coming to know. And she shows us that our own toolkit, with its ample provision of words and concepts, its entire semiotic armature, is radically unsuited for conveying what Kant called "das Ding an sich" (the thing in itself), for fusing with the things it signals. This has little to do with "slippage" or the arbitrary nature of the sign as such. Rather: our terms do not fit what they "say at" (as Faulkner put it in one of his novels). How can words "become" things? Words only point to other words. Dictionaries, thesauruses, and vocabulary lists spill this secret to us early in life. But when do these matters take on a broader urgency, get beyond an academic linguistic conundrum? When do these issues break past the confines of Babel and "noise," so that they can show their true, fiery colors? Dickinson, rarefied though you may think her, enlists these verbal crises precisely to get at the most basic, urgent facts of life.

Consider, as first example, a notion that has immense currency in modern life, with all its strivings and appetites, with the very rationale of going to school and getting a degree: *success*. Many are the writers who have attempted to show the depths and the treacherousness and the price tag attached to "success." It can exact, as Balzac and Dickens and many others have shown, a huge ethical cost: either maiming or killing the one who succeeds. A film such as *Wall Street*, and many that have come out before or since, toils in this familiar vineyard. (My expensively educated students, even the most idealistic among them, ponder these matters intensely, sometimes paralyzingly.) But what if maiming and killing were in fact required for grasping what *success* actually means? What if maiming and killing were in fact the ticket, the only ticket? Listen to Dickinson:

> Success is counted sweetest
> By those who ne'er succeed.
> To comprehend a nectar
> Requires sorest need.

Not one of all the purple Host
Who took the Flag today
Can tell the definition
So clear of Victory

As he defeated—dying–
On whose forbidden ear
The distant strains of triumph
Burst agonized and clear!

I've taught this poem many times, but never quite saw it before as epistemological, yet it is just that. With imagery drawn both from the bucolic world of flowers and scents and foreshadowing the bloody war about to break out, Dickinson revises my central notion, "the cost of knowing," into something more horrible: "the cost = knowing." Everything in these lines says "reversal": Success is "counted sweetest": of course, "counted" means "accounted," but we are meant to feel the incommensurateness between numbers and taste, and this same disconnect is seen in the phrase "to comprehend a nectar"; can a nectar be comprehended? How is anything comprehended? "Sorest need" appears to be the answer: *hurt* and *hunger* fuel knowing. *Lack* drives our engine, on the order of plus/minus pulsions, except that minus always precedes and enables plus, makes us grasp what plus might be, must be. There is a fierce dialectic here, positing that meaning hinges on binaries and opposites, not just for definitional clarity but out of an experiential economy that must be in the red if it is to signal the black.

The fuller deficit-driven topsy-turviness of this scheme emerges in the last eight lines of the poem, yielding one ever-growing image of deadly warfare—rich in color and sound and horrid immediacy, unfolding like a slow-motion film—yet insistently cued to the same epistemological injunction: what is success? How is it knowable? What conditions are required for it to be known? And the same negative logic is in play: the *defeated know* what victory is or would be in ways the victor cannot. This negative logic stamps the grammar itself: *Not one . . .* so that we register the colorful signs of victory ("purple Host," "Flag") as picturesque but irrelevant to the work of *definition* at hand. Instead, the focus of the poem and the work of defining shift 180 degrees in the last stanza, zeroing in on the defeated and dying soldier whose exit is luminous with knowledge; *he knows*. That knowledge constitutes the final assault that will kill him: his "forbidden ear" and his soul are annihilated, ruptured, by the bursting "strains of triumph" whose ringing and lethal truth he—and only he—understands with absolute clarity. Here is a zero-sum logic with the elegance of a guillotine (as it cuts through): success attains its fullest, clearest meaning only via the agony of him "who ne'er succeeds." How sweet this may be counted is another matter altogether. Who would have thought that our secular term "success" would be so blood-soaked? One remembers the quip about a new cure for cancer: human flesh. Dickinson might have relished this.

Dickinson brings extraordinary news to us in this oft-cited poem. We are invariably looking in the wrong direction, asking the wrong people, when we seek to understand things. *Success* is most deeply felt only by those who failed. How much else, in our arsenal of ultimately desired outcomes—richness, happiness, love, grace—can only and fully be *tasted* by those who never got them? Our psychic economy is written in red ink. It is hard to imagine a more calamitous reversal.

The roller-coaster ride of chasing and delivering "clear definitions" appears to be the major business of many of Dickinson's best poems. (One imagines Descartes, the patron saint of the scientific principle that posits *analysis* as route to truth, not just writhing in his grave but feeling outright "inverted," turned inside out, flipped.) Nowhere is Dickinson's zest for negation as route more on show than in what I take to be one of her finest "eclipse" pieces when self and world go over a cliff:

It was not Death, for I stood up,
And all the Dead lie down—
It was not Night, for all the Bells
Put out their Tongues, for Noon.

It was not Frost, for on my Flesh
I felt Siroccos—crawl—
Nor Fire—for just my Marble feet
Could keep a Chancel, cool—

And yet, it tasted, like them all,
The Figures I have seen
Set orderly, for Burial,
Reminded me, of mine—

As if my life were shaven,
And fitted to a frame,
And could not breathe without a key,
And 'twas like Midnight, some—

When everything that ticked—has stopped—
And Space stares all around—
Or grisly frosts—first Autumn morns,
Repeal the Beating Ground—

But, most, like Chaos—Stopless—cool—
Without a Chance, or Spar—
Or even a Report of Land—
To justify—Despair.

Like a research project, this poem examines our conceptual toolkit to
see if the naming equipment (which is all we have, for grasping things)
actually works, and the first two stanzas, valiant though they are, appear
to record failure after failure. Not death, not night, not frost, not fire:
nope, none of these works. But the cunning poet once again wins when
she loses, since the evocation of each of these false leads shimmers with
its own wit and malice, whispers to us that the poem benefits as much
from getting it wrong as from getting it right. The poet sticks her tongue
out at us, defining the dead as lying down and the living as standing up;
true enough in its naturalist way, but then, might you, standing up, still
experience a version of death? Yes, you might. "Night" likewise comes
in for a trial, but it seems to be broad day, as the bells blast away, tongues
out; we also sense that noon has an aural punch of its own, far from innocuous. Not "frost," either, we see, since "Siroccos" (desert winds) are
(like little creepies) crawling in our flesh. Finally, "fire" also fails the test,
since her feet are of marble, so cold they could refrigerate a room. Hmm.
The familiar Gothic bogies that are supposed to stamp our moments of
collapse—death, night, frost, and fire—no longer function as verbal or

conceptual guides, yielding instead to a distinctly nasty picture of suffering: standing up, racked by light, peals of bells, warm currents on our flesh, along with ice-cold feet.

Dickinson's *economy* is again on show. Verbal crutch after verbal crutch is trotted out, and shown to be wrong, yet she makes us see that these are the only tools we have for defining experience, that we can only stand up with the aid of such constructs, even if we then go about replacing them with more accurate labels. Everything is paying its way. And are the hoary tags so wrong? "And yet, it tasted, like them all." Two stanzas for clearing the table, four stanzas now for limning what it was, rather than what it was not. The earlier (erroneous) figures now cohere into the signs of burial . . . my burial. For Dickinson (as for Poe) burial is the beginning, not the ending; it is as if she wished to rebut Hamlet's view that Death is the "undiscover'd country," by staking out her own strange geography and psychic landscape. One's life is shaven—that is, one is purged, scoured, filed, made entirely bare. One is fitted to a frame: here would be a version of the medieval torture called the rack, whereby one's limbs are pulled apart, but in Dickinson they also appear to be repurposed (one's limbs), become components of art, achieve a new form. Breathing does not stop, happily, but a key is required to do so, again suggesting a carceral scheme of significant proportions. And time reenters: midnight. Seems now that "noon" was a trick, intended to deceive.

We are at the witching hour. Things that ticked—clocks, hearts— have stopped. Space itself seems ubiquitous but alienated, staring around, offering no grounding or home. (Pascal territory.) Frosts also make their way back, but revealed now in their natural role as killer, striking on "first Autumn morns," enlisting the power of the bells so as to "repeal"—how nice, that verb here!—the "Beating Ground": the earth, the beating/ticking heart, life's warmth, now under siege. These new arrangements belong to no world we've ever charted: Chaos, beyond all bounds or "frames" of either space or time ("stopless" in Dickinsonian lingo), constituting a setting of utter loss and bereftness: no Chance, no Spar, no Report of Land. This is Despair.

This is Despair. We now—now—realize that the poem "started" with Despair as its origin, its site, unlabelable, unnameable; and the project of the poet is to find for this felt experience a verbal, indeed a narrative, coefficient, a strategy whereby the reader would be led, step by step, via charades that gesture and terms that misfire, toward the ultimate land-scape that wants saying. On the far side of this poem, we do have a kind of dreadful knowledge. It is the very feel, the look, the sound, the regime, the world of Despair. There is no shortcut to such a destination. Beyond "information," it exists only at the end of Dickinson's poetic trajectory. The achieved vista is of Despair—not as it exists in the tidy columns of the dictionary but as it exists in the heart and psyche—but no *reader* who has made this trip ends up feeling despair. On the contrary, the sheer epistemological energies at work here, the gymnastics of trying on and discarding one set of labels in order to move toward further, more novel, ever-more-bristling constructs of seeing/hearing/feeling yields, in my view, a sense of joy. She brings us to a place that exists in our psyches but not in our archives, and that kind of a trip, even when punctuated by fear and trembling, adds heft, adds true data, to our life.

A sibling to this poem about the landscape of despair would be "I Felt a Funeral in my Brain" with its still more explicit focus on *knowing*. Once again, I confess to having long regarded this piece as Dickinson's supreme "3:00 a.m." poem about horror's hold, but the piece reads equally well as manifesto about *affective understanding*:

I felt a Funeral in my Brain,
And Mourners too and fro
Kept treading—treading—till it seemed
That Sense was breaking through—

And when they all were seated,
A Service, like a Drum—
Kept beating—beating—till I thought
My Mind was going numb—

And then I heard them lift a Box
And creak across my Soul
With those same Boots of Lead, again,
Then Space—began to toll,

As all the Heavens were a Bell,
And Being, but an Ear,
And I, and Silence, some strange Race
Wrecked, solitary, here—

And then a Plank in Reason, broke,
And I dropped down, and down—
And hit a World, at every plunge,
And Finished knowing—then—

This piece constitutes the finest rendition of anguish as place that I have ever read. One's initial intuition here is that we're dealing with an imagined death-and-burial—the poem certainly enlists that storyline in its first three stanzas—yet the imagery itself of *treading* and *beating* seems to have a payload of its own, suggesting that Dickinson's ultimate target is "how we understand," itself now understood in terms of pure somatic trauma. Hence, the salient feature of the first stanza is one's sense of being broken and entered, and if it takes mourners stomping on your soul to get that across, so be it. "Till it seemed that Sense was breaking through" announces that what linguists and theorists demurely call "signification" is in fact something far more bruising and penetrating, so much so that its entry into/through our defenses or torpor may be what the death scenario is actually about. (How staid "through a glass darkly . . . but then face to face" now looks!) Something in our former arrangements dies, when "sense breaks through." We'll see more of this at poem's end.

The second stanza works its magic along similar lines, so that "beating, beating" starts to appear to be the main item, enlisting the church service cum drum as plausible backdrop for this relentless physical attack. Much is happening: the drums are beating, the head is beating, the heart is beating, and this awful percussion ruptures all defenses, smashes borders, sets up its own physiological regime, numbs the mind. In the third stanza, we see that numbness is no protection: you are now both *in* the Box/coffin *and* you are the Soul/floor that is being battered by "Boots of Lead" as the horrid stomping finishes its work. This mugging scenario of assault and battery is Dickinson's way of figuring what I call "knowing." It annihilates who we were, and it ushers us into a new cosmos that comes at us—deprived of all shelter, become pure vulnerability, pure target—nonstop. Space tolls, we're told, and this ringing notion is confirmed by the Heavens themselves becoming a Bell, so that the contained music of a church service explodes into a cosmic attack against a creature without defenses. The next three lines amaze: all of *Being* is now converted into an *Ear*, and one feels a horrible transformation at work, as if the entire person turned inside out, became orifice, exposure, throbbing membrane, receiving blows. But there is no more noise. (Has it all gone inside, walled up, unhearable?) Under such a barrage, the battered (dead? buried?) Self experiences the ultimate shipwreck, the ultimate exile, having only Silence as companion, "Wrecked, solitary, here—."

Lest we find this final stage of abandonment too upbeat, the last stanza picks up the pace considerably, turns up the power, makes us realize that "exile" is far too static and gentle a notion, whereas the initiation now at hand is postexile, pure kinesis, a high-speed downfall into the pit. *Downfall* is easily understood as noun; Dickinson awakens us to the ferocious, vertiginous free-fall that now pulls us with utmost brutality down and out of the world, and she makes us see that this is the annihilating voyage we tamely call "knowing." These lines shock in every sense of the term: they describe trauma, they traumatize, they posit trauma as our last station. "A Plank in Reason broke," the poet writes, thereby informing us that Reason *is* a Plank, the very Plank we stand/sit on all our lives as Cartesian thinkers, with nary a clue that it is positioned over the abyss, that it is removable, that it will break. Break it does, and the final trip begins. Science fiction can not go further than Dickinson's notation, "And hit a World, at every plunge," for we are now in free-fall through the galaxy, not as tourists in some nice Elon Musk vehicle but rather as plunging debris crashing into countless other worlds, with the sublime conclusion that this "stopless" series of *collisions* is what "Knowledge" actually is. This is how one "finishes knowing." Remember Dickinson's view of how one "knows" poetry: when it explodes the back of one's head off. And maybe that is the way one knows anything at all. Except that you lose more than your head.

Many of Dickinson's most memorable poems deliver this same violent epistemology. Sometimes they have a religious coloration, imputing these moments of staggering encounter to some divinity who "fumbles at your Soul" the way piano players work their keys. In that particular poem, one is "stunned by degrees," as strategic preparation for the staggering final onslaught that "Deals—One—imperial—Thunderbolt— / That scalps your naked Soul." This murderous encounter is likened to the Winds that "take Forests in their Paws," yielding a picture of God/Nature as fiendish creature that scalps and abducts its chosen victims, as the very price tag of perception and being. Work of this stripe puts paid to any cozy pastoral view of Dickinson as nature's child who strolls and gambols in the woods, sniffing flowers and looking at birds. Instead, the natural world can be alien, immense, threatening, bidding to wipe out the puny observing poet. In one poem she speculates that her very heart would split if she were told the sky was hers, or that the meadows and mountains and forests and stars and motions of the birds might offer visual delight, whereas she is quite certain "the News would strike me dead."

Perhaps the masterpiece in this vein is the seemingly bucolic and witty account of a walk in the woods where the poet meets, one after another, its living creatures: birds, flowers, grass, bees. The familiar suspects, we might assume, for a charming little sortie. But we quickly see that nature's bounty is for Dickinson no less than a perceptual hara-kiri. She so dreads the first robin that considerable time is needed to retrieve her balance. But this gained reprieve is short-lived because the sounds of the forest come across as homicidal and deforming, likened to the power of warring pianos that would *mangle* her. Then come the daffodils whose yellow gown "would pierce me with a fashion so foreign to my own." Even though Dickinson frequently enlists the discourse of fashion and style, this line is not Operation Runway; we are meant to give full weight to *pierce*. (Operation indeed.) The grass might conceivably give protection, if tall enough, so that one could hide, but most likely the bees—the bees!—will come nonetheless, agents of an alien world, a "dim country" they should have stayed in, but they—like all the other creatures—attend the great execution event staged by the poet/Queen of calvary. Staged how? Staged simply by the agony of being there, of looking, by the crushing weight of knowing. She is destroyed by what she sees and hears. It is too much.

There is something astounding about this poem. (And it is accompanied by many like-minded pieces.) The perception of nature—whether it be Kant's sublime or the stunning vistas of a Goethe or Wordsworth or Keats or Shelley or Whitman—stands, for many of us, as the very source not only of poetry, but of beauty, imagination, power, and meaning. Culture is saturated with this belief. Whether it be the sanctity of Walden Pond or the beauties of the Lake Country or the Schwarzwald or the Alps or the Guermantes Way or all those tourist sites named on the World's Most Beautiful Places' lists or indeed your garden variety Sunday excursion, we are taught that such encounters are *good*, that they expand and school our eyes and hearts and minds. Forever, one has thought of poetry as bridge to that world, as passport to wonder and richer intimations of the universe we inhabit, indeed as confirmation of our citizenship and great fortune.

Dickinson tells us something different: that vision is lethal, that we would do best by hiding, that having your eyes put out is a signal blessing. The Creation, in all its glory or in its discrete particulars, is unbearable to look upon, will kill us dead if we make the mistake of accessing it. I cannot help seeing in this conviction a damnation of seeing as knowing that gives great pause, for it whispers to us how lucky we are to have dulled organs of perception, how blessed and strategic our routine torpor and blindness are. (Strindberg was to evoke the brain itself as *penal*: "my bright airy thoughts bound in a labyrinth of fat"; Dickinson welcomes the shelter.) There is no safe haven wherever you look. The nightmarish middle-of-the-night wake-up call with its hallucinatory tidings of Chaos as new home and the putatively pleasant little saunter in the woods are kissing cousins: they bear the same bad news.

When I was a student reading Proust, one of my best professors suggested that the French author seemed the victim of nature's mistake, inasmuch as his outsides and his insides got mixed up, so that he was without protection, without the tough skin that most of us are equipped with. I do not now agree with this assessment of Proust—he seems pretty tough and wiry to me, wherever you locate him—but I feel that Emily Dickinson is indeed shaped along these lines. She is capable of wit and of posing, but I think I understand better why she elected to live, protected, in her "Father's house." The sheer malevolence and violence that run rampant in her work are less the features of her own psychic disposition than the hallmark of a world that wants nothing more than to overwhelm you, to snuff you out. One encounters here a vulnerability toward the Creation such that I have never seen before. It is as if she were born premature, with undeveloped epidermis, with sensory and perceptual organs placed on the outside, without any buffer whatsoever, either physical or conceptual. Her most violent poems open the door onto a roiling world that routinely annihilates. Night, day, frost, blossoms, sun, rain, snow: these are all killers, even if nonchalant and cavalier. (No malice required.) Reading her makes you realize—and appreciate—how asleep you are. Kafka was to say that art is the ax that chops through our frozen sea; Dickinson is poetry's Lizzie Borden, and her ax is sharp. The most elemental forms of knowing—opening your eyes and ears and mind and heart—can betoken murder.

My students, I confess, sometimes see me as fixated on gloom and doom in my courses; and I have to admit that Emily Dickinson—whom I touted as a poet for *everyone*—does not make us delirious with joy, as we negotiate her off-the-charts poems, poems that put paid to most of our complacent views on *knowing*. Hard to argue that these are welcome tidings. But I believe they are aristocratic tidings. I believe she ennobles us as readers, because she invites us to a richer, even if shocking, take on our most elemental affairs: the meaning of success, the unwelcome but undeniable visits of despair, the very texture of panic and capsizing, the overwhelming immediacy and power of a natural world that is alien to the human. There is nothing highbrow or arcane or elitist or even literary about these matters. Her account of the *cost of knowing* inaugurates us into a neural, perceptual, imaginative scheme that wrecks our routinized torpor and does honor to the actual texture of our experience. I'd even say: she adds to our database. Once you've read her, you never forget her. You can decide for yourself exactly what kind of a gift that is, but it is a gift.

Huckleberry Finn and Ole Man River

"The great brown god" is T. S. Eliot's term for the Mississippi River, a river he grew up with in St. Louis, a river he saw as the central pulsing force in Mark Twain's *Adventures of Huckleberry Finn*. The niceties of plot and character, Eliot opined, yield to the sheer power of the river, as it takes the white boy and the older black man on their fateful journey through the novel, following its own willful course. Can it be tamed or channeled? Can it be bent to human or moral purposes? Twain himself spent a large portion of his life learning about these matters, and they bear significantly on the aesthetic and ethical pattern of his novel. As is well known, the novel is widely thought to be flawed (even if ever beloved in some quarters) because its noble moral vision—a white boy in 1840s Missouri coming to understand the dignity and humanity of a black escaped slave—falters badly in the last third of the work, yielding instead to a mishmash of fun and games, as elaborate and unnecessary escape plots are hatched and spun out by Tom Sawyer in his great bid to match the adventure yarns to which he's addicted. Poor Huck and still poorer Jim (imprisoned) become largely accessories in Tom's fantasia of childish pranks and tasteless theatrics. Ethics doesn't stand a chance.

Twain himself would doubtless refer us back to his opening salvo: anyone attempting to find a moral in this story is to be shot. But the author cannot be easily excused for the critics' displeasure, essentially because he himself is to be blamed: the rendition of Huck's ethical growth is among the most beautiful things in American literature. To see it come to so little is hard to take.

Huck's evolution, truncated or not, epitomizes what we might mean by "the cost of knowing," and it might not be far-fetched to claim that the cost was too high—for Twain, but also for Huck—which is why the farcical hijacks the moral and takes over the book. Nonetheless, a closer look at Huck's "trajectory" is instructive. He begins the novel as Tom Sawyer's somewhat lackluster friend. Yet his hardheadedness about Tom's bookish shenanigans (grand schemes of robbery and magic exploits) testifies to a commonsensical center of gravity and capacity for critique that are welcome attributes. Twain's brilliance in this book is to be located on several distinct yet related fronts: (1) the story is entrusted to young Huck's vernacular (this alone is revolutionary; contrast it with the polite language of *Tom Sawyer*, or indeed with the bulk of nineteenth-century classic novels, all written in an "adult," educated discourse); (2) the time frame is set (back forty years) in the 1840s, *before* the Civil War that will forever limn issues of slavery and freedom; and (3) the great sociomoral (ongoing?) dilemma of American culture—Are black people fully human?—is to be "adjudicated" by a high school dropout with zero cultural capital. It is hard to overstate how fertile each of these moves is, since Twain is thereby able to offer us rare insight into how Great Things appear to ordinary folks.

Enlisting the unschooled Huck as scorekeeper is a mark of genius. Huck is as racist as most of the folks in his part of the world are. Worse still, he will find that the institution of slavery is supported *inside* as much as *outside*, by which I mean: not only are adults like Miss Watson and Aunt Sally comfortable with slavery (not to mention Pap, who is vicious on the subject), but the most powerful defense of the racial status quo comes from his own *conscience*. Twain antedates (by two-thirds of a century) theorists such as Althusser by understanding that the dictates of ideology are lodged in our subjectivity, that Sunday school sermons make their insidious way into our minds and hearts (even if we never went to Sunday school). Twain upends a deep-seated American belief in individual freedom, since he knows that there is no such thing as a "free place." There is no "outside" of culture.

That is what Twain knows. What does Huck "know"? He knows that failing to return Jim to his (rightful) owner qualifies as *bad*, and his conscience lets him have it: "the more my conscience went to grinding me, and the more wicked and low-down and ornery I got to be feeling" since, after all, how could he justify "stealing a poor old woman's nigger that hadn't never done me no harm"? "Everlasting fire" is what awaits him. At the margins or not, Huck has internalized the ABC's of his culture and *knows* what kind of punishment is to be his. This same Sunday school code stamps the great relief he feels when he writes his note to Miss Watson, telling her where Jim is: "all washed clean of sin for the first time I had ever felt so in my life." So, why doesn't he turn Jim in?

To answer that question we need first to consult "Ole Man River." As we know, Samuel Clemens took his pen name from the procedure of depth sounding, of measuring how deep the water is: "Mark Twain" meant two fathoms. It is that deep. The trip on a skiff down the Mississippi with the white boy and the black man is also one of measures, acquiring increasing depth as it goes, and Huck's growing recognition of Jim's humanity is often keyed to moments when they are the verge of going under. In this regard nothing surpasses the stunning sequence when they get lost in the fog near Cairo and thereby miss the crucial opportunity to leave the Mississippi and move north on the Missouri. Remember: the rescue plot hinged on getting out of slave territory. But instead they go further and further southward, into it. We know that Twain had writer's block at exactly this juncture. He *knew* that he was supposed to change rivers, and he couldn't, because his most congenial "writing turf" was downriver; it paralyzed him. For years the manuscript lay untouched.

And then we get the sequence with the fog. Here we have a perfect conjunction of Huck-speak and Twain's own river experience, displaying some of the most vivid and echoing language of the novel. It would seem as though nature itself wants to separate the couple; Huck is "shot out into the solid white fog . . . with no more idea which way I was going than a dead man." Water two fathoms deep can be measured by a skillful boatman's call of "mark twain," but solid white fog into which you are shot, with no more sense of orientation than a dead man has, is a different proposition. Orphan Huck now feels his bereftness, hears it in the whoops coming from all directions, sees it in the "smoky ghosts of big trees," and we are meant to consider all these motifs: dead man, ghosts, fog, self as thing shot into the world. One feels that Twain's world, usually so grounded in his vernacular discourse with its wit and sting, is lifting the curtain, revealing the nothingness that lurks behind appearances. No struggle can prevail here: Huck, floating blind on open river, falls asleep. And then wakes up in starry night, sees the raft, mounts it, and finds Jim asleep.

Yet, in the ensuing protracted cruel joke Huck attempts to play on Jim—telling him that there was no fog, no separation; it was just a dream—we see that the corrosive white fog and smoky ghosts remain, for Jim's confusion is outright existential, even modern: "Is I *me*, or who *is* I? Is I heah, or whah *is* I?" These are the most philosophical lines of the novel, spoken by its illiterate black man, and they not only deliver the lineaments of Twain's world but adumbrate the fissuring of self that subtends all this novel's seeming fun and games. Could that be the toxic bottom line, the truly lower depths, in Twain's famous novel: "self as mirage"? Fog, not-seeing-clearly, blindness: these are central motifs in the *Oedipus*, and one remembers that Dickens's elephantine *Bleak House* starts out on the same note, with its rendition of London fog.

Why haven't we seen that Twain is one of our great *undoers*, that Twain sabotages all notions of fixed identity and stable world? Depth sounding is his gambit, and it goes deeper than two fathoms. The fantasia of twins and lookalikes and doubles in not only *Pudd'nhead Wilson* but also *The Prince and the Pauper* testifies to a scheme of blurred and illusory boundaries. (I write these lines as identical twin.) As for our great classic, *Huckleberry Finn,* the maniacal game of disguises and impersonations, stock features of the picaresque genre, stamps everything: the King and the Duke pretending to be the Wilks brothers returning from England, Huck pretending to be Tom, Tom pretending to be Sid. It is not only *carnivalesque* but almost Saussurean in its semiotic hijinks, as is on show when Huck cannot even remember the name of the person he's playing (this time), or in the countless storylets he invents each time he's in a tight corner, or—magisterially—when he swears to tell the truth by placing his hand not on a Bible but on a dictionary. "I never seen anybody but lied," Huck tells us at the outset; we need to see that this is as much a linguistic pronouncement, as a moral one, as if words and truths were forever located on parallel tracks.

A deconstructive reading of *Huckleberry Finn* is possible. In the fog-truth of the book, there are only gliding forms and specious appearances. Names do not bind, and words are slippery, slippery. But this dry assessment will not accord with the novel's passion, even if that passion has nowhere to go and must fizzle. Even if that passion threatens to blow apart the unified self. At its best—and this is why it is an irresistible classic, despite its egregious political incorrectness—*Huckleberry Finn* helps us to see the formation of human character and the acquisition of personal knowledge; and it thereby helps us to realize how arduous and usually invisible such things are, how precarious and elusive their attainment is. (This is a huge claim: the most important, formative events in our lives escape notation, including our own notation; when you consider the bulging, never-ending records kept of/by us today—and bidding to continue growing exponentially—it is astonishing that we may well be in the dark about the essentials, such as "When did I become me?" or "When did I figure out what I wanted to be?")

What is beautiful in *Huckleberry Finn* is the social, ideological, and racial cast of such an education. The human character at issue here is double: Huck's and Jim's. As Huck grudgingly yet heroically comes to gauge Jim's humanity, his dimensionality, we see *both* figures being fleshed out, moving beyond names and categories into something deeper and richer.

The two moments when this moral and epistemological growth is most visible come at the close of each of the scenes I've commented on: being lost in the fog and writing the letter to Miss Watson. They thereby transform the segments they complete in virtually alchemist fashion, making us see what *soul* might look like. As noted, the fog sequence is a nasty piece of work: directionality disappears, the dead trump the living, and racial taunting takes over. But the trickster is about to be tricked, for his final trump card in mocking Jim—pointing toward the rubbish on the raft, asking what it actually is, in order to cashier the "dream-theory" that Jim has had to come up with, by a final look at realia, at reality itself—works against him. Jim looks at the detritus, looks at Huck, comprehends how he's been toyed with, and gives the following answer:

What do dey stan' for? I's gwyne to tell you. When I got all wore out wid work, en wid de callin' for you, en went to sleep, my heart wuz mos' broke bekase you wuz los', en I didn' k'yer no mo' what become er me en de raf'. En when I wake up en fine you back agin', all safe en soun', de tears come en I could a got down on my knees en kiss yo' foot I's so thankful. En all you wuz thinkin' 'bout wuz how you could make a fool 'uv ole Jim wid a lie. Dat truck dah is *trash*; en trash is what people is dat puts dirt on de head or dey fren's en makes 'em ashamed.

Here is, I believe, the response to the fog. Even if—especially if—the world loses its contours, the story of love retains its clarity and authority and responsibilities. Jim looks at the debris on the raft and calls it "trash," and then makes the next call: those who exploit others' tenderness are also trash. The entire one-upsmanship logic that fuels the antics of Tom Sawyer (and the King and the Duke, and most of the people in the novel) yields to a new code: broken heart, tears, kissing, recognition, compassion, feeling, dignity. These are new sensations for Huck Finn. Dry-eyed orphan, victim of Pap's abuse, recipient of orderly concern by the Widow Douglas, quick witted and often quite shrewd, Huck has never experienced *love* before. It dumbfounds him, squeezes his heart, "grinds" out a response: "It was fifteen minutes before I could work myself up to go and humble myself to a nigger—but I done it, and I warn't ever sorry for it afterwards, neither." Twain sweetly uses "humble" as his verb of choice, and in this humble passage, we can see something virtually epic in scale. Moral growth in this book means: depth sounding, taking the strange human measure of an odd couple on a raft floating down the river. Jim makes Huck see its fuller dimensions: caring, anxiety, tenderness, hurt.

Naturally, we will close by revisiting the famous moment when Huck writes his fateful letter to Miss Watson, divulging Jim's whereabouts, and then gets *stuck*. I see Twain's own writer's block here: Huck is encountering something that stops him in his tracks. That "something" is nothing less than the emotional and moral fullness of his trip down the river. Huck accesses this rich quarry in much the same way that Proust's Marcel will recover his fuller past by tasting a tea-soaked pastry years later. So it is that Huck now *sees* Jim—he "re-sees" Jim, and thereby sees him rightly, humanly—as his loving partner: "all the time, in the day, and in the night-time, sometimes moonlight, sometimes storms, and we a floating along, talking, and singing, and laughing." How beautiful and right those present participles are, performing the noble work of "making present," indeed of making real. This retrieval is drenched in affection: "he would always call me honey, and pet me, and do everything he could think of for me, and how good he always was," and it leads to its inevitable epiphany: "I was the best friend old Jim ever had in the world," as beautiful phrase that demands to be rewritten by us: "Old Jim was the best friend Huck ever had in the world."

Toni Morrison has wisely written that Huck—fixated on death and fog, stranger to tenderness—needs Jim more than Jim needs him, but I would invoke Lear here: "Reason not the need." It's not a contest about whose humanity comes first. The mutuality itself is revolutionary. *Knowing Jim* is a revolutionary proposition, and even though Huck remains light-years away from being an abolitionist, he has nonetheless broken free from the orthodoxy of his moment and his world. What we see is "the love that dare not speak its name." Huck rises to its demand, and makes what is arguably the most luminous utterance in nineteenth-century American fiction:

> It was a close place. I took it up [the letter], and held it in my hand. I was trembling, because I'd got to decide, forever, betwixt two things, and I knowed it. I studied a minute, sort of holding my breath, and then says to myself:
> "All right, then I'll *go* to hell,"—and tore it up.

I suspect there are many readers who devoutly wish that Twain had either (a) maintained this sublime level of moral vision or (b) found some quick way to bring his story to an end. Unfortunately, he did neither. But that does not detract from the beauty of this moment, when young Huck recognizes the cost of *knowing* and pays its price. I do not believe this is about courage. It involves something larger, a recognition, fueled by tenderness, that Jim is actually human and therefore cannot be returned to slavery.

Actually human: we need to pinch ourselves to remember what a high bar this is, how arduously "countercultural" such recognition is, given that *othering*, in all its guises and forms, routinely divests entire groups of just this reality. "Pseudo-speciation" is one of the anthropological terms used for such operations, but Twain's manner is more genial, as we see in Huck's interpretation of Jim's pain at being separated from his wife and children, "I do believe he cared just as much for his people as white folks does for their'n. It don't seem natural, but I reckon it's so." *It don't seem natural, but I reckon it's so* is the human spirit's wake-up call. (These moments of surprised insight are life's true thresholds; how often do we measure them?) But that earlier perception did not have the fateful consequences that this one does: going to hell.

Given the subversiveness of Twain's book, few readers believe Huck is en route to hell. After all, hell belongs to that same constellation as Sunday school, and Huck has long intuited that all religious doctrine, much like Tom Sawyer's tales of A-rabs and elephants, has little truck with reality. Nonetheless, he has traveled a far piece down that Ole Man River, to be willing to sign on for hell. For *going* to hell. I believe Twain sensed that he could take his boy protagonist no further. In the nauseating pages of the book's last chapters, dealing with infantile (albeit stolen-from-books), even sadistic stratagems and formulas for freeing Jim, Huck seems almost a background figure. At story's end, Huck learns that Miss Watson had already freed Jim (and that Tom knew it). There is no noticeable reaction on Huck's part. But I cannot read the book's fine last line about Huck "lighting out for the territory ahead of the others" except as acknowledgement that he cannot be returned to business as usual, that he is indeed moving *out*. Maybe that is where Ole Man River ultimately goes: not only past Cairo and through the slave-holding South but all the way into Hell and then some, toward a territory that may signal more than Oklahoma. The River that might conduct him there runs deep, well over two fathoms deep, perhaps unplumbably deep. Twain did not—could not?—write that final leg of the trip.

Instead, the novel closes with a disappearance act. It already foreshadows Ellison's Invisible Man, who stakes out a well-lit hiding place underground to carry out his war with society. Twain understood that the moral growth his child protagonist "sporadically" underwent risked turning his children's story into something denser and more serious, perhaps unwritable; and he refused to go that route. He let Tom Sawyer take over. Just as he earlier had no qualms handing over the adventures of this book to the King and the Duke with their bag of tricks. Just as he later handed over the reins to Pudd'nhead Wilson, who closes up his own story, as well, in the performative mode, with his courtroom theatrics. It is a mode Twain was gifted at. He'd spent his lifetime trying it out, succeeding at it.

But Huck Finn himself is no performer, despite the whoppers he delivers himself of. He exits the story toward parts unknown, but his moments of moral discovery—and they are only moments—have immense gravity. He could not act on his knowledge, but he came to know.

Huck Finn traveled a far piece but he could never imagine "becoming" Jim. In *Pudd'nhead Wilson*, Twain enlisted the genre of swapped infants at birth, so as to get closer at race via the contortions of a plot overloaded with twins and doubles. (Dostoevsky and Conrad had been fascinated by the same motifs. Obviously, for reasons going back to birth, I share their taste.) But what would it look like to go the full existential route, so that Huck actually became black? To *metamorphose* into another. Here would be the final parameters of the project of knowing: to enter the other's heart, brain, *and skin*. Achievable? Survivable?

Emily Brontë, Herman Melville, Franz Kafka, and William Faulkner are all drawn, magnetically it would seem, tragically it will be seen, to just this extreme vista, this farthest pole, as if to say: all talk about understanding others must eventually go exactly that far: becoming the other. And don't write this off as science fiction: can love itself ever disavow this yearning? Mustn't the knowledge-of-the-other always approximate such a journey? What would happen if you got "there"? Could you end up there by chance, by horrible mischance? The works I'm now going to discuss hallow both the beauty and the destruction attendant on such moves.

Knowing the Other: *Wuthering Heights*

Two children—one privileged, one orphan—grow up together in both happiness and sorrow, develop an unbreakable bond, a bond so unbreakable that it essentially breaks them. Emily Brontë's story of Cathy and Heathcliff stands for many of us as immortal love story. Yet a closer look suggests that the novel is more characterized by terror and haunting than it is by love and desire; and it is more cued to *knowing* than we have realized.

As readers know, Brontë's plot indeed warrants my term *haunting*, and it seems shockingly accidental since it arose entirely out of a misunderstanding. As Cathy is explaining to Nellie Dean the difference between her feelings for the "low" Heathcliff and the proper Edgar (who wants to marry her), she has no idea that Heathcliff is within earshot, and thus when she acknowledges his uncouthness and rough manner as "beneath" her, he not only hears it and is hurt to the core but then bolts away from the Heights, to be gone for years. He will later return, to set in motion his fateful machinations. Yet it's worth staying with this haunting moment, since Cathy's continued words to Nellie rank among the most beautiful things in English literature, and every reader is left to wish that Heathcliff had stayed to hear them:

> What were the use of my creation if I were entirely contained here? My great miseries in this world have been Heathcliff's miseries, and I have watched and felt each from the beginning; my great thought in living is himself. If all else perished, and *he* remained, I should still continue to be; and if all else remained, and he were annihilated, the Universe would turn to a mighty stranger. I should not seem a part of it. My love for Linton is like the foliage in the woods. Time will change it, I'm well aware, as winter changes the trees. My love for Heathcliff resembles the eternal rocks beneath—a source of little visible delight, but necessary. Nelly, I *am* Heathcliff—he's always, always in my mind—not as a pleasure, any more than I am always a pleasure to myself—but as my own being—so don't talk of our separation again.

Nelly, I am Heathcliff. One of the central claims in this study is: the world (including other people) only becomes *real* to us when we know it via the heart. Otherwise, we remain in the thin realm of "information." Brontë's novel is out to chart just how much horror, how much fate, is coded in Cathy's simple yet profound words. Forever, we have read this declaration as a thing of beauty, but it turns out instead—to Cathy's

own amazement and doom—to open the door to a succubus-like, pathological, indeed lethal view of human feeling that resembles torture,
disease, and entrapment. Time has, as she says, no purchase on their
bond. Their connection is quasi-morphological—two people fused together, inhabiting each other—even though each appears to be indi-
viduated. "If all else perished, and he remained, I should continue to
be": this will happen. She herself will perish, he will remain, she will
continue to be . . . inside of him.

Cathy and Heathcliff are each "possessed" of the other. The novel is
out to show us the consequences. It is worth noting that although Cathy
suffers when Heathcliff disappears, she soon rallies enough to marry
Edgar and then to experience a goodly amount of domestic happiness.
It is only when Heathcliff returns that the star-crossed pair starts to take
the measure of what their bond portends, that they are fated to crash
upon those "eternal rocks beneath," to be wrecked by this collision. It is
as if each is now to grasp what, in fact, they contain—on the order of a
foreign body—inside themselves. For this reason I read Cathy's remarkable pages-long *meltdown* as the direct expression of her "bond-age."
Reason has zero purchase here, as we see when she bursts into rage at
hearing that Edgar is reading his books: *reading books?* Different ontolo-
gies are on show here. The printed page can indeed seem weightless and
obscene, when measured against the testimony and ravages of the heart,
and Cathy rightly sees Edgar's coolness as alien to her very core being.
But *Wuthering Heights* proposes, in its entirety, a much less sedate view
of what books are and do. They can take us beyond the human altogether. Not for nothing does Ellen tell us that the fierce embrace-before-
dying between Heathcliff and Cathy caused her to think they were of a
"different species." Yes.

For years I saw Cathy's violent emotional breakdown as evidence of
her specific psychological imbalance and emotional precariousness;
now I see it as the grisly consequence of her to-the-death fusion with
Heathcliff. Self is ruptured. Always has been. Not only can she have no
independent life, but the pathological eruption of pain and misery
writes large her contract with Heathcliff, as if there were some kind of
tidal wave or tsunami inside her, wrecking everything in its path,

exposing the fragility, indeed the mirage, of her former bounded contours. Her head wants to explode, her blood pulses with frenzy, her body mutinies: she is coming undone. The two children playing together on the heath sowed far more than they could have understood.

Heathcliff speaks the book's elemental logic when he indicts Cathy's marriage with Edgar as essentially a double-murder, a double-mutilation: his but also hers. She had no right, Heathcliff hisses, to form a union with someone else. And he's right. And she knows it. Cathy's spiraling descent is dramatic and quick: in short order, Heathcliff's return wrecks her life, because it lays bare their intrinsic inseparability, their reality as dyad, joined together, permanently unfree. That neither time nor death can separate them, is borne out by the entire suite of the novel, as the surviving Heathcliff carries out his dreadful pledge to Cathy: to live every single minute, every single day, with her living presence inside him, turned now into gall, demanding that he punish everyone in sight for this haunted state. Each of them is crippled, deformed, bonded; each experiences—one briefly, the other for a lifetime—the active, never dying, presence of the other inside. Each comes to know that "self" is a mirage, a fantasy; worse still: "self' is a cohabitation, a total loss of hegemony, a living out of the "other's" presence and injunctions. The Bible frequently refers to sexual congress as a form of "knowing"; the incessant hounding that characterizes Heathcliff—himself by Cathy, others by him—testifies to a grisly form of "knowing," a plural scheme that puts paid to any notion of individual contours or agency. Such *knowing* bursts the frame of individuation itself. Cathy dies of it; Heathcliff is demonized by it.

Readers have often felt there is nothing erotic in this book. They do not desire each other; they do not seek to possess each other. Au contraire, their devastating truth is that they are already possessed, they compose each other, they can never be quit of each other. Volition counts for nothing. All views of Heathcliff as empowered satanic protagonist (or gypsy or "colonized subject" or some other "othered" figure) seem credible enough but flawed nonetheless, for they overlook the fact that he is inhabited, that his most egregious and sadistic acts are a form of dealing with the imperious ghost who lives in him.

Perhaps the clearest measure of the book's awful view of *knowing* is to be found in the early, almost surreal annunciatory episode when Lockwood—fop par excellence, man least likely to fathom brute life at the Heights, man therefore standing as the (gentle, civilized) reader's own surrogate—has his encounter with the ghostly child who wants in. Here is where we encounter the devastating link between print and blood: Lockwood, at the Heights, has fallen asleep reading, but then hears a rapping at the window, with a hand reaching toward him; Lockwood proceeds to place the child's wrist directly onto the broken windowpane, and "rubbed it to and fro until the blood ran down and soaked the bedclothes; still it wailed, 'Let me in!' and maintained its tenacious gripe." The shocking violence in this image—I find it hard even to make my mind stay focused on it—tells us not so much about a monstrous Lockwood we don't know but about the nature of our contract with art. I'm not sure that we have a more perfect figure for literature itself as violent rending of flesh, as "call of the wild," as intercourse with ghosts, as rupture of self. Lockwood's own unpreparedness for this ghostly hand that will not release his own figures beautifully the liminal nature of art, with its requirement that we move past information and words into something else, more threatening, more rupturing, indeed more bent on taking over.

It is well known that Charlotte Brontë could not fathom how her unworldly sister Emily could have known the things she knew. Where could she have seen or learned them? There is no easy answer here. Yet the world of "Wuthering Heights"—as opposed to the more refined "Thrushfield Grange"—is a place of savagery, unremitting violence, and human bondage. Nothing in Freud's dark picture of the "id" comes close to matching the lawless vehemence that courses through this novel; the number of scenes devoted to kicking, biting, gouging, and beating is huge; the distinctions between animal and human start to blur. That we have construed it as an immortal love story is not surprising, given its gruesome proof that love is eternal; what is not stated, however, is that love is also lethal and omnivorous; that it cashiers any semblance of decorum, agency, or selfhood; that it opens the door to chaos and fury around the clock. The civilized ones in *Wuthering Heights*—Edgar,

Lockwood—come to us as benighted and naive, because Brontë's novel obliterates all polite categories of understanding: "Nellie, I *am* Heathcliff" is a curse worse than that of any oracle I know of.

And that is what we take away from this much loved book: *love* is bondage, glue, erasure, haunting, doom; *knowing the other*—forever posited as the grand triumph of love—is metamorphosis, transmogrification, death-of-who-we-are. The ramifications of this are enormous. My Gothic scenario makes it seem as if such bondage were merely one of love's dangers, but the truth goes the other way: metamorphosis may well be the hideous secret of (final) knowing, as if to say: for x to know y, x must become y. Written with such innocuous letters as x and y, my tidy phrase looks like a minor algebraic equation; but, when engraved in the heart, that same little phrase acquires awful power, for it redefines all "ultimate" knowledge as horror show. Put still more severely, the phrase asks the intolerable question: Is there any other way of knowing?

Wuthering Heights seems so laden with passion, violence, and haunting that we have to reorient our sights, to gauge the terrible things it tells us about knowing. No one would use the term "epistemological" to characterize its energies. Yet how else are we to understand its time-drenched panorama of enraged, hurting, helpless figures? Not just Cathy, Heathcliff, Isabella, and Edgar but, above all, the entire second generation of children (Catherine, Linton, Hareton), reap what has been sown, with the dreadful corollary that the sowing took place in the dark, was seen and experienced (only) as childhood idyl. Emily Brontë was no scientist, but this Gothic text has an almost "laboratory" feeling about it, as if an awful human experiment were being carried out.

Critics have often felt that the story of the children is less compelling than the fiery tale of the first generation is. But we are meant to see the inexorable work of time, the unfurling saga of cause and effect. Brontë's bookkeeping is as unforgiving and inflexible as Sophocles's is. Nothing is ever finished here. Yes, Cathy's agonizing meltdown writes large the novel's curse— "Nelly, I *am* Heathcliff"—but we come to understand that the toxins are longitudinal, as the poison works its will in the next generation, forcing us to see that *it's not over, it will never be over.* Nelly's final words, closing the novel and taking place in a churchyard, ask "how anyone could ever imagine unquiet slumbers, for the sleepers on that quiet earth." It is a sweet thought, but this book is remembered for its turbulence, its coercions, its monstrous view of love as wreckage.

Is self-eclipse the unmentionable price tag for *understanding* our world and ourselves. I have to believe that Oedipus and Lear would say, yes. So, too, as we shall see, do Melville, Kafka, and Faulkner.

Playing the Master, Playing the Slave: Melville's "Benito Cereno"

Melville's best work invariably centralizes the drama and the crisis of *knowing*. Not only is the famous Whale seen and assessed through radically different interpretive lenses, but the very concept of *whiteness* is investigated for its epistemological and perceptual horror. Likewise, the Bartleby mystery continues to haunt the barrister-narrator long after the Scrivener has died. But nowhere are these matters more freighted and far-reaching than in "Benito Cereno," based on the actual narrative written by the American sea captain Amasa Delano. In today's ideological climate, with its sensitivities toward colonialism, racial oppression, and prejudice, Melville's tale of the American who misread everything, who failed to see that a slave revolt had taken place onboard the Spanish vessel captained by Benito Cereno, risks looking embarrassingly transparent. My students assure me that they know, early on in this narrative, that the blacks have taken over the ship, that Babo is their ringleader, Cereno their puppet, and Delano their dupe. So they tell me.

Given that Melville wrote his story in 1855, it is not surprising that today's readers are "sighted" in ways that Amasa Delano was not. As Kierkegaard might have said, we know the *outcome*. In fact, Kierkegaard's representation of Abraham's trial—to obey God's injunction to sacrifice his son, then to find out that God nicely provided, at the last minute, a ram-to-be-sacrificed instead—has uncanny parallels with Melville's own deeper aims—namely, to oblige us to recover the "fear and trembling" that subtend both stories but that are lost once the two tales harden into *information*. In each case, the challenge consists in taking the full measure of the story's horror and affective truth.

What might be the horror that is hidden from view in "Benito Cereno"? Our narrator, Amasa Delano, would doubtless (initially) reply: the threat of being murdered by the weak yet wily Spaniard Benito Cereno whose loyal lieutenants are in hiding, waiting to pounce on the good American. As all readers know, this conviction serves to blind Delano: he demonizes the Spanish, and he pastoralizes the blacks, seeing them as versions of "Newfoundland dogs," seeing their women and babies in "Bambi-like" terms; the entire race is understood as created by God to be amiable and devoted servants for their white superiors. By entrusting the narrative to Delano, Melville not only crafts the most delicious whodunit of the nineteenth century but also exposes the sheer lunacy and outright danger of a peculiarly American form of *innocence*. Much ink has been properly spilled in unpacking the ideological ramifications of Delano's innocence (and arrogance), and, as said, his errors seem all too conspicuous, perhaps all too incredible, to today's readers.

Critics drawn to the question of race have of course focused more on Babo the black servant who postures sweet submission while actually masterminding the entire takeover plot. Figured suggestively as "serpent" in the late passage where he has leapt into the whaling boat, in hopes of murdering Cereno as final act of revolt, he has been termed the "snake in the garden" in nineteenth-century America's disastrously wrong version of Eden. And it is clearly Babo the cunning, Babo the actor, Babo the cruel, whom Cereno has in mind when he offers his gnomic response to the American sea captain at story's end, indicating the true cause of his descent toward death: *the Negro*. Not for nothing did Ralph Ellison cite those words as epigraph for *Invisible Man*, for it makes good sense to see the deceptive little servant as freedom fighter, as the unavowed hero of the story, even as the man of the future.

Ellison doubtless saw Babo also as "invisible man," as perfect image of right-minded Americans' utter blindness regarding blacks. And I believe Ellison had to be no less drawn to the baroque theatrics of "Benito Cereno," with its operatic displays of ritualized behavior, as seen most notably in the presentation of Atufal, the princely "captive" required to appear in chains, every so many hours, before Cereno, to ask forgiveness.

Delano is utterly puzzled by this symbolic display of power and submission, and so, too, are Melville's readers, if they ponder these events, even after they've understood the slave revolt. Why, it can be asked, would the blacks resort to such outré ceremonies? Why all the charades? But the French playwright Jean Genet would have had little trouble making sense of such histrionic moments, since he perfectly understood the power of ritual, especially the power of playacting. His own twentieth-century play *Les Nègres* is cued entirely to the shape-shifting power of such behavior, as if to say, Putting on make-believe chains is the first—and arguably best—step toward throwing them off.

What has all this to do with *knowing*? Is it possible that role-playing is intrinsically epistemological? After all, the slaves-in-revolt are not performance artists as such, nor are they exclusively bent on fooling the American sea captain. Rather, they are tasting a form of freedom that is irresistible. Earlier on, as we later learn, Babo had, once the blacks had taken over the ship, ordered Cereno to deliver him and his brethren to a "Negro country." The song and dance on the ship—and there is both song and dance—constitutes that Negro country. It is a boundless space created by virtuality, by make-believe, by *play*. Each of their countless gestures of submission—not merely the lavish pretended devotion of Babo toward his "master," Cereno, but the no less "saftig" behavior of Francesco as he ministers to the ailing Spanish captain with feigned tenderness and solicitude, and indeed *all* the actions of the blacks as they go through their pretense-motions as slaves—reveals a sublime psychic economy: the (visible) outward display of servitude and the (invisible) inner joy of control and power. Once we realize they are *acting*, we are in a position to understand that this is a priceless form of *action*, perhaps the only form of action that would be commensurate with the depredations they have long suffered. Their *show* is nothing less than their enactment of freedom itself, their coming to know what freedom might be. Fooling Delano pales in comparison with the giddy taste of liberty that their performance allows them to savor. They are *knowing*.

Can power be savored, tasted? Eaten? Yes. The boldest and most extreme move of "Benito Cereno" is its *cannibalism*. Cannibalism haunts Melville as far back as the early *Typee* account of life in the South Seas;

here would be the true Melvillean snake in the garden: savages ingesting human flesh. In "Benito Cereno" it has come full circle. On the prow of the taken-over boat, the blacks place the skeleton of the slave owner, Don Alexandro, friend of Cereno, murdered on board, now replacing the former figure of Christopher Columbus as the text's new shimmering icon of white power transformed by black power. The psychic displacements and exquisite revenge on show in this metamorphosis of Columbus into the skeleton of a slave owner antedate by more than a century and a half our contemporary campaigns against Columbus (and Woodrow Wilson and Confederate statues). Melville our contemporary?

How exactly Don Alexandro became the skeleton he now is, remains a subject of such horror that Cereno pledges to keep its secret to his dying day. He does. But we know what has to have happened: the slave owner's flesh was eaten. In classic cannibalistic logic, or indeed the logic of transferal and transubstantiation, the body of the former leader is ingested so that his potency might be transferred live to the one who consumes him. Once again: *knowing*. The slave *knows* power, in the final analysis, by ingesting it materially, corporeally, into his own body. There could be no more direct model than this.

The scale of Delano's misperceptions and the depths of Babo's machinations scream for commentary and help us understand why so much of the critical literature on this tale is taken up with these two characters. Relatively little discussion exists of Cereno himself, and I suspect that many readers wonder why Melville titled his story with the name of the Spanish captain. I now believe that his is the story, indeed the calvary, that Melville most wanted to tell and that he chose this convoluted narrative scheme to do so. If Delano is the innocent man of the story, what is to be said for—or by—the man who has drained the cup of "experience"?

Melville has to have chewed on this, as it were, and come to the decision that Cereno's *undoing* is to be conveyed indirectly, in muffled fashion, only to be understood by the reader after story's end. The proud Spanish sea captain's demise is aligned of course with the abdication of Charles V, itself an echoing figure of the dying Old World, conveyed by the text's persistent imagery of collapsing power structures. Contrary to

our likely assumption that Cereno's fate would be rhetorically diminished by being veiled, I believe the opposite is the case: Cereno performs exactly the textual moves needed for us to grasp the horror of his
situation. He *performs* the moves of power. He *plays* the Captain. I have
not hesitated to call his experience a "calvary" because he is obliged to
understand—through his very charade—that his own power (thought
to be timeless, essential, authorized by God and King as well as the laws
of the sea) is utterly histrionic, playable, indeed commandable. Hence
reversible.

Let me recall the exhortation I routinely give my students when they
read literature: *Try it on*. Well, Benito Cereno has done just that: he has
"inhabited" the slave-position for the only time in his life, and he has
come to understand the Dickinsonian model of knowing: power must
be lost before it can be understood. The power he thought his is not
merely that of one sea captain but that of an entire colonial world. All
of it is theater. (Lear saw something comparable.) Melville's economy
is so taut, so perfect, that it approaches the rigor of proverb: If the slave
playing the slave becomes, as it were, the captain, then the opposite is
no less true; the captain playing the captain becomes, as it were, the
slave. *As it were*: my phrase connotes an inner world no less teeming
with transformation than the so-called New World Columbus himself
stood for, before being replaced, on this boat, by a skeleton. Yes, Benito
Cereno, Spanish nobleman, finds himself the occupant of a new world:
he discovers his status as minion, as phantom, as text, as construct, as
maneuverable, as joke. This is hard medicine, and he will die of it.

Benito Cereno's entire world is being demolished . . . by his very actions, in front of our unknowing eyes, yet palpable, page by page, word
by diabolic word, in his every move and every utterance. This is what we
realize only *afterward*. If you ever take the time to reread this story, you
will be struck, on every page, by the horrible (but unsignaled) charade
carried out by Cereno. Yes, of course, they all play parts: Babo, Atufal, all
the Africans on the slave ship; but Cereno's is slow-motion suicide. And
that is what a second reading brings home. Reading lives.

(A book on rereading is badly needed, it seems to me, since everything looks suddenly different. Put differently: when is a book over?)

Babo and Francesco and Atufal and company were savoring power in each of their postures—this, too, you can't quite grasp first time around—but Cereno is tasting impotence and even desecration in each of his impostures. His long agony is an affair of disembowelment, for it seems fair to say that his own insides are being wrested from him, his own most sacred and sure convictions are being turned to tinsel, his entire being now transformed into marionette.

And one has to realize that Melville could have conveyed this horror in no other way. To argue, as I do, that this agonizing trajectory is one of increasing knowledge is to retrieve all concepts of "understanding" from the abstract cerebral zone where they are often lodged and to begin to gauge the outright violence that *knowing* entails. Benito Cereno comes to know that his life and beliefs and station have been a mirage, a set of props that can be undone, and this knowledge kills him. He also comes to know that blacks are not Newfoundland dogs at all, and that, too, kills him. "The Negro" is all he says to the uncomprehending Delano, but the reader might well spend a lifetime unpacking his utterance.

A personal reflection is in order. I first read "Benito Cereno" as college senior in 1961, and I know it was one of the catalysts that caused me to commit my life to the study and teaching of literature. I intuited—it would take decades for me to turn this intuition into the type of argument presented here—that the "uncommented" spectacle of Cereno coming undone signaled the dimensionality and reaches of literature itself. Melville's torturous procedure of indirection and getting it wrong became luminous to me as a kind of portal opening onto knowledge, my own knowledge as reader and sentient being, a knowledge I had to make rather than receive, a post-textual knowledge. I understood that I was extending Melville's own byzantine structure, turning its maze into my own exploratory space, mandating a return look at the words and gestures of the story, indeed a return voyage to the story, to espy the hidden crucifixion that was in plain view.

I had not then read Kierkegaard, but I now see Melville's strategy in the service of "fear and trembling," aimed at schooling the heart, by obliging us—in retrospect—to measure the lethal knowledge that a Spanish sea captain comes to when his boat is taken over and he is "minstrelized" by the slaves. These reflections—back then as wondering student-explorer, since then as professor mulling over the moves we make (and ask students to make) when we read literature—were to be for me a kind of Borgesian forking path, revealing the twists and turns that end up constituting knowing. They can take a lifetime, even if Melville's story is read in a few hours, even if the events depicted last little more than a few hours. What clock can measure Cereno's knowing? Or ours?

Knowledge in Kafka: Metamorphosis

Kafka's most famous story opens: "Als Gregor Samsa sich aus unruhigen Träumen erwachte, fand er sich zu einen ungeheuren Ungeziefer verwandelt" (As Gregor Samsa awoke from unruly dreams, he found himself transformed into a gigantic insect). What knowledge does a sane reader make of this? It is hard to see past the fantastic dimensions of this famous tale, and among its most arresting features is its sheer literalness: Gregor is not *like* a bug; he *is* a bug. After all, metaphor and simile are, in some sense, mind's games cued to subjectivity. Melville's Spanish captain became, *as it were*, a slave. Not so, here: nothing subjective in sight. Kafka goes out of his way to make sure we get it: we follow Gregor's awkward and unknowing moves as he tries, many times in the story, to gauge what his body has now become, how he might maneuver that same altered body off the bed (lots of little legs and hard-shelled belly), how he might turn the doorknob of his room (no hands, use teeth), how he might readjust his eating habits (old favorites no good, rotting food OK), how he feels strangely more comfortable under the sofa or on the ceiling than he does in the middle of the room, how his jaws snap at the sight of hot coffee, how huge and threatening his father's feet are, as he is forced back into his room, how his sister Grete's violin music speaks to his heart at story's end, seems to him to be somehow the nourishment his soul requires while his body is starving to death.

It is quite an education for Gregor, and for his reader too. We are made to occupy a subject position (gigantic insect) that I wager none of us ever dreamed of. Gregor finally dies and is cast out with the garbage. The informational payload here—unless you are a zoologist—is a mystery; what does it all mean? I am confident that every single one of Kafka's readers poses exactly that question; Gregor never does, not even once. (This, in itself, is amazing: has he no curiosity? No stake in remaining human? Why isn't he screaming?)

Gregor Samsa makes us realize how much we ordinarily depend on a story's characters to do our thinking for us. He refuses the ticket. I'd suggest that we, like Gregor, undergo a crash course on metamorphosis. I realize that sanity hinges on things remaining stable—I do not expect this computer I'm using to turn into a giant insect—but in fact life is indeed crammed with nonstop transformations, and I'm not thinking of caterpillars becoming butterflies. My advanced age has given me some lights on this: take a walk through hospital corridors or nursing homes, and you'll find altered bodies galore, thanks to the gradual work of disease and of time. In Kafka, it can look more like morphological terrorism.

Anything can happen here; and it will. Gregor's response is exemplary. Against this topsy-turvy, shape-shifting scheme, depicted with the calmness and accuracy of a census taker, we find the incessant pitter-patter of human reason, like a well-oiled machine spinning in the void, trotting out its small-bore questions, adjusting best it can to the changing givens, never once raising its voice or crying out for help or acknowledging the sheer horror of the situation, utterly upended and toothless, a cosmic joke of sorts. The tone is resolutely matter-of-fact. Altered into a giant bug, Gregor's gravest initial concern is: how to get to work.

The absence of affect—Kierkegaard's "fear and trembling" are nowhere to be found—within Kafka's monstrous texts yields something on the order of a palpable *disconnect* between event and interpretation. Kafka is never not reasonable, never not reasoning, but one feels that the mental chitchat has zero traction. One has measuring tools, but they get you nowhere. You are arrested one day, but you get ever further lost in trivia such as finding the courtroom or understanding the charge; you are about to take over decrepit dad's business, but he rises godlike from his sickbed and condemns you to death; you turn into a bug, but what matters is how to go about opening the door so as not to be late for the job; you are called on to evaluate an island's bizarre, even barbaric, penal system, but you remain distant and circumspect, posing few questions, content to observe; you make a medical house-call (via magic horses) to a young patient who turns out to have a gaping worm-filled hole in his side, but you mostly kvetch about doctors' working conditions.

In short, the world incessantly, grotesquely, outruns your ratiocinative powers, but you never stop ratiocinating. Kafka seems always to be showing us the abyss between life's monstrous events and reason's pitiable procedures. Common sense has no bite here. Nor does higher sense: Einstein is said to have been given this story by Thomas Mann when they were both at Princeton, and the man of science, after sampling it, replied: "I couldn't read it for its perversity. The human mind isn't complicated enough."

Einstein could not figure this out. Weinstein suggests that Kafka is examining a tragically recurrent theme in human history: *to exit the human.* Altered in the prime of life, Gregor ceases to be breadwinner, ceases to possess human form. Even though we never exactly "see" Gregor as insect—Kafka (a fine draftsman) pointedly refused textual illustrations for Gregor's new form—we can scarcely fail to see the inexorable physiological tenor of the story. Outfitted with a bug's body and its alien wants, weaned from his familiar furnishings, slowly starving for lack of acceptable nourishment, suffering from festering apple lodged in his flesh, locked out of shareable language, Gregor Samsa loses, page by page, his citizenship in the human family.

Few will forget the horrible scene when Gregor creeps out of his room and his mother and father finally *see* his monstrous shape, leading to a double crisis: (1) Father rises to the challenge of protecting his women by pelting the giant insect with apples, and (2) the giant insect-son finds how difficult it is to go in reverse gear, to make his agonizingly slow way back into his room/lair. Kafka obliges us to process all of this from Gregor's angle of vision, including the huge size of Father's feet as he closes in on the chase.

Hence, Grete's subsequent logical ultimatum to her parents—you must stop thinking that this is Gregor—has, awful though it is, its undeniable ocular truth. How could they think otherwise? Something quite fascinating about competing sources of knowledge is in play here: the testimony of our eyes versus the testimony of books. Consider how dependent we are on each of these conduits of knowing. Formal education tends to put the emphasis ever more insistently on the written word, but none of us exits (voluntarily) the visual regime we entered the moment we first opened our eyes.

The pathos of this story resides in the incompatibility between these two schemes. We the readers are alone privy to Gregor's thoughts, and for us the umbilical cord joining Gregor to the human community is never cut. (The importance of this cannot be overstated, for it points to why literature matters.) We the readers encounter, via Kafka's very prose, Gregor's thoughts and feelings: we learn of his plans to send Grete to the Conservatory, of his undying love for his family, because our own "locus" in the story, somewhat like the apple tossed by Father, is *inside* Gregor. This is exactly where you cannot be, in "real life," where you're always on the outside. What kind of knowing does each position yield?

The Samsa family actually *sees* his monstrous shape, whereas we merely *read* Kafka's words to describe it. But Gregor's thoughts, delivered to us with great pith, are as inaccessible to his family as the far side of the moon might be. (It doesn't help that his transmogrification has canceled out human speech; he can only make animal sounds.) The upshot of this presentation is that we (and only we; oh yes, and also the entire world readership of this canonical tale) become fellow travelers on the voyage out; via Gregor's report, we acquire firsthand knowledge of what it looks like and feels like to be cast out, to cease to be (recognized as) human.

Pseudo-speciation again, quite literally this time: one is forced to wonder just how many people on our planet have had, *as it were*, just this experience. Every war, every incident of ethnic cleansing, every virulent case of racial profiling, perhaps every instance of sexual or religious or tribal discrimination, toils in Kafka's vineyard. (As I write these lines, one encounters daily images of hundreds of thousands of refugees fleeing from failed states, trekking across Europe, encountering barbed wire, tear gas and hatred, regarded [it seems fair to say] as vermin. And, closer to home, every day in America seems to bring news of the potentially systemic abuse and neglect—cued to race, gender, and ethnicity; baked into the operations of justice, policing, work, and community—as particular groups experience being deprived of their humanity.) Kafka's brilliance in imagining—and then telling—this story of transmogrification confers with rare power a knowledge of what *othering* is, what it means, what it does.

The icing on the cake comes when we also recognize just how many metamorphoses are to be found in this tale. It closes with an image of the Samsa family on an outing—"free at last" of their monstrous son who, journey completed, has been swept up and away as garbage—enjoying a moment of carefree pleasure, as the parents, strengthened, review their future options, as Grete, the nubile one, stretches her young body, full of life's promise. This is as rigorous as a mathematical theorem: Gregor has exited—indeed, Gregor has died, been sacrificed—so that they might live. (A familiar fable, this.) What their memories of Gregor might be, we cannot know; what ours might be—knowing, as we do, of Gregor's own knowledge and humanity—are akin to dread, to fear and trembling.

Other Kafka texts enlist the same severe logic, but, if anything the stakes become broader and more resonant, moving from one bourgeois family (the Samsas) to our very institutions of law and medicine. And the metamorphoses reign ever more brazenly, dislocating and reconfiguring virtually everything on the page, removing all footing from readers seeking a perch.

"A Country Doctor" reads like a masquerade, a *carnival*, an explosion of moving parts. First, the hapless doctor witnesses strange figures coming out of his supposedly empty stable: a bestial groom who sinks his teeth into the maid, Rosa, and two magnificent horses that convey him to the patient's bedside with the speed of magic. And then, at the patient's bedside, we begin to wonder, how far has the doctor actually come? Has he left "there" (Rosa's impending rape by the groom)? Or has he brought "there" with him to "here," so that the figure of Rosa-being-raped is insidiously operative in his perception of the boy he's come to see? Worse still, nothing stays still. (Can you imagine this: a world where *nothing stays still*?)

Initially, the sick boy does not look sick. A moment later, noting the blood-drenched towel held by the boy's sister, the doctor revises his opinion and checks out the boy more thoroughly. He now observes (imagines?) a wound as big as the palm of his hand, located in the boy's side; very curious: when did this wound get there? Further inspection reveals the wound to be filled with little worms coming to the surface. Twice, the wound is described as "rose-red," and it is devilishly hard for the reader not to see Rosa herself, perhaps Rosa's targeted vagina, in the description of the boy, now regarded as not only sick but doomed by the "flower" that is blossoming in his side. How does one treat such a wound? The doctor doesn't really know, but the story does: he is disrobed and placed naked on the bed next to the boy.

Metamorphosis of every stripe. People and things jump out of their skin. Animals appear out of nowhere, both two- and four-footed. The wound appears out of nowhere. The sexual violation of Rosa refuses to stay put—who, by the way, is the animal-groom doing the raping? Could it be the doctor's "other" self at work? Why not? Everything is possible, after all, once bottoms fall out—and governs the description of the boy-with-a-hole. Finally, we are asked by this enigmatic, quasi-surreal story to interpret its final astonishing transformation: the doctor lies naked on the bed with his patient. Doctors have told me that this story is their worst nightmare, and indeed the entire tale appears to operate along oneiric lines, as nightmare, for it systematically humbles and humiliates doctors, mocking their white-gowned authority, moving them from place to place, defying their diagnostic powers, literally undressing them and bringing them to the level of a body on a bed. *A body on a bed.*

Is that not the ultimate metamorphosis of this story? The doctor's toolkit avails not, the doctor's analytic prowess is nil, the doctor himself is reduced to being a body on a bed. Kafka's tonality differs entirely from that of Shakespearean tragedy, but proud, mad Lear suffered through to a comparable wisdom regarding our elemental basic condition: poor forked animals. Shakespeare's play deconstructs power, treating us to a baroque spectacle of the strong devouring the weak; Kafka's story is also about power: the social and diagnostic authority of doctors, a power explicitly seen as "modern," as uprooting the older order of the Church: the Parson sits at home unraveling his vestments, whereas the doctor is expected to cure everything with his merciful surgeon's hands.

But this encounter with the sick child, finishing with disrobed, supine doctor, announces major trouble. And Kafka is yet again telling us that reason gets us nowhere when such dilemmas appear—the entire scientific-analytic project of medicine is on the line here—because perhaps the only way for a doctor to *know* his patient's sickness, it now appears, is to lie down naked on the bed next to him. No medical school on the planet would assent to Kafka's radical vision, but there is a very old logic, known to us and at home in Jesus's own beautiful practice as "doctor" healing the lepers and the sick, that doctors must become patients if they are to know and to heal. Remember, again, Dickinson: only the dying soldier understands victory; Kafka's doctor must relinquish all his trumps and be put in reverse gear—bye, bye, attainments, license, and degrees!—if he is to minister to the sick. The story annihilates the old pecking order. The cost of knowing requires no less.

Melville's captain "became" a slave; Kafka's doctor "becomes" the patient. The terrifying fluidity of metamorphosis and its penchant for shape-shifting rules from Kafka's opening page. From the moment the stable doors open, things are on the move: magic horses, Rosa's rape, worm-filled wound. The solidity of hard facts goes up in smoke, and flux rules. Doctoring runs amok. This is not the information highway, but it is a highway, a journey, nonetheless, with its inevitable components of fear and trembling. No wonder this tale seems nightmarish to doctors, for its news about a naked doc-on-a-bed must be the specter that haunts their worst fears. Nightmare: yes. Sublimely *egalitarian* also. That could be the worst nightmare of all.

Let me return, in closing, to Kafka's most "harrowing" fable of knowing as metamorphosis, "In the Penal Colony." As you may recall, I devoted several pages to this story earlier in the book, enlisting the "Machine" at its center as a scandalous model of *immediate writing*. "Es ist ein eigentümlicher Apparat" (It is a remarkable machine) is how the story opens, and we are made to understand the oracular import of those words, given that the Machine is conceived as instrument not only of punishment but also of knowledge. The prisoner, naked, with gag in his mouth to prevent vomiting, lies strapped in, en route to the trip of his life, a twelve-hour-long procedure whereby his "crime" will be *written* by the Machine's needles onto, and into, his flesh, ever deeper, along with the assortment of aesthetic curlicues to frame and spiff up the final design. It is a Writing Machine.

Is this not how Kafka defined literature itself, as ax for chopping the frozen sea inside us? All the potential gore and violation hidden inside this "edgy" definition come to visibility in this tale which emphasizes, over and over, how thick-skinned and uncomprehending most of us are. The Prisoner is presented in insistently animal terms, the Officer and the Explorer converse in French, the very project of communication starts to appear as obstacle course, as doomed. A new linguistics seems needed: a material, cutting one that penetrates and delivers its payload.

But everything in the story announces failed communication. The Explorer is a modern figure: cautious, distant, objective, critical, self-enclosed. The very technique of the story emphasizes, in familiar Kafka style, incompatibility, disconnection, words that never reach their recipient, what the Germans wisely call "aneinandervorbeireden." Lots of verbiage on the part of the Officer, but the Explorer is never reached. It is vintage Kafka: verbal ping-pong, but no bridge to the other, no sighting of meaning. As I have repeatedly claimed, such ping-pong is probably the human race's most common verbal sport: exchanging words, but not meanings.

It will doubtless sound loopy, but I see the elements of a love story here, despite its carnage and torture. We need to see the vehemence, urgency, and stakes of the Officer's pleading: the entire validity of the Machine lies in its translation of language into experiential truth, and therefore the Officer's desperate efforts to convert the Explorer, to make him understand the virtue of the System, are the final gauge of its viability. The Officer fails; the Explorer, man of reason and caution, is not converted. But he does pronounce judgment: he does not approve of what he sees, and he will not support the use of the Machine. He rejects the Officer. Unaccented though it is, this breakdown is climactic, for it constitutes an indictment of the entire proceedings.

The Officer sees this with tragic clarity. He frees the Prisoner. There is only one appropriate step left for him to take, and he takes it. It is to be his logical, signature exit, and he is to do it right. He himself lies down inside the Machine, straps himself in, and turns it on. The captain will go down with the ship. But the Machine malfunctions: it utterly butchers, chews up, the Officer. Looking at his face and mangled corpse, the Explorer can find no sign of the promised grace. An era is over.

The Machine, designed to mete out and embody justice, appears to fail catastrophically. Yet there is a kind of justice being delivered here. But we can only see it if we invoke, yet again, "metamorphosis" as the key to Kafka's world. The Officer has *entered* the Machine and has thereby *become* the Prisoner. The same austere logic that governed "A Country Doctor" is at work here as well. The word bridge, the oral ping-pong, fails. And we then understand: it has never ever occurred to the Officer that the only way to understand the Machine—to understand its enactment of truth or justice or knowledge—is to *enter* it, to place oneself naked onto the Bed, so as to be initiated into it. To be sure, his dead face reveals no enlightenment. Yet his gesture is luminous, for it displays the actual cost and character of knowing, in Kafka: via metamorphosis.

I have termed this story "severe" and "austere." I do so because it utterly rejects the gentler forms of cognition that we are accustomed to. Reading, thinking, talking: these are civilization's wise prescription for understanding; they constitute culture's figurative entry into the other, a virtual form of "penetration" that can be achieved without bloodletting or abuse. This revered idealist model of human reasoning and exchange is "safe," but Kafka seems to say, Yes, it is safe, but it leads nowhere. So, how does one reach the other?

"Empathy," which would bring "fellow feeling" into the equation, which has loomed large in my remarks throughout this study, has no presence or traction whatsoever in Kafka's scheme. Knowing, in Kafka, is, instead, far more radical, indeed far more annihilating than that. It posits, by dint of the despotic structural pattern that we see here and in "A Country Doctor," that we do not understand the other until we become the other. It therefore entails wreckage, because that which is annihilated is of course our former self. That has always been the flip side of metamorphosis.

Most of us look around, and we see no machines of the sort Kafka has devised. In some respects, this tale seems both Gothic—Sade's spirit lurks here—and maniacally high-tech as well. As Haruki Murakami puts it in his recent novel, *Kafka on the Shore*, "What Kafka does is give a purely mechanical explanation of that complex machine in the story, as a sort of substitute for explaining the situation we're in." It is worth mentioning that Murakami, doubtless taking his cue from Hannah Arendt, does not hesitate to hint at a parallel between tech-focus in Kafka's story and the heinous tech-focus that stamped Heinrich Himmler's designs and Adolf Eichmann's work toward exterminating the Jews. Think cyanide showers, rather than cutting beak. The language speculation matters, but it also pales, when we reflect on the political stakes of this fable.

And that is where I want to put my final emphasis. The penal arrangements in this story point to operations of state power that reach beyond the fate of one distressed family on whom a transmogrified son has been billeted. We're talking about executions. If "Ein Landarzt" exposes the hubris of doctoring, "In der Strafkoloni" tackles the questions of justice, law, and truth. And it dares to say that the Empowered—call them Officers or Commandants or Presidents or Führers—are weirdly *innocent* until the moment when they, too, are placed naked in the Machine, to receive the work of justice. It had certainly never occurred to this enthusiastic, huffing-and-puffing Machine-salesman Officer (who has opined breezily and mightily about deciphering the Script) that there might actually be a *view* from that supine victim-slot. There, and only there, does understanding happen. The Officer must "become" the Prisoner.

Becoming the other: Shakespeare's Lear, Brontë's storm-crossed couple, Melville's Cereno, each has made the trip and become undone. This is the cost of knowing, and the law of metamorphosis brings it about. The face of the butchered Officer displays, admittedly, no hint of grace or clarification, but perhaps our sights should be elsewhere: on the knowledge thereby generated within the mind and heart of the ultimate final figure on the receiving end, always the last in literature's chain of command: the reader.

Faulkner: Four Boys on Two Horses

From the beginning of his career, William Faulkner seems to have known that "knowing" might be lethal. Donald McMahon, shell-shocked protagonist of his first novel, *Soldier's Pay*, is an exemplary figure of what experience (in this case, experience of World War I) does to you: it *undoes* you. Many of Hemingway's young men are similar—think the emasculated Jake Barnes or the mysteriously damaged Nick Adams of "Big Two-hearted River"—but Faulkner occupies a place unto himself as writer who has understood *trauma* to be the very hallmark of genuine perception. Hence, Benjy Compson, the idiot-brother in *The Sound and the Fury*, bereft of language itself, wrecked by the loss of his sister Caddy, living in the mausoleum of his memories of her love (triggered endlessly by daily events), is exemplary. He shows us that existence at "ground zero" is, in some awful way, our common vulnerability, our birthright; as the text says, Benjy is the story's "natural," its poor forked animal stranded forever on a heath.

In other Faulknerian texts, the sadistic premises of knowing—of forcing others to know—loom large, as in schoolteacher Addie Bundren's remarkable pedagogy, which I again quote: "I would look forward to the times when they faulted, so I could whip them. When the switch fell I could feel it on my flesh; when it welted and ridged it was my blood that ran, and I would think with each blow of the switch: now you are aware of me! Now I am something in your secret and selfish life, who have marked your blood with my own for ever and ever." As I've indicated elsewhere, everything about this vicious passage amazes: its view of teaching as brutal and invasive entry into others, its near-to-hand view that this model stands for the writer's dream of a language so powerful and coercive that it will enter into the bloodstream of its readers, its conviction that such acts of violence are rapturous two-way streets, fusing together hitter and hit, teacher and student, writer and reader.

Less overt but no less crucial is the "coming-to-know" drama enacted by Byron Bunch, the forgettable little man in *Light in August* who has been chosen by Faulkner for the Joseph role in this version of the Holy

Story. Good-hearted Byron falls for the pregnant Lena Grove the very moment he meets her, but not even her swollen belly quite convinces him she's had sexual relations with another man; yet when he sees her, late in the novel, lying on the bed with the baby, something cracks inside him, gets through to him, etches in his heart the flesh-and-blood seminal presence of Lucas Burch (the baby's progenitor), triggering his tragicomic pursuit of the fleeing Lucas Burch, which will end with Bunch bloodied as a result. But Joseph he becomes. Bunch becomes, as it were, Burch. (B-u-n-c-h becomes B-u-r-c-h. That is the easy part: just a touch of your finger on the keyboard.)

The hard part is the making of knowledge. Faulkner brilliantly writes Byron's discovery of Burch's presence in the woman he loves as a version of the word becoming flesh: *"Why, I didn't even believe until now that he was so. It was like me, and her, and all the other folks that I had to get mixed up in it, were just a lot of words that never even stood for anything, were not even us, while all the time what was us was going on and going on without even missing the lack of words. Yes. It aint until now that I ever believed that he is Lucas Burch. That there ever was a Lucas Burch."* Faulkner is letting the cat out of the bag in this sequence, as indeed he did in the passage where Addie speaks of whipping her students, displaying his full awareness that the world we traffic and truck in every day—including the people we communicate with in it—can be a ghostly regime of dead letters, a weightless nominal scheme that has nothing to do with the immediacy of experience or the heft of knowledge or the possibility for one person to reach another.

It is an unnerving perception. This is not modernist self-coddling about the dubious status of the sign but something more savage, pedestrian, and bleak. The bad news announced here has to do with us, with ordinary people, who strut and fret their whole lives long in their word charades, while actually sensing (now and then) how utterly thin and dimensionless it all often is. Faulkner's baroque novels seem at the antipodes of Kafka's flat style, yet they share a common (tragic) perception that we are unreal to one another. The reasons for this are legion: verbal mediation, ideology, race, gender, historical distance, garden-variety sluggishness, and narcissism. "Get real!" our common cliché has it.

Many of our strongest books are devoted to the fireworks and trauma and outright eclipse involved when this actually happens. It frequently has to do with the most revolutionary move of all: trying it on.

Absalom, Absalom! is Faulkner's grandest novel, and it is his supreme account of the effort needed—perhaps the suicidal effort needed—to grasp the fuller humanity of the other. Suicidal, because the entire white Southern culture (whose poet and imaginative historian Faulkner is) hinged upon denying such "reality" to the black people in its midst. One might expect a novel with these tidings to have a sermonlike punch, but that is not the case. *Absalom, Absalom!* fascinates, because in it Faulkner links this central moral challenge—Are black people (recognized as) fully human in the South?—to an entire array of other ultimacies which, when seen right, are deeply epistemological in character: What do we know of the Past? How do we make knowledge of others? Does the language bridge that carries the talk of the living and the remains of the dead ever actually succeed?

The huge ethical payload (which might, in a different writer, have been presented front and center) of this novel is arrived at—felt—only via a series of investigations about what can be known. Is there a right path to knowing? Put more drastically, Is there a path that leads to the needed miracle: words becoming flesh? Such an absolute query underlies not only the bread-and-butter work of every novelist but also the basic premises of anyone opening up a book and reading its pages. Why else write stories? Why else read them? For that matter, why speak?

No surprise then that *Absalom, Absalom!* initially appears conjectural, stamped by uncertainty, by guesswork, by the impossibility of knowing. We start with young Quentin Compson in Jefferson, Mississippi, just prior to beginning college at Harvard—a stint that will end in suicide, as all readers of *The Sound and the Fury* already know—summoned to listen to the tirade of one Rosa Coldfield (depicted as mummy in a mausoleum) as she thunders forth about the central but mysterious bogeyman of the novel, Thomas Sutpen, one-time plantation owner with dynastic aims, who came to a bad end, and took everyone he knew with him, it seems. Rosa Coldfield blasts Quentin with evocations of the demonic Sutpen: man from nowhere, with a band of "wild niggers," sprung upon the town without warning, wresting a huge spread, Sutpen's Hundred, out of the wilderness, and fated to wreck her family (by marrying her sister) and then herself (by proposing marriage-preceded-by-insemination-to-produce-a-male-heir).

Mind you, it takes pages and pages (many of them late in the novel) to learn quite this much about Sutpen, but Rosa's bile has the clarity and preserving power of formaldehyde. Yet even Rosa is missing key information: *what is Sutpen's past?* and *why was there a murder at the gate of Sutpen's Hundred?* The murdered: Charles Bon, of New Orleans, engaged to be married to Sutpen's daughter Judith; the murderer: Henry Sutpen, son of Thomas, who had helped bring about the engagement by bringing his college friend (Charles Bon) home to the plantation, to meet the family, especially to meet Judith. In fact, the bond between Henry and Charles was so strong that it seemed even to resist the emerging ban on the marriage put forth by the father (who had done a little homework): Henry defied his father, renounced his birthright, went off to war with his comrade, spent four years fighting, returned with his friend to the plantation, and murdered him. Why?

Why? Why the ban? Why the murder? Why the plantation? Indeed: why the Civil War (which is the bristling backdrop for this entire family saga)? This bloated novel is cursed by that question—why? why?—and it should make us uncomfortable, for it signals the pedestrian unseemly little fact that most of us know absolutely nothing about most of the people we know and not much more than that about the people we think we know best. Faulkner does his level best to retain the provisional conjectural status of these matters. In this he differs entirely from traditional writing, which goes about positing its little truths and facts without concern or fanfare. (And we don't even think, "much obliged" or "how do you know?," so natural it all seems.) Here, everything is iffy. We're told here that the servants were the basis for the story of Henry's repudiation of his father in 1861, but it came through as a tale without particulars, as guesswork, as gossip. Likewise, Quentin's initial "audience" with Rosa is equally filled with *lacunae*, especially regarding ultimacies: *either Sutpen destroyed his children or his children destroyed Sutpen.* Which is it, Quentin (and we) wonder?

The first half of the novel is largely made up of Rosa Coldfield's feverish, sometimes apocalyptic memories, complemented by the urbane,
reflective, and balanced storytelling carried out by Mr. Compson (son
of Grandfather Compson, who was the closest thing to friend that Sutpen
had, also father/informant of Quentin soon to go [and then to die] at
Harvard). Gradually emerge the portraits of Thomas Sutpen. If Rosa
offers us a hellish djinni figure who laid waste to her family, Mr. Compson plays the sleuth in a more genial fashion, mulling over the jagged
events of the known tale, trying to figure out why these people did what
they did. He does yeoman's work in giving density and interest to these
faraway shades: through his musings, we get a better grasp of Sutpen
establishing his estate, of Sutpen courting Ellen Coldfield in order to
gain respectability and sire children, of Sutpen building his extravagant
mansion and fortune by dint of sheer willpower allied to ruthless tactics
and brutal resolve. Mr. Compson is also the painter who evokes the
Sutpen family in its mid-nineteenth-century Southern aura: Ellen the
doomed butterfly wife who never had a clue, the sensitive boy Henry,
and the tougher girl Judith—each destined to carry forth the all-
important family line, the seductive visitor Charles Bon, invited to Sutpen's Hundred to light the fuse that would eventually blow everything
up, obliging us to ponder parallels between this family explosion and
the larger national one triggered by Fort Sumter. Again: why? why?

Here, too, Mr. Compson does not disappoint: he sketches for us, on
the family front, the resonant, quasi-erotic friendship between Henry
and Charles: Henry as the angular, innocent, impassioned, Mississippi
Protestant country boy; Charles as the sensual, sophisticated, jaded,
fatalistic, seductive Catholic New Orleans companion. Mr. Compson
goes further still: he muses that Henry's involvement in the engagement
between his sister Judith and his friend Charles is libidinally super-
charged, for it packages together his own incestuous longings for his
sister and his even less avowable homoerotic yearning for Charles in
such perfect fashion that their coupling will also constitute, by dint of
projection and phantasm, his own sublimated congress with the two
figures he loves most, in ways he can never divulge or even acknowledge. When one thinks back to the much simpler erotic arrangements

of *The Sound and the Fury*, one realizes the distance Faulkner has traveled from the earlier text, especially in the murky, bottomless arena of sexual desire and the prodigious displacements it engenders.

We readers get our fill with Mr. Compson: he knows there was an obstacle that prevented the marriage and brought about the murder, and he deduces that Charles was already "married," to a woman in New Orleans of dark skin, via morganatic (hence, legally nonbinding) ceremony; *this*, he realizes, is what Thomas Sutpen must have discovered, and this is why the marriage was forbidden (no matter the legalisms). Well, why not? Won't this do? His pages of narrative sleuthing are wonderful reading, brimming with curiosity, judgment, and generosity. You'd want him to tell your story.

I have wanted to salute the narrative labor of Faulkner's wise and empathizing Mr. Compson (so different from the jaded "same" figure of *The Sound and the Fury* some seven years earlier), in order to return to my basic contention: we know nothing (ultimately) about our fellows. For that is the conclusion that Mr. Compson, the guy who has done most to convert these shadows into people, to make sense of the murder at the gate, nonetheless arrives at:

> It's just incredible. It just does not explain. Or perhaps that's it: they don't explain and we are not supposed to know. We have a few old mouth-to-mouth tales; we exhume from old trunks and boxes and drawers letters without salutation or signature, in which men and women who once lived and breathed are now merely initials or nicknames out of some now incomprehensible affection which sound to us like Sanskrit or Chocktaw; we see dimly people, the people in whose living blood and seed we ourselves lay dormant and waiting, in this shadowy attenuation of time possessing now heroic proportions, performing their acts of simple passion and simple violence, impervious to time and inexplicable—Yes, Judith, Bon, Henry, Sutpen: all of them. They are there, yet something is missing; they are like a chemical formula exhumed along with the letters from that forgotten chest, carefully, the paper old and faded and falling to pieces, the writing faded, almost indecipherable, yet meaningful,

familiar in shape and sense, the name and presence of volatile and sentient forces; you bring them together in the proportions called for, but nothing happens; you re-read, tedious and intent, poring, making sure that you have forgotten nothing, made no miscalculation; you bring them together again and again nothing happens: just the words, the symbols, the shapes themselves, shadowy inscrutable and serene, against the turgid backdrop of a horrible and bloody mischancing of human affairs.

My blood tingles each time I reread this passage—I am certain I've read it at least a hundred times—yet I fear I will somehow wear it out, like the faded fragile old paper it references (even though I'm typing this on a computer), and I wonder: How can Faulkner have gotten it so perfectly? How can he have managed to put into one bravado passage so much wisdom about the impossible challenges embedded in both history and literature, in the very operation of language itself, in the elemental yet profound need to bring dead words to life? For this passage looks straight at the lingual abyss of our kind—the few words that remain of the dead, whether scratched on a tomb or written with Yankee stove polish on French vellum or found today in our temperature-controlled archives or flowing incessantly in cyberspace on electric currents waiting only that we log on and tune in or in the books we assign and read at university or even in the "living" words we throw (or threw) at each other our whole life long—and dares to say: dead, dead, dead.

Initially this passage looks to be a broadside against the very project of history, both private and public. Faulkner published *Absalom, Absalom!* in 1936, the same year Margaret Mitchell published *Gone with the Wind,* and her rendition of Scarlet O'Hara and Rhett Butler and company does indeed write large their "acts of simple passion and simple violence, impervious to time." But this magic trick—the staple ever-reliable seduction of romance itself—fails when it comes to Faulkner's Judith, Bon, Henry, and Sutpen. Even given all the help Faulkner has furnished his narrators with—Rosa's firsthand experience, Mr. Compson's brilliant speculations, the gossip of the servants and the ragtag tales still living in the community—it doesn't fly, their inner lives and motives remain guesswork. We have documents, but no life. Is this not the shipwrecked condition of all of us, when it comes to understanding either the past or indeed others in general? You can't get there from here.

Mouth-to-mouth tales, letters from boxes and drawers—the very sources of so much of our historical knowledge of the past—are as incomprehensible as Sanskrit or Choctaw. But watch carefully as Faulkner switches gears, introduces a crucial scientific metaphor into his archival setting: along with the letters found in that forgotten chest, there is a *chemical formula*; it, too, is old, faded, coming apart, yet still readable, seen to possess some life-giving elixir if its instructions are perfectly followed. They are followed. Nothing happens. They are followed again. Again nothing happens. "You bring them together in the proportions called for," Faulkner twice writes, but the enterprise nonetheless goes nowhere. All you have are "the words, the symbols, the shapes themselves." What is wrong? Why this semiotic failure?

Absalom, Absalom! hinges on this failure. Faulkner's terms are loaded and resonant far beyond what we can initially make out. Do archival notations simply line up, one next to the other? Are chemical formulas a valid entry into the past, a valid way of producing meaning? Do you arrive at knowledge by bringing things together in the proportions called for? Will *data* build the bridge (between words and meaning) that you need? Will life come of this? What makes one person murder another?

Faulkner's baroque confection enlists a passel of narrators trying to get to the bottom of this riddle. The initial focus is rightly on Thomas Sutpen, but he remains crucially opaque, despite his dynastic energies and exploits. Mr. Compson comes up with a remarkable term for characterizing Sutpen: *innocence*. "Innocence," Faulkner implies, was responsible for both the grandeur and the fall. (Fall he does: Sutpen's Hundred falls into ruin and burns down by book's end; Sutpen himself is murdered after inseminating his hired hand's granddaughter.) Here is how Sutpen's innocence is defined: "that innocence that believed that the ingredients of morality were like the ingredients of pie or cake and once you had measured them and balanced them and mixed them and put them into the oven it was all finished and nothing but pie or cake could come out." There can be no doubt that this homily about the ingredients of pie or cake is meant to recall Mr. Compson's earlier remarks about that "chemical formula" (for understanding the past), which required "bringing things together in the proportions called for." As you recall, that model did not do well.

Sutpen's "innocence" can be understood as an *instrumental* picture of reality, a rational program consisting of specific empirical measures, cued to what I've been calling *information*. Why call this "innocence"? Because the mechanistic, quantifying approach to life is grievously flawed. Because there is no evident metric for gauging human feeling, and it is human feeling that explains human behavior, including a murder at a gate. Sutpen is fatally deficient, fatally innocent, in just this way: he instrumentalizes his fellows—Ellen, Rosa, his children—for the sake of his "Design," but he is blind to what drives them or hurts them. It is thanks to the third set of narrators, Quentin Compson and his Canadian roommate Shreve, that we slowly come to understand Sutpen's tragic flaw. There is nothing abstract or abstruse here. They invoke a reality-principle quite alien to Sutpen's thinking; Shreve, thinking back to Rosa Coldfield's "pickling" rage, defines it like this: "What was it the old dame, the aunt Rosa told you about how there are some things that just have to be whether they are or not, have to be a damn sight more than some other things that maybe are and it dont matter a damn whether they are or not."

Here would be Faulkner's credo about final truths: some things just have to be, whether they are or not. I've come to believe that this rustic assertion exemplifies, in razor-sharp fashion, the crucial divide between science and humanities. Proofs have no purchase here; the heart adjudicates, however embarrassing this may be on rational grounds. No historian would ever validate such a model of truth-finding, but Faulkner posits this as his credo. Kierkegaard, were he alive in 1936, would have understood.

Thus, Quentin and Shreve revisit this gory saga of the past, and they are on the lookout for what "had to be." Thus, Quentin and Shreve construct a story of overwhelming human need. Their Thomas Sutpen is a man whose dynastic dream derives from a profound childhood injury: going (as child from Virginia hill country newly arrived in Mississippi) to the front door of the Big House, being told to go around to the back, to never come to the front door again. That's all. Sounds simple, but it isn't. Boy-Sutpen encounters the dehumanizing power of class, and he registers in his person its toxin: it reduces him to nothing. The Design—Sutpen's Hundred—is born of this wound. So, too, is his innocence: to achieve his own big house with servants, he learns to marshal his forces and to instrumentalize all those within his reach. Just ingredients for pie or cake. Just a question of measuring them right and bringing them together in the proportions called for.

Quentin and Shreve also construct their version of Charles Bon. They determine that he is Sutpen's son from a first marriage. And they figure out what "had to be" for him. It was recognition. From his father. Their Charles Bon went to Sutpen's Hundred desperate to see (and be seen by) the man who made him. Sutpen and Bon, father and son, are "brought together in the proportions called for." Charles Bon "saw face to face the man who might be his father, and nothing happened—no shock, no hot communicated flesh that speech would have been too slow even to impede—nothing."

The symmetry here is worthy of Sophocles. Thomas Sutpen's childhood injury of nonrecognition—spawning his Design—is destined to be replayed at the expense of another child seeking recognition: his own. And being denied it: by himself, the father. Yet, even here, the question haunts: why would a father deny his son? There are no records, no data, for explaining this. Quentin and Shreve have to invent their answer, their version of "what had to be." Please note the crucial pronoun: *they*. The two boys in the cold Harvard dorm room *create together* the missing links that would make human sense of a murder at the gate forty-six years earlier, and Faulkner's term for their epic joint imagining is: *overpass to love*. Sounds mushy. But it's not; it's arduous, and it must go *beyond* the known into the unknown: "all that had gone before just so much that had to be overpassed and none else present to overpass it but them, as someone always has to rake the leaves up before you can have the bonfire." This creative heat requires labor, and its results would never pass muster in a laboratory or a courtroom, but they are the truth standard in this novel, the place you must go, to understand: "in order to overpass to love, where there might be paradox and inconsistency but nothing fault nor false."

What can it mean to say that love is the path to knowledge? Faulkner seems to be saying that love is the only creative, projective force that can boost you into the minds and hearts of those you seek to understand. The corollary: if you cannot find or make your way that far—and it is far—you remain locked out. Or, as Mr. Compson said, "It just does not explain." Why Henry and Charles left Sutpen's Hundred in 1861, repudiating Thomas's allegation; why Henry and Charles returned in 1864, for Henry to kill Charles: how do you get there? The metaphor chosen by Faulkner to express the interpretive voyage undertaken by Quentin and Shreve, the overpass, the fusion, is just what it should be: the two youths in Mississippi in 1861 ride away on two horses, and the two youths in a Harvard dormitory of 1910 ride with them: *four boys on two horses.* This is the most beautiful figure for understanding that I have ever encountered.

But Faulkner's wording puts us on notice that this can never be easy, that it may not be survivable: "not the two of them riding the two horses through the iron darkness and that not mattering either: what faces and what names they called themselves and were called by so long as the blood coursed—the blood, the immortal brief recent intransient blood which could hold honor above slothy unregret and love above fat and easy shame." This passage, too, I have read a hundred times, and I am still not certain I fully understand it. Honor and love come across as the supreme impetus for the envisioned waterway of flowing blood that carries you beyond yourself and into the other. "Blood," so often referenced as sign of class, ethnicity, and race, as the signal, often murderous divide between humans, is prized here as current, flow, generic arterial system that contains and binds all of us over time and space. But there is a price to be paid, and it is potentially lethal: you must exit yourself to become the other. Hence, Quentin and Shreve must slough off their faces and names if they are to enter the past and ride on the same two horses as Henry and Charles. They do.

Their fusion with the two boys of the past opens onto a scene filled with Rebel and Yankee soldiers in Carolina in 1864—utterly imagined by the boys in the dormitory—in which Colonel Thomas Sutpen sends for his son Henry and explains to him that Charles cannot marry Judith. Henry replies that he knows Charles is his brother, but no matter. Sutpen then plays his trump card (which we've waited hundreds of pages to see): the marriage cannot take place because Charles's mother (Sutpen's first wife) is part black. The scene then depicts Henry making his way back to Charles, trying *now* to prevent him from going back to Sutpen's Hundred to reclaim his bride, begging him ("You are my brother"), and thereby prompting Charles's final reply, a reply that contains the explanatory venom of an entire culture: "No I'm not. I'm the nigger that's going to sleep with your sister."

Faulkner wrote these words in 1936; they are imagined by two boys in 1910 as they seek to understand a murder that happened in 1864. I write these lines close to a century after *Absalom, Absalom!* was published, and I write with the ever-increasing knowledge that this story makes less and less sense to the young students who come my way. In their multicultural world of the twenty-first century, at least within the liberal university community where I live, Mr. Compson's phrase "It just doesn't explain" is probably how they also see it (and Faulkner's world and possibly me, as well): or, indeed, as "worse than Ben Hur," as Shreve sardonically put it earlier, when sizing up the South for the benefit of his Mississippi roommate.

But I come from Tennessee, which is Faulkner country, and my memories of growing up in Memphis in the 1940s and 1950s—pre–civil rights—bear out Faulkner's dark view that a drop of (putative) black blood was enough in 1864, 1910, and 1936 (and later still) to cancel you out as fully human, indeed to be adequate grounds for murder. And, more to the point, I look around today, at the tribalized world outside my university boundaries, sometimes on foreign shores, sometimes nearby, where terrorists and suicide bombers and other assorted fighters seem to me to be remarkably alive and well, defending or avenging ethnic identity and notions of "blood" on a nonstop basis, and I think, Has it really changed since Faulkner's time?

And I reflect on today's Black Lives Matter movement, which grew out of America's long nightmare of systemic racism, and I ask, Have we gotten any better at granting full human status to people who are said to be "different"? The murder at the gate in *Absalom, Absalom!* stands not only as Faulkner's supreme emblem of a fratricidal war that pitted brother against brother in the 1860s but as a dark model for the blood-letting that seems routinely to stamp humankind. How are we to *understand* such events? Perhaps the only way to do so is to mount those faraway horses ourselves (even if we do not ride) so as to go beyond "data" by thrusting ourselves *inside*, if we are to grasp why "it had to happen."

This overpass can also kill. I believe it kills Quentin Compson, who knows himself to be inhabited by ghosts (just as his creator was). To become four boys on two horses, a price must be paid, and that price is the identity and the contours of who you are, yourself. Quentin and Shreve have sloughed off the names and faces they called themselves and were called by. Faulkner says all too cunningly and seductively, "It did not matter." Can you slough off name and face? Can it not matter? Can you survive it? Faulkner asks precisely the questions this entire study has been wrestling with: What kind of knowledge does the imagination arrive at? Can empathy at its most extreme—pushed to the point of metamorphosis if such were possible (four boys on two horses)—kill you?

I also realize why I always felt uncomfortable with Faulkner's metaphor of "overpass to love." *Overpass*—connoting in my mind the "boosting" power that lifts spacecraft out of the earth's orbit and launches them further on, as Richard Branson and Elon Musk and others want to bring about tomorrow—nonetheless also conjures up highways and concrete, the realia of Interstate 95 rather than transcendence and identification. And then it came to me: what if we reverse it, if we call it *Passover* instead? Faulkner's text signals its Old Testament links everywhere, including in the title; and now we arrive at the bleakest reading of all: *becoming another* is allied with the Angel of Death. And all Faulkner readers know, indeed, that the Quentin Compson of this novel of 1936 is a dead man, because he was the tortured protagonist of *The Sound and the Fury* of 1929, and he committed suicide. Faulkner has exhumed him for the later book, but he is a doomed man. Doomed, here, by an umbilical cord that never stops choking him.

So many of the examples given in this entire study are dire, suggesting that the path to knowing may well be a form of hara-kiri. Above all, sloughing off name and face in order to become another is a severe, perhaps lethal way of understanding, bidding to erase the knower. But at least it does honor to the arduous challenge of moving past "outcomes" and "data," so as to glimpse the turmoil of heart and mind—the fear and trembling—that *knowing* requires.

Cathy Earnshaw dies. Cereno dies. Kafka's Officer dies. And Quentin Compson is dead on arrival, overpass or not. One could claim that Brontë, Melville, Kafka, and Faulkner are pessimistic merchants of gloom and doom and that happier endings are also possible and real. But these books are as they are because they are intent on illuminating the possible death sentence entailed by becoming someone else: *Nelly, I am Heathcliff*; the Captain becoming the Slave; the Doctor becoming the Patient; the Officer becoming the Prisoner. My list seems to be one of individuals, but it is no less about what it might take to see the work of history and culture, to see the air we breathe and the structures, institutions, and ideological formations that we inhabit and that inhabit us. And we are left with the astonishing, chilling, mind-and-body-wrenching possibility that there is no other way to understand the other, as well as its even more toxic counterpart: there is possibly no other way to understand power. That is what these books have to teach us.

But no reader has—to my knowledge—ever died in negotiating these stories. Quite the contrary, these narratives, by dint of their imaginative vistas, invite us to go to places that are found on no map. We go, and—unlike the protagonists—we can return. Art is precious because it enables us to be fellow travelers, to become the fifth rider on the two horses.

Knowing Slavery: Toni Morrison's *Beloved*

I want to close this suite of essays highlighting "the cost of knowing" with an account of the greatest novel we have on slavery: Morrison's *Beloved*. That claim is, I believe, overdue.

Overdue, because Morrison's story, published in 1987, set in post–Civil War Cincinnati, is shockingly of our present, race-riven moment, not only in American society but far beyond our borders, in other cultures with their own racial divisions and nightmares. We are now ready to read it (anew) and to gauge its true portents. The Black Lives Matter movement has, as we know, jostled—even exploded—the thinking of people in all parts of the world about matters of race and justice, thanks in part to the horrific suite of black deaths in America at the hands of the police. George Floyd's final nine minutes and twenty-nine seconds of life, with a policeman's knee on his neck, was the spark that lit the tinderbox, as countless people witnessed on TV screens and iPhones across the globe. Many people saw, some perhaps for the first time, what our awful phrase "business as usual" sometimes means. That agonizingly long period of time during which Floyd died signals, in some impossible-to-track but real way, a four-centuries-long oppression of black lives. Morrison's novel takes that dark measure, makes those connections.

Business as usual is what *Beloved* indelibly renders, but it is not the business or routines most readers have ever read about. Morrison writes, as no one else ever has, what *slavery felt like*. And she thereby provides the necessary complement to Faulkner's *Absalom, Absalom!*, with its beautiful view of the "overpass to love" as the only route toward understanding the racial givens of nineteenth-century (white) Southern thinking. Faulkner, in his intricate novel of delayed disclosures, plumbs right to the bottom of Civil War America's white racial fears by showing that the discovery of "black blood" expelled you from the white human family, so that Henry Sutpen's plea, "you are my brother," to his half-black half brother, Charles Bon, to renounce marrying his sister Judith is met with Bon's tragic rejoinder: "No, I'm not. I'm the nigger that's going to sleep with your sister." The two white, Harvard college roommates, Quentin and Shreve, realize, in 1910, that the threat of miscegenation caused the fratricidal murder, with the unmistakable corollary that the bloodletting of 1861–65, was cued to the same taboo, resulting in fratricide yet again, now nationwide in its scope. They see this in 1910. Faulkner published the book in 1936. What do we in the twenty-first century see?

My students, as I've said, are often stupefied today by the dark logic on show in Faulkner's book. Miscegenation is a word that many of them have never heard, and when one explains it, they are incredulous. This, they think, is behind them. Are they right? The folks marching in Charlottesville in 2018 expressed a rather different view.

Let me now ask, How much does it matter? Does our understanding of neo-Nazis and white supremacists actually illuminate the fuller legacy of slavery? Of course, interracial sexual relations will seem transgressive to the racist imagination. But how far does that get us? *Toni Morrison essentially turns William Faulkner inside out.* Not only does she write about the black women's lives that were simply beyond his imaginative reach, but she helps us see that the entire white problematic has perhaps preoccupied white writers and critics all too long and all too much. What about the black experience? Some critics have noted that Morrison's novels don't much care about white folks' issues and phobias. Her sights are elsewhere. In *Beloved* she shows us how "unknowing" white readers are—and have always been—about black experience itself. Her writing delivers this experience—an epochal story beginning, as more people now realize, actually in 1619, if not even earlier, and still going strong—in shattering ways that do honor to the project of literature itself.

It is no accident that Morrison dedicates *Beloved* to "*Sixty Million and more.*" Many Americans know the figure "six million," the shorthand notation that represents the Nazi effort to exterminate the Jews of Europe. "Sixty Million and more" signals a different kind of holocaust, greater in scale by a magnitude of ten, taking place over centuries, ever since slaves arrived on American shores. The general estimate of how many enslaved people were brought to North America is roughly about twelve million. The only feasible explanation for Morrison's figure must be that "sixty million" has to mean: not only those who died in the Middle Passage or in the historical period of sanctioned slavery but also the many generations of those who were born later, who inherited and continued the legacy. How could you *write* what that means, has meant, and continues to mean?

This is why Morrison focuses as much on *outcomes* as on abuses. I italicize the term because, taking my cues from Kierkegaard, I have earlier argued that our customary—and reductive—grasp of history itself is cued to outcomes, to numbers, to an "informational" scheme that has little purchase on human sentience, on the human price tag that slavery, war, or other forms of violence carry with them *over time*. I've tried to challenge the authority of outcomes and data, at least in the shorthand form by which we know them, by touting literature as unique form of knowledge and truth.

But is it possible we actually do *not* know the outcomes in and of life? When would you take your measures, if you tried to gauge such matters? Even—especially—horrors can perhaps only be fully understood later. Later, when we can see the still living, still "going strong" damage and legacy. When do we finally *know*? Isn't it possible that Paul was talking about outcomes in 1 Corinthians 13:12: "Now we see through a glass darkly, but then face to face." Then. What would the face to face with slavery look like when we come to "then"?

Here is how Morrison, in 1987, writing of post–Civil War America, tells us what Paul D has seen during his travels:

> During, before and after the War he had seen Negroes so stunned, or hungry, or tired or bereft it was a wonder they recalled or said anything. Who, like him, had hidden in caves and fought owls for food; who, like him, stole from pigs; who, like him, slept in trees in the day and walked by night; who, like him, had buried themselves in slop and jumped in wells to avoid regulators, raiders, paterollers, veterans, hill men, posses and merrymakers. Once he met a Negro about fourteen years old who lived in the woods and said he couldn't remember living anywhere else. He saw a witless colored woman jailed and hanged for stealing ducks she believed were her own babies.

It is a tour de force passage. It registers what business as usual was like (before, during, and after the war) for black people. It depicts what they had to do to stay alive. *And it closes with what those experiences did to them*: a boy's mind being utterly erased, a woman jailed and hanged because she stole ducks she thought were her babies. This is the landscape of *Beloved*. Who among us lives—has lived—like this? Ever since Freud, we have been told of the damage done by personal trauma, and there is some awareness in America and elsewhere of PTSD as the

inevitable residue of war and violence, displaying the grisly human afterlife of events from long ago. But, as I write these words, American
society is confronting what *systemic* racism is, does, and has done. *Has
done*: even the term "systemic" (or "structural") says little about the heinous work of time, the undying nature of such injury, the very rationale
of *ghosts*.

Paul D's evocation matters here because its list of horrors bids to reconceive much that I've written in this book. All of the big terms at issue
in the other writers I've discussed—justice, love, empathy, equality,
even "becoming" the other—seem quaint, perhaps abstract, academic,
and elitist here. These people are *undone*. They are the walking wounded.
They are amnesiac. They are the atrocious, blood-soaked materials of
which history is made.

Repression. Both Sethe and Paul D have a past that cannot be pro-
cessed or even faced. Much of Morrison's narrative genius is devoted to
keeping this material initially, partially, under wraps, in the dark: for the
outright mental survival of her two protagonists, and as shrewd, required narrative formula for her readers. (This is not a new scheme:
Oedipus's life is keyed to it, but that dilemma is "informational," whereas
here we're dealing with sanity's requirements, for Sethe *knows*.) Great
writerly cunning is needed to pull this off. Consider this early reflection
of Paul D's: "After Alfred he had shut down a generous portion of his
head, operating on the part that helped him walk, eat, sleep, sing. If he
could do those things—with a little work and a little sex thrown in—he
asked for no more, for more required him to dwell on Halle's face and
Sixo laughing. To recall trembling in a box built into the ground" (41).

The reader must negotiate Morrison's words, without yet "knowing"
fully what they represent or signal, so let me "translate" them into their
actual payload: Alfred, Georgia, will later be shown as the place where
Paul D worked on a chain gang, lived in a cage, and faced sexual brutal-
izing, as his body acquired an unmasterable permanent trembling; later
we'll learn that Halle (Sethe's husband, Paul D's friend) went mad, slath-
ered his face with butter, when he witnessed two white boys on top of
his pregnant wife, sucking her breast milk; Sixo was the group's rebel-
philosopher, the one who challenged Schoolteacher's measures, the

laughing one burned alive and hanged. Paul D keeps, with all his might, these "materials" "in that tobacco tin buried in his chest where a red heart used to be. Its lid rusted shut." What might the cumulative *weight* of these burdens be? When the reader first encounters Paul's shorthand list, these are just words; by novel's end, they have acquired an unbearable density and potency: not just toxic but explosive, in ways no reader could have known at the outset. But, later, "then"? Reading lives. Our knowing builds.

As for Sethe, the withheld "information" is even more toxic, taboo, and lethal: she murdered her baby girl, Beloved. (Will it do to call this "withheld information"? The very term embarrasses.) The entire novel circles around this "concealed crime," giving us bits and pieces of it— Sethe did a stint in jail, Sethe's two sons eventually fled the home, the murder had happened when Schoolteacher and the sheriff appeared in Ohio to recapture the escaped slaves—Sethe and her children—and take them back to Sweet Home "where they belonged." This "material" is what is hidden, what lives in her, what is torturing her, what wants out, and will out. Hidden from the reader; repressed by the character. Morrison needs us to understand what would make you butcher your own child.

And butchery comes in many forms in this text. Listen to Paul D measure who he is, in the slavery economy, and keep butchery in mind as he examines the parts he is made of: "The dollar value of his weight, his strength, his brain, his penis, and his future" (226). This is what merchandizing human flesh comes down to: a market value for each item. Marx would have understood. Except this is not a worker's labor but a person's body and soul. Soul and body. And it is Baby Suggs who offers the fullest, most lyrical tribute to the human body's sanctity and integrity in an ownership scheme that steals, instrumentalizes and, yes, butchers it:

> "Here," she said, "in this place, we flesh; flesh that weeps, laughs; flesh that dances on bare feet in grass. Love it. Love it hard. Yonder they do not love your flesh. They despise it. They don't love your eyes; they just as soon pick em out. No more do they love the skin on your

back. Yonder they flay it. And O my people they do not love your hands. Those they only use, tie, bind, chop off and leave empty. Love your hands! Love them. Raise them up and kiss them. Touch others with them, pat them together, stroke them on your face 'cause they don't love that either. *You* got to love it, *you!* This is flesh I'm talking about here. Flesh that needs to be loved. Feet that need to rest and dance; backs that need support; shoulders that need arms, strong arms I'm telling you. And O my people, out yonder, hear me, they do not love your neck unnoosed and straight. So love your neck; put a hand on it, grace it, stroke it and hold it up. And all your inside parts they'd just as soon slop for hogs, you got to love them. The dark, dark liver—love it, love it, and the beat and beating heart, love that too. More than eyes or feet. More than lungs that have yet to draw free air. More than your life-holding womb and your life-giving private parts, hear me now, love your heart. For this is the prize."

This anthem to flesh, this anatomy lesson, is signature Morrison. Her theme is bodies: first and last estate, granted at birth, stolen by slavery. Further, she writes closer to the body than any writer I've ever seen, showing us up close our various precious parts (the mass of tissue and organ and blood that is/should be you) as well as the systemic theft and violence they are subject to. In so doing, in writing slavery as bodily hijacking, she makes us aware of how desiccated even the most fervent political discourse is. Her writing exposes, by way of contrast, the huge welter of abstractions—what we find in our statistics, our books, indeed our histories—that we all too easily mistake for reality. My students tell me they need time-outs when reading *Beloved*, so they can put the book (just a book, just pages of print) down, so crushing it is, as it calculatedly, unstoppably, delivers its payload of pain and abuse. Morrison's "technique" recalls for me Kierkegaard's "fear and trembling," the emotional dread he sought to restore to the Abraham–Isaac story so that it would finally be understood. And for good reason, for it is the same story: what can it mean to kill your own child?

This novel performs a mind-boggling feat: it "liberates" slavery from the discourse of politics and economy and ideology, of concepts and words, so as to present it in all its awful violations and its never-ending impact. Morrison's injured people are the walking wounded, I said; to stay alive, they "elect"—nothing volitional is meant here—willed amnesia, their system shuts down, since the past is too unbearable to negotiate or come to terms with. This is what they've become; this is their outcome.

Yet it is very possible that no one reading these paragraphs will entirely recognize the novel I am discussing. From the very opening lines—"124 was spiteful. Full of a baby's venom."—*Beloved* is anything but dazed; it pulsates with life and energy and feeling. This is because life fights back. Keeping lids on works until it stops working. The repressed returns: not just because novelists invariably fill in the blanks as they go but because eventually truths do out, must out. As readers, we all know countless mystery stories that proceed along these lines, as the pieces finally fall into place. That's how literature works, from Sophocles to Dickens and Faulkner. Life does too.

What readers do not expect is ghosts. And even less do they expect baby ghosts. We could not be further from some Gothic scheme of spectral figures emerging from shadows. This ghost is *palpable*, and it's been terrorizing 124 for some time: it has earlier led to the flight of Sethe's two boys, and we see it go into action big-time at Paul D's arrival, causing the floorboards to shake and the house itself to pitch. Later in the novel (but earlier in time) when the runaway white girl, Amy Denver, encounters the runaway black girl, Sethe (chokecherry tree on her back, bloody knees, sour milk oozing out of her breasts, baby-on-the-way), we read what may be its most profound lines: "Then she did the magic: lifted Sethe's feet and legs until she cried salt tears. 'It's gonna hurt now,' said Amy. 'Anything dead coming back to life hurts'" (35). This is about more than legs and feet.

It takes perhaps a second reading, perhaps a whole lifetime, to grasp what is so beautiful and awful and all-encompassing in this claim: the dead come back to life, and it hurts. The dead baby, murdered by its mother, is not dead; the hideous materials locked inside Paul D's tobacco-tin heart will out. How to reckon with a still living past, not merely Sethe's and Paul D's but all the buried bodies and wounds and sores, the entire horrible legacy that began (in America) in 1619, seemed to reach apotheosis in 1861–65, and continues into our own time, well beyond 1987, when Morrison's book appeared, perceivable still, marking us still, still demanding to be accounted for. Perhaps we are only now waking up, as James Joyce's Stephen Dedalus put it, to the nightmare of history.

Beloved follows these familiar narrative and psychological laws and injunctions: to bring to light, slowly, incrementally, the occulted horrors of the past. Other great novels play by this rule. But then *Beloved* goes a massive step further: it overcomes all laws of logic and flesh by returning the now grown dead child to its mother. A baby ghost is already strange; a ghost that grows up is off the charts. It is one thing to set in motion a return-to-the-past, to show us its terrible wounds, with as much eventual immediacy (the immediacy of delayed disclosure, of dream, of memory, of psychosis) as possible. But it is quite another to offer us the physical return of the dead one, with her own terrible news, to the mother who killed her yet recovers her. This last piece has still further echoes of what Kierkegaard could conceptualize but not write: how Isaac could be at once murdered (by command) and restored (by command). Morrison has done that. And guess what: the dead daughter returns, not out of some heavenly directive or divine fiat, but because she has a human job to do: to put the pieces back together, to take the lid off, to remember what is repressed, to re-member what has been dismembered. I know of nothing else like this in literature.

Morrison has sometimes been linked to the "school" of magic realism, and we know she came from a family of storytellers interested in folklore and ghosts, but the project here has little in common with, say, Garcia Marquez's *One Hundred Years of Solitude*. Yet, when I read on page 60, a fifth of the way into the novel, "A fully dressed woman walked out of the water," I am jolted, and I think, say, of the wily metaphysician Borges, master of games and ghosts, keen to delineate alternate realities. Even that won't wash. This isn't about magic at all. "Here, in this place, we flesh," Baby Suggs said, and Beloved is just that: new skin, eyelids too heavy, hands soft, head too heavy for her neck, scar on her neck, body wanting to mutiny, appendages to drop off, legs to become unattached. This is the *pieced apart human subject*. Her mission is to piece together.

"Piecing together" conjures perhaps all the wrong things: thread, glue, putting the puzzle bits together. No such static model for Morrison: it is all *fluid*. I know no other novel so composed of water, urine, milk, and blood. Reading *Beloved*, you remember—you understand—that your body is 60 percent water, that the earth is 71 percent covered by water. This has consequences. Morrison helps us see what an *umbilical* world—the one that each of us inhabited before birth, the one that perhaps seems severed and gone once we've exited our mother's body—might look like. A fully dressed woman has walked out of the water. Here is what happens on the next page, when Sethe first sees her:

> And for some reason she could not immediately account for, the moment she got close enough to see the face, Sethe's bladder filled to capacity. She said, "Oh, excuse me," and ran around to the back of 124. Not since she was a baby girl, being cared for by the eight-year-old girl who pointed out her mother to her, had she had an emergency that unmanageable. She never made the outhouse. Right in front of its door she had to lift her skirts, and the water she voided was endless. Like a horse, she thought, No, more like flooding the boat when Denver was born. So much water, Amy said, "Hold on, Lu. You going to sink us, you keep that up." But there was no stopping water breaking from a breaking womb and there was no stopping now.

Morrison's words, in a bodily liquid register you'd never find in a philosophy text, do the work of this novel's returnee: to re-member. Proust had located the return of the past in the taste of a madeleine pastry; Morrison situates it in the bladder. Umbilical: the flowing urine cargoes, memory-wise—for Sethe, then for us—both the dead mother and the emerging baby, reestablishing the mother–daughter continuum as life's indestructible truth-principle and continuum, despite hangings, murder, and our stubborn belief in individuation as our given shape. This passage shows it's not.

Men, too, belong to the fluid world. Once Beloved is installed in 124—stunning Sethe with memories that only the murdered child could have had, pushing Sethe ever further into retrieval of her past, of the old (African) mother tongue she once understood—Paul D also comes under her sway, her gravitational pull. He is moved. From the shared bed with Sethe, then to Baby Suggs's room, finally to the store-room. Storeroom, indeed. Like a guided missile, Beloved is en route to him, comes to him, bent on re-membering what has been severed: "'You have to touch me. On the inside part. And you have to call me my name.'" He tries to send her away, reminds her (and himself) that this is sexual betrayal, but for naught. Morrison writes it like this:

> "Beloved." He said it but she did not go. She moved closer with a footfall he didn't hear and he didn't hear the whisper that the flakes of rust made either as they fell away from the seams of his tobacco tin. So when the lid gave he didn't know it. What he knew was that when he reached the inside part he was saying, "Red heart. Red heart," over and over again. Softly and then so loud it woke Denver, then Paul D himself. "Red heart. Red heart. Red heart."

Sexual fidelity and conventional morality are sent packing in this beautiful but audacious scene, as Morrison continues to restore full circulation and blood flow to her story of slavery, so that the pieced apart objects of the system become subjects, come together, achieve utterance, acquire their own name.

But sexual union pales in comparison with the still bolder, more profoundly boundary-smashing union at the very core of the novel, at the origin of the ghost plot, buried inside Sethe as originary creatural act—birth's opposite number, birth's secret double—namely, the murder of her baby. Murder as union? Murder as birth? One remembers the fate of Sixo: caught by Schoolteacher, tied to a tree, set on fire (his feet cooking, his trousers smoking), yet *laughing,* as he sounds his victory: Seven-O! Seven-O! referencing the baby he's seeded in the Thirty-Mile Woman.

Paul D will finally get the story. As will we. Morrison has wanted to prepare her readers before "delivering" in the fullness of reading-time—not entirely unlike pregnancy, for reading lives—this primal event, an event "known" to everyone in the book *except* Paul D . . . and, yes, the reader. I've already suggested that our detective-story term "withheld information" is obscenely reductive when representing the actual nature of the heart's hidden toxins and wounds, and that is why I put quotation marks around "known" in my sentence. Indeed, much of this book you're reading consists of putting quotation marks around the informational data we have always taken for reality, and no book illustrates my argument so perfectly as *Beloved* does. We are to *know* slavery. We are to achieve a knowledge that goes beyond that of names and concepts, beyond the reach of lists and categories such as those employed by Schoolteacher (and by schoolteachers throughout the world). Toni Morrison has a different lesson plan.

It's about going through the veil, going to the other side (of logic, of life as we know it, of the rules that govern what we've forever been taught of living and dying). No empty tomb in sight, but there will be an ascension into the heavens, this time with the help of birds:

> Simple: she was squatting in the garden and when she saw them coming and recognized schoolteacher's hat, she heard wings. Little hummingbirds stuck their needle beaks right through her headcloth into her hair and beat their wings. And if she thought anything, it was No. No. Nono. Nonono. Simple. She just flew. Collected every bit of life she had made, all the parts of her that were precious and fine and beautiful, and carried, pushed, dragged them through the veil, out, away, over there where no one could hurt them. Over there. Outside this place, where they would be safe. And the hummingbird wings beat on.

Sethe knew that "she could never explain." Yet I feel that we see in her words—about what she saw, heard, felt, and did—what slavery is. It is a system of bondage that makes death, even the killing of one's children, preferable to being sent back. This murder is to be lifesaving, life-preserving. We see Sethe exit, in her mind and via her act, the material realm we call reality. The hummingbirds, with their invasive needle beaks, enter and alter the players: "Simple. She just flew." What we're seeing is that love creates an alternate world, a new set of givens, and at its most desperate and intense and engendering, that alternate world is the only world. Love's law trumps death's. A timeless age-old sacrament comes into view, rules. The mother–child bond is unbreakable, either by slavery or death/murder, despite our rational certainty that this can't be true. And reality must follow its dictates.

Paul D, firmly planted on the ground, can make no sense of this. "You've got two feet, Sethe, not four." At which point "a forest sprang up between them." Nature again intervenes. Morrison has been tagged a "magic realist," I said. If pressed—we are pressed—most of us would interpret her conviction of saving her children, of sending them through the veil to the other side, as the language of faith and miracle, the kind of thing allied with religion or fantasy or madness.

Yet the truth is otherwise, simpler (as she said). What shimmers in her story of hummingbird wings and flying away is the sentient, productive elemental truth of slavery itself: its horror is such that it generates a rival creation, making apparent infanticide into actual salvation, when it comes to mother-love. "Apparent" and "actual" no longer stand for much, in any realist sense, but every reader of the novel not only knows what is meant but, in some sense, endorses it. And this is because the novel is on her side, has been from the outset. First the baby ghost, then Beloved returns.

Yet Toni Morrison is no escapist or fantasist. Remember Baby Suggs's anthem to flesh. Morrison's rendition of bodies, limbs, organs, milk, blood, and urine is about as far from "otherworldly" as you can get. She never loses sight of the force of gravity or the primacy of flesh. Baby Suggs has an aching back, and Sethe has a chokecherry tree etched in hers. Galileo's and James Joyce's truth-principle of thirty-two feet per second per second—the law of falling bodies—hasn't lost its sway. Morrison knows the tug, but also the vulnerability, of flesh. Putting a saw to your baby smacks of permanency. Death is no mirage. Since the beginning of time, we've honored, as well as obeyed, that truth. How can Morrison maintain her balancing act?

Yes, Beloved herself seems miraculous, but the text has hints of her origins that have nothing to do with Sethe: we hear several instances of black children being locked up, even for years, in white men's cellars. Here would be the (secular) detective thread of the book: a putative case of mistaken identity. The author's sights go further still, however, toward a far darker picture of mistaken identity: *"You've got the wrong person."* For that is, tragically, where this book is, and has been, headed from the start: not because of realism's puny requirements but because slavery's wounds can't be healed. And you show that best by trotting out a would-be reversal. What is unbearable about this novel is that it plays its miracle card and then dares to ask, "What, then?" Miracles, it turns out, cheat in more ways than one. The novel puts its returnee into the haunted house, kicks out, initially, the uncomprehending male, then goes about expulsing even Denver, so as to stage the real terror: the dreadful commerce between a mother-who-killed-to-save and a daughter-who-died-and-came-back. *Maldonne*, the French say, when a hand is misdealt. The grieving mother and the lost daughter yield utter cacophony. Each is maimed; neither can be helped.

Denver leaves because she is witness to a monstrous transformation: Sethe shrinking, Beloved growing, a parturition gone wrong, a child devouring its mother. We're reminded of the insect and animal worlds with their iron laws. But worst of all is the sheer pain of apologies and recriminations that go unanswered, that have no answer. Sethe seeks to explain to Beloved how much she loved her and, yet/therefore killed her—I hope you see how grotesque my term "explain" is, how the gap between words and deeds is unpassable—because "her plan was always that they would all be together on the other side, forever," while Beloved offers her own threnody of abandonment, of dead men lying on top of her, of "ghosts without skin" who "stuck their fingers in her," of being abandoned, of having her face stolen. These stories don't match up. And even if they did, understanding and healing are a fantasy, inconceivable. Could there ever be what we lamely call "reconciliation"? I murdered you, but it was for your own good? Could anyone speak or hear these lines? This is what the author has signed on for. This is the dreadful underbelly of fairy tales. No magic realism here.

Morrison enters into each of the damaged people of 124, and she digs directly into the pit. Reading these pages makes you realize you only thought you knew the extent—the ongoing, still playing, virulence—of slavery's wounds in this novel of infanticide. It's a 24/7 fact. So, Denver speaks of having her head cut off by her mother every night, but done ever so carefully so as not to hurt. Reread my sentence. Do we even have words for such a fear? We begin to understand why Howard and Buglar left, why living with mother-the-murderess is itself a death-row sentence, an in-house dread, a threat you can't live with. Begging Beloved to realize how much she loved her, Sethe speaks of making it over, herself, to where her own dead "ma'am" is, praises Beloved herself as a "good girl" who came back, which is what she too would have been and done, if mother hadn't been hanged first. Hanged first. Murdered. The generational mother-daughter consort would still be intact, if only, if only . . .

And Beloved offers the densest, most irreparable testimony of all: her dirge focuses on dead men lying on her, on crouching, on men without skin, on the woman with the circle around her neck, a woman whose face she wants, of her own face being taken away. She speaks of storms, of people being pushed through and going in, of chewing and swallowing, of seeing "her face which is mine," of seeing herself swim away, of being alone, of wanting the join, of a hot thing. None of this is alignable with the murdered-but-returned baby girl, or in some sense, with Sethe herself, even though it closes with the fateful conviction that Sethe's face is the one she lost. What story is this?

Many critics have seen in Beloved's testimony a far older story of how slavery came to America: a story of the Middle Passage with its list of horrors and abuses, of bodies thrown into the sea, of faraway and long-ago origins. And, inevitably, the fluids themselves tell a story, not only of the sea but of the womb, of the liquid home where life begins. Hence, the most capacious reading of Morrison's novel suggests that Beloved is "somehow" at once the dead baby returned, *and* all the lost children, all the desecrated human cargo and pieced apart families that went into the very practice of transatlantic slavery, starting as far back as 1619. A "realist" reading and a "mythic" reading.

The "realist" reading, Morrison has told us, derives from the newspaper clipping the author had read about Margaret Garner, a young mother who escaped slavery and killed one of her children rather than letting it be returned to their "owners." This "source" is real, but Morrison found it "confining," and her larger project, she said, was to create a fuller, even if "repellant" landscape, the landscape of slavery itself, which mandated pitching a tent "in a cemetery inhabited by highly vocal ghosts."

I have earlier referenced the key moment in Ibsen's *Ghosts*, when Mrs. Alving realizes the ghostly dimensionality of newspapers, for she now sees that the ghosts running between the lines are found all over the country: "They lie as thick as grains of sand. And we're all so horribly afraid of the light." Morrison's novel aligns with Ibsen's visionary play. It's not the dark we're afraid of, but the light. Light wakes us up. Light reveals what is actually there in the dark, has perhaps always been there. Morrison's *Beloved* wakes us up. It tells us that our newspapers (and history books) are not the staid, docile texts they appear to be: they are crawling with ghosts, as thick as grains of sand. Knowing slavery means: understanding its toxic hold and reach in America, knowing what it did, as far back as 1619, and what its continued half-life still does today. The woman who walked out of the water bears news of Sethe's dead baby returned, and of the Middle Passage that was the engine of the Atlantic slave trade. We are meant to know their joint costs. We're meant to know that they're not over.

To make us know slavery, Morrison has enlisted the most severe metric known to humankind: death. Virtually everything, we say to ourselves, is malleable, reprisable, rethinkable, except death. It is the end stop. The wall. One exits this novel, knowing that for Sethe the mother—hearing hummingbirds, but far from crazed—the ultimate truth becomes clear: even death is preferable to slavery; and this knowledge is actionable, since the mother who grasps it proceeds to kill one child and to try to kill another. Yes, this drastic act seems to readers, for a while, to be undone, for the dead baby returns as a young woman, proving that Mother was proven right, that the child was indeed saved, taken to the "other side." But Toni Morrison is made of sterner stuff, and the closing portions of the novel take measures such as I've never encountered in literature: the murder cannot be made good, the mother seeking her lost child and the child seeking her lost mother are not only mismatched, but the losses themselves admit of no healing. Sethe's act and the Middle Passage are not alterable, fixable. The damage does not cease, it does not die. But it must be known, to become our knowing.

It is the fuller picture that contains the greatest horror, for it extends into today. Ghosts tell us that the past lives; some of us may smile and dismiss such claims as Gothic and unreal. But the very term "systemic racism" is a wake-up call, for it urges us to think more longitudinally about our history, and to realize that 1619 illuminates today with a light that many are, as Ibsen claimed long ago, horribly afraid of. Morrison's novel shows us the ghosts that live between the lines of our newspapers and archives. Morrison's term "rememory" tells us that Sweet Home and its terrors do not disappear or fade away. The chokecherry tree in Sethe's back "grows still."

Nonetheless 1619 is but a number; "systemic racism" is but a concept; they belong in history books.

Literature knows these things in a different way. The contoured abstract realm of facts and data yields to a regime of fluids: water, urine, milk, blood. The Middle Passage of caged Africans sent across the Atlantic merges here into the liquids of the body, for it is the body that is the supreme currency of slavery. It is also the elemental, precious, despotic truth of life, as we experience it from birth to death. Yet you'd never know that by reading books. Most of our books seem written by the ilk of Schoolteacher, with his lists and categories. I include books of literature here, which so often give us a mind's view of reality. But there is another view. We can glimpse it in this account of the brief period of freedom that Sethe experienced on the other side:

> Sethe had had twenty-eight days—the travel of one whole moon—of unslaved life. From the pure clear stream of spit that the little girl dribbled into her face to her oily blood was twenty-eight days. Days of healing, ease and real-talk. Days of company: knowing the names of forty, fifty other Negroes, their views, habits; where they had been and what done; of feeling their fun and sorrow along with her own, which made it better. One taught her the alphabet; another a stitch. All taught her how it felt to wake up at dawn and *decide* what to do with the day . . . Bit by bit, at 124 and in the Clearing, along with the others, she had claimed herself.

This may be the most utopian, even if doomed, moment of the novel, for it depicts a community of capable women practicing their arts and living together in freedom. This luminous notation is cued entirely to a female logic as old as the species, a logic that counts out events by monthly cycles in connection with the moon and the womb, a logic that finds its purest expression in the creatural flow of mothers and children. Could any male have written this? Women's periods and Schoolteacher's periods have nothing in common.

Epistemology is an abstract Latinate term most at home in the academy. But *knowing* is, as Morrison shows over and over, preeminently visceral, sentient, of-and-in-the-body. Let me invoke as contrast, yet again, Kafka's formidable beak-like Machine that is said to inscribe justice into human flesh. Now Morrison: her reverence for the human body as bedrock truth shines everywhere, not only illuminating the primal sin of slavery as body desecration but also living on the very page, shimmering in her depiction of flesh itself: Sethe and Halle making love among the corn stalks, Amy Denver massaging Sethe's legs and helping her to bring her baby into the world, Paul D kissing the grooves in Sethe's mauled back, on show in Stamp Paid feeding blackberries to the baby, no less visible, even if horribly, in telling us what it does when a horse bit is forced into a human mouth or what it means when a mother's milk is stolen. Flesh is our lot.

If a slavery-future is so awful that one is not only willing but obliged to kill one's children, to prevent their being returned to it, we have something blindingly clear, almost Cartesian: it cannot be doubted. This is slavery's inhuman and indubitable truth. After reading *Beloved*, we know that, because we've been obliged to "dive into the wreck" that is our collective racial past. Not just to dive in, but to "see it, feelingly," as Shakespeare's blinded Gloucester says of the truths he came to, at play's end. "We flesh" is what Baby Suggs said, and that plural claim (embracing all of us) is no less than an ethos, a commandment for living and for writing.

CHAPTER 5

Literature's Map of Human Dimensions

I hated maps as a child. They bored me with their cookie-cutter view of how the oceans, continents, and countries of the world are disposed. It seemed a bit like memorizing the list of American presidents or going alphabetically through the lower forty-eight, both of which exercises my demographic dutifully carried out. That these names and dates and borders were big with the evolving life and crises of my country and other countries never fully occurred to me. My grades were good, but I was asleep. And I suppose my current obsession with *understanding*—displayed in the preceding long chapter about the costs of knowing—is nurtured by an abiding sense of the factitious, superficial "knowledge" that I myself was larded with, during my early years.

Obviously, my history courses obliged me to take maps more seriously. Even thick as I was, I saw that whole swaths of the world came into view during the age of exploration, and that most of the major wars ended with considerable reshuffling of national borders, sovereignly agreed on by the victors and forced on the defeated. But terms such as the "Virgin West" still existed when I was even a graduate student, Columbus was still feted as unproblematic hero of the West, the West itself was breezily understood to be the source of all necessary learning. As I've said, at my arrival at Brown in 1968, even my professional field, comparative literature, was comfortably Eurocentric. No longer.

But one of my favorite poems, William Blake's "London," helped me rethink altogether the very notion of *mapping*; Blake's first lines go like this: "I wander thro' each charter'd street, / Near where the charter'd Thames does flow / And mark in every face I meet, / Marks of weakness, marks of woe." As the poem unfurls, we see an emerging indictment of power itself as it existed in 1794, ascribed to the institutions of church and throne. But Blake's victims fight back, in visionary fashion: the "Chimney-sweeper's cry / every blackning Church appalls, / And the hapless Soldier's sigh / Runs in blood down Palace walls." Pain and exploitation become a visible indicting script, like graffiti—this is amazing in itself, a version of art's "ocular proof"—and the poem closes with the apocalyptic claim that London is diseased and dying, that "generation" itself is doomed by plague, both physical and moral. It is as if Blake were reprising Lear's grasp, on the Heath, of system-wide pain and abuse and turning it into a visionary event: we *hear* the dying soldier's sigh, and we *see* it become blood running down palace walls.

But I now realize that those initial lines are arguably just as revolutionary, along "mapping" lines: Blake knows, as we know, that the city's streets can be chartered, but he also knows that the natural world has a will of its own, that the "charter'd Thames" is a fiction, for rivers can flood, can even become (here) blood on walls. "Marks of weakness, marks of woe" is a simple but sublime assertion: pain (normally what is deepest inside you, unknown and unknowable to others) *marks*, and the poet's task is to read and decode those marks, those markings, so as to illuminate pain's reaches and causality, its victims and its sources. The poem widens, deepens and bids to explode our conventional, inert view of humans placed in their setting, by bringing to visibility what goes otherwise unseen and unaccounted. This is what the poem is *charting*, and it differs radically from any geographer's findings. Reading it cargoes you into the London of 1794, and it initiates you into a regime of power-turned-visible (something your eyes or mine could never see), a far-flung network picture that our more contemporary discourse would call "systemic." This is literature's map of human dimensions.

Pascal

To fill out this map still further, I want to reach still further back far in time, and to enlist the work of the seventeenth-century philosopher, Blaise Pascal. He is one of the stranger guides for this study, most known for his remarkable collection of aphorisms, perceptions, and metaphysics titled *Les Pensées*, a text for all times, with its famous "wager" about salvation and the state of the soul. (Using logic like that of folks optimizing their retirement plan, he suavely proves that you have much to win and little to lose in electing to believe in God. Go figure.) Mathematician, internationally recognized scientist, inventor, satirist, polemicist, and visionary poet: he is a man of many traits. Why, you may wonder, invoke him as guide for the institution of literature?

Pascal's most famous cri de coeur is doubtless the following: "Le silence éternel de ces espaces infinis m'effraie" (The eternal silence of these infinite spaces fills me with dread). It is an amazing utterance, given its author's religious convictions and his scientific program. Stately in its form—virtually constituting a classic Alexandrian verse in its notation of the universe, followed by the presence of the human being stunningly positioned as object rather than subject, indeed as terrorized object—this declaration goes a far piece in the direction of homelessness, of what Heidegger was to call *Geworfenheit*, our cast-out condition. The two adjectives, "eternal" and "infinite," spell out with utmost clarity our lostness in a spatiotemporal scheme that ever outruns us. We have, as I said, no perch. Pascal—albeit a *believer*—looks up at the heavens and finds them terrifying in their alienness, silence, and reach. For all practical purposes, he finds them empty.

In seeking the answers he needs, Pascal-the-scientist is out to trumpet the profound rebuke to human reason that is lodged in this condition. "Disproportion of man" is the rubric Pascal assigns to these arrangements. One of his favorite taunts is found in this stinging binary: "Infiniment grand et infiniment petit." The heavens, we've already seen, dwarf us by their immensity; but Pascal is equally drawn to our locked-out status when it comes to small/smaller/smallest, as he zeroes in on the intricacies of the human body, filled with immeasurable systems within

systems. (Modern imaging takes up this challenge.) In proclaiming that
the ends of things (large and small), as well as their principles are irretrievably, unknowably, hidden, Pascal seems to me as much the man of
science as the man of faith. He is obsessed with "situational" ignorance
as the defining trait of humans: "'I do not know who put me into the
world, nor what the world is, nor what I am myself. I am terribly ignorant
about everything. I do not know what my body is, or my senses, or my
soul, or even that part of me which thinks what I am saying, which reflects about everything and itself, and does not know itself any better
than it knows anything else.'"

Pascal obviously had never heard of information technology, but one
can assume that (1) he would have been, quasi-professionally, intrigued
by it, and (2) he would have found it profoundly inadequate. I had my
reasons for calling Pascal a soul brother to Kierkegaard, because many
of his most beautiful axioms tell us that the path to truth—especially to
the highest truth—is not via "thinking" but rather via "feeling." "Dieu
sensible au coeur, non à la raison" (God felt by the heart, not by reason),
he famously proclaims. Further, the heart outruns the brain, has its own
intrinsic order and purchase: "Le coeur a ses raisons que la raison ne
connaît point" (The heart has its reasons that reason has no knowledge
of). This is an astonishing utterance. I wonder if Freud knew it. It certainly underwrites a good bit of my view of life and literature, even
though I do not bring God into the mix.

Nothing touchy-feely in sight. Further, Pascal is immensely aware of
distortion, error, and prejudice in human affairs and human laws; he is
wise about the blindness of affect, the morass and bias of self-interest,
the skewed optics of appetite and fear. Many of his sharpest aphorisms,
such as the suggestion that Cleopatra's nose altered the shape of the
world, or that morality differs on each side of the river, display his acer-
bic mindset. He termed "imagination" itself "une puissance trompeuse,"
a power that deceives.

Yet, Pascal makes the case that the quest for knowledge must (also)
attend to the testimony of the heart as compass in human affairs. What
is so striking about his vision is its scope: the immense wider world falls
into his purview, and that is what most rebukes the metrics put forth by

reason and logic. The eternal silence of infinite spaces is environment it-self, the huge mute stage where puny lives play out. And literature (a term Pascal had little interest in)—more even than geography or history—brings these arrangements home to us, made both visible and audible; and our compass is the heart. I need him for my book because I think this is a drastic territorial assertion. In what sense could this be true?

It's true because we are incredibly spread out (all over space, all over time), because every life has such far-flung coordinates; Thoreau's claim that he'd traveled a great deal in Concord supports (rather than chal-lenges) my claim. And literature plumbs this, reveals our traffic patterns in ways no diary or GPS or city planner could arrive at. At the outset of this book, I boasted that literature is always a form of science fiction, underscoring the time–space travel required by (and gifted to) readers. But the mobility at issue is more intimate than that, on show in the books themselves, in their very texture: such "travel" often constitutes, on the page and in the reader, the very warp and weft of the human mind, posit-ing us as careening figures, writing us large in ways we rarely consider. I have already lamented the distressing poverty of tombstone inscrip-tions, beautiful though they may be. In my youth the TV detective Friday had a mantra: "Just the facts, ma'am." Well, name, birth, and death are factually right but experientially (absurdly) reductive, given our carnival lives, and literature is the place to go, to depict the larger stage. And to see, more surprisingly, up close, a version of connectivity that preceded all our modern gadgets. That would be Pascal's legacy for me.

Literature's News: The Open Heart and the Opened Heart

My claim: literature alone affords us an adequate picture of the human heart. A new map. Hmm.

In medicine, we go to cardiologists and cardiovascular surgeons for a picture of the human heart. When the system is truly clogged or fail-ing, beyond the reach of pills, the doctors are obliged to "go in." We call this "open-heart surgery," and we know what it is: using a scalpel, the surgeon cuts through our flesh and bone all the way to the life-giving heart, usually removing it and placing it aside temporarily, so as to do the necessary work of reparation, reaming, and cleaning, performed on muscles, valves, or arteries. This procedure is performed in order to save our lives, so that our blood can again flow properly through its channels. Anyone who has had it, or who knows someone who's had it, is well aware of its gravity and of the slow healing that follows. In this context, "open heart" actually means "opened heart." Having your heart physically opened is life-threatening even if sometimes necessary.

We also know that in ordinary (nonmedical) parlance the phrase "open heart" is invariably meant as tribute to one's generosity or compassion, one's capacity to extend human feeling outward, toward others. I have repeatedly claimed that the act of reading is precious because it triggers this kind of blood flow, of human empathy—"mitempfinden" was Goethe's term—by dint of our imaginative, vicarious entry into the lives and fates of fictional characters. I've also claimed, a bit more brashly, that my existence as identical twin likely fostered my interest in these matters, on almost a morphological level. (Let me be clear: my own heart has, regrettably, as much frozen sea or plaque in its conduits as the next person's.)

What needs saying is that literature offers us a picture of both open and opened hearts that is perhaps as valuable and illuminating as the MRIs used by the physicians to get a sighting on these matters. I think that four boys on two horses is an exquisite (equine, literary) figure for the open heart as conduit of both blood and empathy, limning for us what the author termed an "overpass to love." Faulkner's tragic books depict the frequent failure of such conduits, and they also tell us why: not only the "frozen sea" of indifference and egoism but the racial taboo that forbids love across the black–white divide, that denies the status of "human" to large swaths of people.

Literature's imaging goes still further in its findings. What happens when the open heart becomes the opened heart? Not by dint of scalpel but by invasion of a different kind, by the breaking and entering of human feeling that comes unannounced, sometimes surprising its recipients, sometimes delighting, sometimes destroying them. Literature's testimony of human connection illuminates an entire hidden grammar of loves and losses, constituting a new map, not unlike an MRI or CT scan, but entirely sentient, affective, and cubistic. Its scariest, weirdest feature is that it consists of *traffic*, coming from afar and invading our present, hijacking us, turning us into a temporal roundabout, where you never quite know what vehicle has the right-of-way or is about to collide with you. Here it all happens on the inside, moving with the speed of neurons. I know something about the printouts that imaging machines deliver, but only in books do we find pictures of the kaleidoscopic flows and nodal points that are our living history.

Not only does the most interesting literature, along these lines, enable us to perceive the larger stage(s) where we go and went through our moves, where our moves go through us, but it does justice to the immense drama born of these arrangements, still playing. The most sedentary life possesses a dizzying mix of places and time, but no machine today, no matter how complete its notations might be (as in getting second-by-second measures for blood pressure or blood sugar), can record what these times and places *signify* in your personal history and geography. This distinction, by the way, is precisely why Proust disliked cinema: he felt it could depict reality's surfaces but was locked out of the personal human meanings they inevitably possess for us. And he knew a good bit about the awful mobility of this scheme, the way it can suddenly move in and take over. I spoke of roundabouts, but perhaps dodgem or bumper cars (that I used to love driving when I was taken to the circus as a child) convey more of the shock and vulnerability at issue here.

How this happens, what it feels like, and why this matters is at the core of the works—some famous, some less so, and one of them cinematic— I now want to discuss: poems of Baudelaire and James Merrill, prose of Strindberg, Proust, Joyce, and Calvino, a film by Godard. These artists announce, well before the internet did, a regime of connectivity, of neural meshes in which we are caught and "reached," yielding a surprising composite form, short on hegemony, long on linkage. But they also sketch its moral, indeed civic and political, dimensions, and, by breaking into our frozen sea, they reveal us to be interpellated by these tidings. Art can be said to awaken us to this vista and these responsibilities. Is it possible that our *current* moment, addicted to the immediate electronic reach of information technology, has willy-nilly outsourced our fuller story? Will your iPhone register memories or dreams? Can it depict the actual mesh, far beyond data, that contains and queries you, that comes to visibility in literature? Can it tell us where we really live?

Charles Baudelaire: Poet-Explorer

Let me embark on this account of literature as map with one of Charles Baudelaire's grandest, most mythic pieces, studded with references to the classical past, yet significantly anchored in the day-to-day sights and scenes of the burgeoning Paris of his moment; I am referring to the time-shifts that stamp what is arguably the greatest city poem of the nineteenth century, Baudelaire's "Le Cygne" (The Swan), published in 1861, under the grouping "Tableaux Parisiens." I approach this poem with Pascal in mind because the philosopher's vision of radical human homelessness is of a piece with the poet's. And this perspective is surprisingly suited to urban representation because it obliges us to note, counterintuitively, that cities exist along axes of time as well as space.

"Le Cygne" is stamped by a distinctly elegiac note, for it depicts the "price" of a Paris undergoing (what we'd have to call) "urban renewal" at the directive of Baron Haussmann, carrying out Napoleon III's imperial designs for a new capital. The poem achieves a further pathos in its rendition of time–space via its cardinal motif of *exile* as the unifying experience (unifying for the reader only) of the extraordinary cast of characters involved: Victor Hugo, the poet-critic to whom the piece is dedicated, self-exiled and living on the island of Guernsey; the classical figure Andromache, Hector's widow, kidnapped by Pyrrhus and now living out her post–Trojan War exile as wife of Helenus; Ovid, briefly referenced, as the poet banished from Rome and living by the Black Sea; the central eponymous figure of the swan itself, recaptured in memory by the poet as having escaped from its cage, scuffling the dry Parisian pavement, bathed in the dust, longing for rain, for its "beau lac natal" (beautiful native lake); and the final image of the tubercular black woman, trudging the mud, seeking behind the "muraille immense de brouillard" (immense wall of fog) the absent palms of Africa, the far-away homeland.

The first line of the poem announces its energy system: "Andromache, je pense à vous!" (Andromache, I think of you!). This sinuous yet discontinuous poem writes large the kinetic power of *thought*, now understood as a kind of tentacular but enlivening reach, propelling the speaker toward the bereft widow of Classical Antiquity. Her plight is linked to poet's evocation of the "Old Paris" still existing (in the poet's memory) behind the "nouveau Carrousel" of Haussmann's doing, and there, among remembered hovels and bric-a-brac is where we espy the pathetic figure of the swan, febrilely seeking water, its element, now become urban detritus, yielding what the poet calls a "mythe étrange et fatal."

That myth is about the entropic work of time, about its incessant dismantling of place and person, also about the ceaseless transformation of cities: "le vieux Paris n'est plus." ("Old Paris is no more.") But this undoing is countered by the neural retrieval of memory, "mémoire fertile," as the no less incessant building project that defines human doing. To see this in terms of "exile" is to understand the displacements and uprooting that characterize modern life; and we sense something still darker: although the mind of the poet may well bear witness, may evoke the lost homeland, there can be no homecoming. Loss is the primal condition, and even if it communalizes (*in* the poem) the exiled figures, each of these actors is irretrievably alone, cut off.

"A quiconque a perdu ce qui ne se retrouve / Jamais, jamais!" (To whomever has lost that which can never be found / Never, never!) writes Baudelaire late in his poem, underscoring the impossibility of retrieval; yet the poem itself is nonetheless a countercharge, for the very processes of thinking that call up these exiles flaunt the muscularity of mind, of mind as agency in a decentered scheme that permits no other form of assertion. This is also what is most modern about this piece, with its examples of fragmented lives and broken narrative arcs, formed by (and cut off from) different histories, each jostling with the other, yielding a panorama of arrested figures, none achieving closure or related to the other, while finishing its run with still others, many others, endless others, spawned by the sheer power of poetic imagination:

"Je pense aux matelots oubliés dans une île, / Aux captifs, aux vaincus! . . . à bien d'autres encor!" (I think of sailors forgotten on an island / Of the captives, of the vanquished . . . of many more!). One need scarcely be a poetry scholar to see why this bristling, far-flung poem is foundational for future poets; Eliot's *Waste Land*, with its radical use of fragment and fragmentation, with its seesaw between past and present, would be a primary exhibit.

Ever since I first read this poem a good sixty years ago, I have thought its ending was lame—how can you close a poem in such random and featureless fashion ("à bien d'autres encor")?—but I now think its last words document the only strength we have: the strength to register all the lost, all the losses, so as to begin the work, at once imaginative and ethical, of diving into the wreck. "Captifs, vaincus . . . et bien d'autres encor": we are all included among the dispossessed and the homeless. And we sense the list could go on forever.

And it has. I write these lines at a moment when the dislocations brought on by ever greater waves of refugees have led to massive political unrest and resistance in the countries they have come to. A good century and a half after Baudelaire, I find him annunciatory, and I salute his prophetic imagery of dispossessed people, as far as the eye can see and the mind can imagine: in unending hordes, they trek today across Africa and the Middle East, across Central America, they drown in rubber boats or die crossing deserts, they encounter barbed wire and tear gas and family separation, as they exit war zones, seeking a perch somewhere. And of course it's not only refugees from afar on the march, today's homeless line our streets right on our own shores, as exiled as the thirsting swan, perhaps even remembering some "beau lac natal." Even the most dispossessed have dimensions. Have they a poet?

Baudelaire is not easy to love. His pose as dandy, his mix of sympathy and disdain for the city's victims and riffraff, his sexist convictions, his superciliousness, indeed his queasy voyeurism: none of this easily passes muster in today's ideological climate. And yet his poetry is shot through with a kind of rare generosity that does honor to the human imagination even where—especially where—it acknowledges its own inevitable egocentrism. The islanded figures in "Le Cygne" derive no benefit from the poem's resources; they remain islanded, unsavable. But, to use the title of one of his earlier major pieces, these "Tableaux Parisiens" are also a beacon light, "un phare," by dint of their focus on the lost and undone, and in this they do the signature work of poetry itself: to create interest, hence to create life. To see human figures as cut off or exiled is at the same time to widen and deepen their parameters, to sense their longing even when it is doomed.

Hence, this poet rightly uses the word "allégorie" to denote the "remembered" city—the place that exists *only* in mind and heart—and we come to see that poetry's allegorical mission is to gauge the reaches of mind and heart, to coerce us into seeing what these diverse victims have all lost, to take the human measure of their separate exiles. It is here that Baudelaire is "Pascalian," for he produces a fourth-dimensional *sentient* city map filled with exiles. My terms make this seem straightforward and manageable, but the greatness of this poetry derives from how unobvious and arduous it is and must be, for none of us can ever *see* what is hidden and lost and irretrievable in the lives of those we meet, whether on the streets of Paris in 1861 or in our own cities today. Our retinal evidence of others (and world) is flat and thin, even ghostly, and the project of imagination is to fill in these bare shapes, these silhouettes on our path, to reinvest them with the sentience that (must have) bathed their existence, and with the pathos that comes from their losses, from their transformation into debris.

We will all be debris. But who among us will be taken up—later, "unhelpfully," yet generously—by a Baudelaire? "Liberté, égalité, fraternité": this poem has no populist bombast, but it makes good, at least, on the last of that famous French triad: *fraternité*. Maybe that is the office of poetry. In a sense quite different from the financial instruments of today's brokers and investors, Baudelaire writes about *municipal bonds*.

Nowhere is this dialectic more visible than in the haunting, accompanying piece, "Les Petites Vieilles"—it, too, dedicated to Victor Hugo. Here the human wreckage caused by time and "oubli" is in still plainer sight, as we encounter the "little old ladies" wandering the Parisian streets, enduring the insults of life and of a poet of considerable brutality.

Baudelaire's terms include "décrépits," "monstres disloqués," "brisés," "bossus," "tordus," "fantômes débiles," and "ombres ratatinées" (decrepit, dislocated monsters, broken, hump-backed, twisted, feeble phantoms, and shriveled shadows), yielding the spectacle of grotesque crones on parade, but it would seem that the worse they are for wear, the more the poet urges us to care for them: "Aimons-les! Ce sont encor des âmes." The poet devotes considerable time to noting their deformities and peculiarities: they are like wounded animals, like marionettes, their tiny bodies in coffins resembling those of children.

But all this sordidness *adds* to their value, to their richness as object/subject of poetry. For that is where the poet is headed: to show—no, to create—the splendor and beauty that they (must have) had when young, and thus he disinters/invents their glamorous—but forgotten—pasts as actresses and ladies known to all, *in their day.* The poem obliges us to see that they had a day, even if it is now night for them. The poem exhorts us to "love them, because they are souls," yet that familiar, even clichéd, command can only be carried out by an act of creation. They must be "birthed" if their plenitude is to be grasped. That is what he is going to do.

Why does he do this? Here is where the poem yields its signature flavor of voyeurist libidinal interest. "Toutes m'enivrent," says the poet: all of them—widows, drunks, courtesans, mothers—inebriate me. Given what we know of Baudelaire's interest in hashish and his series of poems on the power of wine, "inebriate" seems indeed the right verb. The grotesque relics crawling our streets become—for him, only (one suspects) for him—a source of fascination, inspiration, indeed pleasure, quasi-libidinal pleasure. And still more. Much of the poem's force derives from its certainty that the ordinary Parisians going about their affairs have no interest in or knowledge of these wrecked figures, but that he—the poet—has a mission to restore them to their rightful stature and place. And that he gets inebriated doing it.

"Nul ne vous reconnaît!" (No one recognizes you!), he cries, and we understand that he is articulating a virtue that is urban as well as humanitarian: the city must recognize its own, and it must credit them for their lived lives. "I watch you tenderly from far away," he claims, and goes on to add that he does so as if he were not only their father but a father who is deriving a secret but profound gratification out of what he sees and imagines: "Je goûte à votre insu des plaisirs clandestins: / Je vois s'épanouir vos passions novices; / Sombres ou lumineux, je vis vos jours perdus; / Mon coeur multiplié jouit de tous vos vices! / Mon âme resplendit de toutes vos vertus!" (I taste your clandestine pleasures: / I see the blossoming of your innocent passions; / Dark or luminous, I live your lost days; / My expanded heart thrills to all your vices! / My soul shines with all your virtues!).

There is something sublime as well as parasitic in this proclamation: the life that the poet sees/imagines in the little old ladies is then reincorporated into himself as a kind of double or ersatz existence, expanding the poet, giving him a high that is quasi-erotic (his "multiplied" heart thrills to their vices), and fueling his own energy system with light and life. We cannot fail to see that he is glomming on to them, absorbing them, instrumentalizing them for the "kick" they yield, stealing from them precisely the affective energies he has lent them in the first place. A strange feedback loop comes to light here, as if we can reap only what we sow, as if we have to imagine the pleasure of others to then experience our own. He lives through these exchanges. It is more than a little vampirish. There's no mention of *blood* as such in this poem, yet it asks us to consider "imagination" as a blood enterprise, whether we call it blood-sucking or—more generously—a blood transfusion. The poem is *creatural*.

This is why his final assertion—"Ruines! ma famille!"—is so moving; he has brought them vicariously into his own sphere, into his own libidinal economy, and has thus experienced the only form of *family* he was to know. (His own humiliating, bitter, quasi-crippling arrangements in this area are on record.) There are simply no normative codes for measuring the displacements and appropriations on show here. Baudelaire testifies to an ongoing libidinal carnival that can take place on the streets of the city, day and night, and no one the wiser, and no way of proving or disproving it. This is the commerce of literature. "Multitude, solitude" is the binary he spells out in his prose poem, "Crowds," where he claims that poets must know how to "épouser la foule,"—"marry the crowd": erotic insinuation intended—and we are to understand that this type of borrowing and lending, of getting and "spending," is forever under the radar of our smartest machines and social scientists, resisting all notation except that of the poet.

I want to say that there is something grand and mythic about this project because, no matter how voyeuristic, it is indeed *civic*, requiring of all of us that we become "invested" in the (invisible) lives of others, that our own affective system hinges on, feeds on, lives through, these inputs and outputs. This, too, amounts to "working for your bread," and even if the riotous, more than a little "louche," Baudelairean version of such matters is not for the timid or squeamish it nonetheless articulates a code of feeling and projection that is the very law, the modus vivendi, of art and literature: to furnish the world with feeling. Let me rephrase this last point: Baudelaire's two poems—despite their relative brevity— write large an ethos regarding the dimensions of people, people you walk by with ne'er a glance or a thought. They offer us a kind of generosity, indeed a kind of gift, we find only in literature.

Like all gift codes, it requires an "outward" opening of the heart if one's own heart is then to be moved. Sentient weights and measures— and responsibilities—are in play. Remember this the next time you look at a tombstone with its etched data, or at a map of a city, or at the homeless standing in your path or lurking in the shadows, or even at the CV of any person you wish to know.

As I reread these lines on "Little Old Women," I'm moved to add a postscript: *age* is one of the cruxes of this poem. Any poet can write about the beautiful young people who waltz down our city streets, and Baudelaire himself did, in other, lesser poems. And I'd say that anyone can take the predictable moral high road and indict the young for not revering, or granting dignity, to the old (as is often the case in modern Western society). But what we see here is different: the poet has "youthified" them, has imagined (for himself, for them, for us) a glamour and radiance nowhere now to be seen (by himself, by them, by us). And I think about my young students on their trip through time, of which some four of their younger years are spent in my vicinity; and I realize why love stories fascinate them but stories of ageing leave them cold, because they cannot see themselves in such colors and forms.

I recall, many years ago, seeing an article in the *New York Times* highlighting a kind of high-tech space suit (named Agnes) designed at MIT to help younger folks imagine what it *feels like* to grow old, to inhabit an old, used-up body. As a democratic fellow, I suggest that it is no less arduous (albeit far more painful) for the old to recapture what it *feels/felt like* to be young. Agnes, tricked out in her cumbersome space suit, resembling an astronaut, sends perhaps the right visual signal: the old and the young are different species, and the experiences of the one are no less than science fiction for the other. The old of course can remember. What about the young? Can they "feel forward?" Agnes must have cost MIT a small fortune to build; Baudelaire's poems can be had for a pittance.

James Merrill: Urban Convalescence

James Merrill's "An Urban Convalescence," published in 1962, does not have quite the canonical status that Baudelaire's swan poem does, but it toils in the same vineyard—or to use a more appropriate figure—it also maps an urban landscape big with extensions and trips into time and space. Like Baudelaire, Merrill is drawn to the amnesiac aftereffects of "urban renewal," and his first stanza denotes a familiar modern sight: buildings being torn down: "watching a huge crane / Fumble luxuriously in the filth of years. / Her jaws dribble rubble," yielding the inevitable law of 'out-of-synch' life in the city: "As usual in New York, everything is torn down / Before you have had time to care for it." Whereas Baudelaire remembers vividly the Vieux Carrousel (with swan) that preceded Haussmann's imperial new version, Merrill's speaker is unsure, can't be certain what was here "before," even though he's lived on this street for a decade. Here would be the incessant, relentless, unfelt infidelity, outright sacking, that time brings about, with its implication that each of us is a graveyard of forgotten structures, those of stone and those of flesh. "Je suis un cimetière abhorré de la lune" (I am a cemetery abhorred by the moon), as Baudelaire put it in one of his "Spleen" poems. Merrill is out to shine his own moonbeam on the cemetery-self, to see what kind of connective tissue might still exist, in some kind of half-life, between us and our dead. How does one turn on such circuits?

Hence, the poem goes about humanly examining—exhuming, as it were—the "rubble" that the huge crane's jaws dribble with. The building is coming down, but the memories are now rising. The convalescing speaker recalls a lintel, over which "A single garland sways, stone fruit, stone leaves, / Which years of grit had etched until it thrust / Roots down, even into the poor soil of my seeing." When, the speaker wonders, "did the garland become part of me?" (A good question: how much do we know about the furnishings of our mind? Using MRIs, neurologists are adept at gauging decay and plaque, even at zooming in on unwanted growths; can they measure the stirrings and waning of love? the deposits of memory?) Now begin the metamorphoses: "a particular cheap engraving of garlands" appears, bought for "a few francs long ago"—signaling a transatlantic shift—and it becomes "calligraphic tendril and cross-hatched rondure," "crumpled up to stanch / Boughs dripping, whose white gestures filled a cab," which brings into near-visibility—to clasp the boughs—"the small, red-nailed hand / Of no one I can place." *She*—name, features, "words she must have spoken"— won't quite materialize, even in memory, yet her ghostly presence is palpable as unrecallable, unresolvable lost shade, neither quite audible nor quite understandable today. But there, dimly envisioned, beckoning still.

The almost-achieved human memory must now enter the entropic city-code the poem started with: "So that I am already on the stair, / As it were, of where I lived, / When the whole structure shudders at my tread / And soundlessly collapses, filling / The air with motes of stone." The post–Proust poem achieves no parturition, no miracles, no madeleine-in-a-teacup, no rescued "essences," but rather a complex pledge to stand vigil without flinching, respecting (as a code of honor, it would seem) the "massive volume of the world" that closes again, because it is inhospitable to human desire, because it is the law (of fact and matter) no one—including swans—escapes.

This loyalty test acknowledges that buildings crumple and lives become amnesiac, and it goes further still, intuiting that the fight is yet further lopsided, that "still standing" is somehow felt (by the universe) as hubris and cannot be allowed: "The sickness of our time requires / That these as well be blasted in their prime. / You would think the simple fact of having lasted / Threatened our cities like mysterious fires." It is a remarkable perception: permanence is either intolerable in a culture obsessed with change or—worse—permanence is inherently fraudulent, even when it comes to stone. I am no less struck by its tidings in the realm of human relations, or in the individualist psyche, filled with ancient buried strata, yes, but ever bent on novelty, discovery, and the romance of tomorrow. However you turn it—the termites are winning or architects need work or stasis (and its sibling "fidelity") equate with boredom and paralysis, if not living death—Merrill's stanza is strong stuff.

Too strong, it turns out, according to the verdict of the poet himself who indicts himself for rhetorical legerdemain: "There are certain phrases which to use in a poem / Is like rubbing silver with quicksilver. Bright / But facile, the glamour deadens overnight. / For instance, how 'the sickness of our time' / Enhances, then debases, what I feel." The modernity of Merrill's verse is keyed to its vigilant, indeed severe, principled distrust of verse's own resources, of the poet's own rhetorical keyboard, yielding a "scrubbing" or "scouring" effect whereby anything remotely tinsel is caught, exposed, and expelled. Except that it isn't. The flashy phrase and its austere rebuke both remain on the page, testifying to Merrill's shrewdness that he now has it both ways, and that this self-awareness is itself a kind of muscularity—"toughening" words as one "reinforces" concrete—a reprieve against erosion and entropy, keeping the vision alive beyond "overnight," as the quixotic quest for permanence gets its final formulation.

So, the faraway, long-ago Parisian memory that got only to the threshold of the mind is called up one last time, as a kind of "adieu" (not "au revoir"), evoking a couple strolling on the Champs-Elysées as final urban setting ready for disappearance, ready for its return to "oubli," yet bequeathing a final "earned" residue of core truth: "the dull need to make some kind of house / Out of the life lived, out of the love spent." At last the architectural motif becomes one with the existential poetic injunction: to create a living form—a form that somehow hallows the dimensionality of living—as the homecoming mission of both art and life. But Ithaca, we see ever more clearly, is not merely the place of origin or even destination: it is also one's fuller personal estate, that plenary composite form extending far beyond the here and now, peopled by our own ghosts and the shades they loved, waiting to be called up, on the order of a secular Last Judgment, whereby there is no judgment but merely the miracle or memory or mirage of possession.

Strindberg: "Avenue de Neuilly" and Other Traffic Patterns

August Strindberg is Sweden's most important writer, but certainly not its most beloved one. His misogyny, his paranoia, his egomania, have made him a complicated figure, for teachers even more than for literary historians, because the flagrant political incorrectness of so much of his work raises ever more red flags (and anger) in today's classrooms. He stands close to the top of my list of difficult, unteachable figures— I must enjoy losing battles; more on this later—and as I think about retirement, one useful reason for me to exit the scene would be to sanitize the curriculum, to remove from student syllabi some of the noxious writers whom I nonetheless revere, despite (not because of) their ideological vices. But Strindberg most demands a place in this study because of the astounding neural self-portrait he consistently proffers, in work after work: astounding for its permeability, its (prophetic) status as *wired*, its precariousness as receiver/emitter of stimuli. His work is about traffic and connectivity.

Known largely as dramatist, Strindberg can also be seen as one of Sweden's greatest poets, and he can surprise us. Those who know something of his bombast and virulence may be astonished to encounter the delicacy of one of his most luminous poems, such as "Vid Avenue de Neuilly," depicting, as Baudelaire and Merrill did, life as map, filled with faraway coordinates and nodal points. Strindberg turns the humdrum question "Where am I?" into something at once pedestrian and exotic, beyond the reach of your GPS:

Vid avenue de Neuilly
där ligger ett slakteri,
och när jag går till staden,
jag går där alltid förbi.

[On the Avenue de Neuilly
stands a butcher shop,
and when I go into town
I always pass by it.]

Det stora öppna fönstret
det lyser av blod så rött,
på vita marmorskivor
där ryker nyslaktat kött.

[In the large open window
the blood gleams so red,
on the white marble slabs
where steams fresh butchered meat.]

I dag där hängde på glasdörrn
ett hjärta, jag tror av kalv,
som svept i gauffrerat papper
jag tyckte i kölden skalv.

[Today there hung on the glass door
a heart, I think of calf,
which, in its paper wrap,
seemed shivering in the cold.]

Då gingo hastiga tankar
till gamla Norrbro-Bazarn,
där lysande fönsterraden
beskådas av kvinnor och barn.

[My thoughts then went quickly
to the old Norrbro Bazaar
whose gleaming window shelves
are looked upon by woman and child.]

Där hänger på boklådsfönstret
en tunnklädd liten bok.
Det är ett urtaget hjärta
som dinglar där på sin krok.

[There hangs in the bookshelf window
a thin-clad little book
It is a torn-out heart
dangling there on its hook.]

It is not clear that Strindberg ever wrote a more perfect poem. His Paris years in the mid-1890s are known for the psychic upheavals and breakdown he experienced there, but whatever pain and anguish are to be found here—and there is much: one's book as torn-out heart on show for all onlookers is an unforgettable figure for exposure and vulnerability—are exquisitely contained, at least in this piece, by the dyads of Paris–Stockholm, realia–private sentience, and world–self. Strindberg's most striking (late) work is ever cued to this dialectic between externals and intimacy, an invasive dialectic (if I may put it that way) because it consists of *jolts*, of repeated instances of that *frisson nouveau* seen already in Baudelaire's urban poetry. To read Strindberg is often to be thankful for the thickness of one's skin and for the customary inertness of the objective world.

The flaneur, familiar to us in Baudelaire, is no longer for Strindberg a casual city-roamer, but a figure doomed to meeting himself writ large at every turn, a figure virtually splayed by a type of semiotic backlash, whiplash, bruising him with news of himself wherever he goes. Open heart, opened heart. Strindberg reaches Ithaca on a daily—perhaps hourly—basis. There is no homeland to celebrate here—I do not believe the "exiled" Strindberg is yearning for Stockholm in these lines—but one sees nonetheless the remarkable homecoming traffic that is proper to poetry. And the exposed little book on old Norrbro Bazaar is indeed like a torn-out heart inasmuch as its pages house the poet's "insides," his organs and blood and bones—what you might find on a marble slab in a butcher shop—as well as his thoughts and language. I am stunned by the back-and-forth of this poem, a pas de deux that moves not only through time and space but through matter and spirit, fusing them together, insisting that one's "own" heart is written everywhere, displayed in shopwindows as well as printed poems, on show, for better or worse.

Is this not what art is: "ett urtaget hjärta"? (a torn-out/removed heart)? The poem leads with its ominous carnal, tissue-laden, meaty images: butcher shop, splayed animals, quivering calf heart. And it therefore acquires a kind of fleshly aura at once somatic and medicinal, the sort of thing you'd expect from a cardiac surgeon displaying delicacies. But if we are to think metaphorically about this exposed heart, we realize that the poem is a perfect rendition of "inwardness" turned into flesh, of the heart now brought to view. This can be invasive, garish, and bloody, but it can also be visionary and precious, for it succeeds with art's primary mission of *writing the soul*, of making visible to us precisely the inner world that eludes retinal perception. The thin-clad book of poems exposed in Stockholm morphs into the no less exposed affective wiring of the poet himself, who tells us about his fuller "coordinates," about the muscular reach of heart and mind that we experience incessantly in life but that none of our machines can track.

Try to imagine the tally of a camera or a map or a guidebook, and ask yourself if anything remotely like this far-flung portrait could be teased out of those mechanical precincts. Whitman had written, "If you want me again, look for me under your boot-soles," but Strindberg goes him one further: I am liable to be found almost anywhere, in the drabbest places, ready to pop up, en route outward, yet with squatter's rights, waiting to come home. And one is struck by the exploded city-setting itself, breaking free of all maps and charts: visible to us now as both real and trompe l'oeil, as both ground and springboard, as both a path for your feet and a pulsing locus that signals other times, other cities, other selves. The narcissist, often melodramatic Strindberg, prone to nursing his wounds in print, is nowhere to be seen in this clean yet kinetic urban notation, yet the poem is nonetheless recuperative art. It both reveals and harnesses our everyday extensions into time and space.

Strindberg's Circuits

But the weirder Strindberg whom I especially want to discuss now, the Strindberg who brings us explosive news about *connectivity*, is less the writer than the aspiring alchemist, for that is what he documentably was during a fraught period of crisis while in Paris. Alchemy—stamped utterly by transformation and shape-shifting—must convey to most of us an almost prehistoric period prior to the rise of the sciences, yet, by some accounts, there were as many as fifty thousand practicing alchemists in Paris in the 1890s, and their publications were taken with considerable seriousness. To understand this, we need to remember that this was a time where the appeal of the occult—perhaps a last-ditch resistance to the conquering materialist worldview—was hugely influential. Practices and beliefs as diverse as spiritism, theosophy, hypnosis, telepathy, and monism were in vogue, and people spoke of astral waves, doppelgänger, cosmic influences, and the like. (I sometimes think I was born and formed back then.) One might today smile at such extravagance, but there is much we will not get right, such as Charcot and Freud and the birth of psychoanalysis, not to speak of New Age philosophy, unless we grasp the nature of that late mid- nineteenth-century Weltanschauung. The "occult" Strindberg has much to teach us.

If "Avenue de Neuilly" displayed one form of Strindbergian traffic. *Inferno* (1897), which Strindberg originally wrote in French, offers us another, for it gives us a blow-by-blow, harrowing account of the writer's trials and tribulations in Paris during a time of real mania; this period is often seen as the "Rubicon" that divides up Strindberg's career, because the post-*Inferno* works often rank among his most experimental and visionary pieces, displaying organizational principles that have little to do with "realist" poetics. *Inferno* itself is usually read as a window into the writer's mental turbulence and instability. I want, instead, to read it "topographically," where yet again time and space become, to quote Pascal, "sensibles au coeur," resulting in a stunningly decentralized portrait of the human subject. Given that Strindberg is often seen as swollen-headed, it is worth noting that many of his major texts display at their center a remarkably porous figure, plugged into currents of all stripes, under siege, finding himself trapped in a charged world.

What might that *look* like? Perhaps a good starting place, a prefiguration before tackling *Inferno*, would be Edvard Munch's well-known 1894 portrait of Strindberg, in which the leonine bard is shown with massive forehead and crown of hair, worried eyes, and a tiny, tiny mouth; this painting comes into my argument via its astonishing frame: jagged streaks of lightning on the left side, shape of a woman's body on the right, along with an initially misspelled name, Stindberg, which means, in (Munch's) Norwegian: mountain of hot air. (Can you imagine a portrait of Benjamin Franklin, our exemplary earliest American scientist, also connoisseur of electricity, along these lines?) What jumps out at you here is the *environmental* character of the piece: Strindberg is seen as negotiating a force field defined by electricity and libido.

That same force field is figured in another of Strindberg's most affecting poems, "Street Scenes," which closes with a remarkable rendition of the poet's psyche as "humming dynamo" located in a dark cellar, sparks flying, hidden but *grinding* "light for the entire neighborhood." It's an astounding portrait of the artist as energy system (working in the dark) for the entire community. Much to like here. (Chew on the regimes in play in the words, "grinding light.")

Inferno fascinates because it is stamped by connectivity, leading us to understand that a man having a nervous breakdown in Paris is a story

A STINDBERG

© DeA Picture Library / Art Resource, NY

that can—must—be *writ large*. I read this psychotic text as twin, but I present it to you as a spectacle to ponder, even to learn from. What is breaking down are precisely the form-contours of self that customarily glove our hearts and mind, reinforcing the notion that we are bounded integral entities. In Strindberg, the subject implodes, finds himself interpellated, endlessly reachable. Some of this is Zeitgeist, occultist business as usual. Cyclones, we are told, are likely "waves of hatred, surges of passion, or emissions of psychic power." You can be struck down from afar. But there is nothing random about it because the smallest setbacks and humiliations you experience—a dirty look, a knocked-over glass, a pain in your chest—have your name on them, are always a form of payback for earlier deeds and misdeeds. (I personally experience this "affective fallacy" almost every day: wind, snow, slipping on the ice, bumping into objects, being stuck in traffic, *all* have my name on them.) Thus we have the splendid new accounting of hell as supreme environmental tit for tat, as psychic ecosystem: "It is the earth itself that is Hell, the prison constructed for us by an intelligence superior to our own, in which I could not take a step without injuring the happiness of others, and in which my fellow creatures could not enjoy their own happiness without causing me pain."

Inferno is thus horribly, madly coherent. Reason is held hostage to deeper narcissist pulsions. Strindberg walks the Paris streets, and every perception is endowed with private meaning: he sees numbers on a piece of cardboard, and voilà: they confirm his chemical experiments; he takes the train to Meudon, sees a statue who appears to be looking at a wall, and revoilà: on the wall are scratched the letters *F* and *S*, which (have to) signify Frida (his departed wife) and Strindberg, thereby signifying further: "She loves me still!" This is a double bargain because Fe and S are also the chemical symbols for iron and sulfur, hence they "revealed to me the secret of gold." Nice.

Other encounters are even wackier: a man appears in his hotel whose name is the same as his wife's, a man who receives mail with the same Austrian postmark where his wife and child are now staying, yet he is certain that that village has no post office. A subsequent letter has a Swedish name that reminds him of an enemy, to be followed by a letter from a firm of analytical chemists, thereby proving (to Strindberg!) that "someone was spying on my synthesis of gold." We know that birds feather their nests, but have you wondered what that means? Strindberg seems to be saying that humans also feather their nests: they take bits and pieces of random bric-a-brac (twigs, leaves, notations), and they make a nest/home out of it. That is happening here. Nothing has alterity.

Hence everything speaks to/of Strindberg. (When I teach *Inferno*, I ask my students, "If you walk down the corridor in your dorm, and see two people who are whispering to each other stop and become silent as you go by, do you suspect they're talking about *you*?")

Gradually these matters take on more density and urgency. Strindberg hears someone playing Chopin and is certain (!) that it is his rival Przybyszewski (gifted pianist, also Satanist, also sexual rival, last seen in Berlin, now called Popoffsky here) come from Poland to Paris to kill him. Other threats are more devious but even further reaching. A stranger comes to the hotel, occupies the room next to Strindberg's writing desk, never speaks a word, seems to be writing constantly, seems in fact to repeat each of Strindberg's own motions, including going to bed at the same time as Strindberg does, but this time in the room on the other side, the side where Strindberg's bed is located. Strindberg hears him lying there, reading, turning pages, putting out the light, falling asleep. "Besieged on both sides at once" is our man's conclusion. Hmm. One reading here is: *reading* itself (or language) is now understood as flux, as force field, as connectivity, linking/glueing people over time–space. Reading: sedentary yet kinetic. But soon enough these "perceptions" ratchet up to another level, take over the scene, produce magnetic fluid that enters Strindberg's room, become increasingly toxic, and finally constitute the repeatable *invasion* he is to endure wherever he goes: electric current that passes through him, yielding the classic "personalized" response, "'Someone is killing me! I will not be killed.'"

Thus begins the frenetic *chase* that parses this text: Strindberg finds himself pursued—in Paris, in Dieppe, in Ystad, in Austria with (his wife) Frida's family—by electric jolts (likened by him to the Furies) that suck at his heart, blast him out of bed, provoke horrible palpitations, charge him with suffocating fluid, are bent on destroying him. Consequently (!) he reliably, inevitably, finds the electrical paraphernalia (wheels, spinning wheels, bedsteads with uprights surmounted by brass knobs, springs of copper wire) required for such attacks everywhere he goes: in the hotel room(s) over his, in whatever guestroom he occupies, as predictable as the recurring furniture in today's hotel chains. Our expression "going abroad" would have no meaning for Strindberg since the scenery—whether it be Parisian streets or Austrian woods—soon enough reveals the same despotic features. The Swedish mystic Sweden-borg is enlisted as Baedeker, helping Strindberg to discern the iconog-raphy of hell, in whatever precincts he finds himself.

Such a scheme would appear to be horribly stifling, scalping the var-iegated "real" world of its alterity and neutrality, turning every setting into a torture chamber, but the essential counterintuitive point that I want to make here goes exactly the other way: Strindberg's incessant personalizing operation yields something remarkably resonant and far-reaching. Yes, he experienced, at the height of his crises, an electrical invasion, a blast of current, or something sucking at his heart. This was indeed his heart "in code." He gives, as I've said, nightmarish flesh, blood, and horror to today's fashionable term, "connectivity." Of course, we can throw our diagnostic labels at him—paranoia, mania, hallucina-tion, persecution complex—but he himself, at select moments when the assault is hyperintense, does just that: he trots out exactly these medical terms, says he's heard them all before from the doctors, *and it doesn't help.*

What good is a label? Therapy is not the issue. What kind of a field-picture is this? Could this be a teaching moment? Could all of us be as spread out and invaded as Strindberg was? Freud wrote about the "psy-chopathology" of everyday life, having in mind our slips of the tongue, our moments of the "uncanny," when "inside" goes "outside" and wires are crossed: Strindberg goes a lot further. As teacher, I find him irresist-ible fare because he exposes something fascinating about the bizarre way our equipment sometimes works (or explodes). He is unfettered. He is a carrefour.

Inferno dramatizes Parisian troubles of the mid-1990s; but worse was to come later. Strindberg's third marriage to the (much younger) actress Harriet Bosse was predictably tempestuous and short-lived, but less predictable, and amazingly longer-lived, was the telepathic sexual con-gress that he "experienced" with her from 1901 to 1908. In the so-called "real" department, sex between Strindberg and Harriet appears to have been rocky: she notoriously complained that he was not a "man," and he himself groused that she had a uterine prolapse that locked him out, not to mention that he (in his later years) felt actual sexual congress to be a gross arrangement on nature's part. But, on the "astral plane," as it were, things were quite different. He records in his *Occult Diary* countless episodes of ecstatic erotic pleasure felt during the many *visits* "she" made to him over these years, beginning before they were married and lasting long after their separation. Please note: he experienced her "storming" him repeatedly, and at all hours, but *she* was not there "materially," in any provable, documentable way. Telepathic sex. At its best—and many were the times it was best—such encounters left him in postcoital awe, with the taste of roses in his mouth. (If you call this simply wet dreams, how much do you learn?)

At other times, however, it shades into something darker; consider the following: "In the early morning H—-t was gone. But at about 10 o'clock she stormed me so that my epigastrium was nearly shot to pieces!" In the last months of the diary, such entries (emphasizing a "shot" epigastrium) are frequent, and one is not surprised to learn— Strindberg himself was not surprised to learn—that these sensations were the first signs of the stomach cancer that was to kill him a few years later. But his immediate interpretation of his pains was quite different: "Does that mean that he is beating her?" Translate: does my pain actually signify the pain she (far away) is feeling (maybe)?

I do not believe we have a diagnostic logic for assessing forays of this stamp. Not only does he have frequent sex with her (without her), but he goes on to consult his own body to measure what else is going on with hers, such as the onset of her period or of some sickness or of some setback. Further, the telepathic, virtual *entente* displayed in these notations is utterly in contrast with the dissension and persistent *misunderstandings* that always arose between them when they were actually together. "Love thrives on absence"; rarely has such a cliché been actualized in the way it happened to Strindberg.

What most intrigues me here is the long-distance erotic connection. She needn't be physically there for him to "experience" sexual congress with her. And it goes further. He claims also to "experience" sexual congress that she has with other men. He says that each time it happens, *he* is *defiled* by her sexual encounters with others. (The Corsican brothers may have waded in over their heads.) In an article he had published in the *Revue Blanche* in Paris in 1896, devoted to the (newly exhibited) paintings of Edvard Munch, Strindberg had interpreted the famous *Jealousy* painting in exactly these terms: "holy feeling of purity of soul which despises being conjoined with another of the same sex by the mediation of another person." It is as if she, "cheating" on him, is also pimping for him, transmitting (into him) unwelcome erotic input. As card-carrying research scientist on alchemy (he was respected by the leaders of the field), however, the ever speculative, erudite Strindberg sometimes posited a material "seminal" basis for such unwanted coupling (or tripling), as we see in a letter to Lidforss in 1894: "Buffon writes that fructified eggs have been found in men's penises. *Sansclou* are a *Dröppel*. A *Dröppel* is a heap of male semen found in a vagina. Now, if one mounts a woman overfilled with semen, a man can get another man's semen in his penis or testicles, and so the seeds grow and the *sanscloued* man finds himself in a perverse state of pregnancy. . . . Everything moves, even semen. Wombs are only birds' nests in which the cock lays his eggs." It is hard to know which trap is worse: to have sex with a woman and receive another man's semen or to be alone and experience another man fornicating with your loved one. Ah, the company we keep! When the boundaries of self go up in smoke—or are simply overcome by intense libido—all kinds of amalgams, wanted and unwanted, become possible. Brave new world.

As I've said, we have no metric for the kinds of "contact" that Strindberg says he experiences, but no matter what label we apply, we are struck by the *traffic* being registered in these notations. Radical feeling was seen as a readerly injunction in Kierkegaard, geared to producing fear and trembling if one was to understand Abraham's trial, whereas in Strindberg's accounts of both misery and pleasure it has become something far more uncontrollable, invasive, immediate, and shape-shifting. The more one is struck by its coerciveness, the more one sees in it an onslaught utterly at odds with today's app-supported digital experience of reach, control, and *invulnerability*. The quasi-aphrodisiac appeal of our eversleeker contemporary gadgets is that they *bring* you everywhere at a touch of a finger, and that they *bring* the world *to* you in like fashion.

We have long sensed the commercial dangers implicit in this model, and one cannot log on today, without receiving boatloads of enticing ads and the like, all cued to our own earlier digital consumer history, knowing us perhaps better, we're told, than we know ourselves, "writing us large," as it were. We are also admonished, along more political lines, that "they"—Big Brother, the Kremlin, four-hundred-pound trolls, Google, whatever name you care to give to the evil Wizards of Oz directing it all behind the scenes—have access to our data (our whereabouts, our communications, our purchases, our tastes, our proclivities, ours secrets) on a nonstop basis, making the notion of "privacy" a wistful concept of the old-tech past. These are familiar dangers about being wired.

What Strindberg brings to this mix may border at times on the psychotic—his libidinal history is *playing*, and it is playing *him*—but there is something tonic as well as terrifying in the energized dimensional portrait that he proffers, for it obliterates any notion of agency or protection or choice. You cannot turn the machine off.

What is moving about Strindberg's testimony is that he offers us a fully externalized image of the wired subject, of the human being as magnetic field, of one's own life as extravagant far-flung playground of interacting forces. His fourth-dimensional portrait figures not only a remaking of Pascal's map but, going even further back, a modernizing of Leonardo's Vitruvian man, now splayed out in all his linkages and nodal points, fueled neurally and affectively. There is nothing pleasant in this. His tidings are the direct opposite of the current digital scheme in which we *select* which images, voices, sounds, and sights are to caress us: instead we are under siege, and it is the "emancipated," "exploded" *figure* of our life that is coming into view.

Let me, in closing, offer another visual metaphor for the Strindbergian self, rather different from Munch's famous portrait of him: the *Hypercube* developed by the mathematician Thomas Banchoff; this is an ungainly construct of a formerly docile six-sided cube having "exploded" (or "imploded") by being rotated on each of its sides, as it sovereignly makes its spatial way into the fourth dimension, thereby revealing extensions that baffle and outrun our limited, constricted Newtonian three-dimensional scheme. No cube we know looks like this. But August

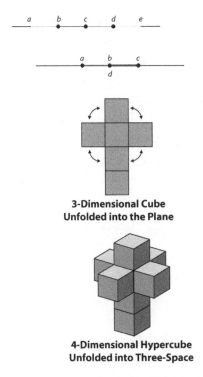

**3-Dimensional Cube
Unfolded into the Plane**

**4-Dimensional Hypercube
Unfolded into Three-Space**

Image Courtesy of Thomas S. Banchoff, from *Beyond the
Third Dimension* (Scientific American Library, 1990)

Strindberg does. He is one of our great explorers; I consider him an
"affective geometer," for he has tracked the very morphology, the "forking path," of human emotion over time–space, yielding a "hypercube"
rendition of our fourth-dimensional selves.

From daydreaming to masturbation, from taking a walk to taking a
nap, from sharing a conversation or a bed, there is *traffic*: we are *out there*
and they are *in here*. Those are the tangents that Strindberg reveals. He's
nuts, you might say; and he probably was. Yet this clearly paranoid text
thrusts into visibility that same mesh that undergirds and fuels his other
poems and plays. Remember Paul's murky mirror. "Face to face" is the
payload of Strindberg's work: his ghostly intercourse with his absent
third wife is the dance of ghosts that each of us participates in, that goes
through its paces in each of us, except that he experienced it "in the

flesh," "am eigenen Leib erfahren." Take a hard look at your own résumé and consider how many (forgotten? dead?) selves (and others) are on display, how many places you've inhabited and are inhabited by, and then do your tally. Remember "Je suis un cimetière ahborré de la lune," as Baudelaire acknowledged for so many of us, but Strindberg's buried relationships don't die, are lit up by more than moonlight, are cancerously active, take him over. His writings speak to us today, for they reveal a tentacular world of living, invasive links, connectivity. Such paranoid work may not yield a picture to one's liking, but it does pack a punch.

Proust: The Trip to Buttes-Chaumont

Who has heard of Buttes-Chaumont? It is a pleasure park in northeast Paris in the Nineteenth Arrondissement. I have never been there. But Albertine, the elusive lover of Marcel, the eponymous hero of Proust's massive *In Search of Lost Time*, has, it seems, spent time there, with her friend Andrée. The relationship between Marcel and Albertine takes up some four or five of the novel's seven volumes. It is a vexed, often tortured relationship—she frequently bores him, yet the threat of losing her causes him immense pain, leading to arranging a sequestered life where she is virtually held "prisoner"—that closes with the young woman's escaping her "prison," thereby triggering a manic search on the part of her lover. And then, abruptly, absurdly, she dies: riding her bicycle, she crashes into a tree, and is instantly killed.

Except that nothing is ever instantly done with in Proust. Time plays its hand, and our life-chapters acquire often unanticipated contours and extra innings, not to mention new beginnings. The "trip to Buttes-Chaumont" is my rubric, and we'll see that it is a temporal, affective, vicarious trip, to be taken by Marcel, taken in the mode of all essential travels in Proust: in the imagination, in the heart. I have of course omitted from my account of Albertine the crucial toxic "fact" that she is *likely* lesbian. Likely but not quite documentably, it seems. ("Ocular proof!" Othello insists on, to determine Desdemona's fidelity; does one ever have it?) Hence, *after* her death, Marcel—ever more tortured by her putative betrayals, betrayals all the more gruesomely "free" to lacerate him as he goes about imagining them, now that she is no longer alive to deny them—actually employs his man Aimé (good name, this) to go about *tracking* her past jaunts and escapades, in hopes of finally getting to the truth. And he finds gobs of it, including unbearable, close-up intimate reports of her being pleasured in ways he cannot compete with. It's as if each of Albertine's trysts acquired a ghostly stalker, coming afterward, doing his own masochistic pilgrimage to Mount Moriah.

Proust, Pascalian par excellence, is one of our great map-makers when it comes to charting the meandering course of grieving or suffering. Marcel never does actually go to Buttes-Chaumont. He doesn't need to. In some awful sense, it comes to *him* . . . via the newspaper. Even in our contemporary culture of unpredictable violence, where crazies are capable of shooting up schools or restaurants or shopping malls, who has ever felt that opening a newspaper could be a dangerous, life-threatening, activity? In Proust it is.

> I tried at times to take an interest in the newspapers. But I found the act of reading them repellent, and moreover by no means innocuous. The fact is that from each of our ideas, as from the crossroads in a forest, so many paths branch off in different directions that at the moment when I least expected it I found myself faced by a fresh memory. The title of Fauré's melody *Le Secret* had led me to the Duc de Broglie's *Secret du Roi*, the name Broglie to that of Chaumont, or else the words "Good Friday" had made me think of Golgotha, Golgotha of the etymology of the word which is, it seems, the equivalent of *Calvus Mons*, Chaumont. But, whatever the path by which I had arrived at Chaumont, at that moment I received so violent a shock that I was far more concerned to ward off pain than to probe for memories. Some moments after the shock, my intelligence, which like the sound of thunder travels less rapidly, produced the reason for it. Chaumont had made me think of the Buttes-Chaumont, where Mme Bontemps had told me that Andrée used often to go with Albertine, whereas Albertine had told me that she had never seen the Buttes-Chaumont. After a certain age our memories are so intertwined with one another that what we are thinking of, the book we

are reading, scarcely matters any more. We have put something of ourselves everywhere, everything is fertile, everything is dangerous, and we can make discoveries no less precious than in Pascal's *Pensées* in an advertisement for soap.

This is not the trip to Mount Moriah, but it will turn out to be equally full of fear and trembling. Kierkegaard claimed you had to put yourself in Abraham's place; you had to take the human measure of those momentous three-and-a-half days. It is all sedentary in Proust; the only kinetic activity is the brain/heart busily processing language. At issue is not the sacrifice of a child, but the abyss of jealousy, an abyss into which you can fall even when you're sitting down, reading. It is well known that etymology is of interest in Proust's world: the curé in Combray is an amateur at it, and Brichot in the later volumes is quasi-professional; both characters risk being huge bores. But the origins of words, the remarkable journey over time that their successive changes display, surprisingly matter: here is a word-version of the play-of-time so central to Proust's interests in memory and the past. And, initially, that is how this long passage seems to announce itself: as potent verbal kinships— Chaumont/Calvus Mons, Golgotha—signaling something nonverbal altogether, crucifixion.

But upon closer inspection, we realize that the dictionary linkages are merely the outward delivery system of a *traffic pattern* that spells out Marcel's condition as permanent *target*, as utterly "nailed" by the associative chain triggered by the seemingly innocuous newspaper notation concerning Fauré's melody. Very curious. Nothing in the newspaper speaks overtly of Marcel or Albertine. (How often does the newspaper have your name in it?) Indeed, no one but Marcel could have read this newsprint in the way he did. Only he sees in this extensive chain of references (the Duke of Broglie exiled by Napoleon to Chaumont-sur-Loire) a private code, one that rightly says via its etymology "crucifixion," but which also shows why "crucifixion" is indeed the right referent here: Chaumont triggers in Marcel's mind "Buttes-Chaumont," and in turn that park site triggers (on the order of a detonation) the memory of Andrée's testimony that she and Albertine were there together

(contrary to Albertine's claim), which can only mean: clandestine lesbian sex. Please note how many sentences it took me to spell out this
trajectory; and then realize: it takes the brain (of the jealous lover) no
time at all to make this trip; it is instantaneous, faster even than the
delayed sound of thunder that follows lightning; it is a form of neural
crucifixion catalyzed by casual newsprint.

Now, this may seem fanciful, even esoteric, but I'd want to say it is
foundational, absolutely bedrock, in its shimmering display of what we
might again call the psychopathology of everyday life. Going beyond
Freud, enlisting the vocabulary and terminology of our own digital electronic world, I'd claim, as I did for Strindberg, that this passage is a
portrait of a man who is *wired*. In putting it that way, I want to contrast,
yet again, the situation of Marcel with that of today's millions of denizens who are permanently hooked up to devices that stream nonstop
"information" (music, podcasts, tweets, you name it) into their ears and
brains . . . and hearts. None of what is coming through into them has
anything to do with their own secret itineraries of the heart (love, sexual
betrayal, etc.); none of what goes through them proffers a map of their
life; none of them feels either thunderstruck or crucified by the currents
coursing through them. (Maybe they do; but what I see, everywhere I
look, is faces intently poring over a small screen or listening to ear-
phones, getting their rations; no Cross in sight.)

Proust's scenario is not a happy one. What we lazily call "jealousy" is
to be understood as a gruesome romp through time and space, with the
added spice that we do not control this voyage; rather, it hijacks us in utterly unforeseeable ways. Your affective past (past? ha!)—who among us
has no terrors better kept in the dark?—is fueling the ride, and it can enlist
virtually anything you run into to send you on your way. You thought it
was only a newspaper (the ultimate impersonal, neutral object, yes?), but
lo and behold: it becomes, via associative logic and etymological play, a
personal-delivery torture system. You have, in "merely" living your life,
"put something of yourself everywhere" as Proust brilliantly says, and
hence the so-called objective outside world, utterly unattuned to your
psyche, is nevertheless utterly polluted by your private story, your private
garbage, a kind of refuse that cannot be refused.

What a brave new world—a world we "leak" into every day—is coming into view here! All of our definitional categories and binaries about inner/outer, major/minor, or subjective/objective are imploded, go down the tubes. Meaning—personal meaning—is *not* packaged in any of the ways we have been taught. The world resembles those pinball machines I grew up with, and you find yourself colliding into flippers that send you careening into pain, hurling you into your own muck. And not just yours, but others'. Proustian jealousy: the fruitless but lacerating trip into the spatiotemporal reaches of the loved one's (hidden) life. The trip to Mount Moriah is now a libidinal torture-trek. We began this essay with Pascal, and now we return to him, and find him outdone (impact-wise) by an advertisement for soap. The loved one's time and space become *sensibles au coeur*: no need to consult the *Pensées* to find this out; a newspaper will do.

It may be thought that the newspaper encounter that triggers the hidden past has a soap-opera, "literary" feel to it, but I see a kind of quotidian dynamite here, a radical indictment of the surface world (of neutral objects, of information and stable dictionary meanings) always thought to be irrelevant to your subjective life, except at those collision moments when it synchronizes with our personal history. At that juncture, nasty stuff happens: the objective public world sloughs off its skin—whoever thought it had a skin?—and a different set of private coordinates and markers take over. (We are not far from Strindberg here: *anything* can become a mirror.) Do you now see why Proust thought cinema to be an impoverished art form, shackled to the surface appearance of things, hence locked out of the only realm that matters: *what things mean to me*?

What, I now rhetorically ask, would you or I ordinarily make of a pastry called "madeleine" (which you can find in any French bakery)? Would you, unprompted, uninitiated, ever see dynamite there? Yet his novel makes us understand that seemingly innocuous "things" are of crucial private importance because they are the counters (the generators, the retrievers, the humming dynamo) of one's actual inner life. They are a magic script. To make this point, as a kind of ocular proof, I offer a "triptych" of images for your perusal: two of them are world-famous icons, known

Mona Lisa at the Musée du Louvre; Notre Dame, image by Peter Haas. Licensed under
CC BY-SA 3.0; madeleines, image by Karen Booth. Licensed under CC BY-ND 2.0

everywhere (Notre Dame and the *Mona Lisa*), whereas the little one on
the bottom left is a piece of pastry (yes, a madeleine). Only readers of
Proust's book will realize that the world-changing item in my "triptych" is
the measly little pastry, the one that "contains"—the way a bottle might
contain its genie—the narrator's entire past. As for the cathedral and the
painting, of course they are momentous in themselves, but they don't say
squat about one's private, hidden, huge interior life. (Unless, perhaps,
your first love affair was in a dark gallery in Notre Dame or the worshipped
painting on your bedroom wall happens to be the *Mona Lisa*.)

To complete this argument about the sentient dimensions of time and space, I want to go back—Why not? It's easy to do—to a crucial prior earth-shattering moment in the novel: the instant when Marcel fully understands, *at last*, that Albertine might be a lesbian. (Kierkegaard's law: live it forward, but understand it backward.) Significantly it happens on a train: Marcel and Albertine are returning home from an evening with the Verdurins, and Albertine informs him that she was virtually brought up by two older girls—namely, Mlle Vinteuil and her friend. Aha! These two girls are *documentably* lesbian: textually, Proust had given us and Marcel "ocular proof" of it (volumes ago), when he, by happenstance years ago, fell asleep by the window of M. Vinteuil's house (how convenient!), woke up (still more convenient!), and then, lo and behold, espied the two girls making love (and desecrating the photo of Mlle Vinteuil's dead father, while they were at it). This was a serious eyeful from long long ago. But it did no damage then; no "lasting damage," as we might say.

We (want to) think time heals, that a chance eyeful long ago would be lost in oblivion. But nothing heals or is lost in Proust. The young man's memory of what he saw back then is now characterized as possessing a "noxious power," and he (wonderfully) likens its time-defying potency to the figure of Orestes, kept alive by the gods pointedly in order to avenge the murder of Agamemnon. He then codes the pain he now feels as punishment for his own sins, in particular "allowing" his grandmother to die. (Once the lid comes off the garbage can, a lot of refuse can come out.) All this, he comes to understand, testifies to the undying virulence of the libidinal data stored inside us, ready to leap out and lay waste to us if somehow triggered by events in the present. One feels, as reader, that this "stored" lethal power resembles radioactive energy or nuclear waste or outright IEDs, with a half-life of hundreds of years, unstillable, undying, waiting.

One is unaccustomed to thinking oneself larded with poisonous deposits that can lie dormant for decades before suddenly releasing their toxins, on the order of a slow-growing cancer or melanoma, "acquired" unknowingly and known to us only the day its malignancy erupts or is finally detectable. Do you ever know what is cooking inside you? Do you have a clue what might make it flower or explode? Here is cognition of a special kind. This sequence reads as the polar diabolic opposite of the angelic moment of the beneficent, ecstatic madeleine experience, for it makes us realize that the life experiences of the past—what happened in another time and place, long forgotten, thought to be dead—can, when a chance encounter opens the bottle and lets the genie out, jolt us with great pain as well as great delight, *shock* us the way a live electrical wire would if we touched it.

What most strikes me here are the immediacy and reach of the hurt, the sheer scale of the new map coming into view. Please note the remarkable telephone metaphor that Proust enlists:

> The notion of Albertine as friend of Mlle Vinteuil and of Mlle Vinteuil's friend, a practicing and professional Sapphist, was as momentous, compared to what I had imagined when I doubted her most, as are the telephones that soar over streets, cities, fields, seas, linking one country to another, compared to the little acousticon of the 1889 Exhibition which was barely expected to transmit sound from one end of a house to the other. It was a terrible *terra incognita* on which I had just landed, a new phase of undreamed-of sufferings that was opening before me.

Proust is rightly regarded as a psychological novelist, yet his interest in the emerging technologies of his day was vivid, and the metaphor of pain as an unmapped, quasi-planetary space that turns out to be *wired*, linking us neurally and viscerally to events far away and long ago, seems luminous to me. I see in Proust's formulation McLuhan's revolutionary view of the media as extension of our central nervous system, but now inverted—so Proustian, that: *inverti*—so that the human subject is on the receiving end, rather than being the person extending his reach. Just as the "trip to Buttes-Chaumont" was (for Marcel, for readers) neural, so, too, does this notation speak of affective pathways that extend our whereabouts in time and space, in order to nail us.

In this light, Proustian jealousy—the tortured experience of your loved one's imagined "freedom" and whereabouts in time and space—is akin to Kierkegaardian fear and trembling, inasmuch as each constitutes a kind of narrative theory, a storytelling injunction that obliges us to "measure by the heart." But whereas Kierkegaard is urging us to grasp the terror in Abraham's faith, Proust's example is about terrorism itself: love regraphs our coordinates, enmeshes us in currents and pulsations, destroys all sense of control or agency or hegemony. Proustian jealousy hinges on the changed direction-signals that reverse the current(s), proving that *there and then* can waylay you *here and now* at any moment.

The Proustian telephone, linking entire continents, can get through at any moment, constituting, as it were, a pulsating cybernetwork without security. Whether the senders are lovers or friends or corporations or the government or hackers, you are exposed, when you're online, and you're always online. Baudelaire, drawing on Swedenborg, had titled one of his early poems "Correspondances": in it, he posited a world of linkage and connection, where the physical and the spiritual beckon to each other. Strindberg showed us the potential toxicity of this scheme, as the human figure becomes a punching bag for incoming messages and pain. Proust takes this model still further, and although there is little to celebrate in his findings, they add a strange kind of dignity to our arrangements, by dint of the connectivity now on show. The rewards of such literature will not fatten your bank account, but they do, oddly, increase your circle of friends (and enemies), by illuminating your hidden circuits. No machinery is required, not even the tiniest microchip. Anything can set it off. It's fueled from the inside. Curriculum vitae. The course of your life.

James Joyce: Goodbye, Ithaca

When Joyce's *Ulysses* made its much vaunted and heralded arrival in 1922, it launched a kind of "private" yet capacious modernist writing—it was to be termed "stream of consciousness" or "interior monologue"—that has become a staple of narrative literature ever since. It is crucial to note that Joyce's novel enlists this mode of writing in fewer than half of its chapters—they are largely to be found at the beginning; they are actually what is "easy" and manageable about this daring, daunting book—whereas other later chapters essentially go berserk, exploding with narrative invention of the freest and most inventive, maniacal sort, shorn of the traditional allegiances and uprights that gave shape and coherence to what used to be known as "the novel," most especially the nineteenth-century novel outfitted with a cogent mix of character and plot.

Berserk in what ways?, the novice reader may ask. Joyce set out to wreck all earlier conventions. To compose one chapter ("Aeolus") in "newspaperese" using headlines as rubrics, to compose another chapter ("Wandering Rocks") from a bird's-eye view of Dublin streets so that the characters appear as ciphers, to compose another chapter ("Sirens") according to the "sound-principle" that works along predominantly phonic and aural principles, to compose another ("Oxen of the Sun") that recounts the birth of a child (a child of zero significance to the narrative) in an evolving stylistic discourse that mimics the evolution of English prose from medieval Latin to modern slang, to commit yet another ("Circe") to dramatic form, but a dramatic form so democratic that bars of soap and statues and paintings and dead people speak in it as players. All of this is mind-boggling and magnificent—no novel I know has come close to matching it—but each of the rhetorical gambits I have (reductively) sketched preens in its own inimitable way and advertises a complete disregard for the "life story," for those core sentient truths that make or break life, that I've claimed as the very mission of literature. Homer's Odysseus ran into one huge trial after another en route to Ithaca, but none of these hurdles was *textual*. Could they be? Why would an author elect such a strategy?

The project of mapping the fuller reaches of one's life—as seen in Baudelaire, Strindberg, Merrill, and Proust—comes a cropper in *Ulysses*, because the novel is so larded with discrete realia and immense systems (symbolic and otherwise) that the authority and integrity of individual life must fight for their life on every page. ("They" of course do not fight; "we" fight to espy or retrieve them.) Even the stream of consciousness—which we'd imagine to be ego-driven, close to one's heart, the real thing—is egalitarian, inclusive, full of flotsam and jetsam, tons of atomistic notations, exploding any obvious notion we might have of proprietary, bounded character.

For first-time readers, therefore, this book is a massive assault against their expectations and habits-of-reading. Joycean scholars have spent endless days and years and entire careers teasing out putative correspondences, linking (through intricate critical and erudite calisthenics) the dazzling textual high jinks to the presumable, inferable Homeric ur-story of man–wife–child. But the nonprofessional readers (if there are any) often go hungry. One upbeat way of assessing these matters is to say that story of the heart or soul is all the more valuable if we need to work around the clock to tease it out of the magma of discrete realia in this utterly *egalitarian* text. (Students rarely appreciate this perspective.) And it is a little embarrassing to be obliged to "bend over backward to find meaning" in a book; Harry Levin once remarked that bending over backward is physically impossible and (if possible) aesthetically or visually rather grotesque. Neither productive nor pretty.

But just maybe that is how the psyche conducts its affairs: moments of clarity and pathos are real but are few and far between. Is it possible that we have forever cooked the books, pretended that our sentient and moral affairs held center stage, governed the inside picture, stamped consciousness with human cogency? (I have to plead guilty here, as this book documents.) But imagine a truthful pie chart of how you actually spend each day, and ask how much space the moral/existential actually takes up, given that such "serious" bookkeeping cohabits with using the kitchen and bathroom, napping, doodling, and more. Worse still, do some eavesdropping on what it actually sounds like inside your head on a 24/7 basis. Big things? Little things? Or unholy mix of bric-a-brac?

Bloom's roving perspective, often like a camera taking in the sights or a recorder jotting down the inside and outside noise, is capacious and often eludes the "girdle" of *story*, a girdle that traditional literature reveres. And that is why the precious moments when the "signifying" needle is found in the textual haystack are so moving. My favorite instance takes place in "Lestrygonians," the "restaurant chapter," where Bloom is eating/drinking/observing with his usual freewheeling pungency. In the sequence that interests me, we see Bloom pondering and parsing the farce of food intake—"Do ptake some ptargmigan . . . May I tempt you to a little more filleted lemon sole, miss Dubedat? Yes, do bedad. And she did bedad." Playful ruminations of this stripe continue for a few lines until Bloom spots two flies stuck together on the windowpane. At that point imbibed wine starts to exert its force, leading to a sequence of grapes, sun's heat, "a secret touch telling me memory" as Bloom's wine-moistened senses retrieve the central erotic event of his past:

> Hidden under wild ferns on Howth below us bay sleeping: sky. No sound. The sky. The bay purple by the Lion's head. Green by Drumleck. Yellowgreen towards Sutton. Fields of undersea, the lines faint brown in grass, buried cities. Pillowed on my coat she had her hair, earwigs in the heather scrub my hand under her nape, you'll toss me all. O wonder! Coolsoft with ointments her hand touched me, caressed: her eyes upon me did not turn away. Ravished over her I lay, full lips full open, kissed her mouth. Yum. Softly she gave me in my mouth the seedcake warm and chewed. Mawkish pulp her mouth had mumbled sweetsour of her spittle. Joy: I ate it: joy. Young life, her lips gave me pouting. Soft warm sticky gumjelly lips. Flowers her eyes were, take me, willing eyes. Pebbles fell. She lay still. A goat. No-one. High on Ben Howth rhododendrons a nannygoat walking surefooted, dropping currants. Screened under ferns she laughed warmfolded. Wildly I lay on her, kissed her eyes, her lips, her stretched neck beating, woman's breasts full in her blouse of nun's veiling, fat nipples upright. Hot I tongued her. She kissed me. I was kissed. All yielding she tossed my hair. Kissed, she kissed me.
>
> Me. And me now.
>
> Stuck, the flies buzzed.

This is the most lyrical—indeed Proustian—moment in the novel, and it shows us with great feeling what it is that Bloom has *lost* in all the "sexless" years of his marriage, "sexless" ever since little Rudy died shortly after birth, over a decade ago. Yet it is sandwiched between stuck flies on a windowpane, and even if it "grounds" our understanding of Bloom's sentient life, it commands little textual authority, a kind of "one-off" memory that no reader forgets, but that coexists with Bloom's countless other musings: about advertising, about a host of Dublin characters, about sights and smells, about hundreds of other random recollections and echoes and notations, all composing the ever-changing landscape of his one-day peregrinations throughout the city.

I have wanted to construct a "centered" Bloom, keyed to marital loss, but to do so I am obliged to ignore the textual container Joyce has made for him (and for us), which frustrates all such underlining or italicizing, which presents this haunting memory as merely a modest dish in a massive verbal smorgasbord (in keeping with Joyce's restaurantese). In short, I the reader am playing the Ithaca card, am seeking to grasp and evaluate the affective density and dimensions of this character, by highlighting one ecstatic moment that took place years ago. Consider our past examples: Baudelaire's community of exiles (Andromache, Ovid, the swan, the tubercular black woman) nursing their losses; Strindberg passing the Parisian butcher shop and returning (in his mind) to the book of poems exposed on the Norrbro bridge in Stockholm; Merrill's speaker moving from the spectacle of urban change to the elusive memory of past love in an "architectural" bid to create a frame for his life; Proust's Marcel propelled, via a chance reading of the newspaper, into the crucifying narrative of his lover's former erotic betrayals. Literature, I am insisting, performs this role of "harvest" as we take the measure of who we have been and (thus) still are. Joyce's egalitarian model—briskly, defiantly nonanthropocentric in its inclusiveness—seems to sink my argument, indeed my entire armada.

But can it sink?

If called on to defend my homing-move in Joyce's resistant book, I would cite the brief utterance that closes this lyrical memory and book-ends it far more hauntingly than the stuck flies: "Me. And me now." For a brief moment, Joyce tips his hand, informs us that Bloom, too, is taking measures, gauging his losses, thinking about his sentient life. How to interpret "Me. And me now"? Tragic or comic or absurd or simply factual? You choose. No matter how we assess Bloom's remark, we must see it as a kind of "harvest," as a parsing of what time has wrought in his life. It is an Ithaca moment. "Me. And me now" has the brevity and clarity of notations on a tombstone.

But how far will this take us? I have already declared war on the meager testimony of tombstones and "information." Joyce is open to

the widest range of testimony ever seen in fiction, but individual hegemony (a.k.a. the shape of a life) is under attack. If Odysseus had
been obliged to construct a résumé—I like this question—you can
bet that Calypso, the Cyclops, the Sirens, Scylla and Charybdis, and
everything else in Homer's epic poem would have been included. But
poor Bloom's CV doesn't stand much of a chance, in the Joycean mix.
Is it possible that the helter-skelter of *Ulysses* exposes the rampant
selectivity and bad faith of the entire CV project? If so, my humanist
argument goes down the tubes. And I promised I would not bend over
backward to save it.

If final accountings and homecoming are our difficult goal, then it
makes sense (and makes my life easier) that we move, as we must, to the
novel's penultimate chapter, "Ithaca": after many long chapters of per-
egrination throughout Dublin, Bloom is indeed going home (bringing
the drunken Stephen Dedalus with him in tow.) It is here that the going
gets tough because Joyce now stages a grotesque war between human
truths and the immense realms of things, data, and history that dwarf
those truths. Like the Empire, *information is striking back*. It is as if my
entire humanist argument were on trial.

Note, for example, what happens when Bloom is preparing to boil
water for hot cocoa for his guest. Nothing soulful here. This should be
easy. Bloom turns on the faucet to get water, and we get this:

> Did it flow?
>
> Yes. From Roundwood reservoir in county Wicklow of a cubic
> capacity of 2400 million gallons, percolating through a subterranean
> aqueduct of filter mains of single and double pipeage constructed at
> an initial plant cost of £5 per linear yard by way of the Dargle, Rath-
> down, Glen of the Downs and Callowhill to the 26 acre reservoir at
> Stillorgan, a distance of 12 statute miles, and then, through a system
> of relieving tanks, by a gradient of 250 feet to the city boundary at
> Eustace bridge, upper Leeson street . . .

I have cut rather drastically the passage that continues into a factual account of current summer drought and the various strategies and subter-
fuges put into action by Dublin officials to meet the potential water
shortage, replete with numbers of gallons and dates of earlier such

challenges. Metrics galore. One reads this passage and one asks oneself: is this an engineering manual? A Dublin water-supply history? (If dead people could read books written in later centuries, the dour Pascal would be smiling in his grave. Yes, he might feel, this, too, is what "the disproportion of man" could look like.) Is this passage of any conceivable significance for our understanding of either Leopold Bloom or his guest Stephen Dedalus? The answer is no. Which then raises the question: should a novel be character-centric? How hospitable can narrative be toward "realia," toward the "environment"?

Joyce is bent on exposing—then exploding—the entire host of conventions that confer meaning in literature. One such convention is that plot and character are in the driver's seat. Joyce might have replied: plot and character are in the driver's seat *only* in literature, but never in life itself. Some critics have felt that precious little *happens* in this long novel. Joyce might have replied: *happens* is a myth. Or he might have replied, citing the very passage that I cited, that the Dublin Waterworks are a happening of sorts, even if they have little to do—"characterologically"—with Bloom or Stephen. This leads me to repeat that *Ulysses* is the most egalitarian novel ever written, "egalitarian" in the sense that a dictionary is egalitarian. (We used to think that dictionaries and novels are different beasts.)

(Joyce makes me wonder how he'd represent me-the-author sitting at my desk, typing out these lines: I can only imagine the intricate array of cooperating muscles and nerves and tissues in play with my moving fingers, or perhaps the mechanistic wizardry of my electronic keyboard as its receives my taps [a keyboard replete with its own energy sources, going back further than the Dublin Waterworks], and then there is the chair I'm sitting on, the eyes I'm using to see my screen, the neural/verbal calisthenics at work as I perform the act of writing. Hmm. Would this be in the least interesting? Would the long, devious, forking, haphazard voyage starting in my brain and making it all the way to the page you're reading be *worth* tracking in all its many constitutive phases?)

Story is being hammered. Its conceptual shelter—the architectural project subtending most literature—is being obliterated. Most of us, in fact, do not think of Homer or Ithaca or the "wife and child," when we turn on the faucet or make a pot of tea, but origins are origins, and once you start tracing where anything comes from—much less what it returns to—you can go on a long trip or indeed off a cliff. Joyce offers in this chapter a magisterial, often hysterical centrifugal model, where the directionality of the textual activity is incessantly *outward*, toward the circumference, a circumference that seems to explode any centripetal fantasy of centering, of recuperation, of making an estate, of homecoming.

Much of "Ithaca" is a screwball, often hysterical rewrite of Pascal's "infinitely great" and "infinitely small." But Joyce, in general, has no interest in making any of these vistas "sensibles au coeur." There are rare exceptions, such as when Bloom escorts Stephen back onto the street and then looks up at the sky; we then see what kind of strange poetry Joyce can wring out of Pascal. He first allows himself a brief lyrical outing: "The heaventree of stars hung with humid nightblue fruit." This is exquisite, and it is a lovely rejoinder to the silent, empty heavens Pascal had pondered. But Joyce then moves predictably into scientese as Bloom meditates "meditations of evolution increasingly vaster: of the moon invisible in incipient lunation, approaching perigee: of the infinite lattiginous scintillating uncondensed milky way," which then goes on to ever greater dizzying notations of distance and scale, so as to close with the familiar contrast of a human life of "threescore and ten" forming "a parenthesis of infinitesimal brevity." So much for the centrality of *character*.

Still greater fireworks emerge when Joyce changes directions and goes small/smaller/smallest, depicting ever greater yet tinier vistas located in "microbes, germs, bacteria, bacilli, spermatozoa: of the incalculable trillions of billions of millions of imperceptible molecules contained by cohesion of molecular affinity in a single pinhead," moving thence (with panache) to still smaller bodies within the blood, "themselves universes of void space constellated with other bodies, each, in continuity, its universe of divisible component bodies of which each was again divisible in divisions of redivisible component bodies, dividends and divisors ever diminishing without actual division till, if the progress were carried far enough, nought nowhere was never reached." This sublime conclusion, *nought nowhere was never reached* makes me want to clap, so grand and baroque it is, yet its tidings are not good news for human measure or human "fit." And home? "Home" seems locked in an unwinnable war with abstract Latinate terms that Joyce demonstrably enjoys playing with, rhyming, deconstructing, having fun. Can you imagine Oedipus or Lear or Cathy Earnshaw or Benito Cereno or Huck Finn or Strindberg or Gregor Samsa or Proust's Marcel running into this kind of trouble? Ultimate truths? A lark.

What, it may now be wondered, am I doing by enlisting *Ulysses* for my apology of literature as recovery of our human dimensions? Molière would doubtless ask me: *Que diable faites-vous dans cette galère?* (What the hell are you doing on this boat?) Well, it's answer time: Joyce's salute to scientific lists, numbing data, endless *things*, in "Ithaca" requires facing up to, not merely for the integrity of my book but for making visible the uphill, indeed unnatural, perhaps heroic proprietary task of character itself, character as the centripetal drama that takes the measure of our sojourns through time and space, through mind and body, in order to posit, as their "home," some kind of plenary self. Self matters most, as Joyce himself helps us see, because it is *made* rather than *given*, because it is the grand fiction of life, the single nonstop (even if sporadic and inconclusive) work of art that thinking and feeling people go about constructing from birth to death, as they muddle through. Joyce makes us see what a wild ride it is, how much selectivity and cheating and corralling and inventing go into it, how much we are obliged simply to factor *out*, if we are to manage home.

Joyce is never simply an encyclopedist, despite his willingness to include the kitchen sink and the laws of gravity in his book. And no one has ever opened up the vistas of fiction as he has, taking the reader for quite a ride. Might "character"—*bounded* character, right?—also go on a ride? Namewise, no problem: they can become Blephen and Stoom; a paragraph can be written about that pair, conflating their educational trajectories. Or we can think anagram: Leopold Bloom, Ellpodbomool, Molldopeloob, Bollopedoom, Old Ollebo, M. P. Joyce also turns the age differences between Bloom and Stephen into a dazzling arithmetic fantasia, which I've already commented on, so you know the bad news already: numbers may do some fancy flying but they do not ground the self any better than names do.

Proust once observed how surprising it can be to wake up and be the same person who went to sleep, given the kaleidoscopic transformations that can take place in dreams, and I have indicated my own slippery sense of self as twin. The dance of identity is real.

Yet Joyce's "Ithaca" has little dancing in it; remember those waterworks. Instead, we are treated to anonymous, breakout, systemic notations, interspersed with whimsical meanderings of habit, routinized lists, nascent thoughts and thoughtlets, fantasies, remembrances, sound bites, flotsam and jetsam, accounts, questions, free association—all orchestrated by the hectoring rhetoric of Q&A that governs the chapter—and cumulatively demonstrating how utterly bizarre and inclusive the spectacle of a man getting ready for bed might be, if seen truly close-up, if seen through a microscope, if seen in its slow-motion entirety. Imagine an ant taking stock of either its or your day, and consider what kind of a complicated spreadsheet and inventory that might yield. This kind of potpourri screams out the reductive fraudulence of our labels and tags, including those meted out by classical psychology, for it tracks the quicksilver promiscuous activity of (neural) life and the endless density of the material world at a level where no categories hold. How can "homecoming" get a perch here?

At some point, as all readers expect, Bloom will move past his extensive domestic inventories and finally make his way to bed. It is the law of nature, and it is the law of this plot. We see Bloom, heading to the bedroom, ruminate on photos and clothing (female wearing apparel strewn out) and objects (commode, hat, basket, washstand), as he removes his own clothes, puts on his nightshirt, and enters the bed. *How?* the narrative asks. "With circumspection . . . with solicitude . . . prudently . . . reverently." *What,* the text then asks, *did his limbs, when gradually extended, encounter?* The answer includes new bed linen, odors, "the presence of a human form, female, hers, the imprint of a human form, male, not his . . ." We also learn of crumbs and flakes of potted meat, which he removes. A forensics team with cameras and microscopes couldn't improve on this.

At this point Joyce does something wonderful: he becomes *subjunctive*. The reign of the factual and the measurable is—for a moment—interrogated. The text asks: *If he had smiled why would he have smiled?* I know no cannier line in literature. Here is the homing moment—what do you make of your trip?—but it is perfectly hedged by the question's speculative fudging. And what reader is thinking about "smiling" at this juncture? What is there to smile at, when you enter your conjugal bed and find there the body of your wife, the imprint of her lover, and bits of potted meat? Joyce enlists Homer in the text's reply, for he is replaying Odysseus's killing of Penelope's suitors, but the Homeric list (of finite, enumerated, males to be slaughtered) matters most because it becomes here just a *list*, a *series*, an unending *sequence* that puts paid to any and all "privatist" illusions. Here, by the way, is why Bloom "would" have smiled, "if" he had smiled:

> To reflect that each one who enters imagines himself to be the first to enter whereas he is always the last term of a preceding series even if the first term of a succeeding one, each imagining himself to be first, last, only and alone whereas he is neither first nor last nor only nor alone in a series originating in and repeated to infinity.

Poor Pascal had felt that human reason and human dignity were sufficiently rebuked and humiliated by the immensity of the large/small worlds we are and are thrown into, homeless and unequipped with any measuring tools that work. This is a tragic, indeed violent perception, meant to open us to the divine. Joyce finds this condition bracing and is quite willing to locate it in the cuckold's bedroom rather than the philosopher's study. Again, I think Blaise might have chuckled.

Hence, Leopold Bloom will think about his marital drama—the staple of both comedy and tragedy since time immemorial, but always thought to be meaningful—as a worldly man whose range of vision is truly multiperspectival and inclusive. (Open the scene [any scene] wide enough, and *you* risk falling out of the equation.) After reviewing some twenty-five candidates who've theoretically cuckolded him, Bloom experiences the following sentiments: "Envy, jealousy, abnegation, equanimity." This list is distinctly un-Homeric. But, being the rational adman he is, Bloom coolly sizes up the pros and cons of each term on the list. "Envy" is short-shrifted: sexual envy toward a better endowed male; "jealousy" is coded as a physics formula for increase, decrease, circular extension, and radial reentrance; "abnegation" harks, bizarrely, back to an unnarrated event a year earlier, but also features altruism, egoism, racial attractions, and inhibitions, closing with info about a musical tour.

"Equanimity," thus, is—not surprisingly, given this book's democratic manner—the item that fully gets the text's attention: for we now see the act of being cuckolded held up and measured against a host of other calamities large and small, ranging from annihilation of the planet to theft, forgery, corruption, arson, treason, felony, trespass, poaching, usury, manslaughter, and still other examples of major bad news. It is as if you just had a stroke or a coronary, and the doctor handed you a medical anthology of somatic misfortunes, so that you could properly align yours, and find its place in the encyclopedic list. (In a sense, this is precisely what medicine does: lines "you" up against the generic data.)

Bloom seeks to do just that. In an astonishing paragraph that states the problem with utmost clarity by grammatically parsing (in hifalutin linguistic terminology, "masculine subject, monosyllabic, onomatopoetic transitive verb with direct feminine object," etc.) two simple but imperious, unstoppable (even if never stated) locutions—"he fucks her" and "she is fucked by him" are the obvious payload—Bloom reaches his evaluative conclusion (the conclusion we've been waiting for, over many hundreds of pages): "the futility of triumph or protest or vindication; the inanity of extolled virtue: the lethargy of nescient matter; the apathy of the stars." Your wife is cheating on you: this infraction, when examined through the lenses on show in the "Ithaca" chapter, is small beer indeed. Pascal, man of faith though he was, is, as said, now squarely in the bedroom, financing the party, offering us a new version of the "wager." It's no longer about saving your soul but about measuring your life. What can the sexual significance of your marriage signify when seen against the backdrop of the infinitely great and infinitely small? As Iago might say, "cuckoldry: a fig!" Yet, yet, these pages do indeed respect literature's "contract" to depict our lives' fuller extensions. As we saw in Strindberg, this may not feel very good, but it does have scale.

Joyce elects to close his chapter by aligning husband and wife head to foot in their marriage bed. Joyce's candidate for Ulysses finds his way at long last back to the anchor of his existence, the reclining body of his wife. In so doing, he is stripped of all particulars, so that he can join in the mythic parade of other wanderers: Sinbad the Sailor and Tinbad the Tailor and Jinbad the Jailor right on through the alphabet, including Vinbad the Quailer and and Linbad the Yailer and Xinbad the Phthailer, finally completing his planetary circuit as Darkinbad the Brightdayler. It is High Society. It is language on a roll. It is a creation myth: night marries day. As for our protagonist himself, he finishes as a tiny point (.) in the text. Welcome home, Leopold Bloom! And maybe that is how each of us finishes: erased in our particularity, disappearing into the void. What chance does soul have against the Dublin Waterworks?

It may well be the masochist in me who insists on including in this book this long section on *Ulysses*, since Joyce makes sovereign sport out of the existential and humanistic creeds that ground my entire argument. My strategy is not merely to put the enemy into my text but to salute the novel that dares go furthest in challenging my beliefs. And my inner Mephistopheles wants to say: the sheer intellectual and imaginative brilliance of Joyce's roasting is itself a testament to mind, to the exuberant (galvanizing even if annihilating) power of thought, as it roams through the carnival of material and mental frames we inhabit. Pascal's map has been transformed beyond all recognition.

Proust, seeking to represent human life in its vertiginous relation to the expanses of time, evoked, at novel's end, a man on ever-growing stilts, stilts that eventually become so high at the end that we fall off and die. Joyce is no stranger to such circus imagery, but he is strangely even more our contemporary: big data enters his book and the mind of his protagonists, and even if it takes a wrecking ball to our fond notions of character and plot, it does indeed position the human subject on an exploded stage rarely ever seen in literature before. Reading and teaching *Ulysses* is certainly a form of working for my bread—yes, I am paid by the university to teach books such as this; no one will be surprised that most university students choke on it—and Professor Weinstein does his level best to save it for humanism. You could ascribe this either to tenure or insanity.

Some people like saunas. I don't, especially. But James Joyce gives me a sauna's harsh pleasure: he keeps me honest; he weans me of some of my puffiness and grandiose claims; he sweats it out of my system. He's purgative. A stint with *Ulysses* sends me back to the humanist aspirations I seek to believe in because he makes me see both their constructedness and their necessity.

The Information Necropolis: Godard's "Alphaville"

James Joyce exploded, about a century ago, all comforting notions of literature as story of the soul. Explosions rip things apart, but they also testify to energy itself, reminding me of that "humming dynamo" Strindberg earlier posited as the very machinery of art, locating it in a dark cellar and claiming that it "ground" light for the entire neighborhood. Put enough neighborhoods together and you have a city; it, too, fed and kept alive by energy systems, seen in the Dublin Waterworks, but seen also in the street life and street talk of human beings (where Joyce remains incomparable). Could those systems dry up? Can cities die? What keeps them alive?

Already in mid-nineteenth-century America, Emerson offered a stunning reply to that question by claiming, "The city lives by remembering." I've already discussed the life-giving retrievals and productions of memory in the poems of Baudelaire, Strindberg, and Merrill. But no one has offered a more magisterial apology for the city along these lines than Lewis Mumford has. In his classic *The City in History*, published in 1961, he gives us an institutional model of the polis as place of transmission and storage:

> Through its concentration of physical and cultural power, the city heightened the tempo of human intercourse and translated its products into forms that could be stored and reproduced. Through its monuments, written records, and orderly habits of association, the

city enlarged the scope of all human activities, extending them back-
wards and forwards in time. By means of its storage facilities (buildings, vaults, archives, monuments, tablets, books), the city became
capable of transmitting a complex culture from generation to generation, for it marshaled together not only the physical means but the
human agents needed to pass on and enlarge the heritage. That remains the greatest of the city's gifts. As compared with the complex
human order of the city, our present ingenious electronic mechanisms for storing and transmitting information are crude and limited.

More than half a century later, it is salutary to revisit Mumford's definition, with its spirited put-down of "ingenious electronic mechanisms
for storing and transmitting information." The twenty-first-century
modern world is, of course, utterly stamped by information technology,
and its array of devices—from the internet to iPhones and all the paraphernalia in between—seem fully in line with McLuhan's thesis that
such technological breakthroughs (and he had in mind the same world
that Mumford was looking at) display an ever widening and more
powerful extension of human reach. For we can now see, hear, and process material in such dizzying, instantaneous, and seemingly unmedi-
ated fashion—at the speed of electricity that fuels our digital arsenal—
that Mumford's privileging of "old world" urban structures such as
vaults, archives, monuments, and books may seem quaint indeed.

So we return to the original injunction that lies behind this entire
suite of readings: art as the means by which the lived reality of time and
space is made retrievable and sentient. To close my argument about why
the arts matter, and how they fight it out with information as rival source
of knowing, I propose looking at two extremist (and opposed) works
of the same period when Mumford and McLuhan were writing: Jean-
Luc Godard's campy film masterpiece, *Alphaville* and Italo Calvino's
dazzling collection of vignettes, *Invisible Cities*. Both texts map our
dimensions.

Alphaville is at once a hoot and a film that seems overtly to resonate
with the theses of both Mumford and McLuhan. The film's hero, Lemmy
Caution—a quasi-cartoonish figure portrayed by grade B cult actor

Eddie Constantine (whom Godard compared to a Martian)—does battle with the evil controller of the futurist Alphaville—namely, a giant computer, Alpha 60 (whose unforgettable voice comes from an actor whose vocal cords had been destroyed by disease but artificially reconstructed). The giant computer, shown over and over with its endless circuitry—reminding us today that the sleek miniature marvels of our moment were not only huge and clumsy and colossally expensive but also in-your-face *visible* when first invented—stores all known information on earth, processes it logically, and then governs the city dwellers with its dictates of order and control. It not only performs its own kind of transmission and storage but has grown rich and powerful in its programming, as the citizens of Alphaville have been despoiled of their language and poetry, their darkness and impulses. Each day they lose a few more words; they don't understand *conscience*; for *amour*, they have only *volupté*; they've lost *rouge-gorge* and *lumière d'automne*; they've lost *tendresse*. Finally, the city knows only a timeless present; over and over we hear in voice-over that no one has ever lived in the past or the future.

For all its campiness and comic-book elements, *Alphaville* is prescient in its critique of "information technology" as socially toxic, and the film can be aligned with contemporary arguments put forth by critics such as Sherry Turkle about the cost in human sentience that today's social media produces among the young. Turkle documents diminished capacity for empathy in her many case studies, and she issues a warning that the stunning achievements of artificial intelligence and ever-increasing digital arsenals take an existential toll that warrants our concern. Needless to say, Godard is no sociologist, yet he does offer a program.

Lemmy Caution is the man to carry it out. It is worth noting that Caution is also invested in transmission and storage. He records all he sees with his little Brownie camera, reminding me of today's selfies. And, bruiser-thug though he often is, beating up or killing most of the males he encounters, he turns out as well to be a hero of intertextuality, since whenever he opens his mouth, we're likely to hear large, literal (but unnoted) chunks of Pascal, Baudelaire, Eluard, and Borges. Intertextuality itself (older texts embedded in more recent ones) signals the living reach of the past, and Lemmy rejects Alpha 60's claim that only the present is real. He teaches Natasha the (French) word *conscience*: signifying both consciousness and conscience, human awareness, and human values. He makes her remember that she has an origin, that she is not from or of Alphaville. Godard's dystopian city is one of incessant tranquillizers, dazed human automatons, choreographed executions, routinized sex, and an enslaved populace ruled by the giant computer. The film closes with Lemmy and Natasha escaping toward freedom.

They are escaping Alpha 60. That is perhaps what is most nostalgic and fairytale-like in Godard's film: that you could escape, that this giant machine is only a machine. Not unlike Fritz Lang's apocalyptic film, "Metropolis," both of these texts are heinously prescient, announcing the new city and the new technology to come. My students rightly laugh at Alpha 60, but at least they *see* it and the nefarious work it does. What is not visible at all are the microchips in their own pocket versions of Alpha 60, the ubiquitous screens and gadgets that map our modern moment. The Swedes like to say, "Det var bättre förr," which means, "It was better before," which in turn means a great deal: life was simpler; we were younger; things seemed to work. Many myths doubtless fuel such an expression, but there is something beneficent in *seeing* the technology that has taken over the functions of memory and consciousness.

The city lives by remembering, as Emerson says, and Godard shows that the opposite is also true: the city dies by forgetting. Alphaville is a necropolis, a city of the living dead, where electronic storage and transmission have entirely replaced human memory and narrative. Think back—*thinking back* is a large part of my argument, indeed of my very posture as I write this book—to the poems of Baudelaire, Strindberg, and Merrill: each one highlights the neural traffic between the sites where we've lived, a traffic suited to the retrievals of both mind and verse. Joyce's Bloom is more reticent in this department, but "Me. And me now"—textually following a lyrical memory of lost passion—goes a long way toward establishing such measures. Even if the outcome is self-lacerating, as in the creative but masochistic obsessions of Proust's Marcel, the past comes to voice.

Each of these texts is big with a kind of sentient human history and plenitude that elude the so-called factual record; each displays the dimensionality of art. Let me go further: each displays the cartographic, homecoming responsibilities of art. Information technology cannot deliver this. The neurologists can pinpoint which part of the brain is receiving neural input, but they cannot translate this into either story or value. They cannot plumb its existential or moral payload.

Godard's dystopian Alpha 60 constitutes an ideological warning that warrants our attention today as the grandiose claims of artificial intelligence are trumpeted ever more insistently, as human memory is ever more (silently) outsourced to our machines and devices. "Alphaville" makes visible, by dint of its giant "old-tech" computer-king and its dazed urban denizens, what it can look like when human interiority—the very currency of literature—is shut down. Campy, overtly cartoonish, it depicts a future no one wants. Yet there is a striking parallel between the technological "boosting power" that extends our reach "outward" and the pulsing energies of brain and heart that fuel both imagination and interpretation. Both activities are expansive, generative, and spawning. What about remaining a self? What about Ithaca? What about home?

There's No Place Like Home: Calvino's *Invisible Cities*

Face to face, final harvest, coming home: these injunctions fuel my book, but also my texts. "Outward bound" is how all of us start and how all of us make our way—and I see my teaching career entirely in those colors: dissemination, human chain—but coming home is, I've come to think, the inevitable closing move, inwardly, of art and life. I know this from my dreams as well as from my books. Those dreams—so often dark and nightmarish in their recurring plot of being lost or locked out or too late, of missing the boat or plane or bus—are, it is said, indications of stress or anxiety. What kind of anxiety? I know nothing of Homer's personal oneiric life, but he was demonstrably no stranger to the landscape of impediments, on show in Odysseus's many adventures and tribulations after the events in Troy, ever en route to an Ithaca he cannot reach. *Ithaca* might be seen, yes, as a conservative proposition, a constant reminder of origins, of (over?)tending the center at the expense of the circumference. One remembers Candide's exhausted conclusion after all his far-flung misadventures: "Il faut cultiver son jardin."

And, yes, I do know that "You cannot go home" is the nasty secret that a life-in-time teaches all of us. It's the message that Dickens's Wemmick leaves for Pip (in *Great Expectations*), and which the boy, unable to sleep in strange quarters, conjugates mentally in all its forms: "Do not thou go home, let him not go home, let us not go home, do not ye or you go home, let not them go home. Then potentially: I may not and I cannot go home; and I might not, could not, would not, and should not go home."

This is not far from Joycean play, and for good reason, for when you get there (Ithaca)—if you get there—neither you nor it will be the same. Pip learned this. (I suspect all of the older ones among us have learned it: I still see, in my mind's eye, the now white [but once redbrick] house I had grown up in, but now sold and transformed, when I last "returned" to Memphis as my mother was dying in a nursing home, and I realized that more than my mother was disappearing; and I tasted the bitter fruit that time feeds us.)

Cavafy's lovely poem, "Ithaca," is especially wry in this regard: it closes with an admonition to focus on the voyage itself, not the actual return:

> Always keep Ithaca in your mind;
> to reach her is your destiny.
> But do not rush your journey in the least.
> Better that it last for many years;
> that you drop anchor at the island an old man,
> rich with all you've gotten on the way,
> not expecting Ithaca to make you rich.

Yet Cavafy also pays homage to the ur-yearning that fuels the entire quest: "Ithaca gave to you the beautiful journey; / without her you'd not have set upon the road. / But she has nothing left to give you any more." Home as starting point, rather than destination. Balzac's Rastignac and Dickens's Pip exit the countryside, never to return; their fates are locked in Paris and London. Other nineteenth-century texts tell the same story.

Baudelaire's tubercular black woman will never return to Africa; his little old ladies will never retrieve their youth. I'll never return to Memphis. You can't go back.

But *thinking* and *feeling* are different propositions altogether; this is more than an issue of memory. In some of our finest texts, the voyage out shades inexorably into the return home in front of our eyes, even if we "know" this to be impossible, undoable. The mind and heart have anchors and loyalties they cannot lose or renounce. We find this beautiful sentiment in the strangest places. I want therefore to focus on Italo Calvino's beguiling, at times surreal *Invisible Cities* (1972) to argue that this lovely, seemingly nonstop, semiotic explosion of new vistas is nonetheless homesick, homeward bound. How can that be? And what might it teach us?

Calvino's entire text is a series of "conversations" between Marco Polo and Kublai Khan, in which Polo reports back to the emperor about the manifold *marvelous* cities that make up the empire. One could not be further from documentary. Calvino's chapter headings reveal the projective, imagined nature of the enterprise: cities and memory, cities and desire, cities and signs, trading cities, cities and names, cities and the dead, hidden cities, et cetera. Polo weaves his spellbinding verbal tapestry via the shimmering description of the fabulous cities he has visited, and one is awed by the generative powers of language and imagination, for it is clear that Polo is hardly dependent on a priori givens or fixed data. Instead, he has discovered the life-principle itself in fiction-making, in endless invention, in pure semiosis. (Do these cities even exist, outside of Polo's words?) And this is why the Khan listens so intently, for he hopes to espy a rival world beyond entropy in Polo's depictions, enabling him to "discern, through the walls and towers destined to crumble, the tracery of a pattern so subtle it could escape the termites' gnawing."

The elegance and litheness and sheer virtuosity of Polo's accounts remind us how drab and inert most critical discourse, whatever the field might be, is, by contrast. Over and over, Polo evokes vistas, patterns, movement, contrasts, cities within cities, cities as objects of changing perception and valuation, cities as mobile kaleidoscopic sites, cities as quicksilver entities that shine, alter, conceal, reflect, and insinuate, ceaselessly stunning both the Khan and the reader with their refiguring of both time and space, as well as the human observer/inhabitant who is part of the dance. Polo's far-flung constructions seem as free and un-limited as the human mind itself is, and it therefore comes as a surprise when the Khan asks him:

> "Did you ever happen to see a city resembling this one?" Kublai asked Marco Polo, extending his beringed hand from beneath the silken canopy of the imperial barge, to point to the bridges arching over the canals, the princely palaces whose marble doorsteps were immersed in water, the bustle of light craft zig-zagging, driven by long oars, the boats unloading baskets of vegetables at the market square, the bal-conies, platforms, domes, campaniles, island gardens green in the lagoon's grayness.

Now, of course, we know, and it seems that the Khan also knows, what city this is, but Polo appears not to, and he speaks on, through the entire night, until dawn, describing all the inexhaustible cities he has seen. Finally, he concludes:

> "Sire, now I have told you about all the cities I know,"
>   "There is still one of which you never speak."
>   Marco Polo bowed his head.
>   "Venice," the Khan said.
>   Marco smiled. "What else do you believe I have been talking to you about?"
>   The emperor did not turn a hair. "And yet I have never heard you mention that name."
>   And Polo said: "Every time I describe a city I am saying something about Venice."

Here, for a very poignant moment, the high-flying Polo comes home, moves from circumference to center, from fable to history, from the ozone layers of fantasy and invention to thirteenth-century Venice, from semiotic carnival to birthplace. Polo's response does not slight the power of the imagination to invent a world, but it humbly acknowledges that the imagination is housed in a body that was born in a particular place at a particular moment in time and that all its glorious freedoms will nonetheless be conditioned by those facts of life. We learn, in fact, nothing of Polo's actual biography—Calvino seems not to care—but we do see the enduring presence of *home*, of origin itself as unerasable and ever present, even if irretrievable. Perhaps the finest legacy of *Invisible Cities* is its gentle insistence that mind games—even the most sublime mind games, those which preen in this text—have an Ithaca behind them, fueling them, an Ithaca you may leave but which does not leave you.

Calvino's Polo is *of* Venice, but he occupies a special place in this book, as our final mapmaker. He charts the cities he has seen, and he charts the unseen and unseeable ones as well, the invisible cities of mind and memory and feeling, where all of us also live, whose citizens we also are. Literature helps us see our estate.

CHAPTER 6

Gaffes . . . and Worse

Despite the unrelieved cheerleading about both teaching and literature that may seem to stamp this book, no teacher can be free of the suspicion that the enterprise itself might be a big question mark. One without answers, no matter how much testing and soul-searching we might do.

My campaign about deepening or challenging our views of *knowing* and *understanding*—a central mission of teaching and of literature, as I've repeatedly claimed—has one major blinder to contend with: teacher screwup, right here at home. I've avoided, up to now, talking about the pratfalls, errors, and imbecilities we professors blindly but routinely make or succumb to. When do we sit up and take notice?

As I've argued throughout, invoking Kierkegaard (to give myself some cover), we're so often in the dark as we plough ahead, that the bad news regarding what we actually accomplished comes late in the game, if indeed at all. (Can you imagine a final grade score meted out to teachers, gauging what they accomplished during their career? How would it be determined? Who would you ask? When would you ask it? I see some overdue justice here: the folks who spend their lives evaluating the young, often enough impacting their students' futures and pathways, finally get their own grades.)

So, now, near career's end, that reckoning moment is here for me. Remember how the Greek tragedies always finished with a satyr play; well, after pages of earnest exhortation, here comes the comic relief. Along with some less funny things.

One of my favorite writers, as you've seen, is the crazy August Strind-berg, world-class misogynist yet brilliant writer. His poetry and his breakdown text, *Inferno*, come up for discussion elsewhere in this book, and I've referred to 2×2 fiasco in *A Dream Play*. He also brings up, in that late play, the hardwired *reversals* that seem to govern human con-sciousness: you have been a dazzling conversationalist at the dinner party, but you realize, in the middle of the night, how pompous, boring, and insipid your inspired remarks were. Do you, dear reader, recognize this? It is a familiar psychological mousetrap that most of us have expe-rienced: the sting of retrospect, the puncturing of our little balloon.

Sometimes, however—the bad times—this unpleasant exercise goes beyond the sporadic 3:00 a.m. second thoughts or heartburn, and takes aim at the bigger picture, examining the fuller longitudinal perfor-mances of a lifetime. Reviewing a career in teaching cannot easily steer clear of dyspepsia.

Afterward. Later. Looking back. Reviewing. Taking final measures. Time is financing this particular party, and my balance sheet may well be more in the red than in the black. Literature, I've been claiming, radically *expands* the snapshot testimony that cameras and résumés and tomb-stones yield. But what about *shrinkage*? You may recall that I posited, in my discussion of the three R's, *subtraction* as the hidden ugly law that bids to reverse the "adding-up" logic we want to assign to our trip through time. Recognizing our errors and failures threatens the entire "progress" scenario that learning seems to believe in, for it is no less plausible (and far more disturbing) that the achieved, face-to-face, fuller picture lessens—rather than amplifies—our tally. Now that I am old enough to be going seriously downhill as well as looking back, it's time to report on some of the fiascos I've encountered and engendered while just working for my bread.

Gaffe One: Journals

As you doubtless know, in French, the word *gaffe* connotes more than just "mistake" or "error"; it smacks also of stupidity, of doing something dumb as well as wrong or unsuccessful. It seems sensible, as well as less chest-thumping, to report on a few of these. I can do that now, oddly enough, because only now can I see them. It can take years before we truly grasp how large our gaffes were. One wonders, Might they be "growing" inside us, like tumors, slowly coming to visibility, at last demanding an accounting? And why were they gaffes at all? This would be my "underground" critique, my belated performance-MRI, of what I've been laboring at for decades. Time to get it out, while I can still tell the tales.

I begin with a course on French fiction that I taught in the 1970s. This was the heady beginning of the Brown New Curriculum, so I was open to experimenting. A number of the texts we read—most notably Sartre's *La Nausée*—made use of the journal or diary form, and I was especially intrigued by the narrative and epistemological surprises packed into this scheme, in particular, its capacity for reversals as the narrator, over the course of time, "reprises" earlier events, seeing in them prophetic signs that could only be understood in retrospect. (A bit like this entire book; a bit like my life.)

So, I informed my students that the major writing requirement for our course was to keep a journal, to make entries in it every day or so, and then to examine it at semester's end to see what lurking patterns or shocks it revealed—for example, the unknown person who sat next to you is now your lover; or your grandmother has died in the interim, changing your perspective; or you've unexpectedly realized in mid-course, in mid-reading, something new and life-altering about yourself: in short, the pieces of your life have gradually cohered or come apart over time. Use Sartre as your model, I said. Pack into this project something of the experiential, unfolding texture of your life-in-time at Brown. Capture and deliver your own living-and-breathing, accretive sense-making drama, open to reversals and peripeteia in journal form. I thought this was a pretty cool assignment. I was asking them, young though they were, to do, some fifty years ago, what I've been trying to do now, in this late book.

The students were thrilled with my scheme—What's not to like about it? they must have thought—and they took to this project with gusto; thus, I had some thirty journals turned in to me at the end of the semester. Virtually all of them went out of their way to indicate how authentic and eye-opening this experience was for them, how much they'd discovered and learned, how satisfying such an assignment turned out to be. I myself was excited to read them, figuring I'd come up with a really promising educational concept, a smart way, for all parties, to conclude a course. The exercise could be a keeper, I felt, usable in still other courses down the road.

I cannot gauge whether or not any of the students "cooked the books" narratively (i.e., wrote the whole journal in the final days of the course), but I tend to think they were honest, because what I was reading was a rare, direct, ongoing, unfurling, relatively uncensored account of their *lives*. I learned about their roommates, their friends, their enemies, their lovers. I learned how undergraduates pass their time at Brown, and what it is they think about as they do so. I learned about the stress of entering the huge dining halls and looking (anxiously) for others you knew and could sit with, about the joys and trials of friendships made and later unmade, about the parties and the pairings, about accidents and family crises, about ongoing murk and confusion sometimes sprinkled with moments of big-time clarity when they sensed who they really loved, who they themselves really were, as well as smaller bore breakthroughs concerning what changes they now envisioned making, what new things they'd be on the lookout for, as they completed their four-year Brown tenure. It was heady stuff, yes, often pedestrian, but sometimes far-reaching. They wrote, as I had hoped, of surprises and discoveries, of reversals and changed views. The journals were, moreover, well written, as I recall, and I could see they had enjoyed doing this project. They had taken me seriously. Even though they wouldn't have chosen the term, they were testing the reaches and payload of *narrative*.

Only one thing was missing, missing entirely, in journal after journal: *there was no mention whatsoever of the faculty or of the courses they were taking*. This surprised me. It upset me. It startled me. For three months these young people kept a record of their lives at my university, but not one of them felt the need to document the fact that they were actually enrolled in courses: no mention of books read, ideas discussed, grades given. Nada. And I thought to myself: my colleagues would be amazed (I think) if I were to describe my experiment and my discovery to them;

I felt they'd be stunned (as I was) because we professors (think we) have every reason to believe that we are playing a role in our students' lives, that we are, if not central, at least visible and pertinent in their everyday experiences. Wrong. Au contraire, it is conceivable that these journals were fun for the students to write *because* their coursework and exposure to professors could disappear entirely from the picture, or from the story they were telling. And they'd even get credit for it!

A former colleague of mine loved to quip: "Brown would be a great place if it weren't for the students." Is it possible that the opposite is also true? "Brown would be a great place if it weren't for the professors." Maybe there is a creatural wisdom and logic in play here: each group hangs out with its own. These young people between eighteen and twenty-one are going through so many momentous experiences and life alterations, are encountering so much that is new, are so ensconced in their own vital demographic's joys and trials that I dimly realize we (largely clueless) oldsters are not invited to the party. And wouldn't understand or appreciate it even if we were.

This occurs to me more and more in my classes these days, as I go about practicing my trade and then bother to actually *look* at my students; oftentimes, I'm jolted by what I see. It's as if they are made of different material, as if they obey different laws, as if they belong to a different tribe, as if they inhabit a different planet, not years but light-years distant from me. *I* spend my life reading and writing books, working up lectures, grading papers. What occupies *them*? Their lives take place, in some sense, in a different universe altogether. It is a miracle we communicate with each other as well as we do. But, as for any lurking conviction of how much we actually matter to them, how large a role we actually play in their day-to-day lives, those long-ago journals promptly and permanently cleared up my preconceptions on that front.

This is not a depressing realization, but it is a humbling one. I have nothing, even today, against journals, but I've never again used them as writing assignment. Why document your insignificance? Laurence Sterne once wrote: "A dwarf who brings a standard along with him to measure his own size . . . is a dwarf in more articles than one." As for sharing with others my unwelcome discovery that professors have a

low—perhaps a zero—profile in the experiential lives of our undergraduates: I've kept mum until now.

Gaffe Two: CEOs

The French have a well-known phrase: "L'habit ne fait pas le moine"
(Clothes don't make the man). You can't judge a book by its cover. Most
of us know about this sartorial warning. I remember it being explicitly
applied to me many years ago at a Brown Commencement. Dressed in
my doctoral gown—a brilliant scarlet affair, far more off-the-charts
crimson than Harvard's current pink-toned doctoral robes—I finally
met personally a French business tycoon with whom I had corre-
sponded (he was the head of Hermès), and we agreed to have lunch at
the Faculty Club the following day. That day, dressed now in slacks,
blazer, and tie, I seemed initially unrecognizable to him, as I heard him
mutter under his breath, "L'habit ne fait pas le moine." This was not a
remark in my favor. I haven't forgotten it.

Why do the monk's and the scholar's robes have the (deceptive) impact they do? Proust wrote, somewhere in his long book, that women
fall for men in uniform, irresistibly drawn to the signs of stature and
power. It is easy to laugh at such expectations, but then, can we be so
sure that those trappings of power don't carry right on through, invest-
ing these lovers with an aura that stays around (for a while, anyway)?

I had been thinking about these issues, these modalities of power, its
iconography, for some time, so it made a kind of obvious sense, many
years ago, when I was asked by a very enterprising young dean to come
up with an afternoon seminar topic for a new program he had developed. Some of Brown's most distinguished alumni would be invited to
campus for a special seminar, centering on a single text, to be taught by
some of the place's well-known professors. Flattered, I accepted this
invitation with alacrity, since I'd always felt that my approach to literature was "meat and potatoes": nontheoretical, attuned to broad human
issues, perhaps especially suited to mature adults who had lived longer
than my undergraduates had and who could read literature in the light
of their experiences and careers. My particular group was about a dozen

high-placed leaders in the Brown Corporation: many were CEOs, others were judges and high-ranking officials, all had reams of real-world savvy and acumen. And they had signed up for this event because they wanted to see what the humanities, today, long after their own student years, had to offer. This was going to be fun, I felt.

In fact, I felt so buoyant about this assignment that I deliberately chose an extremist, provocative text about power, a text that was sure to engage, perhaps challenge, these worthies: Jean Genet's play of the late 1950s, *The Balcony*. When I had been a student in France, Genet was hot stuff, seen as the bad boy of modern drama, taken seriously by Sartre (who wrote a massive tome on him) and by all those who followed the French wave of Beckett and Ionesco and what was reductively called the theater of the absurd. *The Balcony* is the name of the brothel run by Mme. Irma, and Genet has elected to focus his story at a moment of crisis in the city: a revolution is underway. Now, what could a political uprising and a whore-house possibly have in common?

More than you might expect, all having to do with the clothes that make the man, all having to do with forms of power. It turns out that *The Balcony*'s specialty is to offer its clients some very special sartorial choices for the sexual activity they are to undertake at the brothel: the clients can choose between the following three *roles*—each replete with full-scale robes, clothing, uniform, and assorted accouterments—*Judge, Bishop* or *General*. We're not talking about disguise or even playacting in the ordinary sense of the term; no, the "johns" come to the brothel and undress, in order to then clothe themselves ritualistically in the garments of these key positions of societal and political authority, *in order to have sex.*

The plot is especially sauced up because the city's Chief of Police, the man expected to maintain order (and quash any revolution), not only has a permanent liaison with Irma but has been waiting for some time now, outright hungering, for someone to add to the brothel's Nomen-clature (Genet's term) and to elect "him" (Chief of Police) as the "en-abling" role. No luck yet; seems that Bishops and Judges and Generals have been providing sufficient erotic currency. By the way, all these ges-tures and performances are routinely on camera for Mme. Irma and the

Chief of Police. (Genet understood both power and voyeurism—and their connection?—better than any playwright of his time.)

The great crux of the play comes when Roger, the chief of the Revolutionaries, comes to the brothel, and changes the rules by choosing you-know-who—the Chief of Police—as his "persona" of choice. But Roger has a surprise planned: outfitted as Chief of Police, in the presence of the prostitute who is to service him, Roger castrates himself. Hmm. Himself? That is the question we should be asking. Has Roger understood that his most "potent" act as Revolutionary is to castrate . . . (himself as) the Chief of Police? (The real Chief watches this sequence with understandable disarray but then quickly places his hands on his testicles and notes that they're still there, still intact.)

One might argue that Genet is drawn to kinkiness and that he wants to entertain us with the bizarre acts available in brothels. But the more productive approach—the reason I served up this risqué fare to my CEOs—might go a good bit further. Genet's gambit in having "ordinary people" come to the whorehouse in order to achieve their sexual release *via role-playing as Judge or Bishop or General* gives us some bad news about myths of self-realization and social change. (Here, too, I thought the CEOs, folks with a stake in the status quo and its hierarchies, would be intrigued.) Revolutionaries and anarchists, according to my text, are simple, deceived literalists who actually believe that if you blow up the Church or Courthouse or Palace, you achieve the political ends you seek: to overthrow power. But, Genet would counter, the Bishop or Judge or General or Chief of Police you're trying to kill is *not* "out there," in some material real-life place you could blow up, but rather *in here,* inside the minds of ordinary people, internalized as site of power. And required (subliminally, sartorially, projectively) for sexual release. (Big-time CEO aura here.)

That is what the sexual game is all about. The moment regular johns get outfitted as power-figures in order to perform sexually, we should realize that no revolution is conceivable. What Genet rightly calls the Nomenclature is located inside the minds of the populace, alive and well, secure and undestroyable. It's hard to imagine a more conservative vision, yet it hinges beautifully on *imagination* itself: we "realize" or "actualize" power—we naively and wrongly call it "our" power—by oc-cupying, vicariously, the space and uniforms and rituals of the Powerful, of the Nomenclature. Erving Goffman, the sociologist who believed that all street life and human exchanges were forms of everyday theater, would have understood Genet perfectly, since the Frenchman's play sug-gests that theater is everything, that role-playing is the central gambit in human social life, that we only come to experience power by internaliz-ing, in our minds and psyches, the potent others who already embody it.

What's not to like in all this heady stuff, I had figured, as I instructed these august chieftains of the worlds of law, finance, and industry to read Genet's play in advance of our discussion? Give them a new per-spective on the exalted positions they occupy, and the libidinal games that hinge on such arrangements, I felt. We're nothing if not bold, we literature professors.

The seminar was a disaster. My enabling premise—men in power would be intrigued by the eroticized rendition of their station as imagined by Jean Genet—was catastrophically wrong. Asking these (publicly) straightlaced male authority figures to find any hint of self-reflection in the events staged at Irma's brothel was a prize-winning moronic assumption on my end. No more than Melville's tragic sea cap-tain, Benito Cereno, my own CEOs and judges did not savor this cor-rosive exposé intended bring to (kinky) light the props that (Genet claimed) held them up. Gaffe. Stony-faced executives sat around the table, saying very very little, but doubtless wondering about the wisdom of granting tenure at this university they cherished, if it (tenure) re-sulted in authorizing professors to trot out sick and arguably satanic theses of the sort I have just discussed. I was not invited back to give any further sessions. I understand why.

As I review these lines in our own much later moment, when we are told of (almost exclusively male) sexual harassment and improprieties at quasi-epidemic level all throughout the echelons of American society—the worlds of entertainment, journalism, and politics singled out for special attention—I get a weird sense that old Genet's theories are getting a new workout in the public sphere. I'm especially intrigued by the *specular* cast of many of these torrid revelations: men not merely exposing themselves to female view but seeking a female audience to watch them (to enable them?) masturbating. Genet's baroque theatricality, with its array of libidinal substitutions, may seem simply lewd to many folks, but his deep insights into the modalities, mechanisms, and levers of male power seem to fit our scandal-ridden moment. Might today's CEOs be interested in bringing me back?

Gaffe Three: The Faster

There was a long period in my career when students flocked to my courses. This was good. Yet, at semester's end, I was always irked when I would read reviews of my teaching and see that *enthusiasm* was often the feature that took honors in their praise. Enthusiasm? (Why didn't they speak about brilliance?) Gradually it occurred to me there might be still other, even less exalted reasons for my popularity. Conceivably the thing about my courses that most appealed to students was my championing of the *creative project* as final exercise for the course. I was inordinately proud of this option, and each semester I would explain to the students (who already knew, who perhaps were taking the course for this reason) that they could choose between writing a final critical essay or, instead, opting for a creative project. I saw the creative option as consistent with both my view of literature's reach and also Brown's liberal-education philosophy.

Further (I reasoned to myself), the materials we'd studied—novels, poems, plays, sometimes paintings and films—were never packaged in the sacrosanct *critical prose* that we always demand of our students when they dutifully show us, at course's end, what they've learned. So, it seemed strangely *equitable* to allow these young people to have their "say" about my course in a wide range of media and forms: creative writing, paintings, films, ballet, sculpture, photography, song, group performances, and still other forms of expression that they were free to propose. Why not? It seemed right.

I did need, of course, to calm the nerves of my graduate-student teaching assistants who would do their share of the grading in these large courses; they had a point, for they had no training or expertise whatsoever in the huge host of fields that I had legitimized as fair game for the students. "Not to worry," I'd smugly explain; "you'll see, you'll even be blown away by what you see." And often enough this was just what happened. Each student would first explain to the group what he or she or they set out to do—I required a careful (and teacher-approved) prospectus for each creative project—and then *all* of us (students, TAs, and me, gathered together in a performance space during exam period) would usually be gratified, often stunned, by the talent, ingenuity and surprising vistas made visible by these undergraduates.

After all, many, perhaps most of them, had strengths we never suspected: few of them were going to be professional writers or critics, but a good number of them had genuine artistic and performative talents that my liberal scheme had nicely allowed to come into play. Almost invariably, these creative projects—presented and performed with considerable drama, even if some nervousness was on show—provided a satisfying end to my courses. As the smoke cleared and the adrenalin diminished, I always felt "extended," as if the students were now teaching me, but using their skill set rather than mine. Generally some half of the class would elect this option; I had no regrets, from a discipline perspective, given that I'd already obliged everyone to write some five or six short critical papers during the semester, and it seemed fitting that they could now branch out and stretch their wings. (And they had to choose Brown's "Satisfactory/No Credit" final grading option if they elected this model. We weren't going to affix As or Bs or Cs to amateur work of this sort.)

What I did not enjoy considering was how this creative option might be a dodge or an evasive maneuver by my students. And there were always several utterly lame projects, such as collages that appeared to have been put together the night before the due date (or in ninth grade) and then proffered as concluding document for three months of reading; each time one of those came in, I had a serious twinge of anxiety—what, I wondered, would I say if one of my colleagues saw this embarrassing collage or ditty or crayon drawing, and asked where it came from, and what it was doing—so I made sure to keep the bad ones under wraps. A small percentage, I told myself, a very small percentage of the projects were dreadful, and the good ones made it quite worthwhile. Fortunately, no other professors or deans ever checked up on me. (You can get away with a lot in universities.)

For all these reasons I kept to my beliefs and announced to my Scandinavian literature students some fifteen years ago (when the story I'm now telling took place) that they could turn in a creative project at course's end. The following week one of the students came to my office hours to discuss his ideas for the project. I did not know him—he was in a TA-run section—but I was willing to hear him out. He explained that his favorite text in the course was Knut Hamsun's *Hunger*, a novel about a starving writer whose experience of starvation "feeds" his writing. Yes, I agreed. (Elsewhere in this book, as you know, I salute Hamsun's view of writing as a welcome, inspiring alternative to the sober critical model we're accustomed to.) The student was also a fiction writer. His project was simple and straightforward: he proposed to *fast* for some two to three weeks, but to keep scrupulous notes during this time, about his perceptions, about how the world appeared to him, day by day, as he went without food. I was taken aback. It made sense. No one had ever proposed anything like this, and for the life of me, I could not quite see my way toward refusing him. I urged him to be careful, not to overdo things, but I authorized the project. It seemed remarkably promising.

And so he began fasting. I received a few sparse emails from him, saying he was proceeding apace, keeping a diary to record his evolving psychic state (and his evolving weight loss). After about a week into this, I attended a trustee meeting in Boston for a Study Abroad group I had worked with for decades, and, during the course of our conversations, I happened to mention this daring, unusual student project that was taking place on my home campus, under my direction. The director of the program, a close friend, could not believe his ears; he was a man with substantial legal experience regarding student programs, and he told me in no uncertain terms that I had just committed a colossal—and colossally dangerous—blunder. Didn't I understand, he said to me, that I was in grave personal liability here? What would happen if the student became seriously ill? Or even died? It would then come out that what killed him was a "creative project" authorized by Professor Weinstein. There was only one thing to do, he said: contact your office NOW, and have your secretary go directly to this student's dorm room and explain to the student that Professor Weinstein has explicitly "commanded" that the fasting project stop at once. If the student is not in the room, then a note conveying this order can be left. Hearing this—feeling quite faint—I immediately phoned our secretary, and she undertook to carry out my assignment: she went to his room, he was not there, she left a note.

I returned to Providence the following day, much occupied by this dilemma. I repeatedly tried to contact the student myself, but he was elusive, hard to find, and—worst of all—even after I'd laid down the law, still fasting! He was learning so much, he told me; his writing was benefiting, he told me. He would not stop. Meanwhile, I was imagining being fired (at best) and either a stint in jail or utter bankruptcy (at worst). I had opened a Pandora's box, and there was no closing it. About a week or ten days thereafter, we had our public closing event for the course: the creative projects. I watched the performances, looked at the visuals, listened to the recitations, but with a dreadful taste in my mouth. The faster was not there. Finally, a full week later, my department had its Christmas party, and lo and behold, who should show up, but him! He was pale, visibly thinner than I'd remembered him, and he told me that this experience had been so enriching for him that he simply had to go through it all the way to the end. He apologized if he'd caused me any worry or anxiety.

I did not answer.

I never saw his final account of the fasting. He was not in my discussion group, so the graduate TA read it. But he did indeed have a great impact on me: I decided, then and there, to dispense forever with creative projects.

I've already said that these freewheeling projects frequently reversed the traditional teacher–student arrangements, because the teacher was at last in the learning slot. And that was true here as well. He taught me a lesson that no other student ever had: the queasy underside of my adventurous pedagogy, the price tag and the outright exposure attached to the liberties I had so cavalierly pontificated on and extended to my students for decades. No more. I guess I'd have to say he taught me (without ever suspecting it?) that I was a fool. And I haven't paid much of a price, enrollment-wise, regarding student disappointment at the removal of this option; the institutional turnaround for students being no more than four years, new crops have never heard of Weinstein-and-Creative-Project. They therefore do not know enough to miss it.

Yet, upon reflection—the kind of autumnal reflection that is generating this segment on gaffes—I am still further embarrassed. The *faster* did me the honor of taking both my books and myself seriously. He proposed to cross the border between text and life, by actualizing in his experience what the protagonist of his novel had done. I had been singing exactly that song forever, and now I saw that it led me right over a cliff. I am reminded of Kierkegaard's fine remark (in *Fear and Trembling*) that if anyone in the congregation, listening to the preacher speak of Abraham's willingness to obey God's command by killing his son, were *actually* to do just this, we would put them either in jail or in an institution. (Woody Allen was drawn as well to this side of the story.) How seriously should we expect our books and ourselves to be taken? What authority do we have? I know, I know that most of my students will never be tempted to go all the way, to live out the lessons of their books; but I now learned that the real trouble might come if they did, and I mean trouble not just for the student but for the professor as well. Lesson learned.

Gaffe Four: Ordinary People

I came to Brown with an ardent (if naive) conviction that literature both addresses the world and changes the world. This conviction is more tested now but still (more or less) intact. The story I want to tell goes back to my very first year of teaching.

In the first months of my time at Brown, I had been approached by an older colleague in philosophy who invited me to participate in a large citywide conference, devoted to issues of "mental retardation" (the term then used by everyone). My only credential for this invitation—I assumed my colleague had no doubts about my cerebral equipment—was that I had written a big chunk of my doctoral dissertation on Faulkner's *Sound and the Fury* and had, like Faulkner himself and all Faulkner lovers, come to the view that this was his most beautiful and daring book. Having therefore written some twenty to thirty pages on the character Benjy, the novel's "idiot" (who justifies the title drawn from famous lines in *Macbeth*: "Life is a tale told by an idiot, full of sound and fury, signifying nothing"), I was the fellow who was going to use material from this notoriously inaccessible masterpiece of high modernism to persuade a huge room of attendees (doctors, health care folks, mentally impaired people, and their parents and families) that great literature gets us into the nitty-gritty of life's rawest situations.

So, in the large hotel conference room, I confidently explained to this group of people involved with daunting human and medical challenges that Faulkner helps us to see that Benjy is the only *whole* figure of the book, that his cognitive inability to sort out present from past, or even to speak, is the flipside of an emotional purity of great, sometimes unbearable, intensity and beauty. I spoke passionately about the injustice of enlisting "psychometrics" as a requirement for citizenship in the human community; not being able to tie your shoes or pass an IQ test had little to do with the life of the heart. Benjy loves his sister fiercely, wholly, and helplessly: now an "adult," he still goes to the fence every day awaiting her return from school (awaiting the return of the only love he received), despite the fact that she is long gone. The impaired Benjy can neither remember nor forget nor heal: his sister Caddy is ever present in his psyche; that entire segment of the novel is punctuated by his moaning. Hopelessly damaged, he is nonetheless the book's moral compass.

I was still in my twenties then, my salad days; yet, as I listened to some of the families speak out about their responsibilities and burdens, I nonetheless began to sense the gulf between my high-flying bookish moral convictions and these people's day-to-day, unromantic, tedious, patient, demanding lives. Many parents and doctors spoke about the unrelenting stress and cost of tending to such disorders, either with patients or loved ones. And they also implied, without quite saying it, that to expect great changes or improvements in the mental capacities of the impaired was quixotic at best, blind at worst. Life had taught them that.

But my enthusiastic talk nonetheless touched a nerve, and after the presentations were over, an older woman approached me with a singular request: would I be willing to tutor her thirty-year-old daughter? The daughter was mildly "retarded," her mother said, even though she spoke easily enough, and my job would be to help her reach the point that she could score a high enough level on a basic IQ test, to receive further medical services from the state.

This story goes back some fifty years, and my memories of it have dimmed, but after agreeing to the mother's request, I met with the daughter once or twice a week at her house for hour-long sessions devoted to prepping for the test and received a very modest stipend from the state for doing so. My tutee was a good-natured, earnest woman who was eager to make progress, and our conversations resembled, to at least some degree, those I had with my friends and family, maybe a little more plodding and slow-paced, but exchanges nonetheless.

But, whenever we went through the sample tests that she would have to take, we collided head-on with her ratiocinative and cognitive deficits, her inability to reason or remember (as the test required). I remember (sneakily) tweaking the tests, finding ways to elevate her score, reassuring her that we were moving forward. It was what we both wanted to believe. Needless to say, I was not daft enough to ask her to read Faulkner, but I threw myself into this unusual *teaching* challenge, so different from what I was doing in my Brown classrooms, yet so attuned to real-world challenges. I felt a kind of commitment at once ethical and literary. Why shouldn't Faulkner's Benjy be useful?

After two or three months, when the evidence was overwhelming to both of us, we discontinued these sessions. I never saw her again. I have no idea how she has fared since that time long ago, but I did learn something sobering about myself and my pretensions. I have never wavered in my love for Faulkner, and each year I help my students see the beauty of the Benjy section in *The Sound and the Fury*. But life differs from books. I had neither the know-how (nor perhaps the moral fiber) to aid the young woman who wanted to learn. My free flights (several hours a week) in Brown classrooms were easy-peasy; this was a different test, a different responsibility altogether, at once more arduous and with less upside; and I failed it.

That episode, that disturbing sense of the daunting rift between literary and behavioral truths returned to my mind a decade or so later, after I had thrown myself into the new burgeoning interdisciplinary field of "literature and medicine" and was asked to take part in an exciting venture at Kent County Hospital outside of Providence. They were using a grant to put on a two-day conference focusing on ways in which film and literature could be of real use to the community in dealing with issues of mental health and illness. On one of those days the topic was "the death of a child." It's a topic that is central to several of the books I love most—Ibsen's magisterial play *Little Eyolf*, in particular—but since film was on the docket, I selected Robert Redford's early directorial triumph of 1980, *Ordinary People*, about a family become dysfunctional following the death of their oldest (and most promising) child. Hence, the film was screened during the week for the community people attending the conference, and I followed suit, on a Sunday afternoon, to discuss with them the merits of the film and how it might ease suffering and pain.

I love this film: it is the single greatest performance of Mary Tyler Moore as a grieving mother who cannot get past the death of her favored son, and it features a fine Donald Sutherland as the gentle father, trying to focus on the surviving child (Timothy Hutton), who is eaten up with guilt: he and his brother were out on the water, the boat capsized, and only he survived (whereas the athletic, high-achieving older brother perished). Perhaps the most memorable role is that of the psychoanalyst (Judd Hirsch) brought in to minister to the damaged boy, to help him find his way toward recovery. Redford was especially proud of making a film about ultimacies—love, death, family—without a scrap of violence or sensationalism. I was proud of my film choice.

I appeared at the allotted time and saw that there was a substantial crowd of adults in the audience, which pleased me, since I was convinced this would lead to a vigorous discussion, which in turn would lead to a conviction that films such as this have unsuspected utility. As tireless promoter of the humanities, I anticipated this event would be grist for my mill. Gradually, however, as the questions began to come, and as I got a clearer sense of who these folks were, it began to dawn on me that *all* of these people had lost a child, and that was the reason they were there. As soon as this realization got through to me, I started to understand the sheer hubris and meagerness of my tidings. How could this story, which is brutal in the end—the mother essentially exits the family, cannot make peace with the loss of the charismatic son and the survival of the weaker one, and we are left with a father and son trying to pick up the pieces—possibly aid these wounded parents?

But what struck me most in the questions that were asked was how puzzled these folks were by the role of the psychiatrist (done with ethnic chutzpah by Hirsch); what, they asked me, is he there for? Redford has his story pivot on the work of the humane analyst who helps convince the younger son that life is worth living, that he bears no guilt, and that the very fact that *he* survived the accident is a kind of horrible but real proof that he has what it takes to live. Hirsch is outright *saftig* in getting this across, and we watch the wounded boy begin to mend. Psychiatry pays off. But that is not how this audience saw the film. Their recurring question was: *where is the priest?*

At that juncture the gears began to turn yet again in my brain, and I looked still harder at those assembled adults at Kent County Hospital outside of Providence, and I realized a great many of them were Portuguese immigrants—Rhode Island has long had a vibrant Portuguese-American population—with a firm religious belief system still in place. Redford had not thought it strange at all, had indeed thought it self-evident, to haul in the medical man to help heal these existential wounds, whereas my audience found it monstrous that the man of the cloth was nowhere to be found. And the recognition that followed, for me, was: *film* may not be of real use here at all, *art* has perhaps no serious place in these family tragedies. As literature professor, I felt as superfluous to them as the Judd Hirsch character must have seemed. With this insight, I grasped what a special (secular) audience I routinely have for my courses: young bright people, largely unwounded by life's blows, eager to try out new ideas, needing no special pleading to believe that film and literature can be of immense service. I was chastened by these people's grief, but I had to realize that *my* medicine bag (furnished by the humanities and a good bit of arrogance) would not help them.

Much later, it dawned on me that Kafka's surreal tale, "A Country Doctor," prefigures much of the dilemma I found myself in. Faced with a monstrous wound—an open, worm-filled hole in a boy's side—that nothing in medical training could possibly have prepared him for, Kafka's doctor fully understands the transfer of realms that modernity and its secular ethos have ushered in, as he muses that his sick villagers are "always demanding the impossible from their doctor. They have lost their ancient beliefs; the parson sits at home and unravels his vestments, one after another; but the doctor is expected to be omnipotent with his merciful surgeon's hand." My Kent County families in mourning had not read—likely not heard of—Kafka; for them, the miracle of healing was to happen via the spiritual power of the priest, and I saw that the good(s) I had to offer were not what was needed. I'm not sure what kind of wisdom is derivable from this story other than a recognition of the assumptions I take for granted and the limitations I do not easily see.

Gaffe Five: Literature and Mortality

"Literature and Mortality" is the title of a lecture I gave for a large audience in Richmond, Virginia, some years ago. In it, I culled together texts and arguments deriving from a career-long involvement with "literature and medicine," seen especially in the course on that topic that I routinely teach to large numbers of Brown undergraduates, most of them premeds. I also wrote at length on this dark topic in my book, *A Scream Goes Through the House*, published in 2003. In short, I have a real repertoire here. How could I not? Writers have been drawn to the dark themes of death and dying like moths drawn to light, and we see this testimony in the Hebrew and Christian Bibles, in Greek tragedy, and in the work of Shakespeare and many subsequent writers right up to our time. Whether it be Hamlet's famous soliloquy about suicide or Poe's tales of being buried alive or Tolstoy's "Death of Ivan Ilych" or Emily Dickinson's exploratory, sometimes surreal death poems or Ingmar Bergman's hallucinatory film (*Wild Strawberries*) of an old man discovering, at the end of his life, that he's never lived: works of art are filled to the brim with tidings about death and dying.

So, I pranced through my lecture, peppered with eloquent literary references, and closed with a close-up on Faulkner's *As I Lay Dying*, one of the most brutal accounts of death's rituals that I know, since it records, via the interior monologues of the surviving husband and children, the epic journey of a coffin containing Addie Bundren's corpse (the dead mother) from country farm to town cemetery in broiling Mississippi summer heat. Faulkner throws everything he can at this pilgrimage: including Biblical obstacles such as flood and fire. The writer seizes upon the (unspoken, obscene) urgency that characterizes all burial rituals: fine to have flowers, prayers, eulogies, but *get that body into the ground*!

The central question haunting the living Bundrens during their epic quest is: is that still Mother in the coffin? When do you—dead—stop being you? Here is how Faulkner writes it at a late moment in the book, when the coffin with its rotting cargo is parked in a barn: "The breeze was setting up from the barn, so we put her under the apple tree, where the moonlight can dapple the apple tree upon the long slumbering flanks within which now and then she talks in little trickling bursts of secret and murmurous bubbling." This is the voice from the coffin—*the voice from the coffin*—and it may be thought to be both the hideous decomposition of the body and, yet, also a wondrous figure for the very fate of the Writer, since Homer, Shakespeare, Dostoevsky, Faulkner, and company are, themselves, now voices from a coffin.

But our own low-to-the-ground, unheralded, seemingly silenced voices come out of the coffin as well, the humming, vibrant voices of teachers and doctors and lawyers and husbands and wives and children, the entire human tribe that writes and speaks, may still live, long after our deaths, through the melodies and memories of those who lived with and among us. Reading books, looking at photographs, recalling our dead: all this propels us into the incessant conversation with those who are said to be absent and gone. What is enduring love if not a cashiering of mortality, voices from coffins?

I closed the lecture on this high note and then looked about me. First, I noted—how could I not have seen this earlier?—that the median age of this group was advanced, perhaps in their seventies and beyond. Second, I thought harder about the lecture series itself, designed by a man I'd had correspondence with for years but whose mission was dealing, as counselor, with end-of-life issues for the sick and dying and their loved ones. And I began to realize that this audience had all too much firsthand experience with mortality: their closest ones had succumbed to it, they themselves were in the overt danger zone age-wise, and they were heavy, hurting, and needy, because of personal experience, flesh-and-blood experience. As with *Ordinary People* at Kent County Hospital, I sensed that my breezy—perhaps even eloquent—tidings about death and dying as reflected in literature might well seem pretentious, "unearned," even vacuous or offensive to them. I saw that *mortality* is an awfully freighted topic, perhaps too freighted for any lecture hall, especially one like this. "Mortality" is not a topic at all; it is human fate, and it is hideous. My audience was polite, I was thanked for my fine words, and I headed back to Providence the next day; but I was left to ponder the misalignment I had encountered.

I've been reflecting on this ever since, although its meaning has become clearer to me in recent years. My signature, my trademark, both as teacher and as writer of books, has been my full-throated conviction that literature deals with the essence of life—love, death, consciousness, the whole schmear—that it (literature) should not be exclusively the purview or preserve of learned scholars with historicist or theoretical or ideological approaches, but rather it should be disseminated and discussed with "ordinary people," not unlike our water-supply system that serves the entire community. That's how I serve up the books.

Well, I was realizing . . . not so quick. I began to understand the very nature of *resistance*. One of my campaigns in my "literature and medicine" course concerns the "denial of death" that seems hardwired in American medical practice. This denial has been recognized for years, by Sherwin Nuland some time ago and by Atul Gawande most recently in his fine book *Being Mortal*. Gawande rightly points out the obscene price tag of our evasions: the old-and-dying routinely undergo expensive, almost certainly useless, procedures, protocols, and surgeries. Our entire system—not only patients but especially doctors—is held hostage to this form of blind desperation. I have railed for decades against this misguided notion, but my thinking on this issue is now becoming more complicated. A medical career spent in tending to the body's frailties and fate has to be, conceptually if not literally, awash in death. Doctors begin their education by a long acquaintance with a cadaver, and it's likely that that cadaver never fully disappears from their thoughts. It matters that both Nuland and Gawande go to great lengths to confess that they themselves practiced for decades, made countless medical decisions, guided by this same "automatic" view of death as failure, as unacceptable outcome, *until* they had the eye-opening revelation of how deeply flawed their position had been; in each instance, it required the dying of a family member—Nuland's brother, Gawande's father—before they ultimately came to the vision that made them write their crusading reformist calls for change.

And me, with my literary bag of tricks? It pains me, in retrospect, to realize how smug I actually am, all semester long, in my "literature and medicine" course, how my literary texts stack the deck against doctors, how the "human cost" of illness (my great theme, the quintessential payoff for using the testimony of literature) blindsights me and my students to the grinding, death-inflected, relentless truth of doctoring. I still believe in the necessity of a paradigm shift in medicine, with a saner view of death as the hardwired truth of somatic life, despite the experiments in Silicon Valley and elsewhere to cryovac us for a deathless future. So, in that spirit, I have always tried hard, over the years, to jolt my premed undergraduates—coming largely from science majors, sampling my course as a change from their normal diet—into considering the human underside of medicine, the subjective experience of the sick person and not merely the professional work of the physician. (It can be shocking to see how incommensurate these two realms are.) These issues are very teachable, and it gratifies me to see the students' reactions; they frequently tell me, at course's end, that my course has been invaluable at this stage of their life, since it will arm them in medical school and the career beyond, by instilling in them a reverence and imagination for the feelings of the sick.

"Gratifies," I said, yet, for all the reasons mentioned, I at the same time experience more than a twinge of guilt, guilt at my privileged preaching, at my protected perch as literature professor holding forth on a field very far from mine, in terms of books or life. Guilt also at how easy it has always seemed to reach these bright young people with my humanistic message. But reality will have its little card to play—I don't ever quite forget that—and something inside me whispers that my teaching will fade, that medical school (and its depersonalization) will have its way, as will a real career of practice involving sick people, a career that will start and end with cadavers. The lectures and books and poems studied in college will yield to anatomy, biology, specialization, hospital exposures, no sleep, grand rounds, sixteen minutes per patient, and the huge systemic reality of medical training and medical practice in the United States.

My teaching will fade. It's a hard lesson to learn. And a weird lesson, too, because it soothes as well as hurts. One wants one's students to be *marked* by having come one's way, yet this is also a fearful proposition: do I really want to mark them? (Remember Addie Bundren's words as she whipped her students: "I would think with each blow of the switch: now you are aware of me." And I cringe.) It is (also) good that they will forget my golden words.

The lecture at Richmond rubbed in my face the privileged existence I have at Brown, with its eager students on the front side of life, hungry to sample our wares. Not so, the group in Richmond. Their education, what it may have been when they were twenty, had, well beyond the classroom, continued and altered through the years, with significant installments of sickness and death. What is becoming clearer to me is that I myself—despite the immense age difference between my students and me—have been as innocent as my Brown students are, as sheltered by my books, my tenure, my life in the humanities. (Is this why one becomes a professor? Is this what tenure actually provides? Shelter?) All this is becoming clearer to me because my shelter is harder and harder to maintain. I have been unable to ignore the fact that this particular course, "literature and medicine," gets more and more painful to teach each year, no matter how inspiring my students occasionally tell me it is. The reason for the pain is simple: I myself am dodging bullets, I am feeling the yoke of mortality with ever more force and fear, each year that goes by, and many have gone by.

What is also coming undone is my (prior) preening certainty that literature offers us a vicarious conversance with things we cannot afford to experience. I have forever sung that song. Reading books brings the world into us and brings us into the world. This is true. But I now realize that much of my own teaching repertoire—the actual books I assign— has a toxicity and virulence that are hard to contain, hard to keep "virtual." "Hurrah for art!" has long been my battle cry. It offers us, as I have preached to generations of students, a unique perch nowhere else available. But no one told me that this might be a fair-weather model, that there may well be things I myself cannot afford to imagine, because so many of these very things are on my door step wanting in. I am beginning to learn that. This is the humanities' darkest secret: many of their truths become unbearable over time. I cannot believe that mathematicians or physicists or computer scientists or even political scientists ever run into (fall into) this existential quagmire at the end of the road. Yes, they get old and will die, but they don't spend hours each week *teaching* it.

For example, when I teach Tolstoy's *Death of Ivan Ilych*, I discuss: Ilych's persistent pain (that will kill him eventually), Ilych's descent into the "medical regime"; Ilych's unwonted discovery that he has never really lived but has traded his soul for secular success as magistrate in nineteenth-century Russia; Ilych's display of anomie, of tepidness of spirit, of unconcern for wife and children, of selfish life-management. But now this stuff depresses me hugely because I see myself, my quandary, in Ilych. Or take Margaret Edson's brilliant play *Wit*, which the students like less than I do, for it tells the story of a Donne scholar battling with stage-four ovarian cancer and finding herself to be the *text* this time around, to be examined and dealt with by the men of science. I find myself telling my students that cancer (or any other mortal disease) proves our ultimate enslavement to a somatic regime where, eventually, no matter how long and well we live, we must come and, once there, come apart and die. Therefore, *wit* is the meaning as well as the title of the play, because wit testifies to the mind's (fabulous but timebound) authority to stand up, with style, to flesh and death; wit is the cradle-to-grave contest through which we perform our verbal part, go through our moves and repartees, before eventually succumbing and going down.

My supply of wit is dwindling. Tolstoy, Edson, *all* my writers in this course tell us about the unfair battle that we win, win, win until we finally and permanently lose. And I am reaching the point where this is simply too hard, too close to the bone, too akin to the skirmishes and crises that are now working their way more fully into my own life. As mentioned, this issue of painful, even unbearable subject matter never presents a problem in many other disciplines, where there is, as it were, "nothing personal" in the materials one presents; not so for my field. "Literature and mortality" or "literature and medicine": let it go. (I do know that the course will die when I stop teaching it. So what. Too hard to keep talking about these matters. And the specter of collapsing while in the midst of teaching it is poetically fine, but humanly nasty, very nasty.)

Gaffe Six: #MeToo

My last instance of gaffe, of wiping out, is of very recent date, and it still hurts; I am still making knowledge of it, even as I put the finishing touches on this book. And I realize that *gaffes*, as concept, plays me false here, fails to take the measure of where I went wrong, which is why I added ". . . and Worse" to my rubric. Not too long ago (fall 2017) I taught J. M. Coetzee's remarkable novel *Disgrace* in my course "The Fiction of Relationship." That course, often mentioned in this book, examines narratives from the early eighteenth century right up to Coetzee, and I often close with him because he is defiantly and unhingingly of our moment, but his book—which I love for its intelligence, honesty, and, yes, moral vision—*offends*, and it does so precisely because its issues are today so inflammatory that no multiperspectival or neutral classroom hearing for it is imaginable.

Worse still, once again I find my own position—this time as old white male professor—to be embarrassingly and definitively in the way. My undergraduates are incensed by the sexual abuse they see in the protagonist's affair with his student; she is thirty years his junior. When they see that this transgression costs the man his job, they want to cheer. I can't quarrel with this, since (male, older) teachers coming on to (female, younger) students is a vile business and has been for a long, long time. Such infractions are egregious and must be exposed and rooted out.

But I am unhappy that none of my students seems to care in the least about the other side of Coetzee's story: the account of a man in his fifties discovering that he has taken far too many male privileges for granted and that his time for philandering is now coming to an end. Leaving the banquet, recognizing that it's "quittin' time," has resonance for me—it goes well beyond erotic improprieties—since I believe Coetzee is exploring the same hard fate that Freud saw in *King Lear*: the necessity of making friends with death. This issue has little traction for them.

I do not expect the pathos of aging to loom large for my twenty-year-olds. But I had thought that even the toxic issue of sexual abuse could be productively discussed and examined. I now wonder how I could have been so naive, so blind, so . . . "out of it." I title this segment "#MeToo," to signal the perfect storm I both produced and suffered: ever since the election of Donald Trump and the staggeringly large international Women's March following his inauguration, the extent of routine, never called out, ubiquitous male trespasses in Western culture has become increasingly visible and, for many, galvanizing. Since the fall of 2017, the felling of mighty males—Harvey Weinstein, Roger Ailes, and the list goes on and on, seems to be updated every week—has become the order of the day, on show on our TV screens, adding new names on a regular basis, and roiling the hearts in our populace at large. #MeToo announces something grand yet horrifyingly simple and ugly: *most* women have experienced, sometimes repeatedly, sexual harassment and oftentimes worse. This "community of victims" spans the earth. And folks have had enough. Something is beginning to boil over.

My Brown students were no exception. The majority of these seniors were women, and their seemingly unanimous response to Coetzee's novel, especially to his womanizing protagonist-professor, David Lurie, was clear and immediate: he was deemed repulsive, even "monstrous." This is what I learned, during eighty minutes of taut, painful, grudging exchanges, all the more taut, painful, and grudging because they saw that my own judgment did not align with theirs. The great majority of these students were women, as I said, but not all, and as I later read their written essays, I saw that young people of both genders were equally incensed by Lurie's behavior, notably by his having "nonconsensual" sex with a female student far younger than him. I wrote "nonconsensual" in quotations, because I personally (still) feel that this epithet is tricky—at once right and not quite right—when applied to this novel. The scene in question centers on David's "storming" of Melanie at her flat—they have already had sex once before at his place; he is besotted with her largely because she seems to awaken all his ardor at a time when he had thought it gone—and Coetzee writes it like this:

> She does not resist. All she does is avert herself: avert her lips, avert her eyes. She lets him lay her out on the bed and undress her; she even helps him, raising her arms and then her hips. Little shivers of cold run through her; as soon as she is bare, she slips under the quilted counterpane like a mole burrowing, and turns her back on him.
>
> Not rape, not quite that, but undesired nevertheless, undesired to the core. As though she had decided to go slack, die within herself for the duration, like a rabbit when the jaws of the fox close on its neck. So that everything done to her might be done, as it were, far away.

What I learned in our discussion is that a male professor's liaison with a female student admits, in today's classroom, of no ambiguities, no uncertainties. Further, I learned that rape is rape is rape and to suggest otherwise is untenable. To my (old male) mind, Coetzee is not going easy on his protagonist, and the text does not shy away from faulting him, as he himself (ruefully?) gauges what he has done, but it nonetheless turns its key discriminations about "consensual" versus "nonconsensual" rape into something more complex, equally reprehensible but complex. Especially the resonant animal images of hunter and victim signal the scene's further reaches, as will later become clear in the novel. Much, I had naively thought, to unpack and chew on. No: that is no longer how these matters are seen.

I title this segment "#MeToo," too, because I ran smack up against a kind of solidarity I've seen little of before, as these young people expressed their revulsion and contempt for this man's behavior. To even suggest that these matters are in the least nuanced and murky is not only to display a kind of arrogance and obtuseness but even to appear on the wrong side of history, as far as my students are concerned. These matters, they feel, have been adjudicated.

To suggest, further, that Coetzee himself has quite intentionally paralleled the professor's transgression with the ghastly episode where the professor's daughter is raped by three black African men—so as to oblige his character and his readers to ponder both the similarities and the differences (much food for thought here, I had thought: the entire structure of the book mandates such a comparison): this, too, comes across as bullheaded and in poor taste (on my part). In fact, the actual rape of the daughter is not narrated as such, but I know, from firsthand conversations, that people of color will read it differently than white readers will, indicting it for being a colonialist racist cliché about black people. This issue was also not explored; perhaps it, too, has too much heat to handle.

Finally, as mentioned, the animal imagery Coetzee enlists to describe the supine Melanie is telling, for the last third of the book recounts David's slow but real spiritual education as he becomes a champion for euthanized dogs and devotes his remaining energies to preserving some kind of final dignity for their dead bodies as they are fed into the incinerator. At book's end, David has renounced desire itself. Coetzee's novel is about *animal rights*, the rights of the four-footed and of the two-footed, and he inscribes this issue in the inexorable logic of aging and death, as well as privilege. I feel there is something almost Shakespearean in this gathering indictment. Few students respond to this line of argument. The rape of the student is what they see. A long history has sharpened their vision on this front. It was their professor's vision that was blurred.

This anecdote does not have a good ending. One of these students actually complained to my department chair about my handling of this class discussion, alleging that I somehow defended rape. What stuns me in retrospect is how I failed to see this coming. There is a rising, overdue, tsunami of rage in our society about male sexual abuse. This novel was, in 2017, an enormous piece of ordnance just waiting to go off, and woe betide the professor who crassly ignores that. #MeToo not only characterizes the solidarity of my students, but I sense that it positions me, too, as aging white male professor in a dreadful box (coffin?) as fellow traveler, since I experience sympathy for the professor *also*. (This is unimaginable to them; and I have to acknowledge it is unimaginable as well to my wife, daughter, and granddaughter: all of them teachers. The Luddite is me.)

I now realize that I must also have deeply offended my students in my earlier lecture on the book when I claimed that David Lurie is "good company." I have said the same of Iago. And of other characters whose behavior is dubious, even evil, but whose intelligence and lucidity never falter. (I point out to my students that they were admitted to this institution on exactly the same grounds: intelligence ever trumps goodness in college admissions and in college classrooms, and perhaps in [this] life too; these remarks are likewise unappreciated.) I am still, a few years later as of this writing, smarting over this last debacle regarding professors and rape. My students and I—the core audience of my life, the congregation every teacher must have—can, it now appears, be at complete loggerheads. And no amount of good will—these students genuinely like and respect me—will get us across the bridge that leads to understanding one another's viewpoints. I myself am now in the way.

My final reflection about #MeToo is this: it stands for my view of literature itself: I preach myself hoarse each semester urging my students to "try on" the books I assign, to see these characters and their dilemmas as sites for subjective appropriations and virtual experiences. Have I not been claiming all along that reading itself enables us to try out other selves, to *imagine* otherness? I now know, firsthand, the dark truth of so many of my books: that this is neither easy nor safe: Lear, mad, sees the baroque spectacle of system-wide exploitation that stamps his kingdom; Melville's Cereno dies by dint of experiencing an otherness that exposes his whole life as an affair of props; Faulkner's Quentin Compson, by dint of an "overpass to love," grasps what it can feel like when "black blood" cashiers one's humanity, and this insight is mortal.

And today in hallowed Ivy League halls, a stubborn white comparative literature professor collides with a story that has forever been stifled or hidden or disbelieved—and discovers that *others'* subject positions have an unsuspected bruising, wounding, even shaping power, that they may know something firsthand about both our society and the academy that transcends polite, well-balanced discussions of texts. The old teacher is, late in the game, learning a lesson: it seems to resemble, in a minor key, the one that Lear, Cereno, Quentin, and Lurie learned: "quittin' time" is nigh. It may also be: open your eyes and check your syllabus for ticking bombs.

Quittin' Time?

Six gaffes. I have delved at some length into these six, but obviously there are many more than six errors of judgment in my practice, more than six instances where my song and dance went utterly flat, where I collided with my "time" (both my age and the age we live in). In my senior seminar on Proust, Joyce, and Faulkner a few years ago, one student categorically wondered, when presenting on *Absalom, Absalom!*, why anyone would read a book such as this, about a bygone Southern culture with outlandish, evil views on race. (I wondered why he was taking my course.) Yet, in his way, he was right. My (Swedish) wife asks me, with more gentleness and understanding, the same question: Why do you keep on teaching Faulkner? I'm not sure I have an answer. It would seem I have an ax to grind. Do you ever outgrow your past? (And what kinds of contortions and blind spots are required to make Arnold Weinstein, residing in Providence, Rhode Island, for the past fifty years, born and raised [yes] in Memphis but of Jewish extraction, from parents whose own parents hailed from Poland and Hungary, think of himself as Southerner?)

More gaffelets. I still remember vividly tackling, in my younger days, one of the twentieth century's most dazzling and radical texts, William Burroughs's *Naked Lunch*, and routinely lecturing on it in my "Fiction of Relationship" course. This savage, obscene book—"a basket full of crabs," Mary McCarthy memorably called it—inevitably shocked and angered some of my Brown undergraduates, and I recall one principled young woman simply walking out of the classroom, hissing, "I shouldn't have to read material like this in a Brown University course." The amount of violence and body-rending and sadistic rituals in this drug-filled narrative obviously makes it extreme, but I always felt I was capable of delivering it to my audience. (They need to confront books of this stripe, I told myself, showing as well as telling us what hallucinogens produce, both in writing and in behavior.) Yet a day came when I simply could no longer stand at the podium and quote some of its most "ecstatic" passages, dealing with frenzied fornicating bodies flying end over end and exploding in flames. It became too *unseemly* to pull off. I was (only) in my fifties then, and I sensed that I was colliding with a limit situation that was new, since earlier I had had no trouble dishing up this material, just because of its fiery, hallucinatory power. I had not now all of a sudden become squeamish; I had simply registered—finally—the huge age gap between me and my audience, and I could no longer cross it; I could not mouth the words Burroughs had written.

Something comparable happened recently, when we were discussing Proust. We were focused on the remarkable sequences where Marcel (the narrator) describes his sexual maneuvers with his mistress, Albertine. I call them "remarkable" because the young man waits for the young woman to fall asleep and then observes, with some lust and even more awe, her breathing but unconscious (hence "emancipated") body, now akin to sea waves and breezes and the life of plants, now (at last) approachable for intercourse. (Her subjectivity had been his enemy, his undoing, throughout the novel; it will continue to be.) He "mounts" her now docile, fully pliable body and experiences something akin to serene ecstasy. And one feels that the young woman is strangely consensual in this sequence (Ha! There I go again! "Consensual"? "One feels"? I wonder how my women students felt), for this strange kind of lovemaking would appear to be the "final solution" to their sexual wants, even if it doesn't seem all that far from necrophilia (not to mention its gender problematic, a problematic that shines in the dark for today's students, whether or not Proust saw it that way).

I had naively assumed that my twenty-one-year-old undergraduates would feel no qualms in holding forth on this sequence, but instead I encountered only silence and surly faces looking down. *They wouldn't talk.* And it finally got through to me that this material was not intrinsically too hot to handle—it is in fact lyrical and decorous throughout; and heaven knows these young people have seen and read far worse— but simply off-limits to discuss with a seventy-five-year-old male professor. You don't talk about such stuff with grandpa. This episode took place several years ago. #MeToo has added more urgency to all this, as my sixth gaffe made all too clear. It didn't get through to me, back then, that decorum is the least of my problems; Coetzee's *Disgrace* lifted the veil. I've entered the phase where "my" texts either blow up in my face or embarrass my students into silence (because of me).

The old don't like being lectured about sickness and dying because their own proximity to these dark matters is too close. Deconstructing power and sexuality is not a topic geared to please CEOs. The young cotton to coming-of-age stories because they themselves are coming of age; aging itself seems abstract to them. Love stories seem to work for every group, since I imagine they speak their delights and fears to folks at every stage of life's parade. But love is a half step away from issues of power and gender, which yields a heady brew, filled with victims and victimizers, filled with landmines. Our entire country is undergoing an education on that front, but old professors can be slow to learn. Gaffes happen, and there will be more of them, until it is over.

Living Chain

Fifty years of teaching, and you do have to wonder what you've wrought. How many times have I said that? As I've also said, many former students have sent generous, sometimes moving, tributes my way over the years—I reread these when needed—yet the most productive teacherly work is likely invisible, unknowable to *all* parties, happening in the dark. Hazelwood and Kronwald probably went to their graves without the slightest clue of the seed they planted in me and my wife when we were sixteen. And Larry Holland, as I've said, performed that role for me at Princeton in 1961. They were not sages with divine lessons. No single utterance remembered, no philosophy unveiled, no intimate exchanges, but rather a door was opened by our encounter, and it was to have consequences, to have "legs." They embodied a mission—the word would have probably appalled them—which is perhaps better put as a *transmission*, a hookup to a living chain that beckoned to us as students, as would-be readers, as would-be teachers who themselves continued the chain, continued the dance.

(Holland died in his late fifties in a bizarre drowning accident at Bread Loaf Summer School many years ago. It was said that the faculty had formed, yes, a human chain in the water, older teachers hand in hand under the surface, while the young walked over them as bridge. Holland, I was told, had had a coronary while performing that ritual. I now know this story to be apocryphal—he died in rapids, by sudden drowning; no chain of any kind—but there is a shimmering truth in the fable as I first heard it: it was a luminous, emblematic death, for it shed light on a service he, and so many others, had performed for decades and decades.)

A living chain: I like the continuity this figure offers. Each of us constructs, via work and memory and love, the living chain of his or her life. A life in teaching "parents" us, brothers and sisters us, still further, making us into fellow travelers with the books we teach and the people we reach. Given the seeming privacy of reading—one reads alone; one thinks—it is good to close this account on such a note. Yes, our errors, our gaffes still resonate; perhaps they even outlive us, but much else does too.

CONCLUSION

Delta Autumn

It is hard to write this final part of my book without recalling Flaubert's famous warning: "l'idiotie de vouloir conclure" (the idiocy of wanting to conclude). I've had lots of time—decades—to make sense of the Frenchman's words, and for years I thought them essentially *conceptual*: you cannot "conclude" because things do not add up to any conclusion. I still think that has its nasty share of truth. But it shares its bad news with still other odious outcomes, the worst being: becoming an idiot is how you conclude—that is, how you finish; that is, what the work of time does to you. We're far away from literary or writerly challenges now and facing a darker, baked-in threat, akin to entropic damage and progressive dismantling: we end up undone (rather than done).

And even that grim perception is trickier than it may first seem. The damage wrought by time is located in the body, the mind, and perhaps the soul. The body and the brain plus heart that it houses *age*, move deathward, are slated to lose their powers. Not a pretty scenario but a well-known one, which can be attested to by hordes of old folks, as well as geriatricians and therapists. The spiritual piece is counterintuitive and more heinous: you can go—morally and conceptually— increasingly bankrupt or defunct or impaired, the longer you live. Your ethical bearings—that backbone one wants to believe in—are systematically eroded. You fall out of the world by no longer being able to understand it or contribute to it.

Seen together, these two gloomy vistas would suggest that writing this last little chapter of my book—getting the conclusion right,

book-wise—is the least of my problems. Maybe it is. But it has not escaped my attention—and likely not yours either, given all the trumpet-
ing I've done about these issues, about final wisdom, about ultimate
knowing, about literature as truth—that these foreboding threats of
disintegration and nullity target my entire project: the book itself is little
more than my form of conclusion.

But let's examine these tidings. You have already witnessed my losing
battle with delta. I was sacked by its unmasterable mystery as I got hammered in my freshman calculus course. For all I know, that defeat seeded
my future in literature. But you may remember that I tried very hard for
a bit of uptick as I completed my commentary on arithmetic in my segment on the three R's, and I even had the temerity to call delta in for a
last curtain call. I felt I had found, at long last, a "fit" between delta and
my own unknowing incremental voyage through time. Delta found its
allotted place, I thought.

Long after writing those lines, I had a "duhhhhhh" moment, a eureka
moment, that simply stunned me and made me wonder why I had never
thought of it earlier: none other than my beloved Faulkner had titled the
bleakest, saddest story of his novel *Go Down, Moses*—a text I discussed
in part in my pages devoting to "reading"—by the very words you see
above: "Delta Autumn." Faulkner does not have calculus in mind (I have
to believe he'd never even encountered the word, given the rudimentary
math he must have studied in school), but—this was the explosive
insight—the delta of calculus has nonetheless an awful, indeed razor-
sharp bearing on Faulkner's narrative and on my conclusion.

I make this claim in full awareness that Faulkner is unmistakably referring to the Mississippi Delta, a place dear to his heart and his writing.
In this penultimate story of his book, taking place many decades after
the earlier stories in the collection, the once immense and awe-inspiring
Delta (the site of the ritual annual hunts of the past) has drastically
shrunk, shrunk so much that the hunting party of this story, heading its
way, has to travel countless miles and many days by car (no longer by
buggy) to reach it. We are meant to note this encroachment on the majestic wilderness of yore. Time has taken its toll.

And the white protagonist of the novel, Isaac McCaslin—once upon a time the boy going through his life-altering rites of passage to become a hunter—has now become Uncle Ike, a very, very old man whom no one (except Faulkner) seems to take particularly seriously, as he reminiscences and pontificates to the other hunters of the party, still youngish men in their forties, still in mid-life. And it's a different time in America too: the early 1940s, when Hitler was taking over Europe, when the gathering winds of war and threat and change were in the air, when the future was anything but clear. (*Go Down, Moses* was published in 1942.) We're a far piece from the halcyon days of the past and the mythic pursuit of Old Ben.

But aging and dying have always been front and center, and they remain there. It's no longer the totemic old bear or the no less totemic old Sam Fathers, Ike's mentor, half-red–half-black man, whose time has come. Now it would seem it's time for old Uncle Ike himself—who, as a boy, relinquished the rifle and the compass and the watch, as a way of *seeing* the bear; who later relinquished his birthright and inherited farm, as a way of *saying no* to the ownership of land and of people—to think about the last item on his bucket list of things to relinquish: his life. (Remember the physiological clock ticking; Faulkner remembers it: this old man is genuinely old, has trouble moving around, is not far from being bedridden, even though he's out there with younger men for one last go-around, one last fling).

Old Ike is not, however, to die, in this narrative, and it matters. The deaths of Old Ben and Sam Fathers were each swift, possessed of poignance, propriety, and stature, marking the end of an era. Nothing so definitive to be found in "Delta Autumn." If anything, Ike is slated for worse than dying: to outlive himself and to fail the test meted out to him by the future that he and his land are facing. Hence, we are treated to the saga of his young kinsman, Rolf Edmonds's liaison with the black woman who has borne his child and come out to the Delta to see her lover; Rolf's strategy for getting clear of this bond is packaged inside the sorriest bargain of the story: an actual envelope filled with money is what she is to receive, *and she is to receive it at the hands of Rolf's very old relative, Ike McCaslin*. Every detail in this sequence hurts: not only Rolf's evasion and ethical rot but also Faulkner's very *manner*. The young woman is "othered" textually: she wears a hat and man's raincoat as she enters the tent, unplaceable in her features and gender; she even bears, the text says, an odor that Ike gradually identifies as "black" (confirming one of the South's oldest racist beliefs). Slowly she reveals her lineage and racial identity to Ike, for we learn that she is, in fact, the grand-daughter of James Beauchamp, Tennie's Jim, himself the black grand-child of Carothers McCaslin, hence Ike's own black kinsman.

What does Ike—initially supine in bed, half-dressed, flustered—do in her presence? He ends up bequeathing her the ivory hunting horn given to him by General Compson ages ago as the sign of becoming a man. It's a moment worth examining: when Ike gives it and the cash-filled envelope to her, for a brief but heartbreaking instant their two hands meet; Faulkner writes this in terms that no Faulkner reader will forget: "He didn't grasp it, he merely stroked it—the gnarled, bloodless, bone-dry old man's fingers touching for a second the smooth young flesh where the strong old blood ran after its long lost journey back to home. 'Tennie's Jim,' he said. 'Tennie's Jim.'" And he can go no further.

I cannot help but recall the moment in *Absalom, Absalom!* when Rosa Coldfield speaks some of the most sublime words in all of Faulkner: "*Because there is something in the touch of flesh with flesh which abrogates, cuts sharp and straight across the devious intricate channels of decorous order-ing, which enemies as well as lovers know because it makes them both:—touch and touch of that which is the citadel of the central I-Am's private own: not spirit, soul; the liquorish and ungirdled mind is anyone's to take in any dark-ened hallway of this earthly tenement. But let flesh touch with flesh, and watch the fall of all the eggshell shibboleth of caste and color too.*" I have long thought this to be Faulkner's supreme testament: as writer and as Southerner. "Touch" makes others real, overcomes taboo. Touch is knowing.

Ike McCaslin touches the black woman's hand, feels the "strong old blood" running after "its long last journey back to home," but all he can offer her are bank notes and advice: *go North*. I see a massive, tragic failure here. Yes, she bears Roth's child; yes, she *might* finally bring to-gether the white and black strands of the McCaslin legacy. She *might* indeed begin to make Faulkner's fractured world whole. Instead, the existential leap that the two lovers might have made is commodified and outsourced to a tired old man at the end of his rope. This brief shimmering moment of possible redemption fizzles, comes to naught.

In *Absalom, Absalom!*, Faulkner had called love's hope, love's magic, a "might-have-been that is truer than truth." But, here, it is not to be. "Maybe in a thousand or two thousand years in America but not now, not now," Ike tells the young woman. We do not know where she will finally take this child, but we do have the searing, indicting, hard-to-forget words she pronounces to this man who has relinquished so much: "'Old man,' she said, 'have you lived so long and forgotten so much that you don't remember anything you ever knew or felt or even heard about love.'"

Delta Autumn: the time of death is nigh. The Delta is shrinking, the world is under siege, and the heart fails. It may be the most damning speech in all of Faulkner. It stands as testament to decay, to corrosion of spirit, to the collapsed bridge between self and other, man and woman, black and white. The work of time is delta: not the once grand wilderness that borders the great river, but the delta concept that sank me at Princeton in 1958, that bids, I fear, to threaten me even today. Ike McCaslin fails a test far worse than my calculus tests. His heart cannot keep pace—just as William Faulkner's could not, just as I'm not sure mine can—with the work of time and the cry for change. Faulkner knew the racial sins of the South—no other writer has plumbed them so profoundly—but his old hunter cannot envision a future. Delta Autumn: our hearts fill with plaque, of a sort no MRI can depict. We harden. We grow afraid. We shrink: not only in size but from the great tasks in front of us. That mysterious evolving force that mystified me in calculus, that is defined as "the change in the value of a variable," may well be the implacable mutations that time produces, as the world changes but we do not.

Gaffes are one thing, but this is far worse, far more damning. My greatest fear, as I look at the world about me—at the young people who come my way each semester, as well as at my own children and grandchildren—is that I unwittingly, unknowingly, unalterably, resemble

Faulkner's old Ike McCaslin, that I am at risk of forgetting what love means. I repeat to myself Eliot's lovely exhortation, "Old men ought to be explorers," and even though I want to view this very book as my last professional exploration, I fear the warping and drying up and sheer shrinkage brought on by the years I've lived. And I sense that I can never exit the carapace that contains me. The bright shiny high-tech world of the new and the young—a world I've often railed against, here, in my campaign for literature and in my war against information technology— seems more alien to me every day. It's on the other side of my looking glass. Literature is the shell that houses me. Its words will not die. But delta's law of change is real.

Adieu, Bob et Nancy

If the spiritual conclusion might be grim, what about the verbal one? Literature's words will not die, I said, but those who write, read, and speak those words will. If you start a book of words with your own start, and you continue through your voyage out—Bob and Nancy, Hazelwood, Princeton and Paris, Brown, The Great Courses, Coursera, the life-altering books I love and teach, the entire lifelong word-fueled feast—then how do you see it finishing? (The idiocy of wanting to . . .) Words have been the engine, the driving motor force, for all this. As long as the tank is not entirely empty, the machine works. But, unlike my perch at Brown, no tenure security exists for this creatural appointment; it's subject to delta.

Therefore, in finishing up properly, I want to zero in still further on the basic energy source that has enabled all these gambits and projects: language, the not-very-secret hero of my book, of my life. The language of teaching, the language of writing. And the mind that generates it, delivers it to my vocal cords and my fingertips. Might *words* also be concluding their run? Might they have a faithless, even mutinous, will of their own? Might they "ultimately" be out for themselves? Do you remember *Kuboaa*? It is the word that Hamsun's protagonist *created* as a gesture of absolute verbal freedom: to *make* a word that has no prior meaning. I claimed this as the pinnacle of Hamsun's book, and posited it as a shimmering example of writing's own freedom, its own inventive and creative possibilities, as contrasted with the penitential model of thesis-argument-conclusion that has acquired so much authority in school. Words need not copy, I asserted: they can spawn. Words: mine and my students'. Language is a *transport*, a force-multiplier; it is propulsive and world-engendering. "Nothing will get you nothing," Lear had growled to Cordelia; but the imagination and the writing fingers and the tongue produce something from nothing on a nonstop basis.

At my most rhapsodic—doubtless cued by my earliest school years, when I would be called to the blackboard to *diagram* sentences, using a piece of chalk to denote sites in time and space—I sometimes think of grammar itself as a launchpad, as a means of accessing/producing just those whereabouts in past, present, and future, or as even further exploratory in articulating might-be (or might-have-been) realms via the subjunctive or conditional. Verbs are means of transportation, and no car, train, plane or spaceship is required or can rival with them. Likewise, we access space and via prepositions and direct objects and all those things you can do to verbs. And adjectives and adverbs fill out the picture, give it point and color. Any self-respecting linguist would laugh at what I've just written, but I won't back off.

See it this way, in a diagram on a blackboard, and you realize "graphically" how beautifully the mind is furnished, how colonizing its energies and reaches are. And be sure to recognize how allied this muscular yet neural/verbal power is to the antics of our psyche, so that fear and dread generate their own visions, just as desire and happiness create theirs. These territories are found on no maps, but we engender them around the clock; and *literature* enables us, for a while, to inhabit them, to live elsewhere and to be other. Furthermore, the sheer affective carnival that books offer to us in their vicarious fashion is culture's greatest workout plan. The full play of language outdoes any exercise program you can imagine, asking only that we try it on. Take it out for a spin.

This is why *Kuboaa* both enthralls and frightens me. Hamsun's addled protagonist has done what Ibsen (Hamsun's archenemy in many respects) called for: *torpedoing the ark*. *Kuboaa* short-circuits the entire machine. A "free" word, an outlaw word, a word without fealty or allegiances: this is the anarchist dream. One imagines poor Saussure with his founding binary, "signifiant/signifié" (word/meaning) writhing in his grave, for Hamsun declared war on all mediation and connectivity, on the very bridge that links sign to referent, word to meaning. *Hunger* has a number of exquisitely mad scenes where this anarchic pulse rules the day, and where words seem to go on an excursion, inventing their meanings at every turn, rejecting any and all dependencies. Hamsun's actual Norwegian grammar and syntax behave, but they stage a wilding and make us sense their weird potential independence, coiled in wait, like ammunition, like a lightable fuse; in doing so, they point to definitive troubles down the road. And even before the road. The language of babies is like that. *Infans.* Babble. Cooing. Just noise. That's how we started.

And that's where all of us are eventually headed. The wreckage entailed by *Kuboaa* is not merely the breaking of the oldest verbal contract we have—making sense to each other, tying words together to express meaning—but it foreshadows a further, still more radical breach of contract: the dissolution of individual language brought on by time, entropy, senility, and dementia. The verbal cost of living is a bill that will come and that we will pay. Here is the breakdown we are headed for, if we live long enough: the gradual, then increasing, malfunctioning of our verbal equipment, as we sputter our way into incoherence and toward silence and the end. The words will fail. But, absent a stroke, they do not fail all at once. The process is slower, more insidious, and harder to size up.

The Eddie Constantine character in Godard's film *Alphaville* had spoken of the city's inhabitants losing their words, so that *amour* is replaced by *volupté*, they've lost *tendresse*. Godard works as a poet-ethicist, not a geriatrician, whereas the actual human pillaging that I am discussing is democratic in character, without program: all kinds of words, high and low, important and insignificant, are hinting at possible mutiny and disappearance, "down the road." I've always revered the lovely French phrase, "l'esprit de l'escalier," which means: the word or brilliant repartee that you were looking for in the conversation (but didn't find, didn't find) that comes to you later as you mount the stairs, having exited the room. And as long as the equipment still works at all, many of the missing words do show up, later, somewhere on that stairway, useless of course, but nonetheless there, loyal, standing and accounted for.

But a day will come when they go altogether on strike, on holiday, on vacation, on permanent leave. I saw it happen, in graduate school, to a famous scholar of Puritan America in mid-lecture: he began to mumble; sounds came from his mouth that were not words; a graduate assistant came out to the podium and assisted him off stage; he never returned. So it will be, for many of us, teachers or not, off stage as well as on. There will be no staircase in sight, no return to be hoped for. And we will, I fear, encounter, with pain but perhaps not surprise, the absolute (hidden) "otherness" of language, its pure conventionality, its unnaturalness. A trusted and *enabling* friend will have died. For what will go lost is the *contract* between word and meaning. That lifelong partnership, more intimate than our deepest love relationships, is eventually headed for divorce, rupture.

I have regarded language as an immense keyboard to be played on, and a very large portion of this book is about that keyboard, that instrument for expressing oneself, for inventing oneself. But time is holding its own cards: I can be in mid-lecture and find myself, unbeknownst to the students, searching for a word, a metaphor, perhaps even a tangent or segue, and it does not come. I know this will only grow and take on more scope, that it has all the time in the world (all the time that I have) to pick me apart more fully, to ransack and dismantle me, more definitively.

Nothing personal here, for it's not exactly *me* that's being picked apart. No, it is that conjugal pair: word and meaning, or body and mind. That glue is coming undone. Eloquence (and much else, including our bond with others and with the world) hinges on that inspiriting consort, that unassailable semiotic linkage that cements the sounds we make and the sense we make; all communication (from mind to mouth, from mouth to ear, from ear to brain) hinges on harnessing that old faithful team. But it is subject, like so much of our somatic equipment over time, to eventual undoing.

Everyone is familiar with the old game of pronouncing a word aloud so many times that we no longer quite know what it means, that we "hollow" it out. I'm now finding that this "hollowing" process is gaining ground, is infecting my goods, is turning my words more weightless. I say "weightless" because nowadays I often actually feel the iffy-ness of my terms, as if I were afflicted with "uptalk," closing every utterance with a question mark. Until this happens, until your words start to become uncertain and insecure, to misbehave, to be husks without a core, to acquire an unwanted freedom, to move toward being empty signs, to begin approaching *Kuboaa*: until that happens you are still the ruler in your kingdom. I still make sense when I speak and (hopefully) when I write; but I feel the tug, the loosening of bonds, a queasy lightness and promiscuity of these implements that were so firm and true before.

Kuboaa signals more than dissolving words; all patterns start to waver. The glue I've alluded to, the glue that makes sounds and meanings stick together, is subject to a broader, more sweeping dissolution, a wider perceptual erosive plague that is no doubt waiting in the wings. *Cohesion* and *adhesion* refer to the propriety of all those forms that never wavered or came unstuck in the old days, that used to be docile in containing their significance, a containment or a pact so taken for granted that one was never even aware of it. These forms contain and package the content of our lives: our humanity, our longitudinal identity, as well as our sanity and our umbilical cord with others. They eventually give way. Here is a passage from the Dutch writer, J. Bernlef's novel of dementia, *Out of Mind*:

> Behind me in the doorway stands a woman. Her brown hair falls in a lock towards the right across her forehead. Remarkably smooth cheeks in an otherwise old face that seems to move away ever further and comes closer again only I have briefly looked away from the mirror to the wall beside it. She is keeping an eye on me. (Could she have been assigned to me? By whom?) Tie, where is my tie?

This is what a long marriage now comes to. Your wife's face is describable in great detail, but my phrase "your wife" has been emptied of meaning; you now inhabit an increasingly egalitarian, democratic world, one where your "tie" has parity with your "wife"; it (the tie) is oddly recognized as "yours," even though it is missing, whereas your spouse, right there, has indeed gone missing.

I look in the mirror and I see a face I recognize, but it has more independence than it used to; it seems readier to jump the fence. And I look at my family and my surroundings in the same eerily emancipated way, knowing (of course, still, mercifully) who they are, yet seeing them in a contingency that I never noted in the past. Things and words are asserting their muscular freedom, their unownability. I discussed earlier the freedoms James Joyce takes with his characters. Hence Stephen and Bloom—the two central protagonists—can become Blephen and Stoom. As for (Leopold) Bloom himself, I've noted how he used to doodle with his name, creating anagrams for it: Ellpodbomool, Mollopeloob, Bollopedoom, and Old Ollebo, M.D. I then, as critic practicing my interpretive trade, enjoyed subjecting those (delightful) monikers to a psychological reading, imagining that each has a peculiar psychological bite, a purchase. But I now, as crumblier, edgier old man (a man who's crumbling, whose edges are coming undone), am most struck by their *parity*, their weird independence and integrity. Why not? I think. Are your borders intact? Cohesion, adhesion: the old corral is being breached, coming undone. The rustlers are coming.

I have repeatedly referred to words as *ordnance*, to reading as *transport*, but that wonderful, all-powerful vehicle is ultimately, as we arrive at the end of our voyage, in Lucifer's service, slated and fated to tell us, *Non serviam.* "Take it out for a spin," I fatuously tell my students, but what if it is destined to go out for spins all on its own? What if one becomes the helpless passenger, rather than the driver? I sometimes wonder if Bob and Nancy are completing their run. "Adieu, Bob et Nancy" does not mean that *they* are leaving, but that *I* am slated to lose the controls: both the steering and the fueling.

I have many times referenced the French mandarin poet, Mallarmé, in these pages. He was one of my great literary breakthroughs in Paris in my junior year, and I've described the headiness of navigating this exotic, suggestive, sometimes impenetrably allusive verse, especially given that my command of French was not yet what it would become. But, as I've said, somehow my double apprenticeship with Mallarmé and with French was a marriage of sorts, enkindled by the joy of new words, new vectors of meaning, new signals and echoes. I often (in a goofy way) thought of myself as the ideal Mallarmé reader back then, because my limited French enabled me to see his poems as *entirely* alien landscape, filled with strange markers, whereas "real" French readers would be partially blocked and deceived by what they (thought they) already knew.

Mallarmé's most extreme poem may well be the one known as the "sonnet en yx," because its rhyme scheme consists exclusively of two sounds: "or" and "yx"; "or" is a common term and means both "gold" and "for/because" in French, but "yx" is radical, and I know of no other poem that has risked finding six words to end six lines with the sound of "yx," coming up with "onyx," "Phénix," "ptyx," "Styx," "nixe," and "fixe." That is the extravagant side of the poem, but the line I want now to cite—the line that haunts me—is the most self-erasing of all the "or" verses: "*aboli bibelot d'inanité sonore*" (abolished bauble of sonorous inanity).

My English butchers Mallarmé's exquisite French. "Abolished bauble" keeps the poet's guttural consonants but has the elegance of a ten-ton truck, and it utterly loses the singsong, ballet-like, chiasmus of "aboli bibelot." Bauble: cheap trinket, knickknack, but also shiny stone, undone, literally deconstructed. The line is brutal: why begin with "aboli," why beat up on bauble? Language and meaning are a bauble, one that time will eventually abolish, derealize, hollow, turn inside-out, turn into gibberish, cooing, pure sounds of "sonorous inanity," as if we might still rhyme but can no longer reason, so that whatever pith may once have come from our utterances is just sound, unjust sound, empty sound, sound. Bauble, babble, Babel.

Mallarmé's exotic French had sent me, in Paris in 1960, searching both my dictionary and my brain for the right English equivalents, for the dance of word and meaning that was performed so beautifully on the pages of that slim volume of poems. I feel that I am now returning—not by choice—to that open-ended lingual field of guesswork and imagination, for my English words now gesticulate in ways they never did before, as if they were uncomfortable, unharnessable, en route to being unusable. And that fanciful little exercise of "My name is ...," which I allowed myself in the discussion of "Reading," whereby I put onto the very page all the lingual variants of my moniker (French, German, Spanish, Italian, Swedish, Russian, Chinese, Japanese, Hebrew, Arabic), now seems more ominous and threatening than playful, more hesitant and interrogatory than decipherable bear tracks, because *all* the codes start to seem mechanical, arbitrary, equivalent, interchangeable, nonbinding. Is major divorce—definitive liberation, uncoupling— coming my way?

Literature's Lives

I did not title my book "Literature's Deaths," even though my books have their fill of dying. Characters die, authors die, teachers die. The makers, speakers, and readers of words not only perish but, as I am coming to know, as I have wanted to show, will likely be hit where it hurts: their capacity to make or speak or understand words may eventually fail. The contract that underwrites my book, career, and life—transmission, living chain, language bridge—will be breached. That is how things *conclude*.

But do they? "Aboli bibelot d'inanité sonore." Look one last time at Mallarmé's exquisite line: it is anything but empty sound or the reign of darkness. Like a finely cut diamond, it is prismatic, and it radiates light even now, just as it did when he wrote it well over a century ago and when I discovered it over sixty years ago. This word-bauble—which is what poetry is—cannot be abolished, for it relives on the page each time you or I or those to come read or say it. Its four perfectly chosen words have the strength, order, and beauty of the atom. Composed by a person now moldering in the grave, it shines, it smacks of human doing, not undoing. It's for the long haul. Virginia Woolf said of painting: "Beautiful and bright it should be on the surface, feathery and evanescent, one colour melting into another like the colours on a butterfly's wing; but beneath the fabric must be clamped together with bolts of iron. It was to be a thing you could ruffle with your breath; and a thing you could not dislodge with a team of horses."

Teachers die. My own teachers are dead: not only Hazelwood and Holland but the still larger, fuller, echoing gang who formed me: Sophocles (406 BCE), Shakespeare (1616), the Brontës (1848, 1855), Dickinson

(1886), Melville (1891), Twain (1910), Proust (1922), Kafka (1924), Joyce (1941), Faulkner (1962), even Morrison (2019). Dead? *Echoing*, I said. Echoing still. Their words live on, in their work but also in me, and I have passed them on to others during my years as teacher and writer. That transfer, that traffic, is how we work for our bread.

Yes, our personal equipment—"ours" only on loan—is subject to entropy, mutiny, and a host of ills, and we ourselves must eventually exit. But literature, which offers us, as I've said over and over, a unique form of *knowing*, does not know death. It hallows life, makes life. Those beautiful children, Bob and Nancy, were my very first "characters," and they magically opened the door, for me, to the undying figures who people this book: literature's people. Like all the other tutelary ghosts mentioned in this volume, words were their gift as well as their source. Morrison had it right: ghosts are real. None of the lives I've discussed— from Oedipus to Lear to Heathcliff to Huck to Marcel to Quentin and Shreve to Leopold Bloom to Sethe—can die or be displaced, no matter what happens in their stories, for they still reside, once we've met them in our books, in our minds and hearts. There, they have squatter's rights, which cannot be taken from them, and the institution of reading will preserve those rights, that presence, for those who come after us. Their gifts have no expiration date. Their nurturance does not go bad: it can be consumed, and reconsumed, right on through the years, as I personally know, having had the profound good luck to put my life into their company. Books are beginnings, not endings, even after the last page is read.

Literature itself can be thought of as the fellowship of spirits. I've tried to say some of the ways that fellowship grows us, extends our reach in both mind and heart, and differs entirely from the realm of facts, data, and information. Such trips are the stuff of reading and teaching. Such are literature's lives. Time, space, and knowing get plumbed through these word-driven, imagination-fed ventures, these little but epic odysseys through which literature takes us out and takes us home.

BIBLIOGRAPHY

Aristotle. *Poetics*. Translated by Malcolm Heath. New York: Penguin, 1997.

Barth, John. *Lost in the Fun House*. New York: Bantam, 1969.

Baudelaire, Charles. "Le Cygne." In *Les Fleurs du Mal*. Paris: Garnier, 1964.

———. "Les Petites Vieilles." In *Les Fleurs du Mal*. Paris: Garnier, 1964.

Beckett, Samuel. *Molloy*. New York: Grove Press, 1994.

Bergman, Ingmar. *The Seventh Seal*. In *Four Screenplays of Ingmar Bergman*. Translated by Lars Malmström and David Kushner. New York: Simon and Schuster, 1960.

Bernlef, J. *Out of Mind*. Translated by Adrienne Dixon. Boston: Godine, 1989.

Blake, William. "London." In *The Selected Poetry of Blake*. Edited by David V. Erdman. New York: New American Library, 1981.

Brontë, Emily. *Wuthering Heights*. New York: Norton, 1971.

Burroughs, William. *Naked Lunch*. New York: Grove Press, 1959.

Calvino, Italo. *Invisible Cities*. Translated by William Weaver. New York: Harcourt, 1972.

Cavafy, C. P. "Ithaca." In *Complete Poems*. Translated by Daniel Mendelsohn. New York: Knopf, 2012.

Coetzee, J. M. *Disgrace*. New York: Penguin, 1999.

Defoe, Daniel. *A Journal of the Plague Year*. Oxford: Oxford University Press, 1990.

DeLillo, Don. *White Noise*. New York: Penguin, 1986.

Dickens, Charles. *Bleak House*. London: Penguin, 1994.

———. *Great Expectations*. New York: Penguin, 2002.

Dickinson, Emily. *Final Harvest: Emily Dickinson's Poems*. Boston: Little Brown, 1961.

Dostoevsky, Fyodor. *Notes from Underground*. Translated by Richard Pevear and Larissa Volokhonsky. New York: Vintage, 1994.

Edson, Margaret. *Wit: A Play*. New York: Farrar, Straus and Giroux, 1999.

Faulkner, William. *Absalom, Absalom!* New York: Vintage, 1990.

———. *As I Lay Dying*. New York: Vintage, 1990.

———. *Go Down, Moses*. New York: Vintage, 1990.

———. *Light in August*. New York: Vintage, 1990.

———. *The Sound and the Fury*. New York: Vintage, 1990.

Genet, Jean. *The Balcony*. Translated by Bernard Frechtman. New York: Grove Press, 1994.

Godard, Jean-Luc. *Alphaville: A Film*. New York: Simon and Schuster, 1966.

Hamsun, Knut. *Hunger*. Translated by Robert Bly. New York: Farrar, Straus and Giroux, 2008.

Ibsen, Henrik. *Ghosts*. In *The Complete Major Prose Plays*. Translated by Rolf Fjelde. New York: Penguin, 1978.

Joyce, James. *Portrait of the Artist as a Young Man*. New York: Penguin, 1993.

——. *Ulysses*. New York: Vintage, 1986.

Kafka, Franz. "A Country Doctor." In *The Complete Stories*. Translated by Willa Muir and Edwin Muir. New York: Schocken, 1971.

——. "In The Penal Colony." In *The Complete Stories*. Translated by Willa Muir and Edwin Muir. New York: Schocken, 1971.

——. "The Metamorphosis." In *The Complete Stories*. Translated by Willa Muir and Edwin Muir. New York: Schocken, 1971.

Kierkegaard, Søren. *Fear and Trembling*. Translated by Alastair Hannay. New York: Penguin, 1986.

Mallarmé, Stéphane. *Collected Poems of Mallarme*. Translated by Henry Michael Weinfield. Berkeley: University of California Press, 2011.

McLuhan, Marshall. *Understanding the Media*. New York: McGraw Hill, 1964.

Melville, Herman. *Benito Cereno*. In *Billy Budd, Bartleby, and Other Stories*. New York: Penguin, 1986.

Merrill, James. "An Urban Convalescence." In *Collected Poems*. Edited by J. D. McClatchy. New York: Knopf, 2001.

Morrison, Toni. *Beloved*. New York: New American Library, 1988.

Mumford, Lewis. *The City in History: Its Origins, Its Transformations, and Its Prospects*. New York: Harcourt, 1961.

Pascal, Blaise. *Pensées and Other Writings*. Translated by Honor Levi. Oxford: Oxford University Press, 1995.

Proust, Marcel. *Remembrance of Things Past*. Translated by C. K. Scott Moncrieff and Terence Kilmartin. New York: Random House, 1982.

Shakespeare, William. *The Tragedy of King Lear*. Edited by Jay Halio. New York: Cambridge University Press, 1992.

Sophocles. *Oedipus the King*. In *The Three Theban Plays*. Translated by Robert Fagles. New York: Penguin, 1984.

Strindberg, August. "Vid Avenue de Neuilly." In *Sömngångarnätter på Vakna Dagar*. Stockholm: Norstedts, 1995.

——. *A Dream Play*. In *Miss Julie and Other Plays*. Translated by Michael Robinson. Oxford: Oxford University Press, 1998.

——. *Inferno/From an Occult Diary*. Translated by Mary Sandbach. London: Penguin, 1979.

Tolstoy, Leo. *The Death of Ivan Ilyich*. Translated by Richard Pevear and Larissa Volokhonsky. New York: Vintage, 2012.

Twain, Mark. *The Adventures of Huckleberry Finn*. New York: Norton, 1977.

Whitman, Walt. "A Noiseless Patient Spider." In *Leaves of Grass*. New York: Random House, 1993.

INDEX

reading (*continued*)

pedagogues and, 84; humanities and, 93; identification and, 9–10, 13, 205; information and, 87–90; interpretation and, 97; iPhones and, 64; Joyce and, 95; Kindles and, 64; language and, 82–84, 86, 91–93; lusläsa, 96; Mallarmé and, 91–93; one's environment and, 84; poetry and, 91–93, 95; prose and, 86, 88, 94; prospective, 9, 96–97; Shakespeare and, 91; slavery and, 86–89, 93, 96; taint of the South and, 86–93; understanding and, 12, 89, 91, 96, 110, 191

Redford, Robert, 300–301

retrospect, 22; cost of knowing and, 140–41, 147, 182; education and, 24, 28, 33; Melville and, 182; Sophocles and, 4, 8–9, 140–41, 147; sting of, 285, 305, 312; truth and, 96, 305; understanding and, 286

Revue Blanche (Strindberg), 251

Rimbaud, Arthur, 2–3, 31, 105

"Rites of Passage" (Weinstein course), 75, 90, 97

Rousseau, Jean-Jacques, 10

Sanctuary (Faulkner), 79

San Jose State, 58

Sartre, Jean-Paul, 290

satyr play, 24, 284

Saussure, Ferdinand de, 324

Schiller, 139, 143

Scholes, Robert, 68

Scream Goes Through the House, A (Weinstein), 302

Seventh Seal, The (film), 77

Shakespeare, William, 51; cost of knowing and, 2, 131, 147–50, 188, 192, 223; education and, 44, 48, 62; enrichment from, 50; gaffes and, 302–3, 311; *Hamlet*, 1–2, 17, 114, 156, 302; illusory appearances and, 148–49; impact of, 21, 24, 50, 329; Kafka and, 188, 192; *King Lear*, 1, 8, 41, 91, 120,

131, 147–50, 309; mathematics and, 120; reading and, 91; understanding, 48; writing and, 114, 120

Shelley, Percy Bysshe, 29, 161

Silicon Valley, 128, 305

Slack, 74

slavery: cost of knowing and, 163–65, 169–70, 177, 179–83, 189, 206–23; Faulkner and, 18, 75, 87–89, 206–8; Godard and, 278; Lincoln and, 79; Melville and, 18, 177–83, 189; Morrison and, 206–23; reading and, 86–89, 93, 96; Twain and, 86, 163–71

social media, 15, 62–63, 104, 277

Socrates, 15–16, 19, 57

Soldier's Pay (Faulkner), 193

Sophocles: cost of knowing and, 131, 137–47, 176, 202, 213; education and, 78, 80; feeling of murder and, 141–42; impact of, 21–22, 329; information and, 133–43; *Oedipus the King*, 2, 4, 8, 137–47, 332; retrospect and, 4, 8–9, 140–41, 147

Sound and the Fury, The (Faulkner), 85, 193, 195, 198, 205, 298–99

Stalin, Joseph, 117

Stein, Gertrude, 104

STEM fields, 24, 36, 41

Sterne, Laurence, 127

Stone, Phil, 83

"Street Scenes" (Strindberg), 245

Strindberg, August: "Avenue de Neuilly," 241–45; Baudelaire and, 241, 243; circuits of, 245–54; connectivity and, 244–45, 248–49, 254; cost of knowing and, 161; Dickinson and, 161; *A Dream Play*, 122, 285; gaffes and, 285; Godard and, 275; hypercube and, 252–53; impact of, 21; *Inferno*, 245–50, 285; Ithaca and, 243; Joyce and, 263, 270; map of human dimensions and, 230, 241–54, 257–58, 262–63, 266, 270, 274–75, 278; mathematics and, 122–26, 126; misogyny of, 241, 285; Munch and, 245, 251–52; poetry